SHAME
Theory, Therapy, The

G000243604

Shame provides an invaluable, stimulating resource for all those who
are concerned with understanding shame and assisting those who
live in its shadow. Psychologists, philosophers and therapists will
find this a fascinating source of new insight into the theory and phenomenology of shame. It will be of particular interest to those who
are interested in relationships between religion and mental health,
to pastoral workers and counsellors, and to religious thinkers and
theorists.

Stephen Pattison considers the nature of shame as it is discussed
in the diverse discourses of literature, psychology, psychoanalysis,
philosophy, history and sociology and concludes that 'shame' is not
a single unitary phenomenon, but rather a set of separable but
related understandings in different discourses. Situating chronic
shame primarily within the metaphorical ecology of defilement,
pollution and toxic unwantedness, Pattison goes on to examine the
causes and effects of shame, including its use as a means of social
control, before discussing means of healing shame and integrating
individuals and groups whose lives are blighted by it. He then considers the way in which a particular religious tradition, Christianity,
has responded to and used shame as a preface to suggesting ways
in which religion might alleviate rather than exacerbating shame.
His analysis raises fundamental questions for religious thought,
organisation and practice in what is increasingly regarded as an age
of shame.

STEPHEN PATTISON is senior research fellow in practical theology
at Cardiff University. Formerly a senior lecturer at the Open
University, he is the author of *A Critique of Pastoral Care* (1988), *Alive
and Kicking: Towards a Practical Theology of Illness and Healing* (1989),
Pastoral Care and Liberation Theology (1994) and *The Faith of the
Managers* (1997), as well as being editor of *Reducing the Risk of Cancers*
(1992), *Medical Knowledge: Doubt and Certainty* (1994), *Mental Health
Matters* (1996) and *The Blackwell Reader in Pastoral and Practical Theology*
(2000).

SHAME

Theory, Therapy, Theology

STEPHEN PATTISON

Cardiff University

PUBLISHED BY THE PRESS SYNDICATE OF THE UNIVERSITY OF CAMBRIDGE
The Pitt Building, Trumpington Street, Cambridge, United Kingdom

CAMBRIDGE UNIVERSITY PRESS
The Edinburgh Building, Cambridge CB2 2RU, UK   www.cup.cam.ac.uk
40 West 20th Street, New York, NY 10011-4211, USA   www.cup.org
10 Stamford Road, Oakleigh, Melbourne 3166, Australia
Ruiz de Alarcón 13, 28014 Madrid, Spain

First published 2000

Printed in the United Kingdom at the University Press, Cambridge

Typeface Monotype Baskerville 11/12½ pt.   *System* QuarkXPress™ [SE]

A catalogue record for this book is available from the British Library

ISBN 0 521 56045 4 hardback
ISBN 0 521 56863 3 paperback

This book is for
Edmund Clarke
in the hope that he will never want to read it,
and for his parents,
John and Cressida,
in the hope that they might

A theologian is born by living, nay dying and being damned, not by thinking, reading, or speculating. (Martin Luther)

His disciples said: When wilt Thou be revealed to us and when will we see Thee? Jesus said: When you take off your clothing without being ashamed, and take your clothes and put them under your feet as the little children and tread on them, then shall you behold the Son of the Living One and you shall not fear. (*The Gospel of Thomas*)

Contents

Preface

It has been said that authors know how their books are going to end as they start at the beginning. If this is generally true, the present volume is a dramatic exception. Almost until the last moment of writing, I have lived with the anxiety of not been able to see quite where the book was going and how it would finish. It has been a confusing and daunting voyage of discovery, replete with wrong turns, false leads and conceptual mirages. In other words, this book is the product of a genuine process of research, with all the excitement and frustration that implies.

I owe substantial authorial debts. Alastair Campbell first stimulated my interest in shame by requiring me to write an essay on chronic guilt. His book *The Gospel of Anger* also offered an important, inspiring model of how practical theologians might begin to think about emotions. Donald Capps, an American pastoral theologian, always seems to have visited the topics I am interested in before me. His own work on shame, though I am sometimes sharply critical of it, has been a constant stimulus to me. Alex Wright at Cambridge University Press commissioned this volume and encouraged me enormously by reading it in draft. I am grateful to him and to his successor, Kevin Taylor, for the patience they have exercised in waiting for it gradually to emerge. On the technical side of this book's production, I would also like to thank Joanne Hill, the assiduous copy-editor at the Press who greatly improved the text in the final stages of its production, and James Woodward, an old friend who kindly compiled the index.

This book would never have seen the light of day without the privilege of uninterrupted time for thinking and writing. This came in the form of a research fellowship in the Department of Religious and Theological Studies at Cardiff University. Cardiff has been extraordinarily generous to me, both institutionally and in the form of forbearing colleagues who have tolerated more absence than presence on my part. I want to thank the University and, more particularly, my line manager,

Paul Ballard, for appointing me to my post and supporting me in it. In addition to this, Paul has probably done more than any other single individual in Britain over thirty years to maintain and develop pastoral and practical theology as a serious area for research and teaching. I would like to pay tribute to him as a valued friend, critic, editor and colleague.

Throughout the period of writing, my drafts have been read and commented upon by two heroic friends, Gordon Lynch and Janet Bellamy. Janet also edited down the first draft. Thank you, Janet and Gordon. Without you, I would simply have drowned.

Amongst my other creditors are Peter van de Kasteele, Sue McKinney, Pat Bradley, Geoffrey Whitfield, Michael Griffith, Peter Graham, Thomas Dixon and Nelson Ould. The anonymous readers at Cambridge University Press deserve my gratitude for their supportive critical comments and suggestions.

I am deeply grateful to Patricia Allderidge and the Bethlem Royal Hospital for permission to use Marion Patrick's 'The Cross' on the cover of this volume. This moving work was painted when the artist was an inpatient suffering from depression at Bethlem. It sums up the quality of alienation and abjection in shame better than any other picture I have ever seen. I am only sorry that I cannot thank Marion Patrick personally for her inspiring art; she died some time ago. It is a parable of stigma and shame that the picture could only be anonymously attributed in a public exhibition of Pictures at Bethlem in Sheffield a few years ago when I first saw it, while now she can receive the public credit for it that she deserves.

Finally, my particular thanks to Jean Way who was my psychotherapist for fifteen years, and to Charmian, Lewis, and Eliot for all their shame-dissolving love and support during the writing of this book.

Introduction

Sin is respectable and highly poetical, shame is not.

(Ellmann 1987: 54)

Shame itself is an entrance to the self. It is the affect of indignity, of defeat, or transgression, of inferiority, and of alienation. No other affect is closer to the experienced self. None is more central to the sense of identity. Shame is felt as an inner torment, a sickness of the soul. It is the most poignant experience of the self by the self, whether felt in the humiliation of cowardice, or in the sense of failure to cope successfully with a challenge. Shame is a wound felt from the inside, dividing us both from ourselves and from one another.

(Kaufman 1985: ix–x)

Writing at the end of the 1960s, the psychoanalyst Charles Rycroft asserted that shame was 'the Cinderella of the unpleasant emotions, having received much less attention than anxiety, guilt, and depression' (Rycroft 1972: 152). If this claim was justified at the time, it has been eroded over the last thirty years. A plethora of books with a huge variety of perspectives in disciplines ranging from literature, sociology and philosophy to various kinds of psychology has emerged on the topic of shame in recent times, especially in the USA. This particular Cinderella is now one of the main objects of attention at academic, cultural and clinical balls that consider the negative or shadow side of existence. Shame is recognised as a major phenomenon of the times, a basic and prevalent condition of individual and social life in late capitalist society (Lasch 1991; Giddens 1991). Contemporary theologian James Fowler writes, 'Now that I have eyes for it [shame], I see it everywhere' (Fowler 1996: 91). He is not alone in acquiring the gift of sight.

Shame is not only an entrance to the self, as Kaufman (1985) has it. It provides an *entrée* to many other important features of individual and social life, as well as being a nexus of attention for many intellectual and clinical disciplines.

I

There are any number of good academic reasons that might justify examining shame as a phenomenon. However, my own reason for undertaking this study was personal. At the outset, I simply wanted to understand the phenomenon of shame in my own life.

Beyond seeking to understand my own experience, this book has three main aims. The first is to provide an overview, and to try to make sense, of the very different understandings, languages and experiences that surround the phenomenon loosely labelled as shame today. Is there a set of core understandings or experiences that unites all phenomena that are characterised as shame? Or is there a variety of different, incommensurable uses and phenomena that are confused by what is basically a coincidence of terminology? There is considerable doubt and debate about how shame should be conceived and responded to.

The second aim is to attempt to understand what might be called chronic or dysfunctional shame. While shame is an integral, and often very important, positive element in all social relationships, it seems that some people get caught in an enduring experience of shame that blights their lives and limits their potential. It will be important to analyse why this happens and to survey some of the ways in which individuals and groups might be helped from such a situation by therapy and other means.

The third aim, which is both distinct and over-riding, is to consider the relationship between the ideology and practice associated with Christianity and human experiences of shame. Shame provides a rich seam of exploration and discovery from which the interaction between the Christian religious tradition and human well-being can be scrutin-ised anew. It acts as a kind of 'hub' from which many theological and practical issues can be explored (de Sousa 1990: 1). The dialogue of reli-gious belief and practice with shame is situated within the discipline of practical theology which also provides the structure for this book.

I shall say more below about practical theology. However, it is not nec-essary to be interested in theology or religion of any kind to make use of this book as an interdisciplinary source and survey of approaches to, and insights about, shame.

I envisage at least two main different and possibly overlapping audi-ences for this work. One readership consists of therapists, counsellors and academics who are interested in shame alone, especially chronic shame, and who wish to gain a broad overview of perspectives, findings and techniques relating to this phenomenon. They will find in the first two Parts of the book much straight discussion of shame that has nothing specifically to do with religion. The second main readership is likely to consist of theologians, pastors and others who are concerned with religious thought and practice. For them, there is much material about the ways in which shame and Christian thinking may interact, particularly in the third part of the book.

To facilitate usage by these two groups with different needs and interests, I will outline the structure of the book at this point. I will then turn specifically to some background introductory material, some of which is concerned with setting the book in a theological context.

The content of this book

This volume is divided into three main Parts. Many readers, particularly those of a practical bent, may wish to omit, or to return later to, the first Part, 'Approaching shame'. It provides preliminary theoretical orientation to the phenomenon of shame and considers methodological and epistemological issues that are relevant to understanding the approaches and discourses surrounding shame.

Shame in the modern world is often understood fundamentally as an emotional state. There is much debate, however, about the nature of emotions. The first chapter provides an overview of perspectives that will challenge any assumption that emotions can easily be defined.

The kaleidoscopic vertigo that may be induced by the consideration of emotions in general is intensified in chapter 2. Here it will become apparent that shame, too, is variously understood in different academic and clinical discourses. A family resemblance theory of shame is advanced whereby it can be maintained that different uses of the concept 'shame' in various discourses may have overlapping meanings, but that shame cannot be narrowed down to any one set of agreed meanings or phenomena. Shame remains a family of meanings and phenomena, not a single experience or definition.

Part II, 'Encountering shame', is more practical and immediately accessible than its predecessor. It is to this Part that practitioners of various kinds might like initially to turn. I first consider the experience of shame and make some fundamental distinctions about different kinds of shame as they appear in contemporary discourses. Having situated shame into various broad ecological contexts, at the end of chapter 3, I move towards discussing the kind of shame that is to be the focus of this volume, chronic or dysfunctional shame. The focus of chapter 4 is upon the diverse causal factors that may be implicated in producing and maintaining chronic psychological shame from early infancy to adulthood. Chapter 5 goes on to look at the effects that reactions to chronic or character shame may have on behaviour, attitudes and pathology. It also discusses the ethical and moral effects of shame, advancing the argument that shame prevents people from taking responsibility in community. In this way, shame has a pernicious effect upon morality. This can be signalled by suggesting that more guilt and less shame is needed in individual and social life.

Chapter 6 attempts to broaden the understanding of chronic, dysfunctional shame away from seeing it simply as an individual phenomenon. Some socio-historical aspects of the generation and use of shame are considered and the place of shame as a tool of social control and disapprobation is discussed. Shame is a powerful force for social conformity. However, the stain of shame is difficult to control, limit and direct. Having considered both individual and social aspects of the causes and effects of alienating shame, chapter 7 suggests ways in which both individuals and groups may be integrated within themselves and within society. Integration dissipates the defilement, alienation and dishonour implied in the toxic unwantedness that characterises chronic shame. Various therapeutic and other responses to shame are surveyed. Unfortunately, there appear to be few, if any, effective solutions or cures to this condition. This somewhat pessimistic conclusion ends the Parts of the book that are devoted to trying to understand shame in terms of psychological and other non-religious discourses.

Part III critically examines the relationship between contemporary Christian thought and practice and shamed groups and individuals. Chapter 8 surveys modern Christian theological responses to shame and finds them to be generally rather limited. They are mostly oblivious to the insights provided by 'secular' academic and clinical disciplines. This makes them inadequate. The next chapter considers ways in which Christian ideas and practices might generate or nurture dysfunctional shame and alienation rather than alleviating it. Finally, chapter 10 tentatively outlines some ways whereby Christianity might begin to change itself so that its capacity to integrate would be enhanced and its use and exploitation of shame might be diminished. Christianity, I maintain, is ambivalent in its effects, having the power to heal and to harm. If it is to maximise integration and minimise alienation, it may have to change its theories about itself and its practices. This kind of conversion or repentance is, perhaps, justified and informed by the symbolically inclusive ministry of Jesus who came to seek and save the lost.

In the remainder of this Introduction, I shall discuss the use of my personal experience in this volume. Thereafter, I will consider the nature of practical theology, which provides the field and structure for the book.

The use of personal experience

The starting point for this study was my own experience of shame. I have used this experience to guide, and sometimes to illustrate, all the material that follows, even when this is not directly acknowledged or apparent. A main reason for doing this is to challenge the assumption that shame is a distant phenomenon that only occurs in other people and not amongst academics or theologians. This colludes with the obscuring and objectification of shame and shamed people (S. Pattison 1998). In a work of scholarship, however, what might appear to be self-indulgent solipsism requires some further justification. It will also be useful directly to outline some of my experience and motivation here to ground the examples that occasionally occur in the main body of this text.

Rendering visible the authorial self

Paradoxically, even in an age of individualism and obsession with the self (Lukes 1973; Taylor 1991), it is still frowned upon for authors of academic books to address readers directly and to talk about themselves. This may reflect a desire to maintain an illusion of impersonal objectivity, a concern that writers should not descend into boring solipsism, or even a certain embarrassment about discussing the self in public, based perhaps on reverence or revulsion for what that self might be. It remains difficult for an academic author to step out from behind the words of a text directly to discuss his or her own experience.

The etiquette that requires authorial invisibility is slowly changing. Some postmodern and feminist authors have questioned the illusion of objectivity that is sustained by third person formulations and observations (Karp 1996). There are new demands for honesty and personal authenticity as people learn to, and assert the right to, speak for themselves (Read and Reynolds 1996). Narrative, especially personal narrative, has become an important field for serious academic enquiry (Frank 1995; Freeman 1993; Karp 1996). It has been noted that creating personally meaningful and socially credible stories or narratives is essential to understanding and coping with the world (MacIntyre 1981). Further, it has been suggested that the process of individuals manufacturing their own narratives out of the socially available materials that are extant may be helpful and liberating for themselves and for others: 'When any person recovers his voice, many people begin to speak through that story' (Frank 1995: xiii; cf. Bolton 1999). It has become apparent, too, that both persons, and the accounts that they give of themselves, are socially funded and constructed (Scheff 1997; G. Pattison 1998). Thus, a personal account is also in many ways a social account of existence. Individuals participating in the world of language and concepts are not self-constructed atoms; the accounts they give of them-selves are not relevant to themselves alone. Finally, all enquiry, however 'academic' it may appear, is fuelled by emotional energy or passion that ultimately finds its locus within individual interests and needs (Game and Metcalfe 1996).

Within this broad framework that gives some credence to the impor-tance of persons, narratives and passions within academic discourse I adopt a loosely 'autoethnographic' approach here. This approach is described by sociologist David Karp: 'Instead of viewing the self as a contaminant, it is more reasonable and honest to recognize that "when-ever we discuss others, we are always talking about ourselves"' (Karp 1996: 203–4). While this book is not a work of sociology, 'you will find that I am very present in this text. Every analysis offered in the book . . . is initially guided by personal introspection' (Karp 1996: 204). My text is heavily 'contaminated' (an interesting concept to use in the context of discussing shame and selves) with my interests and experience.

In offering some aspects of my own experience of shame here there are a number of limitations. I do not offer all my experience. The expe-rience that is described is selective and the narratives are shaped by my own interests and needs. This means that, although I attempt to be honest by my own lights, readers must be aware that they are in receipt of an edited account of what I interpret as my experience. Perhaps accounts of my 'experience' in this connection are better seen as truth-ful fiction than any kind of straightforward fact as I narrate and rewrite my self in public (Freeman 1993; McLeod 1997; Pattison et al. 1999).

My experience of shame

It may help readers to understand the nature and significance of what follows in this book if I say some more about the background to my own experience of shame and the ways in which I have sought to understand and come to terms with it.

I am sure that there are many people in the world whose experience of the kind of profound or chronic shame to be considered later in this book is limited, fleeting or non-existent. For such people this work might seem incomprehensible. They may be like William James' 'once born' psychological types with a 'consciousness, developing straight and natural with no element of morbid compunction or crisis' (James 1960: 96).

However, it is likely that most people have some direct experience of shame in their lives, for it seems to be a fairly universal phenomenon. And for some individuals and groups, shame plays a persistent and dominant role whose effects are baleful and destructive. If shame becomes a constant experience, a perennial attitude to the self, a dominant mood or character trait, its effects can be very negative. The habitually deeply shamed or shame-bound person is trapped, self-rejecting, paralysed, passive, and often depressed.

I believe myself to have been a shame-bound person for most of my life, regarding myself as unworthy, valueless and defiled, with a deep desire to hide myself away from the 'legitimate' negative judgment of others (cf. Tantam 1998). It has taken me a long time to realise this, not least because of my involvement with Christianity. At a very early age I developed a strong Christian faith. I believed that the good, powerful Christian God would look after me and allow me to experience joy and salvation if I served him faithfully and obeyed his laws. The fact that I continued to feel bad about myself, even after confirmation and ordination in the Church of England, I attributed to the fact that I did not try hard enough to trust God and do his will. Of course I felt bad – I was a sinner, guilty of many continuing offences against the deity who graciously loved me and just wanted me to trust more and try harder!

My sense of ontological guilt, fundamentally defiled identity and basic badness was first problematised when, in 1977, I had to write an essay on the theory and therapy of guilt. I was intrigued by this topic. However, I came away from it puzzled; the category 'guilt' and the methods used to deal with it did not seem to address my own condition. The literature on the theory and therapy of guilt suggested that this emotion comes into play when a real or fantasised discrete offence has been committed against another person or a moral rule (Stein 1969). Therapy or forgiveness lies in recognising and acknowledging the offence and making realistic reparation in an appropriate way where that is possible. At this point, the guilty feeling should depart. My problem was that I felt non-specifically bad most of the time, whether or not I had committed any offences against God or other people. Sacramental confession sometimes provided temporary relief (though that was a shaming experience in itself to a scrupulous soul), but I still felt that basically I was no good. I realised this was not real guilt, but did not have a vocabulary to describe my condition.

It was some years later that I came across a short account of Helen Merrell Lynd's book, *On Shame and the Search for Identity* (Capps 1983). Here I found a name for my condition, which was that of shame. Better still, when I read Lynd's original work – one of the very few books about shame in existence at the time – I found a full description of the phenomenology of personal shame which corresponded almost exactly with my own experience (Lynd 1958).

I resolved that I would explore the relations between shame and Christian theology and practice further. The nature of my explorations has been twofold. In the first place, I engaged in personal psychotherapy for fifteen years. Secondly, I researched the different kinds of literature within which shame seemed to figure, overtly or covertly. This ranged from fiction to philosophical treatments of shame and more clinically related material about narcissism, victimisation in various contexts, and child abuse.

At the end of this process, I think I have gained some understanding of why, for many years, I experienced a sense of chronic shame. Broadly, I now believe the roots of my own shame to lie in a certain amount of abuse and neglect in my childhood which was amplified by social institutions like church and school. I have written about this at length elsewhere (Pattison 1998). However, this is just one narrative about shame that makes sense to me personally. Like many shame-bound people, I cannot actually remember my infancy. What I have gained is a story that helps me to understand and make sense of the present and integrates my experience to some extent, as well as relating it to the experience of others in society (McLeod 1997).

I should acknowledge at this point that neither scholarship, nor therapy, nor religion have freed me from a sense of fundamental personal shame. However, there is some freedom in understanding and accepting a shamed identity (cf. Karp 1996). To a much greater extent than when I set out on this personal and academic venture, I now feel I have a sense of shame and defilement rather than it having me. For that I am grateful.

Although this book starts with my experience and is guided by it, it is not limited to it. So, for example, I try to consider a wide variety of views about shame, and I also try to locate it socially and politically as well as personally. Experience is used as an entry point for thinking about shame as a general phenomenon and to illuminate aspects of it, not as an end-point of closure.

The practical theological dimension

This book is basically a study in practical theology. I have used a particular practical theological model, that of critical conversation, to structure it. It is necessary to say something about this kind of theology in general and the model in particular. I will conclude with some questions for practical theology that have emerged from this study.

The nature of practical theology

The term, practical theology, has been variously understood (Pattison and Woodward 2000). Friedrich Schleiermacher (1768–1834), the German Protestant 'father' of the discipline, thought practical theology was the 'crown' or result of the more academic theological enterprise whereby theoretical theological conclusions would be implemented and applied to ministerial activity (Schleiermacher 1988). On a less exalted level, it has been thought of as simply teaching clergy the practical skills needed for ministry. More recently, practical theologians have become aware of the need to make this a more dialectical activity which explores contemporary human experience and practice, both inside and outside the faith community, and critically relates this to theological insights and traditions (Browning 1983, 1991; Hiltner 1958; Tillich 1978).

In an ill-defined area, Whyte defines practical theology as 'the theology of practice'. He suggests that

pastoral theology is triadic, concerned with the interrelationships of faith, practice and social reality, and is aware that the lines of force flow in both directions. (Whyte 1987)

Practical theology can thus be seen as a tripartite interaction between faith (including doctrines and historical traditions), practice (including experiences and phenomena that may lie inside or outside the Christian community), and social reality (including personal reality and insights about that reality derived from the human sciences).

This interaction can be translated into the more concrete model of critical conversation (Pattison with Woodward 1994). Practical theology can then be thought of as a critical conversation between aspects and interpretations of (a) one's own ideas, beliefs, experiences, feelings, perceptions and assumptions; (b) the beliefs, perceptions and assumptions arising from the Christian community and tradition; (c) the contemporary situation, practice or event which is under consideration; and (d) relevant insights, methods and findings that emerge from non-theological disciplines.

The model of conversation has several positive aspects. Conversation often lies at the centre of human encounters, including pastoral encounters. Conversations can be short or long, deep or superficial. They can involve two or more parties. They do not necessarily proceed in a straightforward direction or at the same level. Used in practical theology, a conversational model does not presuppose a lot of previous knowledge about theology or a particular issue, but it does presuppose a willingness to attend, to listen and to learn. The skills and conventions of conversation can be learned. They benefit from practice with other people. Good, creative conversations transform people and their views of themselves and the world. If words are regarded as deeds, as they are in the Bible, they shape events, actions and persons (cf. Cupitt 1990; Schüssler Fiorenza, 1995: 25ff.).

Practical theological process can be seen as an illuminating, often demanding, critical conversation which draws participants onwards and outwards without prescribing exactly where they should go or what they should do (Pattison with Woodward 1994). The richness of practical theological activity is increased by a variety of different perspectives and participants (Ballard 1986). However, practical theology is not just talk for talk's sake. Nor is it an abstract, disconnected intellectual quest. Liberation theologies of various kinds suggest that theological activity must spring from, and feed into, practice in a concrete way. It must resist rather than colluding with oppression in the interests of promoting human flourishing (Pattison 1997a; cf. Jantzen 1998). Practical theology must, therefore, be a transformational activity in the arena of practice as well as in that of theory and understanding.

Practical theology is not just the province of clergy or religious people. Nor need it be confined to the overtly religious sphere. Any inhabitants of an action-influencing world view such as management or the market are likely to find that their activity is undergirded by fundamental faith assumptions about the nature of reality (Pattison 1997b). Many 'secular' practitioners and theorists would, therefore, perhaps benefit from becoming much more self-consciously critical practical theologians, insofar as their own faith assumptions remain implicit and so uncritical (Pattison 1995b).

Structuring the practical theological conversation about shame

To subject shame to a practical theological enquiry is to conduct a structured critical conversation between what is known of the contemporary experience and understanding of shame and some relevant aspects of Christian tradition and practice.

The first 'moment' of the conversation comprises 'listening' to contemporary experiences and insights into shame. It aims to understand the nature and experience of shame in the modern world by using the resources of sociology, psychology, philosophy and other disciplines. The first two Parts of this book are devoted to this activity.

The second 'moment' consists in enquiring into the ways in which the Christian tradition and community has dealt with shame, paying attention to sociological, socio-historical, psychological and theological resources. This moment of the pastoral theological conversation will yield insights into the theological significance of shame as well as opening up important questions about the nature of sin, guilt, personhood and ethics.

The purpose of practical theological activity is the transformation of theory, theology and practice. Having obtained contemporary, historical, secular and religious understandings of the place and significance of shame, it is then appropriate to consider whether aspects of the Christian religious tradition of thought and practice should be changed. This forms the third and final 'moment' of the practical theological exercise conducted in this book.

Ideally, there should be a further stage in which the Christian tradition was allowed to speak more directly and dialogically with the other sources consulted. In this way, a critique of contemporary views might be constructed on the basis of religious practices and insights. For this to happen, however, the religious tradition must become much more knowledgeable and well-informed about contemporary views and experiences of shame as an *a priori*. Only thus can the theological conversation be respectful and pertinent.

Just some aspects of the theory and experience of shame and of religious tradition and practice can be touched on in this book. I necessarily have to be selective in my choice of topics, approaches and interpretations. The book will not, therefore, be comprehensive in content or scope. It will indicate some ways into a particular practical theological conversation rather than completing it. It will clarify questions, criticise assumptions and advance some tentative theoretical and practical conclusions in an area which is still underexplored in terms of methodology and substance from a theological perspective. This volume is thus a suggestive starting point, not the last word on shame, theology, or any kind of practical situation.

Emergent questions and issues for practical theology
This volume raises more questions than it answers for religious belief and practice in relation to shame.

Contemporary experiences and understandings of shame pose many fundamental questions for Christian practice and belief: Is Christianity harmful to some people? Is this religion 'on the side' of the shamed (Batson et al. 1993)? What view of the self should Christians adopt in the modern world (McFadyen 1990; White 1996)? Is atonement theory adequately nuanced to cope with the alienating experience of shame? What view should be taken of theological notions such as sin and religious practices such as confession in relation to shame?

These questions, and others like them, will unfold as the text progresses. Here, however, I want briefly to outline some broader, more methodologically related issues and questions that this study raises. These relate particularly to the field of practical theology. However, many of them would apply equally to other fields of interdisciplinary enquiry that relate to practice and human well-being.

The first and most important emergent issue concerns the purpose and honesty of theological endeavour in general and of practical theology in particular. Theology partly justifies its presence in the secular academy by claiming that it is engaged in open, rational enquiry into religious thought and experience. It will be seen as this study progresses, however, that both general and pastoral theology have almost totally ignored shame, together with many other important 'negative' emotions and experiences such as anger, dementia, and other chronic states. This prompts me to ask whether practical theology is genuinely open and exploratory, or whether it is a kind of rationalising justification for Christian orthodoxy – a species of applied or practically related apologetics.

Shame, together with other negative human experiences, presents enormous challenges to Christian thought and practice. It problematises the 'goodness' of this religious tradition, the truthfulness of its narratives about a caring God, and the effectiveness of its practical responses. If these challenges are veiled or ignored this might indicate that practical theologians are more interested in defending and exemplifying the 'truth' of certain *a priori* assumptions and positions than they are in understanding human experience and promoting human flourishing. If this is the case, theology risks being wilfully deceived and deceitful at the expense of human well-being. It can be seen as glossing over the uncomfortable and the unspeakable rather than honestly facing it. Thus, it might be seen as a kind of 'kitsch' activity that looks past, rather than into, the reality of human experience:

'Kitsch' is a German word born in the middle of the sentimental nineteenth century . . . Repeated use, however, has obliterated its original metaphysical meaning: kitsch is the absolute denial of shit, in both the literal and figurative senses of the word; kitsch excludes everything from its purview which is essentially unacceptable in human existence. (Kundera 1984: 242)

A second, related point concerns the level of seriousness with which practical theologians are prepared to pursue interdisciplinary enquiry. Most practical theologians reckon to use the insights and methods of a variety of non-theological disciplines such as philosophy, sociology and psychology to illuminate their concerns (Pattison 1986). Practical theology is often described as an interdisciplinary activity. However, such activity is fraught with problems. Even in relation to one particular subject such as shame or guilt there are a variety of perspectives that emerge from disciplines that have differing fundamental world views, assumptions, methods and purposes. Often exponents of these disciplines are ignorant of, or indifferent to, the findings of those in disciplines other than their own, so there is no attempt at attaining synthesis or dialogue between perspectives that are in many ways incommensurable.

A range of questions, therefore, arises for practical theology. Which disciplines should be attended to? Of the disciplines attended to, which should be privileged and prioritised? On what criteria should some disciplines be taken seriously while others are dismissed or relativised? To what extent is it incumbent on practical theologians to understand the background and methods of disciplines that produce particular findings that are then used to illuminate a specific issue or subject? Perhaps most awkwardly, what is to be done with the insights and methods of disciplines that do not readily support the drift and purpose of a particular line of theological enquiry?

These questions are raised acutely in the case of shame where many different voices and sources are available for consultation but few seem to be saying the same thing. This highlights the fact that practical theologians are often in danger of adopting approaches characterised by uncritical, haphazard, pragmatic eclecticism. These use a very limited range of resources in the interests of creating a coherent, pleasing narrative synthesis which may accord little respect to the diversity and complexity of reality as mediated through pluriform, sometimes contradictory, disciplinary discourses. Here again, the issue of 'kitsch' may hover around uneasily. The issue of interdisciplinary use and enquiry needs more attention if practical theology is to regard itself as a serious academic endeavour whose findings are to be allowed some authority in influencing thought and practice.

A similar area of concern is that of the use of experience in practical theology. I have somewhat uncritically asserted the importance of using experience, particularly my own experience, in trying to understand shame. At the same time, I have admitted that I only disclose aspects of that experience, heavily edited, within this text. All of which poses the question of the use to which practical theology puts experience. What is experience anyway? What value should be accorded to experience? Is an individual researcher bound to be disclosive and honest about their own experience, or should this be bracketed out for the sake of clarity and objectivity? How much and what kind of experience is to be used? Whose experiences are to be included or excluded? What counts as valid experience that is worth attending to? How should experience be presented and interpreted in practical theological enquiry? How should group and individual experiences be integrated with and weighed against other kinds of relevant evidence? These issues need further consideration if practical theology is to be properly self-critical of its own presuppositions and methods.

Other issues in the same vein can be briefly indicated. For example, how does practical theology cope with gaps in its understanding and knowledge of the contemporary world? How are hiatuses in experience, understanding and knowledge to be dealt with? Should they be glossed over or acknowledged, for example? To what extent is practical theology prepared to be open-endedly dialogical in its encounters with experiences, traditions and interdisciplinary insights rather than moving towards some kind of closure or solution? How should practical theologians involve themselves and their own immediate personal interests in their research work? How far do practical theologians need to be open to the possibility of their own change and transformation through practical theological activity? Do they need to be receptive to transformations that might actually be very upsetting and disruptive of their *a priori* religious and intellectual commitments?

All of the issues and questions documented here have arisen as challenges to me as a practical theologian in the writing of this book. In one way or another, they are all concerned with the fundamental sincerity, identity and integrity of pastoral theology as a disciplinary field and of pastoral theologians as practitioners of that discipline. Despite the best efforts of some colleagues (Browning 1983, 1987, 1991) I suspect that issues like these are presently insufficiently addressed within the discipline. The result is that it is less rigorous and honest than it might be. Thus, it lacks intellectual bite and practical credibility. To avoid the label of kitsch, I believe these questions need to be more directly addressed. Perhaps the contents of this volume will help to make the case that this should occur sooner rather than later.

PART I

Approaching shame

Introduction: *establishing a theoretical orientation*

The present work is an exercise in interdisciplinary dialogue structured by the notion of pastoral theological 'conversation'. The first two Parts of it therefore attempt to 'listen' to contemporary discourses that contribute to understandings of shame.

The two chapters in Part I, 'Approaching shame', will provide theoretical background and orientation to understandings of shame. In contemporary Western society, shame, like guilt, is often thought of as an emotion or an emotional experience. The first chapter, therefore, discusses different concepts of emotion. This shows that emotions can be variously understood. It problematises the hope that a single, clear understanding of shame or any other emotion can be established because there is no monolithic, authoritative understanding of the concept of emotion itself. This is inconvenient from the perspective of trying to create a coherent narrative about shame. However, it may help to establish the integrity of this work. It is concerned to engage in real interdisciplinary dialogue which is faithful to a complex view of reality rather than with opportunistic synthesis.

Chapter 2 problematises the nature and understandings of shame in particular. The concept of shame is to be found in many different contexts and discourses from literature to clinical psychology. The range and instances of this usage and their significance are considered here and a 'family resemblance' approach to concepts of shame is suggested. This allows the diversity, pluriformity and incommensurability of different discourses and understandings to be taken seriously while permitting a certain amount of synthesis in the interests of understanding the phenomenology of shame.

These two chapters provide a theoretical orientation for the interdisciplinary study of shame. This is a necessary methodological prerequisite in a work of this kind. However, for those readers who

18

are more interested in the outcomes rather than the underpinnings of such study, it may be helpful to move on to Part II which is more concerned with the phenomenology, experience and healing of shame.

CHAPTER I

Emotional confusion

Any attempt to review approaches to the emotions is bedevilled by
a certain lack of clarity and conceptual confusion in the literature.
Similar approaches may be given different names in psychology
compared with sociology or anthropology, for example, and even
within these disciplines there is a lack of consensus about how to
label or categorize the various approaches.

(Lupton 1998: 10)

Phenomena such as shame and guilt are widely regarded as emotions
(Taylor 1985). I shall, therefore, begin by considering the complexity and
contested nature of the study of emotions generally. Unfortunately, the
literature that pertains to emotions from different disciplines and
approaches is vast, disparate and often incommensurable in terms of
both perspectives and findings.

Rehabilitating the emotions

Until recently, emotions were mostly hidden from the purview of serious
academic consideration outside the disciplines of biology, psychology
and some kinds of philosophy. In the case of the latter, some philosophers such as Spinoza, Hume, Mill and Nietzsche allotted the emotions
or passions a significant role in moral life (Calhoun and Solomon 1984).
More typically, others, such as Kant, wanted to downplay or eliminate
emotions altogether (Lindholm 1990).

A number of factors may have inhibited the widespread academic
consideration of emotions historically. Perhaps the main reason that it
has been difficult rationally to appraise the emotions is that they have
been perceived to be fundamentally anti-rational and antipathetic to the
intellect (Averill 1996b). Since the days of the ancient Greek philosophers, what moderns call emotions and what ancients would have called
passions, desires and appetites, have represented a disruptive force that

appears to threaten rational life for individuals and groups (James 1997; Nussbaum 1994).

A dualistic attitude has flourished. The faculty of reason has been taken to be separate from that of emotion within the person. Passions and desires have been associated with humanity's embodied 'lower', primitive, and animal nature. In the patriarchal social order they have also inevitably been closely linked with the embodied, 'irrational', devalued female part of the human race: '[E]motion, like the female, has typically been viewed as something natural rather than cultural, irrational rather than rational, chaotic rather than ordered, subjective rather than universal, physical rather than mental or intellectual, unintended and uncontrollable, and hence often dangerous' (Lutz 1996: 151; cf. Lupton 1998; Crawford et al. 1992).

The passions or emotions appear to have the capacity to change and distort everything, threatening rational control and order. This is suggested by their very nomenclature:

> The term 'emotion' is derived from the Latin, *e* + *movere*. It originally meant to migrate or to transfer from one place to another. It was also used to refer to states of agitation or perturbation, both physical . . . and psychological . . . The term 'passion' derives from the Latin, *pati* (to suffer) and is related to the Greek, *pathos* . . . At the root of these terms is the idea that an individual (or physical object) is undergoing or suffering some change . . . (Averill 1996b: 206–7).

In their apparently ungovernable nature, some emotions can seem alien and overwhelming. Like demons or spirits, they cast the human beings who experience them as jetsam tossed about upon a sea of passion. The consequence of seeing emotions as a potent but incomprehensible enigma is that many thinkers have not perceived them as being susceptible to rational analysis or worthy of intellectual attention (Lloyd 1996: 9f.).

Fear, incomprehension and dismissal of the emotions have contributed to their being ignored as important aspects of human experience and thought. Only now, with the rise of feminism, the decline of narrow rationalism, and post-Cartesian holistic thought about the person, is it becoming possible to understand them more adequately. The process of re-evaluation is gaining pace. Unfortunately, the study of the emotions raises more issues and problems than it solves.

Defining emotion

There is no universally agreed definition of what an emotion is, nor of what traits a phenomenon must have in order to be regarded as an emotion (Oksenberg Rorty 1980: 1). Psychologists Kleinginna and Kleinginna suggest the following synthesising summary definition that draws upon textbooks, dictionaries and other sources:

Emotion is a complex set of interactions among subjective and objective factors, mediated by neural/hormonal systems, which can (a) give rise to affective experiences such as feelings of arousal, pleasure/displeasure; (b) generate cognitive processes such as emotionally relevant perceptual effects, appraisals, labeling processes; (c) activate widespread physiological adjustments to the arousing conditions; and (d) lead to behavior that is often, but not always, expressive, goal-directed, and adaptive. (Plutchik 1994: 5)

By contrast, Solomon, like many philosophers who have become interested in emotions (Nussbaum 1994; Oakley 1992; Sartre 1993), emphasises the cognitive, judging or appraising aspect of emotional activity, de-emphasising its physiological aspects: '*[E]motions are judgments*, not blind or irrational forces that victimize us. Emotions are the life force of the soul, the source of most of our values . . ., the basis of most other passions' (Solomon 1993: 15).

Behind these contrasting definitions lie very different theories of the nature and cause of emotions. In practice, many people, especially non-philosophers, would probably generally agree with this characterisation:

emotions involve affect or feelings, often equated with certain physiological
    events;
emotions also involve cognition, however fleeting, in the form of
    remembering or appraising;
emotions are expressions of inner feeling;
emotions communicate our feelings to others;
emotions overcome us. (Crawford et al. 1992: 110)

While there may be some consensus on aspects of the definition of emotions, this is by no means comprehensive and universally applicable to all the experiences that are characterised as 'emotional' in human life.

What counts as an emotion?

There are a number of experiences that most people would probably recognise as clearly emotional. These contain elements of physiological arousal, a clear orientation to an object, and cognitive appraisal in a very immediate way, as in anger, fear, sadness, joy or surprise.

However, this does not exhaust the number of very different experiences that are characterised as emotions. It is possible to experience 'intellectual' emotions (Averill 1996a) as well as emotions that seem passive or which predispose to inaction. So, for example, some would argue that hope, loneliness, regret, despair, or nostalgia are emotions even though they may be long-term states of being that have little sense of physiological arousal, immediate response, predisposition to action, or clear intentional object (Landman 1996; Wood 1986).

Attempts to anchor specific emotions to particular patterns of objective physiological arousal have foundered. Often, when people experience arousal they do not initially know how to label or understand it. They may describe their experience with a number of different emotional terms ('I was so shocked when I got a First. I did not know whether to laugh or to cry. Then I felt quite depressed, even suicidal. I only really felt happy about it the day after I heard the news.') Ginsburg and Harrington note: '[T]here does not appear to be a set of bodily states which are uniquely and reliably tied to specific emotional states and only to them. The bodily instantiations of what we refer to as emotions appear to be variable and unreliable . . .' (Ginsburg and Harrington 1996: 249).

It might be argued that whatever individuals or groups regard and talk about as emotions can be regarded as emotional. Thus, experiences and states that may have very different provoking stimuli and may manifest themselves in very diverse ways, subjectively or objectively, may be included within the category, 'emotion'. This may broaden it until its edges become so blurred as to make the basic concept boundariless. What is regarded as an emotion or emotional may then seem to be in the perception of the beholder, or at least within the agreed conventions of a social group, rather than being a clear label for a universally felt, physiologically related state.

Emotions may be difficult to separate from other categories of experience. The intellectual categories within which particular states are understood are porous and change over time. The Greek therapeutic philosophers, for example, included both the passions and the physical appetites such as hunger and the need for sleep under the category of 'desire', while seeing the appetites as distinct and easier to come to terms with than the passions (Nussbaum 1994: 111ff.). It is not easy to distinguish emotion, or at least some kinds of emotion, from categories such as affect, sentiment, intuition, instinct, disposition, character trait or mood (Ekman and Davidson 1994: 49ff.).

The distinction between emotion and mood is a particularly significant one in the context of the forthcoming discussion on shame (Parkinson 1995: 3). Is one to understand the condition of being chronically shamed or shame-ridden as an emotional experience when it may last for a lifetime? Should it be understood to be a mood because it seems to be a prolonged emotional experience that has an evaluative component together with the affective component of feeling bad without having a definite object? Or has it in fact become a character trait, a sentiment, or an attitude to the self (cf. Tantam 1998)?

Basic emotions?

Since the time of Aristotle there has been an unresolved quest to identify and categorise some fundamental and universal emotions (James 1997). The 'holy grail' for many contemporary investigators working within the tradition of Darwin (1965) has been to try and identify certain core, physiologically based responses which are be anchored in humanity's biological nature and species evolution (Demos 1995; Ekman and Davidson 1994; Plutchik 1994). These are believed to form the bedrock of emotions. They can be universally found throughout the human species, existing independently of culture and social interpretation.

Lists of such basic emotions that manifest themselves in distinctive types of facial expression include fear, anger, disgust, sadness, joy, surprise, rage, love, happiness and interest (Parkinson 1995: 4). All other emotions, properly so-called, are combinations of these basic, physiologically based responses. They can be identified by studying human behaviour, posture, and expression to find common features relating to particular situations. It is argued that all human beings can basically recognise the physiological responses such as facial expression that accompany different kinds of arousal (Fridlund and Duchaine 1996). They therefore act as a fundamental means of communication and information-giving for self and others within groups.

There are problems with this kind of theorising. First, physiological arousal and expression may not correspond to subjective experience or to an individual's labelling of a particular emotional state. Individuals may not to be able to name their own emotions. They may interpret them very differently from outside observers.

Secondly, while some observable phenomena such as the facial expression of anger seem to be highly visible and universally recognisable, others are not. Expressions of shame, sadness or disgust, for example, may be much more difficult to recognise and interpret accurately than that of anger (Oatley 1996).

Finally, identifying such basic emotions does little to help in trying to understand how emotions play out in practice in particular individuals and contexts. Individuals often experience a complex melange of feelings and perceptions that makes it difficult for them, and for others, to identify exactly what emotion they are experiencing. Context and culture are very influential in the causation, recognition and interpretation of emotions. It is, therefore, questionable how much a knowledge of 'basic' emotions is helpful in understanding lived human experience. This is a limitation of the disciplinary ends and methods such as those of psychology that have been applied to emotions and which can easily lead to ordinary and subjective experience being ignored (Crawford et al. 1992: 26–7; Harré 1986b: 5).

'Families' of emotions?

One issue that has vexed researchers into the emotions is the relationship of various emotions to one another. Some believe that there are only a few (say 6 to 10) physiologically related basic emotions such as fear, anger and joy (Demos 1995; Ekman and Davidson 1994: 5ff.). All other emotions are combinations or variations of these. One way of categorising emotions is, therefore, to attempt to find a limited number of basic physiological reactions and origins for them.

Another way is to try and categorise them in relation to their objects or common provoking factors. Lazarus and Lazarus (1994), for example, identify five groups of emotions whose members have a familial resemblance based on the object towards which the emotion is directed. The 'nasty' emotions of anger, envy and jealousy belong together because they all share a desire to hurt oneself or others. The existential emotions of anxiety-fright, shame and guilt all have to do with meanings about who we are, our place in the world, life and death, and the quality of existence (Lazarus and Lazarus 1994: 41). Emotions caused by unfavourable life conditions that militate against the attainment of personal goals include relief, hope, sadness and depression. Those provoked by favourable life conditions include happiness, pride and love. Finally, the emotions of gratitude and compassion, together with emotions arising from aesthetic experiences, form a 'family' because they all depend upon the need to empathise with others.

This schema can be contrasted with that of Gabriele Taylor (1985).

She groups shame and guilt *together with* pride, thus transgressing the boundaries between Lazarus and Lazarus' second and fourth categories. Taylor characterises these emotions as 'emotions of self-assessment' (Taylor 1985).

Another way of categorising emotions is to place them in a bipolar relationship. Thus pride becomes the polar opposite of shame, hatred is the opposite of love, and so on (Plutchik 1994: 65–73). There may be some value in making this kind of broad distinction, as there may be in trying to distinguish expansive, extraverting emotions (such as joy and pride) and contractive, introverting emotions (such as despair and shame).

The most important thing that emerges from the schemata of categorisation considered here is that there is a degree of arbitrariness in them all. Often, it depends on how an emotion is discerned and described as to whether it will satisfactorily fit into any particular family, category, or distinction. Is shyness a milder version of embarrassment which is in turn a mild version of shame, for example (Price Tangney and Fischer 1995)? Or can these categories, which have a certain clear distinction in everyday parlance, be seen and understood as distinct from one another?

Attempts to categorise emotions in rigid ways are liable to break down. This is particularly likely when one moves towards mild emotional states and those that do not appear to have much in the way of obvious physiological correlation.

The structure and function of emotional experience

There is some consensus around the idea that emotions tend to include aspects of physiological arousal, cognition and affective response. However, there is much debate about how these aspects of emotion interact with each other and the sequence that they follow.

William James suggested that the commonsensical notion that perception of a situation led then to feeling which then gave rise to physiological changes was incorrect at least in the case of the 'coarser' emotions like grief, fear, rage and love as opposed to the 'subtler' emotions associated with moral, intellectual and aesthetic feelings. Perception of a situation leads to a motor reaction that is then accompanied by visceral arousal. This is finally (if almost instantly) perceived as emotional feeling by the subject. The perception of emotion is thus a kind of feedback mechanism to the subject (James 1981: 1061; cf. Plutchik 1994: 27ff.).

An early neurological researcher, Walter Cannon, argued for a rather different order of arousal. He suggested that perception of a situation leads to hypothalmic arousal. This simultaneously provokes bodily changes *and* the feelings that are emotions (Plutchik 1994: 29ff.).

Subsequently, more, and more complex, models of arousal have evolved. For example, Parkinson outlines a four-factor theory in which encounter leads to appraisal of some kind which then can give way to evaluative feelings, bodily reactions, expressive responses and action tendencies. All four of these factors can contribute in different contexts and circumstances to the overall emotional experience that eventuates (Parkinson 1995: 16–17).

It is not necessary to provide a global vision of all the possible theories of emotional constitution or causation, nor of the different approaches to these in the present context. It is, however, useful to be aware of the diversity of theorising.

One recent theory of emotional response illustrates the complex intricacy of factors that can be involved and implicated. Lazarus and Lazarus (1994) advance a cognitive-motivational-relational theory of emotions that pays particular attention to reason and cognition in human emotional experience. They argue that emotions are fundamentally 'the products of *personal meaning*' (Lazarus and Lazarus 1994: 5). Specific emotions follow a particular course or 'plot'. This defines what subjects believe is happening to them. It reveals the personal meaning that is assigned to a particular event and its significance for the individual's well-being (Lazarus and Lazarus 1994: 5). The emotions have a logic of their own which varies from individual to individual and indeed from context to context. If one knows the situation of an individual then their emotional responses are actually reasonable and predictable responses to what is going on (Lazarus and Lazarus 1994: 10).

Lazarus and Lazarus conclude that:

Emotions are complex reactions that engage both our minds and our bodies. These reactions include: a subjective mental state, such as a feeling of anger, anxiety, or love; an impulse to act, such as fleeing or attacking, whether or not it is expressed overtly; and profound changes in the body, such as increased heart rate or blood pressure. Some of these bodily changes prepare for and sustain coping actions, and others . . . communicate to others what we are feeling, or want others to believe that we are feeling. (Lazarus and Lazarus 1994: 151)

This is a good example of a theory that removes emotions from the sphere of irrational, visceral response to events and makes clear the place of other factors such as evaluation, goals and meanings. Emotion in human beings is a very complex matter. Particular individuals act very differently in different contexts and situations and, indeed, their responses can change rapidly within the same situation.

This kind of theory allows for individual differences in response to the same situation and for rapid changes. It also accommodates the fact that the appraisal of facts and situations can change in the light of new information or the acquisition of a different perspective. Furthermore, it allows for social factors and norms to influence the way in which situations are experienced and emotions evoked and expressed. Such theorising opens up the possibility that while emotions may often follow common patterns or plots, they are as plastic, educable, manageable, and changeable as the human subjects to whom they belong. They are not eruptions of blind, animal-like instinct. Nor are they incompatible with intelligent judgment, which cannot be controlled or modified by consciousness and reason.

A number of possible functions can be identified for the emotions. Probably the most obvious of these is to motivate and predispose to action. Emotions often induce, or are accompanied by, a state of alertness and preparedness for action. They focus attention and are often associated with the physiological arousal that would allow swift action such as flight or fight to occur, even if that action is not actually performed in the event.

Another important function of the emotions is as informational feedback or communication to the self. By becoming emotionally aware, one becomes cognisant of changes that are taking place in the relationship between the environment and one's own organic existence. Thus, experiencing emotions can teach us much about how we relate to ourselves, other people, our goals and values, and the world (Lazarus and Lazarus 1994: 203–4). This allows appraisal, choice and action and may help predispose towards an appropriate response.

The notion of emotions as communication with the self may cast light on the finding amongst actors, therapists and others that the conscious adoption of a particular posture or set of physiological behaviours can foster a sense of a particular emotion. Emotions or feelings in this context appear to be the consequences rather than the causes of action and behaviour (Laird and Apostoleris 1996). Thus soldiers who screw up their faces and shout while doing bayonet practice may find this actually begins to elicit feelings of hatred and aggression towards the straw bales that they are required to impale.

Changes in posture, expression, etc. may be more visible and easy to interpret by a third party than by the individual who is experiencing them if the latter has not become conscious of her appearance. This brings out a third important function for the emotions, that of social communication. A main theme of biological and psychological research has been the fundamental importance of the expressive, communicative function of emotions in relation to other members of the species. Facial and bodily muscle movements signal to others of our state of being and of our intentions for action (Cole 1998).

Some facial and bodily expressions such as those associated with anger can be 'read' easily and accurately by others. However, other expressions such as those associated with shame and despair are more ambivalent and difficult to interpret (Oatley 1996: 315; Keltner and Harker 1998). This suggests that the 'language' of emotional expression may not be a universal one. It is likely to be affected by social, contextual and other factors. These have to be taken into account when trying to understand the function of emotions.

Some theorists argue that while emotional expressions do indeed perform functions of communication between individuals, this may be much more of a learned than an innate language. In this sense, individuals may be seen to act out emotional expressions as dramatic performances or roles whose function is to give emphasis or energy to an individual's attitudes or actions. An emotional response is taken to be a sincere and meant response in relationships. There are probably few people who have not, on occasion, as at a funeral, consciously assumed a posture or expression with a view to convincing others of an inward attitude or disposition (Sarbin 1986).

Emotions as they are commonly understood within broadly bio-physiological discourse perform a variety of functions in different contexts. In general terms, emotions inform us about ourselves, our goals and values, and our relationships with other people and the world. They help to shape priorities and action and also provide the impetus and motivation to pursue it vigorously. It is difficult to imagine human life without them: 'Life without emotions would be an exercise in boredom' (Lazarus and Lazarus 1994: 203). Indeed, those who are perceived not to have emotional experience are often thought of as being inhuman. Murderers, psychopaths, torturers and other criminals are often regarded as inhuman not only because of their evil deeds, but because they seem to be unable to manifest an appropriate feeling response in relation to them. Life without emotions would not be social and personal life as we know it.

Social factors and emotions

Hitherto, the place of social and cultural factors in the creation, performance, recognition and interpretation of emotions has only been hinted at.

Various stances are possible in trying to understand the relationship between 'individual' emotions and social context and relationships.

Some theorists argue that emotions are social constructions (Gergen 1991, 1994; Harré 1986a; Stevens 1996: 219ff.). Social constructionists start from the presupposition that there is no access to experience or any kind of 'objective' reality beyond language (Rorty 1980, 1989). It is thus impossible to have knowledge of phenomena 'in themselves'. Meaning and understanding is a property of social relationships. Where people share a world view they create local ontologies whereby some meanings come to seem reified, real and unchallengeable. However, these local ontologies remain products of language; they are only sustained by rhetorical persuasiveness and interest. When society and language changes, 'reality' changes too.

Social constructionists argue that emotions are not biologically based, physiological phenomena located within individuals. Emotions have no 'objective' existence. They are not simply there in nature, 'propelling us along willy-nilly' (Gergen 1991: 165). Instead, 'ownership of the emotions' should be 'transferred from biology to culture'. From this perspective, they are performances within relationships that conform to a socially intelligible script:

We are not driven by forces bottled up within us; rather, we perform emotions much as we would on stage. In 'doing' an emotion we recruit biology in the same way an actor needs heightened blood pressure to enact properly the rage of King Lear. The biological system is required to carry out the emotion effectively, but the biology does not require the actions themselves. (Gergen 1991: 165; cf. Gergen 1994: 210ff.)

From the social constructionist standpoint, Gergen questions empirical research into emotions that seems to demonstrate that certain basic emotions in the form of physiologically based responses exist beyond social relationships while it in fact constructs the phenomena it purports to study:

[R]esearch procedures employ a circular form of reasoning. . . . The research first draws from the reservoir of commonsense assumptions. It is an unchallenged truism in Western culture that there are emotions such as love, fear, anger, and so on, and that they are indicated or expressed in facial expressions, bodily movements, tone of voice and the like . . . the research gains initial credibility by virtue of cultural truisms, and with the aid of controlled research and technical measurement proceeds to draw conclusions about the causes and the effects of the emotion. These conclusions serve to objectify the conventional constructions; they give a sense of warrantable palpability to a folk myth. . . . there is no turning back to ask whether there is, in fact, anything there. (Gergen 1994: 221–2)

On the 'hard' social constructionist view exemplified by Gergen there is no physical underlying ontological reality to any emotion. Emotions are entirely constructed and mediated within social and moral orders. Physiological phenomena and feelings are then either loosely related incidentals in emotional experience, or perhaps form part of emotional 'performance' in the same way that particular gestures are an integral part of acting in a theatre.

A 'softer' social constructionist position is possible and has been commended by sociologists such as Lupton (1998: 8) and Hochschild (1983: 28). This allows that society and culture fundamentally shape emotional experience, expression, performance and interpretation. However, it preserves the notion of the possibility of experience existing outside language and some kind of physiological basis of bodily arousal for emotions (Stern 1985).

It is not necessary to opt for either the hard or the soft social constructionist position. Here, I simply want to point to some of the evidence that suggests that social and cultural factors have an enormous significance for the expression and construal of emotions. They must be seen at least partially as social constructions and phenomena, not simply as essences inherent in individual physiology (Harré 1986b).

The evidence for the influence of social and cultural factors upon emotions is varied and diffuse. It is a commonplace of social scientific and some philosophical discourse that language is a social product that reflects, refracts and shapes the nature of reality (Rorty 1989). Whenever someone makes a judgment of a situation, or names an emotion or an emotional experience, language and concepts are used instantaneously, spontaneously and unthinkingly. Without words and concepts, reality lies outside human experience and meaning (Gergen 1991, 1994). Social order and communication are therefore impossible. This is reflected in the empirical findings of Crawford et al. (1992). Without words and concepts people were unable to analyse or even to remember important emotional experiences:

> We reflect on and define our emotions in relation to others' response and in response to others' assessment. Therefore, if we were isolated in our experience or if our feelings were invalidated by adults, we had no grounds for making the experience intelligible. . . . Silence has the power to render us helpless. (Crawford et al. 1992: 189–90)

The importance of the linguistic and, therefore, social construction and maintenance of emotions becomes apparent in cross-cultural evidence. There is enormous variation of expression, description and interpretation of what might be called 'emotions' across cultures (Heelas 1996). Different languages have different numbers and kinds of emotion words. English, for example, contains around four hundred emotion words (Heelas 1996: 174). The number of words applying to different kinds of emotional state also varies markedly. An analysis of Maori vocabulary, for example, reveals a predominance of words relating to anger and aggression while there is a paucity of words that describe states of depression, envy, jealousy, hate and grief (Strongman and Strongman 1996).

Frequently, there is little cross-cultural constancy of meaning. Spanish, for example, contains the concept '*vergüenza ajena*'. This denotes and conflates both shame and embarrassment and seems to be rooted in historically based, social understandings of honour in Spain (Iglesias 1996).

Different cultures attribute the causes of emotions very differently, whether to gods, to social activities, or to the self (Heelas 1996: 186). Emotions are also differently treated and valued across cultures so that 'Apollonian societies tend to treat emotions as dangerous threats to the moral order, whereas Dionysian societies tend to treat them as essential for that order' (Heelas 1996: 187).

All this diversity may be taken to imply that there is little, if any, universal or common emotional experience that is shared in all human cultures.

Dominant emotions and ways they are talked about have tended to change radically over time as societies and cultures have changed (Stearns and Stearns 1988). At one time in English society, 'melancholy' was a dominant emotion (Burton 1932). It has now been displaced by concepts such as depression, boredom and nostalgia (Harré and Finlay-Jones

1986: 222; cf. Ferguson 1995). Similarly, it has been possible to see the apparent rise of 'new' emotions like loneliness (Wood 1986).

An example of the many ways in which the definition, scope, expression and perception of emotions has changed is in the way that grief is manifested (Stearns and Knapp 1996). Giotto's thirteenth-century fresco depiction of the deposition of Jesus from the cross in the Arena Chapel in Padua shows the grieving disciples adopting very different postures than those that would be appropriate to grief in twentieth-century England (Basile 1993). Above all, the mourners have no tears in their eyes (Barasch 1987).

It is possible to see one emotion giving way to another as societies change. Thus it has been argued that guilt as a main social control emotion supplanted shame in early New England over the course of two centuries (Demos 1996).

The social and cultural shaping of emotions is apparent in the contemporary world in their gendered nature. While both men and women manifest emotional responses, the expression of 'wetter' emotions such as grief and depression have often been associated with the latter while the former have been associated with 'hot', dry emotions such as anger (Lupton 1998: 84ff.; Gillis 1988).

Feminist researchers point out that women's experience of emotions such as happiness and anger can be very different from that of men who experience a greater sense of autonomy and often have less sense of responsibility for the emotional well-being of others (Crawford et al. 1992: 110ff.). Lutz suggests that in patriarchal society women are not *more* emotional than men but are construed as being more emotional to justify strategies of control:

In all societies, body disorders – which emotion is considered to be in this society – become crucial indicators of problems with social control and, as such, are more likely to occur or emerge in a discourse concerning social subordinates . . . Because emotion is constructed as relatively chaotic, irrational, and antisocial, its existence vindicates authority and legitimates the need for control. (Lutz 1996: 166)

This brings us to the social production and control of emotions and the role that they play within the social and moral order. Scheff argues that emotions relating to the moral order are ways of sustaining and monitoring social bonds. In this connection, pride and shame, for example, are primary social emotions that 'serve as intense and automatic bodily signs of the state of a system that would otherwise be difficult to observe, the state of one's bonds to others' (Scheff 1990: 15).

This is close to Hochschild's (1983) suggestion that emotional performances act as signals or sources of information to self and others.
Hochschild argues that emotional behaviour and display follow social
rules – 'feeling rules'. These are learned, much as actors acquire the feelings, words and gestures that go along with a theatrical role. When an
actor gets deeply inside such a part he or she becomes engaged in 'deep'
as opposed to 'surface' acting so that s/he appears to act naturally.
Members of society are similarly socialised into roles and gestures so
there is no conscious distinction between the person and their emotions;
their emotions then seem spontaneous, natural and inevitable. They can
be interpreted and evaluated as appropriate or inappropriate in particular contexts by others with a similar socialisation experience. Thus, it is
possible to judge whether someone has displayed the 'right' kind of
behaviour and emotional reaction, for example, at a funeral.

Averill similarly argues that in all societies emotions follow social rules
of creation, appraisal and attribution. Thus, 'getting in touch with one's
feelings is not so much a process of discovery as it is an act of creation'
(Averill 1986: 115). Emotional performances and evaluations can change
from society to society, and it is perfectly possible for individuals to
change their emotional responses as they grow older; thus they are not
innate at birth. Sarbin (1986) also argues that emotions are essentially
socially mediated and shaped dramatic displays of the self in human
interaction. Fridlund and Duchaine (1996) show that when individuals
are experiencing emotions on their own, even in terms of making gestures and and facial expressions, this is done within the context of being
a 'social self'.

Armon-Jones argues that 'emotions are constituted in order to serve
socio-cultural purposes' (Armon-Jones 1986a: 34). This is not difficult to
accept in the case of emotions of social control like shame and guilt
which relate to the upholding of morals, values and standards. However,
she suggests that it is also true in the case of apparently sinful,
inappropriate or undesirable emotions such as envy, hatred and jealousy
which may also help to affirm social norms and values. Thus jealousy
may affirm the value of possessiveness, while hatred allows societies to
mobilise their defences against threats and enemies.

Some sociologists argue that emotions can be changed, manipulated
and 'managed', even deliberately (Fineman 1993). Mestrovic characterises Western society as 'postemotional', maintaining that 'a new hybrid
of intellectualized, mechanical, mass-produced emotions has appeared
on the world scene' (Mestrovic 1997: 26). He believes that while emo-

tional experiences are still to be found in society, these are now less clearly associated with commitment and action. So, for example, engaged compassion has given way to ineffectual, abstract pity.

In her brilliant study of airline attendants, Hochschild (1983) describes the way in which these people are required to manipulate their own emotions and emotional display. 'Emotional labour', the term coined for this process, is 'the management of feeling to create a publicly observable facial and bodily display; emotional labour is sold for a wage and therefore has exchange value' (Hochschild 1983: 7). Hochschild argues that this kind of labour is becoming common in contemporary service-based industries where impression and a 'personal touch' of sincerity and authenticity is desirable.

One must beware, here, of portraying emotions as easily manipulable, manageable aspects of self and society that can be channelled in the direction of social conformity and thus used simply as tools of social control. Insofar as some emotions inform people about their attachment to objects, values and identities, they can be socially and politically destructive, transformational and subversive (Landman 1996). It is the ungovernable, unpredictable aspect of emotions in social groups that has led Gabriel to the notion of the unmanaged and unmanageable organisation (Gabriel 1993).

Another temptation that must be resisted is that of suggesting that because emotions are socially formed and mediated, people's emotional reactions and experience in a particular society will be uniform in response to events and situations. In practice, individuals belong to different sub-groups within societies and their experience of socialisation is different. There is enormous scope for individual and group differentiation in emotional response and expression.

Harré and Parrott sum up the intriguing, problematic, ambivalent relationship between social, psychological and physiological factors in emotions thus:

Emotions are at once bodily responses and expressions of judgements, at once somatic and cognitive. They seem to have deep evolutionary roots, yet they are, among human phenomena, notably culturally variable in many of their aspects. Even the somatic aspect of emotions is complex. There are emotion displays and there are, in some cultures, emotion feelings, and neither is immune from cultural influence. Some displays seem a general feature of human ethology, . . . whereas others are acquired as habits, and yet others are trained in much the same way as manual skills are trained. Yet, considered functionally, emotion displays have their proper places in unfolding episodes of interpersonal reaction: they are acts embedded in patterns of acts; their display is subject to rules and conventions; they are embedded in culturally specific moral orders and normative systems that allow for assessment of the correctness or impropriety of emotions. (Parrott and Harré 1996b: 1)

In due course, it will be necessary to return more specifically to some sociological insights into the nature of emotions of social control such as guilt and shame. These insights form an important counterbalance and complement to psychological and individualised understandings of these emotions or states (Lupton 1998: 10ff.). They help to explain how the emotional experience of particular persons in specific societies might be related to the wider social order with its norms and values.

Conclusion

This chapter has provided background information about the nature of emotions as a prelude to studying the specific phenomenon of shame. I have not been systematic and comprehensive in my consideration of the nature, causes, functions and factors affecting emotions and emotional expression. Nor have I tried to resolve important questions or to give extensive accounts of the very different academic approaches to the study of emotions. However, I have shown that the whole field of study of the emotions is controversial and contested.

Biologists, psychologists, philosophers, sociologists and others all differ within and between disciplines on the nature and understanding of emotions. There is some consensus around the ideas that emotions have cognitive, physiological and affective dimensions and that they usually have some kind of object. However, social and other factors, including semantic differences, obscure any clear vision of the fundamental nature of emotions. Oksenberg Rorty's 1980 judgment still seems accurately to sum up the state of the study of the emotions:

It is too early to construct a unified theory, even too early for a single inter-disciplinary account of the approaches whose contributions are required to explain the range of emotional conditions. The vocabularies of neurophysiologists, psychologists, anthropologists, biologists, and philosophers have not been uniformly or consistently established in a reliable form. Even workers within a single discipline often turn out, on close examination, to be talking at cross purposes. (Oksenberg Rorty 1980: 4)

Apparent 'emotional illiteracy' (Orbach 1994: 3f.) together with ignorance about, and insensitivity to, emotions in contemporary society is underwritten by a great deal of confusion and lack of consensus and understanding of emotions amongst those who study and research them. Experts disagree and talk past each other in the matter of emotions. It is with this discomforting conclusion that I turn directly to the emotion of shame – if, indeed, emotion it turns out to be.

CHAPTER TWO

Problems in approaching shame

Shame is like a subatomic particle. One's knowledge of shame is often limited to the trace it leaves

(Lewis 1992: 34).

Study of the phenomenon of shame is characterised by a huge variety of approaches and insights (Gilbert 1998). For a long time, I hoped to arrive at a synthesis that would accommodate and make sense of them all. I wanted to identify a lowest common denominator to all instances and uses of shame. I sought a controlling meaning or experience, possibly embedded in a basic physiological response, that would permit a synthetic understanding of all kinds and instances of shame.

I now believe there is no fixed essence of meaning or experience that underlies all usages and instances of the category 'shame'. Like an onion, shame is made up of enfolded and overlapping, but also discrete, meanings and understandings; there is no 'essential onion' or 'essential shame' at the centre of meaning or experience. Nor, indeed, to change the analogy, is there any Esperanto or universal set of words and concepts into which all experiences and instances of shame can be translated. The reifying language of substance and essence applied to shame is misleading if it implies that there is a stable, objective core to this phenomenon.

It has taken me a long time to have confidence in the judgment that approaches to shame are mostly disparate and incommensurable. The most useful way of understanding them together is to adopt a kind of family resemblance theory (Parrott and Harré 1996a: 42ff.). This means that while some of a possible range of features will be present in all instances in which the phenomenon of shame is alluded to in a variety of different discourses, not all of them will be present all the time. In this chapter, I will give an account of the journey that leads to this conclusion before discussing the family resemblance approach in more depth.

39

The first part of the chapter considers some of the obstacles that occur in the search for an understanding of shame. Shame has been hidden from view in ordinary human experience and in academic and clinical discourse. It will be useful to understand some of the factors that have contributed to this apparent inscrutability before advancing to look at some of the very diverse approaches to shame that have been proposed in different quarters. In addition to clarifying the range of possible approaches to shame, this second part provides basic information about the content of these approaches. Having briefly summarised and evaluated the usefulness of a variety of approaches, the final part of the chapter considers how to relate these very disparate approaches together in a methodologically credible way. Here, the family resemblance perspective is introduced as a means of taking different approaches to shame seriously without resorting to uncritical eclecticism or to pragmatic synthesis.

Shame: a phenomenon that is hidden

One of the main problems that arises in trying to arrive at a comprehensive understanding of shame is that it is a phenomenon that has been hidden in various ways. Here I will consider some of the factors that may have contributed to this obscurity.

Shame and exposure
It may seem ironic to start by suggesting that it is the quality of exposure that is often attributed to shame experience that partly accounts for its being hidden and ignored.

The word 'shame' derives from notions of covering and concealing:

> The word *shame* is derived from a Germanic root *skam/skem* (Old High German *scama*, Anglo-Saxon *scamu*), with the meaning 'sense of shame, being shamed, disgrace (*Schande*).' It is traced back to the Indo-European root *kam/kem*: 'to cover, to veil, to hide.' The prefixed *s* (*skam*) adds the reflexive meaning – 'to cover oneself.' The notion of *hiding* is intrinsic to and inseparable from the concept of shame. (Wurmser 1995: 29; cf. Schneider 1987a: 29–31)

However, this notion of concealment better describes the reaction to shame rather than shame experience itself. The urgent desire to cover oneself or disappear succeeds an acute sense of unwanted exposure. Adam and Eve find the fig leaves that cover their naked bodies (their 'shame') when they become conscious that they are exposed in a painful, undesirable way. Thus, many writers on shame put exposure at the centre of the shame experience (Kaufman 1993: 8). In *Shame: The Exposed Self*, Michael Lewis notes that:

Shame can be defined simply as the feeling we have when we evaluate our actions, feelings or behavior, and conclude that we have done wrong. It encompasses the *whole of ourselves*; it generates a wish to hide, to disappear, or even to die. (Lewis 1992: 2)

The painful personal exposure that inheres in shame and the desire to escape from or avoid it have meant that, until recently, few sufferers or investigators have examined shame closely and directly: '[J]ust as shame has an intrinsic tendency to encourage hiding, so there is a tendency for the observer of another's shame to turn away from it' (Lewis 1971: 15–16). The unspoken desire to avoid thinking about shame may be buttressed by the 'contagious' nature of this condition. Such is the horror and stigma of shame that people may shy away from it lest they experience some kind of personal or social contamination (Lewis 1971: 15; cf. Lewis 1998). Even to recognise or consider shame may be to risk stigmatising defilement.

Academic and clinical investigation has mirrored the secretive, concealing dynamic of shame. Thus shame has remained a 'veiled' or masked companion (Wurmser 1995) to other states like guilt and anger. Such is the intensity of discomfort with shame experience that it seems to have been surrounded by a shame-bound cultural taboo of shame about shame (Kaufman 1993: 4).

The failure of words
Linguistic difficulties have also played a major part in ensuring that shame remains hidden.

The experience of shame does not readily present as an articulable experience. From a psychoanalytic perspective, Block Lewis suggests that the roots of shame lie in the 'primitive', pre-linguistic experiences of young children (Lewis 1971). This perhaps helps to explain its fundamental resistance to clear verbalisation and articulation in later life. Shame presents as a visual or imagistic experience rather than one that can easily be verbally articulated. Indeed, the experience of shame often reduces the shamed person to speechlessness.

Kaufman points out that scientific language has not had a vocabulary that is adequately nuanced to describe different inner states and experiences of emotion (Kaufman 1993: 4). Within psychology, until recently an emphasis on observing and describing behaviour and 'objective' situations has militated against interest in the development of a pluriform language of subjective perception. This has hindered interest in experiences of emotions like shame.

There is a specific problem with the everyday English language regarding shame. While some other languages have a number of different words that capture significant aspects or types of shame (Iglesias 1996), English uses just one word to cover a wide range of phenomena and experiences:

Although the English language has only one word for shame, Indo-European languages commonly have two or more: Greek has available the various meanings of *aischyne, aeikes, entrope, elencheie,* and *aidos*; Latin can draw upon *foedus, mucula, pudor, turpitudo,* and *vercundia*; German has *Scham* and *Schande*; and French, *honte* and *pudeur* (Schneider 1987a: 18, 145).

A limited English vocabulary means that it is difficult to distinguish between, for example, shame as disgrace and shame as a disposition of respect, modesty or discretion.

The difficulties raised above are compounded by different theorists' variable usage of the concept 'shame'. Broucek, for example, distinguishes four main different uses of the term. These are shame as used in everyday parlance, shame as used to designate an innate affect, shame as a category or family of feelings that share a base in a common innate affect, and shame as an anticipatory affect that influences future behaviour (Broucek 1991: 5).

Many writers are not clear in their usage and some use shame in a counter-commonsensical way. For example, Benedict (1954), an anthropologist, understands shame to be a reaction to other people's disapprobation that comes from outside the individual while guilt depends on an internalised individual sense of sin or wrongdoing. This notion of shame flies in the face of the fact that in the modern world shame is often experienced by individuals on their own, there is no need for an audience or the presence of others for people to feel shame, and shame can feel at least as deeply personal and internal as guilt (Thrane 1979). Benedict is not necessarily wrong in her characterisation of shame. However, the diversity of usage of the word 'shame', often accompanied by lack of contextual clarity and definition, creates an obstacle to understanding the nature of this phenomenon.

It could be argued in response to these points that language constructs rather than reflects experience (Gergen 1991, 1994). Thus it might be suggested that the reason that there is such poor linguistic clarity and nuance in the consideration of shame is that this phenomenon is still in the process of construction and is, in fact, being differently constructed in different discourses and cultures. This does not detract from the main point being made here; presently shame is poorly and diversely articulated and expressed linguistically. This contributes to its hiddenness.

The assimilation of shame to guilt

Shame has been obscured from view by being assimilated to, and hidden behind, the concept of guilt (Kaufman 1993: 4). Both shame and guilt may be described as emotions of negative self-assessment (Taylor 1985). It is probably futile to try and make any absolute distinction between these two concepts or states in terms of common parlance (Cairns 1993: 24f.). However, for the most part, any feeling of self-censure and negative self-evaluation in Western culture has been described as guilt and this usage continues to the present day (Gordon 1996). The reasons for this assimilation are not entirely clear.

One reason may be that these states may occur more or less simultaneously (Lewis 1971: 11ff.). A sense of shame may often accompany a sense of guilt. So, for example, a person may commit some offence for which they feel guilty. But they might also experience shame for the way that they appear in their own eyes or those of society in having violated some kind of ideal. Or a person may feel ashamed, then feel angry that they feel ashamed (an attempt to avoid the painful experience of shame), then feel guilty about the aggressive feelings that they have had. It is easy in such circumstances to describe the whole experience as one of guilt; this is reflected in common parlance.

A second factor may be that, on the whole, feelings of guilt are perhaps easier to handle and do something with than feelings of shame. There are, for example, formal mechanisms for dealing with guilt like confession and atonement. Shame has no such remedies. Block Lewis notes, 'Insofar as guilt is a more articulated experience than shame, and a more dignified one, it may actually absorb shame affect' (Lewis 1971: 42). Shame is an acute, painful, inarticulable experience. It leaves those who experience it feeling exposed, passive and impotent. Compared with this, the state of negative self-assessment surrounding the committing of a discrete offence can seem more bearable. Guilt implies responsibility and the possibility of action through the mechanism of repentance and reparation (Lewis 1971: 42ff.). The guilty person may feel bad because of having committed some offence. However, he or she has the possibility of maintaining self-esteem and self-efficacy by taking appropriate action. The shamed person is likely to feel a sense of personal collapse that implies the loss of self-esteem and self-efficacy. Guilty people feel that they have done some specific thing that is wrong or bad; their shamed counterparts have to face an unbearable sense that their whole self is bad. Unsurprisingly, the latter may attempt to move to the position of the former by interpreting their experiences of negative self-judgment as guilt rather than shame (Miller 1989).

Again, shame is notoriously difficult to recognise or distinguish from guilt, even for those who experience it:

[T]he intrinsic difficulties in identifying shame are: that it is often fused with guilt; that its stimulus evokes guilt so that shame reactions can be confused with guilt; that it is an irrational, primitive, wordless reaction experienced in imagery of looking, and in autonomic activity, and so has little cognitive content; and that it leads either to denial or to by-passed shame feeling accompanied by watching the self. (Lewis 1971: 38–9)

The tendency to assimilate and deal with shame as guilt was significantly reinforced within the psychological community by Sigmund Freud. It has been speculated that Freud himself was shame-prone (Pines 1987). Perhaps he was ashamed of being a Jew in anti-Semitic Vienna, or because he perceived himself to be ugly, and this made him blind to shame in his clinical practice (Pines 1987; cf. Gay 1988: 11f.). His use of a couch in psychoanalysis so that he did not have to see his patients face to face may provide circumstantial evidence of shame in his own personality, as may the fact that he seems to have failed to recognise shame and humiliation in some of his therapeutic relationships (Retzinger 1998). It is clear that, after some initial interest in shame, Freud was overwhelmingly interested in guilt in his clinical practice and theorising. Shame played only a minimum part in his considerations, being seen predominantly as a reaction formation against exhibitionist and scopophilic drives (Pines 1987: 17). By focussing on guilt and sidelining shame, Freud sent psychoanalytic theory off in a particular direction that was not corrected until well into the second half of the twentieth century.

The Western Christian tradition with its emphasis on guilt and sin rather than shame may also have had an ongoing influence in focussing attention on the former at the expense of the latter (Thrane 1979). A large contemporary cross-cultural study found that guilt and shame tend to be far less clearly separated as experiences in White, Anglo-Saxon Nordic cultures which have been influenced by the 'Protestant ethic'. In these cultures, all self-conscious emotions are likely to be tinged with, if not wholly transformed into, guilt (Wallbott and Scherer 1995: 482).

Kaufman notes that most clinicians and investigators have found it 'easier and safer to explore "guilty" impulses rather than the shameful self' (Kaufman 1993: 4). Unfortunately, the general cultural trend, reflected in the clinic, towards assimilating shame experience to guilt has meant that shame itself has been inadequately discerned and understood.

Some main approaches to shame

A major obstacle to a clear vision of the nature of shame is the diversity of approaches to the phenomenon in different disciplines and discourses. It is to some of these approaches that I now turn to provide a broad but compressed overview of the ways in which different kinds of researchers have contributed to the understanding of shame. The contribution of many of the approaches briefly outlined here will be discussed and selectively developed later. Readers should not to be deterred if the material offered here is too concise for full comprehension. If a concept is of significant value for the overall argument of the book it will reappear subsequently.

Psychoanalytic approaches
Psychoanalytic approaches to shame rest on the basic assumption that shame originates in unconscious events and processes. These shape the personality.

Freud saw shame as being part of the psychic mechanism designated the 'super-ego' that inhibits or dams the drives of the libido, specifically with regard to the sexually related instincts of scopophilia (the desire to see others) and exhibitionism (the desire to be looked at by others) (Freud 1977: 45ff.).

It may be that Freud saw shame as something more than a reaction formation function or a drive inhibitor. Miller suggests that sometimes he regarded it more as an affective signal that is 'an expression of internal distress over a belittled image of the self', as an expression of 'narcissistic strain' (Miller 1989: 232). Thus, she argues, Freud allowed for the possibility that emotions, like other psychological structures, may have different functions and serve multiple purposes at the same time.

Since Freud's death, and particularly in the USA, his psychoanalytic successors have been making up for their founder's lack of interest in shame. In 1950 Erik Erikson raised the status of shame as a psychological condition. Within an elaborate stage theory of personal development, now regarded as problematic (Stern 1985), he proposed that all infants pass through an early developmental stage of autonomy versus shame and doubt before advancing to a 'higher' stage of initiative versus guilt. Erikson saw shame as 'essentially rage turned against the self' (Erikson 1965: 244).

Later, Piers and Singer (1971) argued that whereas guilt is a product of offence against the laws and rules that have been internalised into the super-ego, shame results from a failure to reach the goals of a psychic structure identified by Freud as the ego-ideal (Freud 1984: 86ff.). This is held to contain a core of narcissistic ominipotence, the sum of positive identifications with parental images and goals, and an awareness of the ego's potentialities and goals: 'Shame occurs whenever goals and images presented by the ego ideal are not reached . . . Behind the feeling of shame stands not the fear of hatred but the fear of *contempt . . . of abandonment*, the death by emotional starvation' (Piers and Singer 1971: 28–9). Shame, then, arises from the fear of loss of love and abandonment in response to failure of some kind rather than from the inhibition of libidinal desires (Freud), or from turning anger inwards (Erikson).

The next beacon along the psychoanalytic path is Helen Block Lewis' *Shame and Guilt in Neurosis* (1971). This work launched modern studies of shame in the USA in a range of disciplines (Scheff and Retzinger 1997). It advanced a view of shame and guilt as both equally advanced super-ego functions, with the super-ego being understood as 'a regulatory self-evaluation agency' within the structure of the self (Lewis 1971: 26). Identification with the threatening parents stirs an 'internalization threat' which is experienced as guilt. 'Identification with the the beloved or admired ego-ideal stirs pride and triumphant feeling; failure to live up to this internalized admired imago stirs shame' (Lewis 1971: 23). Lewis placed shame and guilt on a par in terms of prevalence, origin and ongoing importance rather than seeing shame as a more primitive state than guilt that was eventually subsumed into the latter.

The final, and perhaps most profound, study of shame to be considered as an example of a wholly or mainly psychoanalytic approach is Leon Wurmser's *The Mask of Shame* (1995), first published in 1981. In Wurmser's complex text two main roots for the emergence of shame are postulated.

On the one hand, Wurmser rejects failure to live up to the ego-ideal as an explanation for shame anxiety proper. He returns to Freud's early formulation that shame is a reaction formation to the libidinal drives that find expression in exhibitionism and scopophilia or voyeurism. Wurmser discusses these drives in terms of a theory of theatophilia and delophilia.

On the other hand, Wurmser argues that a sense of basic flaw and unlovability accounts for the sense of shame:

[S]hame originates on the one hand in anxiety related to theatophilic and delophilic impulses – in traumatic failure in the perceptual-expressive fields – leading to many layers of defenses and wishes. Shame also relates to a basic flaw: being a loser, defective, weak, or dirty – all redounding ultimately to the taint of unlovability. (Wurmser 1995: 168–9)

While both roots of shame lie in infancy, they are quite clearly of different types, complicating an already complex picture.

The approach of self psychology

Self psychology, developed by émigré Austrian psychoanalyst Heinz Kohut in the post-war USA, is closely related to psychoanalytic theory. However, the self psychologists have developed their own distinctive views and vocabulary within which notions of shame are situated. Most notable amongst these is attention to the 'self', which is a distinctive structure in the mind 'similar to an object representation, containing differing and even contradictory qualities' (Siegel 1996: 64).

Kohut himself was not so much directly interested in shame as in narcissism, a notion that he developed from Freud's thought (Sandler, Spector Person and Fonagy 1991; cf. Mollon 1993; Symington 1993). Kohut understands narcissism to be 'the cathexis of the self' (i.e. the necessary investment of energy and attachment to the self) (Kohut 1971: xiii). He argued that there is a distinct narcissistic sector to the personality. In it, there coexist two unconscious archaic narcissistic configurations consisting of needs, wishes, feelings, fantasies and memories. These arise in response to the trauma of disruption of uninterrupted contact (bliss and perfection) with the caregiver.

One configuration is that of the grandiose or expansive self. This arises from the fantasy of a perfect self with unlimited abilities and exhibitionistic wishes. The other is that of the idealised parental imago, the perfect other, with whom union is sought. 'Their central mechanisms may be stated as: "I am perfect" = grandiose self; "You are perfect, but I am part of you" = idealized parental imago' (Siegel 1996: 67).

The narcissism associated with the grandiose self is exhibitionistic. When it matures, it is eventually integrated into the ego in the form of ambitions. The idealising narcissism associated with the idealised parental imago eventually matures into the formation of ideals. Both of these developed states are necessary to successful adult functioning. Satisfactory maturation into a firm, nuclear self with adequate self-esteem depends on an adequate response from others. Where parents, for example, fail to provide adequate mirroring for the grandiose self or the possibility of empathic idealising merger, narcissistic self-development is disturbed or arrested. The consequence can be self pathology (narcissistic personality disorders). This may take the form of depletion or empty depression in which the self feels empty and enfeebled, or of disintegration and fragmentation of the self (Siegel 1996; cf. Morrison 1983, 1989).

This brief account of self psychology (based on Siegel 1996), forms a compressed prelude to the work of Andrew Morrison (1983, 1987, 1989). Morrison highlights and develops the relationship between shame and narcissism, arguing for its implicit importance in Kohut's thought in concepts such as 'self-esteem', 'dejection of defeat', 'defective self', 'mortification of being exposed', 'hopelessness' and 'lethargy' (Morrison 1983: 309–10). He believes that 'shame is an emotion experienced in relation to self-critical judgments, to failures and defects of the ideal self, and as such is specifically relevant to self psychology and to a thorough understanding of the narcissistic character' (Morrison 1983: 308).

The precise relationship between narcissism and shame is unclear. There is little doubt in Morrison's mind, however, that these phenomena are closely linked (Morrison 1989: 66). He claims a central place for shame in self psychology that is analogous to the place of guilt in traditional Freudian theory: 'Just as *guilt* is the central negative affect in classical (conflict/drive) theory . . . *shame* occupies that position in problems of narcissism, in the psychology of the self and its deficits' (Morrison 1987: 274).

This brief discussion of the approach of self psychology to shame concludes my account of basically psychoanalytic approaches to this phenomenon. Two final observations can be made here.

First, while there is some consensus about the importance of shame in the psychoanalytic authors considered, conceptualisation and language vary quite markedly. Even within a particular disciplinary boundary, then, there are significant degrees of conceptual incommensurability.

Secondly, psychoanalytic approaches are difficult to evaluate for those working outside the psychodynamic paradigm within a clinical setting.

This is partly because they claim to be dealing with clinically relevant material, with the unconscious, and with infantile experience, some of which is pre-verbal.

I will not attempt to evaluate the validity of the psychodynamic approach here (Gellner 1985). My own working assumption is that while the foundations and vocabulary of psychoanalytic approaches to shame may be questionable, opaque, or even fanciful in terms of empirical observation (Stern 1985: 11), this perspective highlights some very important aspects of the phenomenology of shame.

Biopsychological approaches to shame

A completely different psychological approach to shame was formulated in the post-war USA by Silvan Tomkins, a psychologist of personality who attempted to construct a theory of human affect. This is now simply known as 'affect theory' (Demos 1995). Tomkins argued that there is a distinct innate biologically based affect system within each individual that amplifies perceptions so that things matter (Tomkins 1987: 137).

Tomkins identified nine basic innate affects that amplify experience. Interest-excitement, enjoyment-joy and surprise-startle are positive affects. The six negative affects are distress-anguish, fear-terror, dissmell, disgust, anger-rage and shame-humiliation. Each affect relates to particular facial expressions, for example, smiling in the case of enjoyment, lower lip lowered and protruded in disgust, eyes and head lowered in the case of shame (Tomkins 1987: 139). In fact, Tomkins designates shame, dissmell and disgust as innate affect auxiliary responses because they follow on from the activation of other affects. Shame, for example, 'operates only after interest or enjoyment has been activated; it inhibits one, or the other, or both' (Tomkins 1987: 143).

Tomkins' affect theory of shame has been widely influential (Nathanson 1992). It is expounded and developed by Kaufman (1993) who explains how the brief experience of a particular affect such as shame can be built upon so that it becomes a dominant character trait. At the most basic level, infants have affects, drives, interpersonal needs and needs for purpose that may meet with a shaming response from adults who destroy or interrupt the child's experience of interest or enjoyment. If this happens repetitively, the cumulative experience gets amplified and magnified into 'scenes' that are then cathected with shame, possibly in combination with other emotions. Scenes that have a similar emotional content can then adhere to one another and become incardinated in memory. They become general or governing scenes that fundamentally shape and determine a person's personality (Kaufman 1993: 58ff.). Governing scenes give orientation and shape to people's lives. They are accompanied, magnified and perpetuated by images (audio and visual) and 'scripts', series of habitual words and actions/responses, which ensure the re-enactment of those scenes into the far distant future (Kaufman 1993: 100ff.).

Governing scenes eventually develop into *states of shame* related to body, relationships or competence. These in turn contribute to character shame. A shamed person at the level of total character is someone whose early emotional responses and needs were met with shaming in interpersonal relationships which ruptured the 'interpersonal bridge' (Kaufman 1993: 159ff.). These experiences were built up into scenes and coalesced into governing scenes or over-riding orientations.

Tomkins' understanding of shame is rooted in genetically determined basic physiological affect responses. These are modified and educated by a complex set of factors such as experience, interpersonal interaction and culture. The affect may be activated more in some than in others. It can leave a profound mark upon some personalities and characters. Kaufman draws heavily upon affect theory. However, he integrates its insights with more psychodynamic theories of shame such as object relations theory and interpersonal theory (Kaufman 1993: viii).

Tomkins' affect theory is not accepted by all psychologists (Broucek 1997: 44ff.). While accepting the physiological, biological basis of emotions in general, empirical child observer Michael Lewis (1992) rejects the notion of shame as a primary innate affect present from birth. Lewis sees shame as a self-conscious emotion that can only occur when objective self-consciousness has come into being in the infant so that s/he has the capacity to compare and evaluate him/herself against others. This means that infants only gradually acquire the capacity to experience shame over their first three years of life. Shame is not a simple automatic response to a particular kind of stimulus that can occur at any moment after birth. Rather, it is a complex secondary emotional response. Where there is no objective self-awareness and no evaluation, there can be no shame (Lewis 1992: 13ff., 36ff.).

Outlining the basic approach adopted in the field of self-conscious emotions by most academic psychologists, Price Tangney and Fischer (1995) assert that all emotions act as functional organisers, moulding, constraining or structuring human activity and thought. They are grounded in bodily expressions and actions, cognitive appraisals, and social interactions. Furthermore, emotions are fundamentally adaptive – they organise action tendencies that promote successful human functioning. Each emotional reaction is pervaded with the appraisal of the meaning of events and follows a prototypical social script (Price Tangney and Fischer 1995: 6). Finally, all emotions are organised into families of related affects. So, for example, shame is closely related to guilt and embarrassment. To qualify as a self-conscious emotion, an emotion must have elements of self-consciousness and evaluation or comparison against some kind of standard (Price Tangney and Fischer 1995: 14).

The notion of comparison situates self-conscious emotions within the social arena. This means they are intimately connected with social interaction, communication and appraisal of others (Caplovitz Barret 1995; Gilbert and Maguire 1998; Keltner and Harker 1998). Within this functional, action-organising perspective on emotions, shame is described thus:

In shame . . . physical signs seem typically to include lowering the gaze, covering the face, and sometimes blushing and staying quiet. The subjective experience of being ashamed includes feeling exposed, heavy, or small, and dwelling on the flaw that one is ashamed of. The organizing action tendency describes the whole sequence from situation to primary actions, perceptions, and reactions. With shame, a person wishes to be judged positively in a given situation but instead is judged negatively (by self or other) for some action or characteristic, especially something that signals a deep-seated flaw. The person reacts by trying to hide or escape, or alternatively, trying to blame others for the event. Emotion refers to all three of these facets (physical signs, subjective experiences, and action tendencies), as well as the categories and labels we use for them . . . (Price Tangney and Fischer 1995: 7)

Self-conscious emotions follow prototypical social scripts. So, for example, shame flows from antecedents such as 'flaw or dishonorable or deplorable action, statement, or characteristic of a person'. The responses to this are 'hiding, escaping, sense of shrinking, feeling worthless'. The self-control procedures that can ensue are those of 'undoing and redefinition', for example by changing the flaw or dishonourable action (Price Tangney and Fischer 1995: 10).

From the point of view of the secondary researcher adopted here two things should be noted. First, psychological approaches to shame are very different in their assumptions, methods and assertions from those in the psychoanalytic sphere. Secondly, there is a good deal of diversity and lack of certainty as to the nature and function of shame in this disciplinary field, as there was in that of psychoanalytic approaches (Price Tangney and Fischer 1995; Gilbert 1998; Andrews 1998a).

Eclectic / synthesising approaches

Many, if not most, theorists are eclectic in their approaches to shame. This is not surprising. Shame is such a complex phenomenon that any one theoretical perspective approach cannot provide a sufficiently 'thick' (Geertz 1993) description or account of it.

In the interests of illuminating practice and offering more effective help, clinicians in particular tend to be eclectic in their use of different ideas and schools of thought in this area. While writers may describe themselves as psychoanalysts or psychotherapists, they often use relevant material from many different approaches. Kaufman, for example, combines the psychoanalytically related insights of object-relations theory and interpersonal theory alongside Tomkins' affect theory (Kaufman 1993: viii). Wurmser (1995) draws on philosophy and literature as well as classical analytic theory and self psychology in his attempts to understand shame. One of the most comprehensive eclectic and synthesising accounts of shame so far undertaken is that of Donald Nathanson (1992). Nathanson is a psychotherapist who has enthusiastically embraced Tomkins' affect theory and other scientific and artistic perspectives to illuminate the genesis, nature and treatment of shame.

Eclecticism is probably both a necessary and a valid approach to shame, particularly in the service of clinical understanding and the imperative to help. It is, however, problematic if one is trying to provide a neat categorisation of approaches to shame. Here, as elsewhere, shame eludes easy comprehension and order.

Sociological approaches

It seems clear that shame as a phenomenon has substantial social roots, functions, implications and effects. People induce shame, it is a product of comparison with others, it affects the nature of relationships, and it can affect the whole nature of a group or society. This being so, it is surprising that, despite recent sociological interest in the emotions (Bendelow and Williams 1998), little specific work has been done on shame.

A notable historical exception to this is Lynd's book, *On Shame and the Search for Identity* (1958). Lynd defines shame as a wound to one's self-esteem, a painful feeling or sense of degradation excited by the consciousness of having done something unworthy of one's previous idea of one's own excellence. It is, also, a peculiarly painful feeling of being in a situation that incurs the scorn or contempt of others. (Lynd 1958: 23–4)

Because shame is so intimately related to assessment of the self, Lynd believes that studying it can provide a unique entrée to identity in modern society.

The perception that shame and identity are crucially linked is further developed by Giddens in his studies of society in modernity. Giddens (1991) argues that a necessary sense of identity, self-esteem and narrative coherence can be problematised by shame. This is a condition which is growing in significance as an emotion in social conditions that produce more narcissistic personalities unanchored in traditional customs, values and practices.

Since Lynd's contribution in the 1950s, Thomas Scheff is the most prominent contemporary sociologist to have devoted attention to shame. Adopting an interdisciplinary approach, Scheff draws on Goffman's sociological work on self-presentation and 'face' in social relationships (Goffman 1956, 1968b, 1971a, 1971b), and from the psychoanalytic work of Helen Block Lewis (1971) to examine shame in society.

Scheff (1990, 1997) postulates that there is a fundamental social bond of attunement between individuals. The state of the social bond, that is, the degree of solidarity or alienation experienced, is routinely registered by either pride or shame: 'Pride signals and generates solidarity. Shame signals and generates alienation. Shame is a normal part of the process of social control; it becomes disruptive only when it is hidden or denied. Denial of shame generates self-perpetuating cycles of alienation' (Scheff 1997: 74).

Scheff sees shame as 'both a genetically determined emotion within individuals, and equally a signal of the state of a social relationship, revealing the degree of alienation (separation or engulfment) of the participants' (Scheff 1995a: 394). From this stance, which 'integrates the individual and social psychologies of shame', Scheff analyses shame-based pathologies in groups and even in nations, arguing that, wherever shame is bypassed or ignored, rage and aggression is likely to occur in a 'shame-rage spiral' (Scheff 1997: 394). For him, the study of shame is an important key to understanding social relationships and structures in general.

Sociological approaches to shame are likely to develop in both scope and extent in the future. They highlight the social as opposed to

the individual nature and significance of this phenomenon. I shall return
to them at a later point in the book.

Cultural approaches

Scholars from a number of disciplines have examined shame in non-
Western cultures. The focus here has been upon the understanding and
use of shame as a mechanism for social and individual control.

The first major study of shame in different cultures was that of Ruth
Benedict, an anthropologist influenced by the work of Margaret Mead
who studied Japanese culture during World War II. In *The Chrysanthemum
and the Sword* (1954), Benedict pointed out that there seem to be two
broadly different kinds of cultures throughout the world, shame cultures
and guilt cultures.

Shame cultures are those that are structured around shame, honour
and esteem. In this context, social conformity is engendered by external
sanctions for good behaviour. Significantly – and confusingly from the
perspective of modern Western notions of the phenomenon – shame is
not perceived or felt to be an internal psychological condition. If people
offend against social mores, they are publicly shamed, ostracised and
rejected by their social reference group as a main form of punishment.
The emphasis is upon appearance and conformity in response to an
external social view.

In guilt cultures, on the other hand, the individual has an internalised
sense of wrongdoing and a sense of conscience. Specific offences are
dealt with by specific, often formally legal, mechanisms of punishment
and restitution that do not depend on the loss of honour and a sense of
global stigmatisation of the person. Benedict associated shame as a main
mechanism of social and individual control with less individualised,
more group-oriented societies such as Japan. Guilt culture was more
typical of Western societies where there is a high degree of individuation from the group.

Benedict's work has been extensively criticised, partly because of its
basic understanding and definition of shame, and particularly because
it is not easy to identify cultures that can be categorised exclusively as
shame or guilt cultures (Parker 1983: 251; cf. Cairns 1993; Demos 1996;
Thrane 1979). Nonetheless, her fundamental distinction between shame
and guilt culture has continued to generate interest and research.

Dodds adopted the notion of shame culture to describe Homeric
society in Ancient Greece, arguing that 'Homeric man's highest good is
not the enjoyment of a quiet conscience, but the enjoyment of *time*,

public esteem' (Dodds 1951: 17). It was only gradually that notions of individual sin, guilt and offence arose together with a clear system of law and rationally based morality. In shame culture, pollution and dishonour affecting one's outward standing in the community were the matters of significance, not one's individual psychological state (Dodds 1951: 28ff.).

While later writers (Parker 1983) have been more guarded about the notion of a progression from shame culture to guilt culture in Ancient Greece, Williams (1993) points out that there was no concept corresponding to the modern Western notion of guilt in early Greek culture. Shame, *aidos*, covers what we might call guilt as well as shame, locating guilt and moral offence within a broad view of character, the person, and the rest of life (Williams 1993: 102; cf. Cairns 1993).

Recent cross-cultural studies recognise that there are significant differences in the ways that shame presents and is used in different cultures. Kitayama et al. (1995), for example, suggest that shame and guilt exist as emotions of self-consciousness and social control in all cultures. However, they are differently experienced, interpreted and regulated according to social contexts, norms and structures. Thus in a culture that prizes individual independence such as the USA, shame occurs when people perceive themselves or others to be dependent. Conversely, in cultures where interdependence between people is valued, such as Japan, shame occurs when the views and expectations of others are unmet. To avoid the psychological experience of shame, individuals need to have a sense of self-esteem and personal worth generated by a sense of meeting social norms and expectations. The source of this self-worth in a interdependent, collectivist society is the positive appraisal of other people. In independence-valuing societies the source of self-appraisal is the self.

Some cultures use the emotional experience of shaming much more overtly to control behaviour than others. Miyaka and Yamezake (1995) argue that in Japanese society characterised by group dependence and perfectionism, shame and its concomitant emphases upon social conformity, maintaining appearance and respect, and avoiding ridicule, are deliberately engendered as a major technique of child-rearing.

Cultural approaches reveal that shame as concept and experience is variably understood in different cultures. They also highlight the ways in which both shame and guilt perform important, if somewhat different, roles in social and individual control according to social structure, norms and expectations, even if the dichotomy between 'shame' cultures and 'guilt' cultures probably cannot be sustained.

Philosophical approaches

Some distinguished philosophers have devoted considerable attention to shame, mostly as a phenomenon relevant to morality (O'Hear 1976/7; Heller 1985). According to Rawls, for example, Kant made shame rather than guilt and law the foundation of his moral system (Rawls 1972: 256).

Rawls sees self-respect or self-esteem as one of the primary goods for the person. He distinguishes two kinds of shame. Non-moral shame arises from 'the injury to our self-esteem owing to our not having or failing to exercise certain excellences', while 'someone is liable to moral shame when he prizes as excellences of his person those virtues that his plan of life requires and is framed to encourage' (Rawls 1972: 444).

Failing to meet standards and values and judging oneself negatively as degraded through the eyes of others is common to many modern philosophical approaches. Sartre notes that 'shame is shame *of oneself before the Other*' (Sartre 1958: 221). Gabriele Taylor argues that:

> There are basically two elements in each case of shame. There is firstly the self-directed adverse judgement of the person feeling shame: she feels herself degraded, not the sort of person she believed, assumed, or hoped she was or anyway should be . . . Secondly, there is the notion of the audience. (Taylor 1985: 57)

Taylor understands shame to be a moral emotion insofar as it is a judgment upon one's morality, one's ideals of how to live and how one ought to be. Shame is a positive, revelatory emotion. It helps people to know what their values and ideals are and urges them towards living up to these. Shame therefore acts as a guardian of self-respect (Taylor 1985: 80).

A more complex, less morally focussed approach to shame emerges in Nietzsche's writings. On the one hand, Nietzsche appears to see shame as a captivating force for individuals from which they need deliverance (Nietzsche 1974: 220). On the other, he seems to regard shame as a necessary protection both for the individual and for things which should be respected and held in awe (Nietzsche 1974: 38). This contradiction is perhaps explained by Nietzsche's dialectical, teasing, aphoristic style (Tanner 1994), as well as by distinguishing two meanings of shame here. In the first case, Nietzsche is perhaps advocating emancipation from the kind of shame as dishonour and inferiority that prevents human beings from attaining their true potential. This is not necessarily incompatible with advocating the maintenance of shame in the sense of reverence in the face of a reality that cannot and should not be treated as wholly comprehensible (Schneider 1987a: 7ff.).

Philosophical approaches to shame have tended to emphasise its significance in moral life and judgment and its relationship to maintaining self-respect. Philosophers have mostly paid little attention to insights into shame that emerge from other disciplines such as psychology. Their vocabularies and understandings of shame can therefore seem idiosyncratic when compared to other approaches.

Literary approaches

Literary concerns and themes reflect social and individual life. Shame, therefore, often forms an important area of exploration for imaginative writers. Some of the works most often alluded to in this context are Fyodor Dostoevsky's *The Brothers Karamazov* (1958) and *Demons* (1994), Leo Tolstoy's *Anna Karenina* (1995), George Orwell's *Nineteen Eighty-Four* (1954), Franz Kafka's *The Trial* (1953) and Arthur Koestler's *Darkness at Noon* (1947). In all these works, there are themes of humiliation, inferiority, boundary violation, personal anguish and self-devaluation.

Three works dealing directly with shame come most readily to my mind: Hawthorne's novel, *The Scarlet Letter* (1903) examines the use of humiliation and exclusion to achieve religious and social control in early New England. Joyce's 'The Dead' is a story in large measure about personal humiliation and inferiority (Joyce 1956). Kundera's postmodern novel, *The Unbearable Lightness of Being* (1984), explores deviance and shame in the last days of totalitarian rule in Eastern Europe.

Imaginative works reflect life, but not academic or scientific discourse. Shame is thus embedded, hidden, partial, undefined, and not systematically anatomised in many fictional works. This often makes it difficult to say exactly what any particular author's understanding and view of shame is. Indeed, according to one's own understanding of shame, one may not find much material about shame at all in a particular work. I am unable to identify much material that really concerns what I consider to be shame in Koestler's *Darkness at Noon*. However, the account of the decline and eventual death of Sebastian Flyte in Evelyn Waugh's *Brideshead Revisited* (1962) seems to me to be a classic account of a man who is abnegated and shamed by being trapped in the dynamics of isolation and engulfment that constitute major threats to personal identity and the social bond (Scheff 1997: 76ff.).

Shame figures in a similarly partial, embedded way in other kinds of literature such as autobiography (Angelou 1984; Gosse 1949; McCourt 1997). It is not possible to list all the biographies and autobiographies that have been written in which shame appears, particularly because almost any unhappy childhood account is likely to be bound up with elements of shame. Many books about child abuse contain case studies in which people talk about their sense of shame or in which shame is strongly implicitly present (Walker 1992). Like imaginative works, biographical accounts illuminate the phenomenology of shame while mostly prescinding from aetiology, definition and close anatomy of this condition. Shame is just one aspect of people's experience. The phenomenon is treated in a commonsensical, uncritical, partial, though engaging and useful way.

Some literary scholars have, through their studies, made contributions to a more academic understanding of shame. In *Keats and Embarrassment*, Christopher Ricks (1974) exposes the importance of the shame-related emotion, embarrassment, to the poet's life and work. James Hans (1991) explores shame in Kundera's novel, *The Unbearable Lightness of Being*. Hans' approach is picked up and developed in relation to Joyce's 'The Dead' in Frederick Turner's (1995) study, 'Shame, beauty, and the tragic view of history'. The main object in these studies is not so much to define and anatomise shame as to enrich broad textual understanding.

Literary approaches to shame, while diffuse and partial, are useful for gaining a wider, 'thicker' sense of this condition in the context of life. However, there is little consistency in the ways that literary authors approach shame. This reflects the diversity of the ways in which shame is encountered in reality, reminding that shame is not a single, unitary, commonly understood and shared condition that stands apart from persons and their life narratives. It also provides relief from the unrelenting attempts at focus and definition which characterise other approaches to shame.

A social constructionist approach?

Social constructionism is a transdisciplinary epistemological stance that has roots in philosophy, sociology and psychology.

A social constructionist approach to shame as a reified phenomenon in different discourses has yet to be formulated. However, it might be a particularly suitable one for examining this phenomenon. There is no set of agreed universal physiological responses that can invariably be noted in connection with the experience of shame. Notions of shame have changed over history and in different societies and cultures. This suggests that there may be no physiological essence to shame. Furthermore, shame has a definite social function in moderating and monitoring social relations between individuals and groups. The concept plays an important part in a number of very different contexts, languages and cultures. It might therefore seem very relevant to look at the nature and function of shame from a constructionist perspective, trying to discern the interests, needs and usages that impinge upon the concept as it is identified and invoked in different situations and discourses.

What do usages of the concept of shame imply and achieve within different kinds of discourse and situation? This question might be more useful than trying to identify the essence or inner reality of shame when that seems bound to remain contested and elusive. Although I cannot attempt a thoroughgoing social constructionist approach here, I hope to use this perspective to arrive at a general attitude to the various approaches to shame considered above.

The value of different approaches to shame

A kaleidoscope of approaches to shame has now been outlined. It reveals an enormous diversity of views on the basic definition, nature and function of shame. However, each approach provides something of value for understanding shame.

Psychoanalytic approaches, with their understandings of shame as a drive inhibitor, a turning of anger inwards, or a failure to live up to ideals, highlight the possible beginnings of shame in infancy before language has formed. Perhaps they can help us to understand or to tolerate the inarticulate and often irrational nature of shame as a phenomenon that seems to go right to the centre of the self.

Self psychology situates shame within the development of the whole self with its narcissistic needs that must be met if people are to grow up to be effective adults. Where depleted and depressed, narcissistic adults with poor self-esteem are found, shame plays an important part as symptom of, or compensation for, unmet needs.

Biopsychological approaches to shame root what is thought of as an emotional reaction within the physiology of the individual organism. They emphasise the universality of a basic shame reaction and provide an account of how it is shaped into a complex emotion. The gradual emergence of self-conscious evaluation as the infant develops cognitively highlights the social shaping of emotional reaction and perception. It emphasises the relational nature of shame and its practical adaptive function in guiding the individual through social life.

Eclectic approaches to shame highlight the fact that no one set of theories and insights into shame provides a comprehensive, exclusive account. Most eclectics are clinicians; this is a useful reminder that the study of shame is usually undertaken to gain practical understanding and insight that is of use in helping people. The study of shame is not a detached academic matter. It is often a search for usable theories and techniques.

Sociological approaches to shame emphasise the fact that shame is not just of individual significance. How people experience shame depends to a large extent on matters of socially constructed identity and upon the nature of social relationships. The incidence of shame may reveal who one is in a particular society. It also provides important information about the state of social relationships.

Attending to shame in different cultures shows how shame is used in social control. Furthermore, it relativises commonsensical understandings of shame in particular cultures. There may be different types, functions, definitions and uses of shame other than the individual psychological shame that is thought to be predominant in contemporary Western society.

Philosophical approaches have a broadening function in helping to understand the nuances of shame. Shame is not merely about a particular kind of 'irrational' embodied feeling or performance. It is, at least to some extent, a judgment of the self by the self using the mind. The experience of shame reveals what one's ideals are and the extent to which one has attained these. It can provide information about the self, the nature of reality, and the grounds for self-respect.

The rational clarity of the philosophical approach is usefully muddied by literary approaches to shame. These show that shame is not an isolated phenomenon in real life. It is mixed up with a host of experiences and emotions within the context of a complex, multi-faceted narrative context. Literature does not define and demarcate shame. It helps us to understand the reality of shame in all its diffusion, pervasiveness and complexity.

A putative social constructionist approach regards shame as a nonrealist, linguistic phenomenon. This permits us to take all the insights and approaches that have been outlined above seriously as important languages about shame. However, it does not require a commitment to any particular world view. We can look at the various ways in which the concept 'shame' is used without being required to make a judgment as to whether one way of thinking or speaking about shame is 'more true' than another. Thus, a springboard for further exploration is provided to take us further into the complexity of shame.

The complexity of theories about shame is best approached with integrity through a version of family resemblance theory. It is to this methodological device that I now turn.

Making sense of diversity: family resemblance theory

Studying shame presents a number of problems for the researcher. Shame is obscured by factors such as human aversion to the phenomenon, linguistic confusion and the assimilation of shame to guilt. This opacity is increased by the wide variety of academic and clinical approaches to shame. These provide a plethora of different definitions, epistemologies, research methods and appropriate responses. Faced with diversity, pluralism, contradiction and apparent incommensurability, how should the transdisciplinary researcher make use of the various perspectives and findings that appear in discourses about shame?

A number of responses are possible. The first is to conclude that what we have here is a set of completely different concepts whose difference is disguised by the common usage of the word 'shame'. If this is so, we are witnesses to an instance of 'accidents of usage' (O'Hear 1976/7: 74). This means that no significant commonality underlies uses of the concept 'shame' in different discourses. When a psychoanalyst uses the concept, this has little or nothing in common with the usage of the sociologist or the philosopher. In these circumstances, the quest to find any commonality or convergence of meaning is futile. The researcher might then best be occupied in mapping and clarifying the nature and parameters of 'shame' in different kinds of discourse. However, it seems too dismissive to suggest that most conceptualities underlying shame have only an accidental relationship. There do appear to be some commonalities in places. For example, most discourses allow that shame represents a measure of distress or pain for the individual or the group.

A second possible response is to try to identify and synthesise a common definition and set of characteristics to shame that takes equally into account *all* the various approaches to this phenomenon. This way of proceeding can only work if the approaches considered have enough in common in terms of methods, findings and terminology to be synthesised without loss of insight and meaning. In the case of shame, the diversity of approaches is too broad and disparate to permit easy synthesis without distorting exclusions.

The third option would involve specifically privileging one set of theories and approaches to shame while excluding or downgrading the

importance of others. So, for example, one might choose to adopt a
psychoanalytic approach as normative and then include material from
other perspectives only insofar as it was illuminative psychoanalytically.
There are two reasons for rejecting this option here.

First, as a transdisciplinary researcher, I am neither competent nor
able to make a judgment about which perspective should be given
primacy. Secondly, I am unwilling to surrender or relativise the findings
of several different approaches in order to produce what would then
seem to be a speciously monolithic clarity about the understanding of
shame. Many, if not most, of the approaches that I have considered in
studying shame have important insights to offer. If thinking about shame
is partial or pluralistic at this time, it would be a distortion to adopt an
over-simplifying approach.

A fourth option would be to conclude that understandings of shame
are still at such an elementary stage that it would be best to wait a while
before trying to say anything about it. The hope might be that, in time,
empirical psychological investigation, for example, might identify a clear
core to shame experience which could then act as a norm for reflection
on this subject. But this response privileges the notion that one disciplinary approach to understanding shame might become normative. It also
falls into the epistemological trap of assuming that there may be some
constant essence or basis to shame.

A more appropriate, positive way forward is to abandon the quest for
narrow definition, synthesis, normativity and theoretical exclusivism for
a broader approach. It is here that the family resemblance approach to
concepts becomes relevant.

It was the philosopher Wittgenstein who first proposed that concepts
could be approached along the lines of family resemblance. This
approach rejects the notion that every use of a concept should be
deemed to have the same essential content and meaning (Bowden
1997:12). Rather, a concept might be used in many different ways and
contexts with only some commonalities with usages in other contexts.
Following Wittgenstein, Hick uses the example of games to explain what
family resemblance means. Games 'have no common essence'.

What makes us apply the name 'game' to this wide assortment of activities,
ranging from football to chess, and from a solitary child playing with her doll to
the Olympic Games, is that *each is similar in important respects to some others in the
family, though not in all respects to any or in any respect to all. Instead of a set of defining
characteristics there is a network of similarities overlapping and criss-crossing like the resem-
blances and differences in build, features, eye colour, gait, temperament and so on among the
members of a natural family.* (Hick 1989:4)

Applying the notion of family resemblance of concepts to the study of shame is methodologically liberating. Instead of trying to identify a single determining essence or definition, one is free to accept that there is a legitimate plurality of concepts and approaches. These may be loosely linked in various ways and degrees by context, usage and content. One is not obliged to rule some usages and approaches in, while excluding others. Rather, one can consider all usages and approaches as *prima facie* valid and useful.

For the researcher using secondary sources, relying on the research and findings of others in wide range of disciplines, the adoption of a family resemblance notion of concepts and approaches to shame allows proper openness and humility. One is not obliged to press towards a particular, narrow understanding of a complex phenomenon. It is possible to attend to the insights provided by different discourses, approaches and instantiations of the concept of shame.

Utilising the notion of family resemblance in relation to the concept of shame obviates the need to find an essence, a narrow foundational definition, or a lowest common denominator understanding into which all other understandings can be resolved. However, it is necessary to specify some criteria of selection and judgment in selecting material to illuminate the understanding of shame that will emerge in subsequent chapters.

First, my use of insights and sources is determined by practical considerations. My aim is to try to understand the significance and implications of shame in contemporary individuals and societies. Insofar as particular approaches or discourses provide material that appears to provide insight into the contemporary experience of shame I shall use their findings. However, I will remain formally agnostic about the validity of their epistemologies, methods, and assumptions. I propose to treat all approaches to shame, whether formal or informal, scientific or artistic, as equal languages or discourses. Insofar as these discourses have rhetorical power to persuade so that they appear illuminative to me, I will mingle their words and concepts with my own. Others may not be persuaded by the picture I present of shame here. They are free to create more persuasive pictures and discourses of their own.

Implicit in the first criterion for using and selecting material from different discourses about shame is a second one. Ultimately, I intend to create an account of shame that is credible to me personally, measuring insights and theories against my own experience of shame. This avowedly personal approach has already been discussed in the Introduction. Since I am a participating, communicating member of my own culture and society, I believe my own experience and understanding of shame is unlikely to be wholly unique, though it may be idiosyncratic in some ways.

Hereafter, there will be little direct evaluation of sources of insight and understanding about shame. I will adopt an eclectic approach. This will draw in material about shame from a variety of discourses using the criteria of experiential congruence and illuminative rhetorical power to determine inclusion and exclusion. I shall remain agnostic as to the 'essence' of shame, or the 'best' methods for determining its fundamental nature. My working assumption is that there is no such 'thing' as shame but that there is a set of discourses, both everyday and scientific, that deploy this concept in family resemblance terms. It may be possible to see or to create links between different uses of 'shame'. However, it is not helpful to try and pin this concept down too definitely. Shame means a great deal to many people in different places, cultures and discourses. Unfortunately, it does not mean the same thing. Users of the concept 'shame' are divided by a common concept – or rather, by the family resemblance between a number of different but related concepts, all denoted by the same five letter word.

PART II

Encountering shame

Overview of Part II

In the first part of this book, some of the methodological and other issues associated with approaching shame were considered. A picture of great diversity in both perspective and understanding was presented. A family resemblance approach to discourses relating to shame was suggested as a device for drawing upon different perspectives and insights with discernment and integrity.

Part II examines aspects of the phenomenology, experience and healing of shame, particularly chronic, dysfunctional shame, in contemporary Western cultures. Within this particular cultural context, shame is often regarded primarily as an individual, psychological phenomenon. Many of the main discourses that are drawn upon, therefore, explore shame in these terms. It will, however, be seen that shame has substantial social and political implications. Discourses relating to the social arena therefore have a part to play in understanding this phenomenon. Integration is a key concept when it comes to describing positive responses to shame whether at an individual or a social level of existence.

Chapter 3 below provides preliminary orientation to a number of issues pertaining to understanding shame in general. It begins by identifying the main features, or family characteristics, that people usually associate with 'shame' when they use it to describe their experience. Having outlined a range of basic meanings characteristic of individuals' experiences of shame, some of the possible functions of shame are discussed. Thereafter, some basic distinctions between different kinds of shame, functional and dysfunctional, are identified. Finally, I offer some discussion of the metaphorical ecology of stain, pollution and defilement within which understandings of shame might be situated. This chapter acts as a prelude to the more focussed discussion of chronic, dysfunctional shame that occupies the following four chapters.

While shame may, indeed, have appropriate and useful functions within the lives of individuals and their social relationships, it can also have very negative effects. Chapter 4 turns explicitly to chronic shame in individuals, pointing up the mechanisms whereby shame may become pathological and destructive.

Chapter 5 examines the causes of chronic, pathological shame and shame proneness as a character trait. People whose personalities are moulded to a large extent by shame and the avoidance of shame often have deeply unhappy lives. To remedy this requires an understanding of the events, situations and other factors that bear upon the production of shame proneness and chronic shame. Many factors in social and individual relationships can produce people who suffer from an overwhelming surfeit of shame.

Chapter 6 looks at the implications and effects of chronic shame. Some of the common defences and reactions to shame are considered, then the pathological associations of this condition are explored. Finally, the effects of shame upon the moral life and involvement of individuals and communities are examined.

Next, chapter 7 examines the social uses and context of shame. Socio-cultural and sociological perspectives remind us that shame has important functions in relationships and particularly in social control. This chapter looks at the historical and contemporary place and uses of shame with a view to examining their appropriateness and legitimacy. Shame-engendering practices and functions in society may sometimes be desirable. However, the use of shame as a main tool of social control has dangers. The chapter concludes with some reflections about the appropriate use of social shame.

Chapter 8 considers some of the ways in which inappropriate, dysfunctional shame in individuals and groups might be resisted, prevented or, if necessary, cured. The key concept here is integration so that people's alienation and sense of defilement is overcome. Restoring a proper sense of self-regard and self-esteem to shamed individuals and groups is not an easy matter. They are, almost by definition, cut off from other human beings and fearful of them. The task of integration is a complex, lengthy and arduous one.

CHAPTER THREE

The ecology of shame

He who is ashamed would like to force the world not to look at him, not to notice his exposure. He would like to destroy the eyes of the world. Instead he must wish for his own invisibility.

(Erikson 1965: 244)

Shame is a pluriform phenomenon with many implications and ramifications in the discourses in which it appears. Subsequent chapters explore the phenomenology, causes and responses that pertain to a particular kind of shame – chronic, dysfunctional shame. Before focussing on this type of shame, however, it will be useful to place shame in ecological context. This chapter therefore provides preliminary orientation to some important issues and discussions that pertain to shame in general terms. The chapter falls into four discrete sections that each situate shame within a particular kind of conceptual ecology.

In the first section, I try to capture the range of meanings and experiences that seem to be suggested when contemporary people in Western societies talk about shame. The second section of the chapter outlines some of the functions that have been suggested for the phenomenon of shame in individual and social life. It will then be appropriate to look at some of the fundamental distinctions that are made in trying to identify different kinds of shame. One major distinction that is made is that of acute, appropriate shame as distinguished from chronic dysfunctional shame. The last section is then concerned to locate understandings of shame within an appropriate metaphorical ecology. Here I suggest that shame, particularly chronic, dysfunctional shame, is best placed within the broad ecology of meanings that are associated with pollution, stain and defilement.

The contemporary experience of shame

Here are some responses that contemporary people have provided independently in response to the question, 'What is shame?'

'A feeling of being dirty, defiled, unwanted'

'Something I want hidden surfacing'

'Feeling demeaned and put on view'

'A sense of unworthiness and badness because of something that I've done'

'My self feels diminished'

'There is nowhere to hide'

'A feeling of exposure'

'Demeaning and affirming exposure'

'Feeling found out and that it is not possible to put things right'

'Wanting not to be seen'

'A sense of deep embarrassment'

'Not being good enough'

'Not coming up to scratch'

'Feeling bad about deeds done'

'Being wrong without knowing why'

These people generally seemed to have no problem about defining what shame means for them. Mostly, shame is taken to be a category that relates essentially to the self rather than to society. Furthermore, most of the respondents define shame as a negative term of unpleasant self-judgment in which one feels bad or uncomfortable.

There are various clear strands of meaning that are shared between some respondents. One group focusses upon a sense of being generally bad; the whole self does not meet the standards that it should. Significantly, one respondent reports the sense of feeling wrong without knowing why – a clear difference between the feeling of shame and that of guilt, perhaps. Another group of responses focusses upon the sense of feeling bad because some kind of offence has been committed. This is close to morality and the notion of guilt. One set of responses centres upon the sense of being exposed, while others allude to the desire to hide which may be the other side of being exposed in an unwelcome way. Finally, some responses emphasise the sense of feeling demeaned, diminished, defiled and unwanted. A sense of unwillingness and lack of control also pervades many of these responses. The degrees of continuity and discontinuity between these responses reinforce the point that shame is more a family of concepts and usages than a unitary entity with a clear single meaning.

Although a random and unscientific sample, these responses contain many of the most important meanings of shame in Western culture that have been identified in the theoretical literature. These meanings locate shame primarily as an individual, personal phenomenon which is to be understood within the discourse of psychology.

It is easy to move from informal definitions to a composite understanding such as this one:

Shame is an inner sense of being completely diminished or insufficient as a person. It is the self judging the self. A moment of shame may be humiliation so painful or an indignity so profound that one feels one has been robbed of her or his dignity or exposed as basically inadequate, bad, or worthy of rejection. A pervasive sense of shame is the ongoing premise that one is fundamentally bad, inadequate, defective, unworthy, or not fully valid as a human being. (Fossum and Mason 1989:5)

I now want to look in more detail at some of the main elements and meanings of shame experience as it is commonly perceived and discussed in modern society. I will draw upon the appropriate theoretical literature as well as upon my own experience of shame to amplify points where necessary.

To anchor this discussion in lived experience, here is an account of one of my own paradigmatic shame experiences:

When I was an ordination candidate of about sixteen years of age, I went to see the Diocesan Director of Ordinands to make my confession, a practice that he had recommended to me as part of my spiritual life. Towards the end of the confession, when I had read out all the sins I could remember, he asked me directly whether I had been having any sexual thoughts or experiences. Actually, I had been having little else for a number of years. Not having heard the adage, 'Ninety-eight per cent of adolescent boys masturbate, the other two per cent are liars', I felt desperately ashamed and guilty about my apparently uncontrollable physical urges. My confessor pressed his question again. My face went redder and redder, the world seemed to sway, and the earth felt as though it was disappearing from beneath my knees. I managed to stumble out, 'No, nothing like that.' The priest looked at me doubtfully – he knew I was lying. Then he gave me absolution and penance. I fled as rapidly as I could from the church.

The main characteristics of shame experience

Picking up on my story of the confessional, one of the main features of the experience of shame is a sense of *uncontrollable exposure*. This is an embodiment of the root meaning of 'shame' with its sense of uncovering that produces a strong desire to be covered (Lynd 1958: 27–34).

Often, this is unexpected. It is usually involuntary. The person experiencing shame feels that they can suddenly be seen to their disadvantage in a direct and uncomfortable way. I had not expected the priest to ask me about my sexual experiences. When he did, I felt horribly exposed and vulnerable, as though I was standing in a spotlight on a stage. This sense of exposure is noted by most writers as an essential element in shame experience (Lewis 1992: 75; Kaufman 1993: 29).

A second distinctive aspect of shame is a sense of being looked at or *seen*. One seems to become an object in a visual field. To feel shame is 'to feel seen in a painfully diminished sense' (Kaufman 1993: 17; cf. Lewis 1971: 37). The language and experience of shame is suffused with visual imagery; for example, 'loss of face' is used as a metaphor for losing respect. Michael Lewis describes shame as the 'eye of the other in the me who beholds my transgression' (Lewis 1992: 92). Andrew Morrison entitles one of his papers about shame, 'The eye turned inward' (Morrison 1987). The sense of being seen metaphorically represents the sense of being judged or assessed. This is often also accompanied by a tacit internal monologue of self-criticism (Erikson 1965: 244; Lewis 1971: 37).

Sometimes, shame occurs in public and before real people. If one then makes a mistake or stands out in some way, one experiences public shame and embarrassment. However, one can have the sense of *audience* or the *critical other* entirely on one's own and in private (Lewis 1971: 39; Price Tangney, Burggraf and Wagner 1995: 344). Susan Miller notes that 'the particular kind of misery-about-the-self that gives shame its distinctive feel does seem to depend on some sense, however vague, of the self standing before another and potentially visible to another' (Miller 1985: 32). This suggests that somehow one internalises a critical gaze. Wurmser suggests that shame always has a kind of objective pole whereby one is ashamed in front of someone else: 'This pole is always originally a person; later it is an inner representation of such a person, usually vested in the superego' (Wurmser 1995: 44).

Feeling that one is seen by a real or imaginary critical audience turns the self into an *object*. There is a loss of distinction between subject and object as these two things become fused in the self. 'In shame we become the object as well as the subject of shame' (Lewis 1992: 34). The sense of being scrutinised from 'outside' provokes a feeling of being objectified. The person moves from a sense of being a person who judges into the position of feeling judged or assessed, even if the assessment is actually internal. This contributes to a characteristic sense of loss of agency and responsibility.

One of the main characteristics of feeling subjectively shamed in front of an internalised other is that it feels that *the whole of one's self is involved* (Lynd 1958: 51ff.; Lewis 1971: 40). It is not so much one's specific actions that are scrutinised, as they might be in guilt. The whole self feels as if it is available for global scrutiny. Although it was only my sexual thoughts and behaviour that were the subject of scrutiny in the confessional, not my whole being, my experience of shame was one of being wholly involved in every part of my conscious being. I experienced a 'crumpling or failure of the whole self' (Lynd 1958: 52).

A corollary of the global involvement of the whole self is that shame is *self-related*, not object-related (Wurmser 1995: 27). In guilt, the object of attention lies outside the self, in the person damaged or the act committed. In shame, on the other hand, the self is the object of concern. Indeed, one of the effects of shame is to exclude the outside world of other persons, events and actions and to fix attention firmly within the self (Lewis 1992: 34).

Experiencing the scrutiny of the self engenders a sense of heightened and tormenting *self-consciousness* and divided functioning (Kaufman 1993: 20). There is a sense of being split between the 'other' and the self, between affect and cognition. This inhibits the functioning of the self (Lewis 1971: 40). Self-functioning is usually smooth, 'silent', unnoticed and unproblematic; one is unaware of one's self most of the time. In shame, however, it is disrupted so that the self becomes 'noisy' and the sole focus of attention. There is an acute sense of dividedness or doubleness as the self evaluates itself (Lewis 1971: 34ff., 81).

The sense of acute self-consciousness is closely related to a sense of *incongruity*. The person becomes aware that things are not as they thought, perhaps that the self is not as it was thought to be in relation to the world (Lynd 1958: 34ff.).

This feeling of incongruity and things being not as they were assumed to be produces a *threat to trust in the nature of things* (Lynd 1958: 43ff.). One's world and one's identity within that world appear to be jeopardised. One does not know who or what one is any more. The experience of shame 'violates both interpersonal trust and internal security' (Kaufman 1993: 19). Shame thus produces a feeling of meaninglessness and hopelessness as the disoriented self drowns amidst its own confusion. It is a confrontation with tragedy (Lynd 1958: 56ff.).

Given the sharp retreat into the self, and the descent into inner division, meaninglessness, chaos and confusion, it is not surprising that a further feature of shame is *difficulty in communication* (Lynd 1958: 65ff.).

Shamed people are left without words or the capacity to use them, as I was in the confessional. The shame experience itself is impossible to articulate at the time, and may be so even afterwards:

[S]hame is a relatively wordless state. The experience of shame often occurs in the form of imagery, of looking or being looked at. Shame may also be played out in imagery of internal auditory colloquy in which the whole self is condemned by 'the other.' . . . The wordlessness of shame, its imagery of looking, together with the concreteness of autonomic activity make shame a primitive, irrational reaction, to which there is difficulty in applying a rational solution. (Lewis 1971: 37)

Goldberg describes shame as 'ironic' because the more intense and present it is, the less easy it is to articulate it or speak about it (Goldberg 1991: 86). Gordon Lynch suggests (in a personal communication) that, within a social constructionist view of shame, the loss of words accomplishes the exclusion of the subject from the world of social discourse and shared narrative. Shame is thus a state of linguistic and social exclusion and alienation even though it is subjectively perceived to be an intensely personal and individual experience.

A corollary of this is the common experience of *acute individual isolation* that often accompanies shame. One is trapped in the self without words and without other people: 'Shame sets one apart' (Lynd 1958: 65) and destroys the interpersonal bridge and social bonds between people (Kaufman 1993: 32ff.). This may be felt as a kind of 'radical abandonment' as the person turns inward, loses social bonds and a sense of the other, and so, being a social animal, loses a real sense of self (Wurmser 1995: 62f.). The functioning social self is lost in shame. It is a lonely, alienating experience.

The sense of isolation can be accompanied by an enormous sense of *despair*. Shame emerges when trust in other people and the self is shattered. Furthermore, the shamed person feels that they have no means of recontacting other people and reconstructing relationships. Thus, 'shame can engulf the self, immersing the individual deeper into despair' (Kaufman 1993: 25). The feeling of despair is exacerbated because shame fixes the self in a sense of *unending present* where past and future are forgotten (Goldberg 1991: 215). In the immediacy of the shame experience, yesterday has gone for ever and the future, with such hope as it may provide, will never arrive.

Shame experience is often described with reference to a set of distinctive, physiologically associated feelings. Perhaps the most uncomfortable of these is a *sense of total paralysis* and the inability to move, act, or do anything (Kaufman 1993: 21). In shame the 'self-machine' stops dead and is unable to function (Lewis 1992: 35). This sense of paralysis includes an inability to act upon the sense of shame itself. In guilt, action can remove the cause of offence or make reparation for it, so guilt is dissipated. In shame, there is no set of redemptive actions that is possible (Goldberg 1991: 53). The self is stuck, immobile, until the feeling of shame gradually fades away or is interrupted by some other feeling state. The affective experience of shame is very *immediate, rapid and generalised*. Shame is 'the most generalizable, most quickly spreading and flooding affect of them all' (Wurmser 1995: 55).

Related to the feeling of paralysis are the experiences of *powerlessness and passivity*. The person experiencing shame has no power of herself to help her self – or anyone else. The self feels small, helpless, childish and out of control (Lewis 1971: 41). The objectified, divided self experiences itself as lacking in power and agency in the face of the hostile 'other'.

A number of other apparently *physiologically related features* come into play in shame experience. Many people describe feelings of freezing, burning, numbing, leadenness, or having a sense of physical weakness in association with their experience of shame (Wurmser 1995: 53). Kneeling in front of my confessor, I seem to remember feeling all these things at the same time! There are more obvious *outward physical manifestations* that can be associated with shame, such as hanging the head, averting the gaze, and blushing (Kaufman 1993: 29; Darwin 1965: 325ff.). 'The body gestures and attitude include head bowed, eyes closed, body curved in on itself, making the person as small as possible' (Lewis 1971: 37).

None of these physical phenomena necessarily have to be present for shame to be experienced inwardly. There is no clear correspondence between physiological phenomena and the inner experience of shame (Lewis 1992: 26). Nonetheless, they are often present figuratively or metaphorically. Hence the popularity of expressions like 'losing face' to describe what happens in situations where shame occurs. One may lose face even if one does not avert one's gaze, hang one's head, or bear witness to one's shame with a facial blush.

Unsurprisingly, one of the main features of the shame experience is the *impetus to hide, disappear or flee*:

The primary motivational instruction of shame is the impulse to get out of the interpersonal realm, usually by hiding . . . Ashamed people frequently wish to get up and run out of the room, which they sometimes do. At other times, they simply look down, avoid eye contact, and lower their shoulders, seeming to shrink in size. (Lindsay-Hartz et al. 1995: 295–6)

'For some, shame is a moment when they wish a hole would open up and swallow them; it makes them want to disappear, for they feel at risk of death' (Nathanson 1992: 158). There are recorded examples of people not only needing to leave the room, but changing address and not telling people where they have gone, or even committing suicide, as ways of escaping shame (Lindsay-Hartz et al. 1995).

Many of the features of shame that I have so far described as being typical of shame experience might also be associated with descriptions of other emotional states such as grief or shock. A distinctive set of features that helps to distinguish shame from other experiences revolves around the perception of the self as being *judged to be inferior, defective, incompetent, undesirable, or unlovable.*

Wurmser (1995) argues that underlying all shame anxiety experience is the conviction of *being unloved and unlovable.* The self has a sense that it is defective and has a basic flaw that ensures its unacceptability and rejection by those whom it loves. Shame thus contains a fear of abandonment, loss of love, and so loss of self: 'Basic shame is the pain of essential unlovability' (Wurmser 1995: 93). The experience of shame often results in people experiencing a sense of self-rejection and loss of self-esteem: 'Deep down, [shame] always ultimately comes down to a painful feeling: "I am an unlovable, despicable nothing; the core of myself is hollow; my self is lost." One patient called it "this black vomit in me"' (Wurmser 1995: 235).

In experiencing the shame affect people experience a sense of *weakness, dirtiness and defectiveness* that contributes to a feeling that their self is fundamentally defective (Wurmser 1995: 43f.). The loss of love of the self experienced in shame decreases the self's sense of its own value. It is dehumanising to the extent that it changes the person into excrement – something low, stained, unpleasant and unwanted in their own eyes (Wurmser 1995: 81).

Shame experience is often described as inducing a *sense of inferiority, valuelessness, or personal diminishment* through failing to meet one's own adopted standards and ideals. Shame is a group of feelings about the self that 'all carry the conviction that one is small or inferior or defective'.

Along with this conviction comes an intense sense of displeasure about one's status and a wish to be changed: to be smarter, stronger, neater, more ethical, or more beautiful. The core of the feeling experience is distress concerning a state of the self as no good or not good enough. To capture the state, one can think of a young boy standing before an admired parent who berates the child as stupid, thoughtless or clumsy . . . He wants to disappear or hide, not to fight, because the self is experienced as not strong enough or valuable enough to proceed into the world. (Miller 1985: 32)

Loss of self-esteem is also associated with shame and is related to a sense of *failure* to meet the unconscious goals and standards of the ego-ideal (Goldberg 1991: 229; Miller 1985: 19). Because these goals and standards may be unconscious, people cannot necessarily articulate why they feel bad about themselves in shame.

A particularly painful characteristic of shame experience occurs when people not only judge themselves as not having lived up to their standards and ideals but actually experience themselves as *embodying the anti-ideal*. When Lindsay-Hartz et al. talked to people about their experience of shame, 'participants talked about being who they did *not* want to be . . . they experienced themselves as embodying an anti-ideal, rather than simply not being who they wanted to be' (Lindsay-Hartz et al., 1995: 277).

The next characteristic is that of *contempt or scorn directed towards the self* (Miller 1985: 134). Contempt is a more all-embracing negative attitude to the self than anger or rage (Erikson 1965: 244). It is characterised by the desire to abandon, to eliminate and to ignore, rather than to restore relationships, as anger might. Contempt 'wants to eliminate the other being, as dirt is thrown away. It is a "cold" affect, treating the object as if it did not exist, and constitutes a very strong form of rejection, using abandonment and isolation' (Wurmser 1995: 80–1). Hatred and anger are emotions that imply an amount of respect for the being of the other. However, '[b]ehind the feeling of shame stands not the fear of hatred, but the fear of contempt' (Piers and Singer 1971: 29): 'Contempt says: "You should disappear as such a being as you have shown yourself to be – failing, weak, flawed, and dirty. Get of my sight: Disappear!"' (Wurmser 1987: 67)

The final feature of shame experience is the curiously *unexpected, irrational and unpredictable* nature of its incidence and causes (Lewis 1971: 82). There are situations in which it is predictable that people may feel shame. However, people are often 'ambushed' by shame. It can occur at almost any time. Causes can be very difficult to identify. They may seem trivial, or more to do with other people than with oneself:

One may be ashamed of almost anything about oneself . . . One may be ashamed at times of anything with which one feels in any way identified – one's ethnic origins, country, religion, family, etc. One may feel shame over failure to be accepted or valued by any person or group whose acceptance is desired. Any perceived loss of love or respect from a loved one may trigger shame. One may feel shame over a lack of competence or over the loss of previously acquired competence . . . Any loss of control over one's body, mental functions, or emotions may elicit shame . . . When personal boundaries are not respected by others, shame and shame rage are apt to be the result. Shame also has to do with one's relationship to one's bodily functions and may be elicited under certain circumstances in association with eating, excretion, and sexuality. Anytime the self experiences itself as ruled by some 'lower' passion, the self may be vulnerable to shame. Failure to measure up to what others expect or what one expects of oneself may elicit shame. (Broucek 1991: 6)

Amongst other things, shame is highly social and can be very contagious (Lewis 1971: 15).

The ecology of the experience of shame is complex and multi-faceted, both as ordinary people describe it, and as it is treated in the relevant literature. Not all elements identified here as pertaining to shame experience are necessarily experienced by all people all the time. Nonetheless, they can all be significant in what people commonly describe as experience of shame.

Some possible functions of shame

Shame in its most direct form is perceived by those who experience it as acute, painful, paralysing, and unpleasant. But what is the function of the experience described as shame?

Answers to this question are pluriform, sometimes contradictory, and ultimately speculative. Most theorists would probably agree that the nature of shame experience is to inhibit action and to draw the attention of the self inwards, towards itself. A major function of the normal reaction of shame therefore seems to be some kind of protection of self and perhaps of others. I will now outline some of the theories that constitute the functional ecology of shame experience.

One function that has been suggested for shame by psychologists interested in the social display function of emotions generally is that it is an appeasement-related response. Shame display occurs when rules are violated that disrupt social interaction. It is an acknowledgment on the part of the offending individual that allows observers to reintegrate that person within the group:

An appeasement analysis of shame suggests that the nonverbal display of shame (1) allows transgressions of social and moral rules that govern behavior and experience related to the sense of virtue and character . . . and (2) is expressed in a distinct display that resembles submissive, appeasement-related behavior, which (3) restores social relations by reducing aggression and evoking social approach in observers. (Keltner and Harker 1998: 80).

For theorists influenced by Tomkins' affect theory, shame registers a disruption in the interpersonal bridge between the self and others (Tomkins 1987; Kaufman 1993). When the interest and joy that characterise reciprocal interest and trust in relationships is interrupted, shame damps down the positive affects that were previously evident. The perception of shame then alerts the self to this disruption. It prevents negative reactions such as violence and anger that might threaten the renewing of the interpersonal bridge by paralysing the self. It also creates a sense of longing for the bridge to be restored, thus maintaining the possibility of re-establishing needed relationships, such as those with carers (Kaufman 1993: 29ff.).

For many psychoanalytic theorists, one of the main functions of shame is to inhibit basic (forbidden) drives associated with sexuality – in particular, the drives to see (voyeurism) and to be seen (exhibitionism) (Freud 1977; Wurmser 1995). Shame prevents individuals from acting upon impulses that might prove dangerous to the self or anti-social to others. This view of the function of shame reminds of the fact that shame often occurs in a sexual context where a person is vulnerable to scrutiny and can easily experience embarrassment, inferiority and humiliation. Shame inhibits all actions of any kind including sexual activity. Some theorists extend this inhibitory function to argue that shame has an important role in regulating intimacy and distance in relations with others generally. Lewis, for example, argues that shame prevents total merger with others while it also stops others taking over or devouring the self. Shame monitors the boundaries between the self and the other. It helps to stake out clearly the limits and identity of the self (Lewis 1971: 23ff.).

The idea of shame as a useful defensive demarcator between self and others in relationships has been a popular one. Broucek suggests that shame is a defence against being objectified (Broucek 1991: 135ff.). The experience of shame returns people to their own sense of subjectivity and individuality. Where merger with another takes place there is a loss of self that can be very destructive – as witness abusive relationships where the abused are objectified and feel they have no will of their own (Walker 1992). Shame experience signals this danger. It is also a symptom of this kind of objectification having taken place. Within this perspective, shame provides a defensive shelter for the inner life of the person.

Broucek (1991) suggests that so-called 'shameless' people are those who either act only as subjects (so others are objectified and treated as if

they did not have an independent existence), or only as objects (so failing
to develop a proper sense of independent selfhood). Where there is no
shame, there is no possibility of proper individuation, autonomy and
selfhood, while the presence of shame allows the possibility of mutual
subject–object relations.

The protective role of shame in relationships is further developed by
several theorists. Wurmser, for example, argues that shame is triggered
when there is a danger of 'contemptuous rejection' by another person.
Shame signals that this rejection may take place. When the rejection and
disruption of relationship has occurred, shame prevents further exposure. It induces a self-protective attitude in the shamed person. Further,
it signals that the person has been exposed in a shaming way, thus pre-
paring the way for the re-establishment of relationship (Wurmser 1995:
53–4). Shame provides a kind of 'fig leaf' or 'soul mask' for the rejected,
despised, weak, exposed, inferior self that enables it to survive disruption in valued relationships (Jacoby 1994: 54). Wurmser further suggests
that when the boundaries of the self are threatened and the self feels
helpless in relation to this, shame covers the weakness that would be
exposed. While guilt limits strength, shame covers weakness (Wurmser
1995: 62).

The notion of shame protecting the inner life and subjectivity of the
individual is an important one in Western psychological understandings
of its function. Schneider suggests that it is 'discretion shame', the shame
associated with the sense of respect for boundaries, that protects the self
from harmful exposure to others. It allows the existence of necessary
personal privacy (Schneider 1987a: 38). To develop satisfactorily as
persons we need masks to protect ourselves (Jacoby 1994: 54). (If masks
become permanently fixed, however, then the pathology of 'false self'
may ensue as a person becomes totally identified with a mask or *persona*
(Richards 1996).) Shame pushes us to develop necessary masks. This
function of shame is close to the notions of proper respect and reverence
for the self. Without a sense of shame, the inwardness and integrity of
the self might be negated or compromised. Shame, therefore, guards the
boundaries of the self (Wurmser 1995: 64).

The positive function of shame as guardian of the self is amplified in
notions of its functioning as a means to self-knowledge and identity. In
fixing attention on the self, shame helps to expose us to ourselves for
what we are and what we might become (Lynd 1958: 20). It can function
as a teacher and as a 'royal road' to the sense of personal identity and
selfhood (Nathanson 1992: 211). Shame can be revelatory in relation to

understanding ourselves and others (Schneider 1987a: 25f.). It helps us to get ourselves into proportion. It is right that we should sometimes realise our smallness and our relative inferiority compared to other people and to the world we live in. It also helps us to recognise our ideals and aspirations, which can be a powerful spur to self-development (Thrane 1979).

Implied in much of the foregoing about the place of shame in relation to boundaries and relationships have been the very definite social and moral functions of shame. The self-evaluative aspect of shame suggests that there are elements of comparison in this experience; these relate to the measurement of self against others, social ideals and values (Lewis 1992). (In this connection, 'social' embraces the intimate relations between parent and child and extends outwards from there.) The social, relational function of shame is thought to be central by sociologists. Scheff describes shame as possibly the 'master emotion' that controls both normal and pathological human behaviour. In social interaction 'signals of normal shame serve to regulate social distance and as a compass for moral behavior' (Scheff 1995b: 1056). Scheff holds that 'pride and shame are the primary social emotions'.

These two emotions have a signal function with regard to the social bond. In this framework, pride and shame serve as intense and automatic bodily signs of the state of a system that would otherwise be difficult to observe, the state of one's bond to others. Pride is the sign of an intact bond; shame, a severed or threatened bond. The clearest outer marker of pride is holding up one's head in public and looking others in the eye, but indicating respect by taking turns looking and looking away. In *overt* shame, one shrinks, averting or lowering one's gaze, casting only furtive glances at the other. In *bypassed* shame, one stares, attempting to outface the other. (Scheff 1990: 15)

Shame thus acts as a kind of barometer of the distance and amounts of honour and respect that are exchanged between individuals in social relationships (Kaufman 1993: 21).

Another social function of shame alluded to by Scheff is that of maintaining and revealing personal ideals and values (these being themselves internalised from other persons). Like guilt, it appears to form part of an internal policing function:

The function of guilt and shame is to interrrupt any action that violates either internally or externally derived standards or rules. The internal command, which I call bringing into consciousness, says, 'Stop. What you are doing violates a rule or a standard.' This command, then, serves to inhibit the action. (Lewis 1992: 35)

The person who experiences shame is internally inhibited or bound from performing actions that might be destructive of relationships or society (Elias 1994). Shame may preserve internal ideals and values, together with a concomitant sense of integrity. It also functions as an internalised means of social control. The fact that shame is such a powerful means of controlling and inhibiting the self and its desires has meant that it has been elicited deliberately and offensively as a tool of social control. Nathanson describes shame as 'the affect of cutting down' (Nathanson 1992: 449). Insofar as it is good at cutting people down to size, making them feel inferior and cowed, it has often been exploited to exact conformity in social relationships of all kinds.

An ecology of possible functions for shame has now been outlined. Suggested functions have ranged from signalling disruption of relationships and appeasement, through the inhibition of forbidden desires, to the protection of the self, the development of self, self-knowledge, the monitoring of social relationships and social control. Shame appears to have important functions for the individual and society – and for the individual in society and relationships. Some of the concepts and ideas outlined here will be expanded later on. However, the critical reader may very well feel dissatisfied with the apparent incoherence of this set of accounts of the functions of shame. Many of them seem to depart from the specificity of shame experiences such as the one I described in my visit to my confessor. Furthermore, many of the functions of shame described here may sound positively useful, helpful and good. It may appear then, that there is no problem with shame. It is just one particular emotional phenomenon that forms a proper part of the human landscape. What has become of the very sharp, painful and dysfunctional aspects of shame? Are we, in fact, dealing with shame experience at all in any direct way in these accounts of the functions of shame?

It will help to get on the track of the negative, pathological aspects of shame, and to sort out some of the conceptual elisions that have been allowed to creep in, if I now outline an ecology of some different types of shame.

Some types of shame

While there may be a group of typical characteristics surrounding the experience of shame generally, shame ramifies itself into many different phenomena and experiences. I want now to make some important distinctions about the different ways in which shame is discussed and understood.

One preliminary point to note is that intense emotional experiences tend to be transitory. The acute sense of shame I felt in the confessional was very immediate and all-absorbing. However, it did not last long. While the experience contained many of the elements of shame that have been discussed, including the unpleasant physical accompaniments of blushing and feeling weak, it eventually passed off, as many shame experiences do. Many people only have intermittent and rare experiences of shame. These may be mainly associated with childhood, adolescence and schooldays when the personality is being shaped and a secure sense of identity is being developed (Kaufman 1993: 43; Schneider 1987a: 36ff.). Acute, sharp experiences of shame may occur most frequently in adolescence when people have a plastic sense of who they are and can easily find themselves in circumstances characterised by novelty, incongruity and uncertainty. As identity, social position, values, and confidence in ways of behaving solidify, directly reactive shame experiences of this kind often become less frequent and less painful.

There is an enormous difference between acute, reactive shame and the chronic shame that shapes a whole personality and may last a lifetime. When individuals appear to experience the whole of life as actually or potentially shame-productive and manifest such symptoms as withdrawal, self-contempt, inferiority, and gaze aversion as a matter of course throughout their everyday lives, shame has become pathological and chronic. Those whose lives are shaped by persistent shame attitudes and reactions are sometimes described as 'shame-bound' characters. They may be shame-prone, insofar as they feel, or act as if they feel, that shame may afflict them at any moment. They live their lives trying to avoid occasions and relationships that might provoke painful shame experiences. When such people experience actual, acute shame, they find it unbearable.

There is, therefore, an important distinction to be made between acute, reactive shame that occurs in particular situations, and chronic shame or shame proneness as a personality or character trait. The former is painful but temporary and limited in its effects which are by no means all negative. While the characteristics of the latter are similar to those of the former – family resemblance again – they are extended in time and influence. They can cast a permanent shadow over a person's life, character, and personality. In this book, I shall be mainly concerned with the negative influence and effects of chronic shame in individual and social life.

A second important distinction that can be made here is between, on the one hand, shame as a sharp, unpleasant, acute experience or as a confining, harmful, character trait and, on the other, shame as an anticipatory attitude of respect. When people talk of others having 'no sense of shame' they are not referring either to their specific experiences of shame, or to negative, defensive aspects of their characters. They are alluding to the need to have a sense of appropriate respect for certain people, institutions, values, ideals, or behaviours. In this connection, the use of the concept of shame denotes a sense of awe, reverence or respect, what the Greeks would have called *aidos* (Cairns 1993; Williams 1993).

This very positive notion of shame might be denoted 'respect shame' or 'discretion shame'. This can be distinguished from 'disgrace shame' (Schneider 1987a: 18ff.). The latter is acute reactive shame that occurs when a breach in social order and normal relations has occurred. The former is less like an intense emotional experience and more like an attitude or a characterological virtue that affirms the social order and prevents its disruption. It acts as an internalised defender of treasured social attitudes, values and behaviours. It can be thought of as 'anticipatory shame' insofar as it acts in an pre-emptive manner to prevent people from acting in anti-social ways. It is linked to the experience of acute, reactive shame by the fact that it is expected that people will feel bad, belittled or humiliated if they fail to give due honour to things that other people regard as valuable.

The difference between the sense of shame as a necessary social attitude and as an emotionally based experience of shame can be exemplified in relation to Bill Clinton, President of the United States of America in the 1990s. Clinton was alleged to have had an affair with a woman on his White House staff, but denied this to a Grand Jury investigation. Subsequently, he admitted to having the affair and was accused of perjury. Many people asked, Does Bill Clinton have no sense of shame? The video tapes of his testimony before the Grand Jury suggest that Clinton was certainly able to experience shame as an immediate emotion. He frequently looked discomforted, red, evasive and embarrassed as he faced questions into his personal life and behaviour. However, the fact that the President committed perjury in the first place suggests that he was deficient in a sense of discretion shame, failing to honour and respect the Constitution that he had sworn to defend by lying under oath and so subverting the rule of law.

As the Clinton example shows, the shameless person is one who, in the view of others, has failed adequately to embrace the ideals and values of society. Thus, he becomes shamed and deserving of contempt, rejection and exclusion in the eyes of others even if he is unaware of this. A person with a proper sense of positive, respect-related or discretion shame will feel shame when she violates the ideals and expectations of the society or group she lives in. However, the things that are protected by the dynamics of honour and shame will differ according to the culture, society or reference group within which a person is brought up and lives.

Another important set of distinctions has been made by the psychoanalyst Wurmser. Wurmser identifies three major phenomenological types of shame. First, there is shame anxiety. This is anticipatory anxiety about the imminent threat of being exposed, humiliated, belittled or rejected. It signals the danger of contemptuous rejection and corresponds roughly to discretion shame. Secondly, Wurmser identifies shame affect proper. This corresponds approximately to acute shame. It is a reaction to an actual situation or event in which exposure, humiliation, inferiority or rejection occurs. The person who experiences shame affect proper is likely to recognise that he or she is experiencing shame. Finally, Wurmser identifies shame attitude. This he characterises as a reaction formation to experiences of shame that helps to avoid shame experiences in the future. People develop attitudes of avoidance, bashfulness, etc. that become habitual. This kind of shame attitude corresponds roughly to the category of chronic or character shame (Wurmser 1995: 49–56).

A further, crucial and very influential set of psychoanalytic distinctions has been made by Block Lewis who identifies three ways in which shame might be phenomenologically present in people's lives in different ways.

In *overt shame*, shame affect is to the fore and the self may be highly conscious of feeling diminished and inferior, and of physical reactions such as blushing. It is this overt, obvious, shame that characterised my experience in the confessional. This form of shame is apparent to the self and also, often, to others.

A second form of shame is *overt, unidentified shame*. Here again, the shame affect is to the fore, but the person experiencing shame cannot, or will not, identify or acknowledge it as shame. Instead all he knows is 'that he feels "lousy", or "tense", or "blank"' (Lewis 1971: 197). Shame may be unidentified here because it is hidden behind ideas of guilt in the person's mind, possibly as a defence against the unpleasant feeling of shame itself.

In *bypassed shame* the self is not conscious of feeling shame affect at all: 'the person is aware of the cognitive content of shame-connected events, but experiences only a "wince", "blow", or "jolt"' (Lewis 1971: 197). While the person does not experience the disruption of the self associated with direct shame experience, there is 'a peripheral, non-specific disturbance in awareness, which serves mainly to note the shame potential in the circumstance' (Lewis 1971: 197). Lewis writes: 'The ideation of by-passed shame involves doubt about the self's image from the "other's" viewpoint. There is frequently an accompaniment of overt hostility along with this ideation, and sometimes clear retaliatory feeling' (Lewis 1971: 197). While a person may experience no direct bodily arousal of the kind normally associated with shame, he or she might find him- or herself consciously making comparisons of the self with others in an unfavourable or hostile way (Retzinger 1995: 1106).

Lewis' notions of unidentified and bypassed shame point up the possibility that shame may not be easily perceived or identified. Shame experience may be much more significant in people's lives than would seem plausible if it were confined to acute, conscious experiences. Unidentified or bypassed shame is real and has a profound effect on individuals, especially chronically shamed or shame-prone individuals, and situations. The real, but covert, effects of shame will be picked up in places in later chapters.

One final type of shame might be denoted 'ontological' or 'inherent' shame. Far from being a psychological condition, this is deemed to be a kind of innate, universal shame that surrounds simply being a mortal, embodied human being and having to cope with the limits of this condition (Kundera 1984; Hans 1991). Animals lack self-consciousness and awareness of themselves in the eyes of others so they do not experience shame. Humans, however, experience awareness of self and others. This produces a sense of autonomy and standing out from the rest of creation, but it is accompanied by a sense of abjection or shame. This emerges from disgust at the body and its functions, such as eating and defecating, from a sense of powerlessness engendered by the force of bodily desires, and from a sense of being critically observed by others in such a way that the individual is objectified (Hans 1991: 71f.). All humans experience abjection even if they are not aware of it. Furthermore, many human institutions and structures such as religion and politics are defences against having to acknowledge and own this kind of shame. While ontological abjection may be normal and inevitable, defences against it are pathological because they prevent humans from recognising their part in the flow of creation. Often the price of denied human abjection is the suffering of animals who remind humans of their powerlessness and embodiment.

This section of the chapter has created an ecology of different types of shame experience. This suggests that the experience of shame is more diverse and pervasive than the basic experience of 'being ashamed' in an acute, momentary way. The ecology of distinctions outlined here will be built on as the book progresses. Now, however, it is appropriate to consider briefly the significance of the images and metaphors within which shame experience is described.

Metaphors, images and shame

It is a commonplace of social constructionist views of discourse that all experience is mediated through language (Gergen 1991, 1994). This means that all understandings of experience are in some sense metaphorical. This is overtly apparent in the discourses that surround shame.

So, for example, visual images and metaphors are used to talk of a sense of exposure in shame (Schneider 1987a: 35). This does not mean that the self is literally exposed to the gaze of the self – we have no 'mind's eye' with which to look at ourselves, even though we often use this term to describe our experience. Nor do we literally 'lose face'. What is meant here is that there is an 'as if' feeling of evaluation in which it is felt that one is evaluated or self-perceived to be inferior and lacking in honour. This has substantial similarities with the sense of actually seeing with the eye.

Similarly, the self can be discussed in terms of having 'boundaries'. The metaphorical use of the term 'boundary' helps to encapsulate the notion that there is a proper separateness to individual persons. When this is 'violated', 'breached', 'overcome', or 'broken down', harm may be done to the individual.

The various discourses concerning shame are saturated with such images and metaphors. These, in turn, crucially affect the way in which we understand and regard shame and the ways in which it is responded to. So, for example, if we understand shame to be a kind of proper awe or respect for ideals or persons, then we may want to promote it in society. If, on the other hand, shame is perceived through the lens of metaphors of disease and disturbance so it is described as 'chronic', or 'pathological', then it might seem important to eliminate shame. Shame described as the affect of 'cutting down' (Nathanson 1992) – a metaphorical understanding of its violent, aggressive function – has a very different value and feeling from shame described as the 'guardian of the inner self' (Wurmser 1995: 64). Images and metaphors power-fully shape reality, explanations, attitudes and actions.

No one set of images and metaphors exhaustively or exclusively describes shame. Instead, there are competing or complementary dis-courses with their own families of metaphors and images. Thus, in some discourses notions of measurement and evaluation are to the fore, while in others those of protection, belonging or uncleanness are emphasised.

Having acknowledged this, however, I would like to suggest a specific set of organising or governing (though not exclusive) metaphors and images for this phenomenon. It is my contention that shame, particu-larly chronic shame, is best situated within the metaphorical ecology that pertains to defilement, pollution and stain. This contrasts with the meta-phorical ecology surrounding guilt, which might best be described as one of offence, debt, and punishment. While guilt pertains to a world characterised by metaphors in which persons offend against rules, incur debts, are punished and have to make active reparation, shame pertains more to a metaphorical world in which persons are excluded, found to be 'dirty' or polluted, and stand in need of cleansing and acceptance in order to be reintegrated into society.

According to Robert Parker, an ancient historian, the notion of defilement lies at the heart of the ancient Greek notion of miasma or pollution (Parker 1983: 7). According to the philosopher, Paul Ricoeur, at the heart of defilement lies the notion of metaphorical stain (Ricoeur 1967: 33ff.). Behind both these perspectives there is a hypothesis that before societies were based on guilt and offence, fault and alienation were primarily dealt with in terms of pollution and cleansing. If the order of society was disrupted, for example by a natural event such as birth or death, or by an act such as murder, purificatory ritual was required to restore normality.

Building upon Douglas' (1969) idea that pollution arises when an ideal of order is disturbed rather than being a product of either anxiety or guilt, Parker suggests that disease and moral offence become 'assimi-lated' to the powerful metaphors of dirt and pollution (Parker 1983: 225). It is not difficult to see why offenders came to be thought of as meta-phorically 'dirty'. The person who murders another dishonours him, and in doing so disrupts the social order and brings pollution and defilement (that is, shame) upon himself. Such was the power of the metaphors of dirt and purification for dealing with matters of order and disorder that many kinds of experience became assimilated to them.

Even today, our notion of legal offence incorporates elements of pollution and defilement – 'dirty crook' being an example.

The modern experience of shame is not a straightforward replication or replaying of the socio-metaphorical structure of ancient society. However, the metaphors of pollution and dirt have continued to have power and resonance. Just as notions and metaphors of evil have gradually become internalised and personalised (Russell 1986), pollution metaphors may also have become psychologised and individualised in contemporary society. It might be argued that in many ways the modern 'psychological' experience of shame is one of 'internalised pollution'. This notion certainly seems to inform the thinking of Kristeva whose notion of personal abjection seems to owe much to the idea that dirt and defilement are now internal, psychological matters rather than external realities (Kristeva 1982). There seems to be a kind of metaphorical affinity between ancient notions of pollution, defilement and dishonour and contemporary experiences and descriptions of shame, albeit that the latter mostly now refer to the experience of individuals rather than describing a primarily social reality.

Some elements of contemporary shame experience are brought into sharper focus if they are deliberately placed in the context of the metaphorical world of pollution, stain and defilement:

– Shame, like pollution, has elements of social dislocation and exclusion. The shamed person feels they stand outside the social order and social relationships.

– That which is polluted is dirty: it is regarded as worthless if not dangerous, contaminating, and unworthy of respect. Similarly the sense of feeling like, and regarding oneself as, dirt often accompanies the experience of shame. Indeed, the shamed person may actually feel either temporarily or permanently like shit.

– Pollution and defilement come upon people not necessarily directly because of moral offence, but because of a disruption in the order of relationships. Those who experience shame similarly may be in a position where they have not necessarily done anything wrong, but find themselves feeling in the wrong, and thus in a state of alienation from others.

– A prominent cause of pollution and defilement is the inappropriate transgressing of boundaries or borders – for example, standing in the wrong place in a temple, or failing to respect the gods or other people appropriately. Shame, similarly, emerges when boundaries are breached or threatened (Walker 1992). While the disruption in social relations represented by offence and guilt can be restored by reparation and punishment that remedies debt, shame, like pollution, has no remedy other than some kind of public cleansing to effect social reintegration. However, the cleansing rituals that were available to the ancients are no longer available for those experiencing shame internally today. Those who experience shame are therefore left in a state of permanent self- and social alienation.

Modern, essentially individually rather than socially related experiences of shame are not the same in terms of content, meaning and context as the much more public, corporate experience of miasma or pollution in the ancient world. Nonetheless, the parallels between the two conditions or experiences may be enlightening. To see chronically shamed people as people who essentially experience a sense of themselves as excluded, inferior, defiled, polluted and polluting, indeed as toxic dirt, is not far-fetched. Understanding their experience with the metaphors of pollution, stain and defilement consciously in mind may thus be very appropriate. For example, the modern notion of stigma or spoiled identity whereby a person feels they have a stain upon their identity that excludes them from valued human relations and society seems to fit well into a metaphorical ecology of defilement and pollution (Goffman 1968b; cf. Lewis 1998). Goffman actually traces the modern notion of stigma back to ancient Greek culture where it was used 'to refer to bodily signs designed to expose something unusual and bad about the moral status of the signifier'. A stigmatised person was externally marked so that people could see that they were 'a slave, a criminal or a traitor – a blemished person, ritually polluted, to be avoided, especially in public places' (Goffman 1968b: 9, 11ff.).

Placing shame deliberately within the metaphorical ecology of pollution and defilement might have a number of advantages. First, notions of pollution and defilement may help to underline and distinguish some characteristic aspects associated with descriptions of shame experience.

Secondly, understanding of this experience is drawn from another source than that of modern psychology or sociology. Having in mind the notion of pollution may obliquely suggest ways in which shame might be comprehended and dealt with in the contemporary world. For example, there are many modern instances and experiences of social pollution, such as stigmatisation whereby people 'enjoying' spoiled, discredited identity are excluded from social participation (Goffman 1968b). Such people – gays, disabled people and others – often experience a sense of accompanying shame to this kind of rejection, even if the particular word 'stigma' is no longer used (Goffman 1968b). Many shamed people – for example, those who have been raped or abused – see themselves as dirty, defiled and polluted. They have to manage a spoiled or stigmatised identity (Walker 1992). There appears to be a sense of 'best fit' here in terms of metaphorical grip that may be very fruitful. The emphasis upon order, boundaries and transgression within notions of pollution also implies a good metaphorical 'fit'.

Thirdly, firmly placing shame within the ecology of defilement helps further to distinguish shame experience from guilt experience which finds its own metaphorical home within the ecology of offence and reparation.

Fourthly, keeping in mind the social nature of pollution and defilement in ancient civilisations acts as a useful counterbalance to any tendency there may be to see shame as only an inward, individual, psychological experience. While the sense of exclusion and defilement implied in much shame experience is certainly a very acute personal phenomenon in our social order, shame is a socially shaped and engendered phenomenon. No-one is shamed in social isolation or without social implications, even if they are on their own when they experience shame.

Finally, this placement may prove suggestive in trying to understand the relationship of religious ideas and practices to shame. For Ricoeur, the development of a sense of sin or fault in human history begins with symbolic notions of defilement and develops through the sense of sin against God to more modern notions of guilt and offence against laws. He argues that '[d]read of the impure and rites of purification are in the background of all our feelings and all our behavior relating to fault' (Ricoeur 1967: 25). He suggests that 'the world of defilement is a world anterior to the division between the ethical and the physical' (Ricoeur 1967: 31). Western Christianity has tended to see the nature of sin, fault and alienation from self and from God as matters of offence and guilt. However, Ricoeur points out that this is underlain with the metaphorical stain of defilement. Defilement is a 'symbolic stain' and every evil is 'symbolically a stain' (Ricoeur 1967: 36, 46). If defilement continues to be an important human experience, perhaps in the form of shame, and it also occupies an important, if implicit, place in Christian religious discourse and practice relating to sin and atonement, then paying attention to notions of pollution and defilement may be an important aspect of evaluating this religious tradition.

In the next chapter I shall consider more of what are perceived to be the effects and implications of shame for individuals, groups and social institutions. Leaving acute, reactive shame largely behind, the focus here will be upon the negative effects of shame that becomes chronic and so limits and distorts human existence.

CHAPTER FOUR

Chronic shame

> [S]hame as a healthy emotion can be transformed into shame as a state of being. As a state of being, shame takes over one's whole identity. To have shame as an identity is to believe that one's being is flawed, that one is defective as a human being. Once shame is transformed into an identity, it becomes toxic and dehumanizing.
>
> (Bradshaw 1988: vii)

Many people experience what is described as shame acutely, reactively, and only for a short space of time. For some, however, shame is a permanent trait or sentiment rather than a temporary state (Tantam 1998: 168). It becomes a dominant characteristic, a deeply engrained habitual mode of reacting to self and others. Such people may be described as shame-bound, shame-ridden, shame-prone, or toxically or chronically shamed. They live permanently diminished, distrustful, unhappy and uncomfortable lives: 'Any human emotion can become internalized. When internalized an emotion stops functioning in the manner of an emotion and becomes a characterological style . . . The person doesn't have anger or melancholy, she *is* angry and melancholy' (Bradshaw 1988: 10–11).

Here are a couple of examples from my own recent experience of what it means to have a personality shaped by a pervasive sense of shame and being ashamed.

A few years ago, I was sitting in a station buffet when a friend of mine whom I had not seen for about ten years walked in. I recognised him immediately but he did not see or recognise me. My first instinct was to go and say hello to him, but quickly a sense of anxiety and reluctance came upon me and I decided to sit where I was. I dropped my eyes on to the book I was reading again and fervently hoped from then on that he would not notice me. He did not, and eventually departed – to my relief. I felt a bit disappointed with myself that I had not made contact with him. It would probably have been nice to have had a chat. I also had a sense of regret. Puzzling over my behaviour afterwards, I think the reason that I did not approach him was that I feared not being recognised and then not being welcomed or valued. My inner sense of shame and my desire to avoid possible rejection prevented my being able to greet my friend. At the time, I 'consoled' myself with the thought that he would not have wanted to speak to me anyway and that I would be being a nuisance to him when he was engaged in his own thoughts and activities. Thus shame-bound people may exclude themselves from human contact and relationships for reasons that are entirely internal.

A second example is more immediate. I often find it easy to write words on paper or on a word processor screen. However, when I am writing a book, a lecture, or a paper for publication, as I am at the moment, I find it very difficult to write the words down, even though I can change them many times before they are published. It feels as if every word has to be squeezed out of me, over my own dead body, so to speak. Reflecting on this experience, I think I am inhibited as well as pleased by the thought that many other people are going to read my words and may find them unclear, incomprehensible, inadequate, or stupid. An internal audience of potential 'critics' looks over my shoulder as I write and discourages me from even trying to express myself in words. I have to overcome my primary and perpetual inner fear of being found wanting, and so being rejected and ridiculed, in order to write. This is a difficult experience that often makes me want to give up altogether. Here again, then, a sense of permanent inner shame disrupts my life and seems to conspire against my personal enjoyment, well-being and communication with others.

These examples are of a fairly trivial and minor kind – though, interestingly, I find it quite shaming to own up to them in public. They give some sense of what chronic or personality shame can feel like and how it can act in everyday life. In this chapter, I will explore some of the factors that may contribute to the evolution of toxic, character shame.

The aetiology of chronic shame

Preliminary considerations

There is no commonly agreed definition of what chronic shame is. Nor is there agreement about the 'symptoms' of the condition, any more than there is consensus on the nature of shame as an emotion. I take chronic shame to be broadly the expansion and prolongation of the features associated with affect shame throughout someone's personality.

Thus, they manifest symptoms of feeling, for example, abnormally self-conscious, aware of being under scrutiny, or that they need to hide. This is not a set of universal, authoritative diagnostic criteria. It is a personal heuristic stance.

Related to a lack of agreement about definition is the fact that there is no epidemiological data about the prevalence of shame in the population. Nor are there nuanced diagnostic criteria whereby chronic shame might be designated as mild, serious, or severe. The evidence for the extent and importance of chronic shame comes from a large amount of clinical experience and writing and a small amount of psychological investigation in the community.

Most of those who write about chronic shame and point up its clinical importance are American. Furthermore, most of their writings have appeared since the last war. This might provide *prima facie* evidence for a social constructionist stance to shame. It suggests that chronic shame, like many other 'diseases', is a construction of the clinical gaze (Seale and Pattison 1994). Chronic shame could then be regarded as an explanatory construct in a particular set of discourses that has some kind of social utility. Just because a concept is socially constructed does not mean that it is not socially 'real'. If many North American clinicians think 'chronic shame' usefully captures an important dimension of experience, as I do myself, it has a reality in clinical, psychological and personal discourse and practice. However, being mindful of the socially constructed nature of a concept such as chronic shame allows one usefully to avoid uncritically reifying it. The loose-knit, ill-defined nature of 'chronic shame' as a concept in both theory and practice allows one to escape from empiricism and narrowness even as its non-specificity makes formal epidemiology and diagnostic investigations problematic (Andrews 1998a).

This raises the question of the relation of chronic shame to other symptoms and disorders of the self. For some writers, chronic shame as a condition exists in its own right (Bradshaw 1988). It is worthy of primary attention. These theorists hold that shame is causally associated with many other negative aspects of the human condition such as depression and addiction. For others, shame itself appears to be more like a sign or symptom of another condition of the self, for example, narcissistic personality disorder (Morrison 1989). Should shame be seen as an independent factor and variable in causing uncomfortable or negative conditions of the self? Or is it itself dependent on the development of such conditions so that it may be regarded as an indicator or symptom of such conditions? There is probably no answer to this conundrum. Within a constructionist view of emotions and the self, indeed, there is, in fact, no need to resolve it.

Finally, it must be acknowledged that since chronic shame is not a tightly defined, reified disease entity or clinical condition, any attempt to examine its causes is bound to be fragmentary and to contain a good measure of speculation and incoherence. There is no agreement on the aetiological factors that contribute to the condition described here as chronic shame. There is a variety of plausible suggestions from various different narratives that might be relevant to the evolution of this condition in individuals. Thus all perspectives and factors considered here should be treated with proper scepticism. Many factors contribute in different measures in different individuals to the evolution of a shamed personality.

There is no 'master narrative' or identifiable main cause that can confidently be attributed in the case of chronic shame. However, it seems plausible to suggest that any experience that constitutes a rejection, objectification, or boundary invasion of the person that induces a sense of social or individual worthlessness, alienation or abandonment if severe enough, long enough, or repeated enough, is likely to contribute to the development of a chronic sense of shame. Many theories of the development of chronic shame dwell on early experiences as stimuli to chronic shame. However, it seems to me that it is possible to develop a sense of chronic or personality shame at any time in life (Tantam 1998: 168). Thus rape victims, abuse victims (Walker 1992) and those who have endured tyranny in oppressive regimes or prison camps (Bettleheim 1986) as adults, for example, may develop this personality trait decisively at quite advanced stages in their lives.

Having laid out some preliminary cautions in trying to identify the factors that may contribute to chronic or personality shame, I shall now work through some of the suggested factors themselves. None of the factors discussed below is necessarily exclusive to a particular phase in a person's life. Thus, for example, it is important for persons to be recognised and respected as individuals and not to be objectified or abnegated at any stage in their life course.

Factors in the creation of chronic shame

Genetic, biological and pre-birth factors

Very little is known about genetic and biological predispositions to particular emotional responses or personality traits. However, if it is accepted that biological and other factors work together to shape personality, then a notional, if unclear, significance must be attached to this factor in the evolution of shame as an affective response and personality trait.

It is perhaps here that the shame proneness of women should be discussed. Block Lewis in empirical psychological studies noted that people who were more field, i.e. context, dependent in making judgments, for example about distances, were also more likely to experience shame rather than guilt (Lewis 1971: 126ff.; cf. Lewis 1992: 10). Women were found to be more field dependent than men. Men, being less field dependent, tended more towards guilt proneness. This kind of finding has been confirmed in other research projects that have found that women are more prone to self-blame and to whole character attribution of fault than men (Lamb 1996: 91ff.).

It might be deduced from these findings that women are biologically predisposed towards shame. However, differential socialisation after birth is a more likely explanatory factor here. Girls may be socialised to have more regard to the opinions and needs of others and to look outside themselves and into relationships for a sense of what is correct and right (Baker Miller 1986; Eichenbaum and Orbach 1985; Crawford et al. 1992: 55ff.). They may be schooled to make global attributions of failure of the self by a society that values female subordination and finds a role for women as oilers of relationships and ministers to male needs. This may also produce a sense of low self-esteem, together with shame-related features such as a sense of ineffectuality, helplessness, self-blame, whole person attribution, and passivity (Andrews 1998b; Lamb 1996: 141ff.). At this point, it should be mentioned that recent writers on men have highlighted their propensity to shame as well (Bly 1991: 147ff.). The present work itself bears witness to the possibility of shame in men.

The basic biological nature of human individuals may have some impact on whether or not they become shame-prone in later life (Zahn Waxler and Robinson 1995: 156–8). However, the dynamics of how this works in with other factors are unclear. Perhaps a more significant social factor that may have an impact on the development of shame before birth is whether or not the child is wanted by its parents. An unwanted child may begin to internalise a sense of itself as alien, undesirable and unlovable. The seeds of shame may thus be sown before a child is born.

Any putative genetic, physiological basis for personal and emotional development is crucially changed and shaped by personal history and events in the social context of development. It can therefore be argued that individuals learn shame and their own sense of self primarily through life experience, particularly through relationships with others. It is, therefore, to the experience of early infancy that I now turn.

Factors pertaining to infancy

Infancy is an important time for the emergence of a sense of self, for emotional development, and for developing ways of relating to self and others. Most theorists accept that persons only become persons, attain self-consciousness, language, etc., insofar as they are communicated with and socialised by other persons. The individual 'becomes an object of himself only by taking the attitudes of other individuals toward himself within a social environment or context of experience and behavior in which both he and they are involved' (Mead 1934: 138). This process is most intense during infancy. However, despite the growth of child observation studies, there is no unanimity as to the mechanisms that come into play to produce the kind of 'healthy', 'normal', well-individuated, sociable self that appears to be the norm in Western society.

Within psychological discourses about early child development there is broad consensus that infants desperately need the focussed individual care and attention of their carers if they are to flourish physically and emotionally:

Alice Miller . . . states, 'the child has a primary need to be seen, noticed, and taken seriously as being that which it is at any given time, and as the hub of its own activity. In contradistinction to drive wishes, we are here dealing with a need which is narcissistic, but nevertheless equally legitimate, and whose fulfillment is essential to the development of a healthy self-esteem.' (Mollon 1993: 57)

The quality of the intimacy between carer and child in the earliest years is significant for shaping the child's sense of self. Winnicott's notion of mirroring is important here. Winnicott (1974: 131) argues that the infant sees itself reflected through the eyes of its primary carer. If the carer's gaze is loving and empathic, the infant's self-esteem is confirmed and enhanced. The baby will develop a sense of being valuable and loved. This is then carried into later life. If the mother's face is consistently absent, or is unresponsive and fails to reflect the baby's feelings, or only reflects the mood of the carer, then the child's sense of self will not be enhanced and may be damaged. This may prevent it from gaining a proper sense of self, including the self's emotions, creativity, limitations and boundaries.

The notion of mirroring is underpinned by the observation that many parents spend much time literally gazing into the faces of babies, reflecting their moods and feelings, often with exaggerated facial gestures of their own: '[M]other and child remain engaged for thirty seconds or more, and during play a mother may gaze at her baby for seventy percent of the time . . . The mother's face is the first place the baby's gaze is directed toward, the first place a child learns about human relatedness' (Cole 1998: 112).

Many theorists have drawn upon the literal and metaphorical richness of the notion of facial communication between mother and child to highlight the importance of developing an empathic relationship (Kohut 1971: 117). This helps to bestow, maintain, and enhance a sense of selfhood in the child:

Love resides in the face – in its beauty, in the music of the voice and the warmth of the eye. Love is proved by the face, and so is unlovability – proved by seeing and hearing, by being seen and heard. A child can be loved without being given the nipple; but love cannot exist without face and music. (Wurmser 1995: 96–7)

The notions of mirroring and gaze that are so resonant with ideas about shame that concern loss of face and self-contempt are metaphorical as well as literal in content. Arguably, 'mirroring' is really a metaphor for active 'empathic response' (Mollon 1993: 57). While a good deal of gazing may take place, infants who are blind from birth can still develop a strong sense of self-esteem and selfhood from being held, spoken to and responded to in non-visual ways, though their emotional experience and development may be subtly different from those who are sighted (Cole 1998: 183ff.). In the light of the limits to visual metaphors, it may be appropriate also to use the more aurally resonant metaphor of 'affective attunement' (Stern 1985).

Stern suggests that while mirroring suggests synchronous robot-like imitation of the infant's behaviour, affect attunement 'is the performance of behaviors that express the quality of feeling of a shared affect state without imitating the exact behavioral expression of the inner state' (Stern 1985: 142). Affect attunement 'involves changing the other by providing something the other did not have before or, if it was present, by consolidating it' (Stern 1985: 144). Carers need to establish interpersonal communion with their infants by catching their experience or feeling state and showing that they resonate with it. When this does not happen, there is either purposeful misattunement, in which the mother deliberately tries to alter the baby's feeling state, or non-purposeful misattunement, in which the mother fails to resonate to the baby's inner state (Stern 1985: 148–9).

Experts have expended much effort trying to understand how the parent–infant relationship works to shape personality, a sense of self, self-esteem, self-consciousness, emotional self-awareness, and social functioning as a person (Klein 1987). This kind of thinking can be aggregated into a crude summary. Infants come into the world with lots of innate potentials. To become persons with integrated selves and personalities they need the intimate physical care, attention, love and esteem of their carers. This is often expressed through facial as well as other kinds of contact. Infants need to feel that their carers understand and resonate with their feelings and moods if they are to learn what they themselves feel and to feel safe with powerful drives or emotions. They also need to feel a sense of efficacy – that their parents are tuned in to their needs and that they will respond to these. If all this happens effectively the infant enjoys a 'facilitating environment' (Winnicott 1990).

Eventually, the baby who enjoys 'good enough' parenting becomes more independent. Even if occasional unpleasant or frustrating experiences are encountered, the loved and cared for infant will tolerate these. Indeed, learning to tolerate 'optimal frustration' (Kohut 1971: 50) helps the infant to learn about identity as an individual that is separate from the carer. The well-loved and cared for infant, to whom carers are available for mirroring and attunement, will develop self-esteem and a proper sense of her own boundaries as a person. She will also be at home with her own emotions and have a proper sense of the limits of her self and abilities.

Shame can enter into this picture in several ways. Infants may be unloved or deprived of intimate relationship. They may be physically abandoned temporarily or permanently so that intimacy is traumatically interrupted. This may expose them to an amount of upset with which they do not have the inner emotional resources to cope. Even if a carer remains physically present, they may abandon the baby emotionally, failing to mirror, attune or respond to the infant's needs and so inducing a sense of despair. Stern (1985) notes the phenomenon of mothers who seem unable to attune to the emotions and moods of their children. Worse, some babies may have to mirror and reflect the emotional needs of their parents instead of having their own needs reflected. Winnicott describes the condition of 'false self' that emerges when an infant has to modify its own feelings and needs to ensure the continued attention of its carer:

The mother who is not good enough is not able to implement the infant's omnipotence, and so she repeatedly fails to meet the infant gesture; instead she substitutes her own gesture which is to be given sense by the compliance of the infant. This compliance on the part of the infant is the earliest stage of the False Self . . . (Richards 1996: 14; cf. Klein 1987: 238ff.)

Some infants develop a kind of compliant self to survive. This means that they become divorced from the unacceptable feelings and energies that constitute the 'true self'. A large part of the child's existence is denied and regarded as unwanted. A related kind of pathology appears to result from carers not recognising the individuality and needs of the child and so treating it as an extension of themselves. Here the child may feel engulfed and deprived of properly separate existence (Mollon 1993: 45f.).

As a helpless being, the infant is vulnerable to learning that it is unwanted, inferior, powerless and disgusting from its first carers. Early lessons in selfhood may easily predispose towards a basic sense of shame, even when parents do not indulge in specifically shaming activities. It is possible that overt, momentary shame is experienced when intimacy and enjoyment is interrupted between carer and child (Kaufman 1993). However, chronic shame and a sense of being unwanted for what one is may be engendered if a child experiences a constant sense of not being wanted, not having its needs met, having to meet the needs of others, having its personal boundaries disregarded, and being treated as an object. If a child is unloved for what it is as a potential subject in its own right, chronic shame, a sense of exclusion, defilement and unlovability, may emerge right at the beginning of life.

Within the metaphorical ecology of the visual, Mollon suggests that there are two kinds of gaze. On the one hand, the infant may experience itself as admired, the apple of its carer's eye. On the other hand, it may experience an objectifying gaze that is essentially dehumanising and disregarding (Mollon 1993: 47). This engenders a sense of violation and shame. Wurmser puts this more graphically:

To be unlovable means not to see a responsive eye and not to hear a responding voice, no matter how much they are sought. The helplessness of the searching and the cry for love is the helplessness of feeling doomed to unlovability. Function and content are one in this primary trauma; they remain combined in the affect of shame. Even love and power, libido and aggression are combined in this experience; lovelessness is powerlessness, object loss is self loss (Wurmser 1995: 97).

The foundations of chronic shame in the personality may be laid in the general tenor of relationships between infants and carers (Mollon 1993: 43). However, specific occasions and practices in childhood may also

help to engender shame (Mollon 1993: 43ff.). The ingression of the unexpected – for example, not seeing the mother's face when expected and
seeing a stranger's instead – can bring about a reaction of shame. If an
infant fails to express itself successfully and so experiences a sense of
inefficacy or inadequacy, shame may arise. (Perhaps this is the root of my
writer's block when it comes to public documents!) Shame, particularly
about the body, may be induced by the carer's reaction of rejection or
disgust during toilet training or when a child plays with its genitals.

None of these experiences need necessarily lead to a sense of prolonged chronic shame. However, if they are searing or persistent
enough, or if all of them are occasions for a rejecting response from
carers, it is likely that they will help to provide building blocks for a
shame-based personality (Kaufman 1993: 58ff.).

Kaufman argues that, from infancy onwards, all kinds of human
needs and experiences can become shame-bound, reinforcing a sense of
basic shame (see Kaufman 1993: 58ff.). The expression of emotions can
become bound with shame either generally or specifically if children are
shamed for expressing them. For example, if parents ostracise their children for expressing anger, rupturing the interpersonal bridge, that
emotion becomes shame-bound. This Kaufman labels the 'Affect Shame
Bind'. 'Drive Shame Binds' occur when needs such as those of food or
sexual intimacy are bound with shame by parents shaming children for
expressing or having such needs. 'Interpersonal Need Shame Binds' are
instituted by failures on the part of parents to meet children's needs for
touching, holding, relationship, identification, differentiation, nurture,
affirmation and power.

Infancy is a crucial time for developing relationships between
parents and children that are either basically self-enhancing or shame-
engendering. It is here that basic lessons about self and society, acceptance and rejection, are learned. These last through life. However,
chronic shame is also developed and amplified beyond infancy in childhood and broader family life.

Familial and micro-social factors
There is a kind of tragedy in the predisposition to chronic shame that
may often arise from the accidents of early relationships in infancy. Most
carers do not set out to induce the sense of unwantedness, defilement,
weakness, inferiority and low self-esteem that constitutes chronic shame
in their infants or young children. There are, however, some 'soul mur-
dering' carers who systematically, and sometimes even knowingly, use

shaming and shame-related behaviours as a main way of bringing up their children.

'Soul Murder' is 'a dramatic term for circumstances that eventuate in crime – the deliberate attempt to eradicate or compromise the identity of another person' (Shengold 1989: 2). If children are traumatised by too much stimulation or deprived by being under-stimulated, they will experience soul murder and erect personal defences along the lines of a kind of false self.

A consummated soul murder is a crime most often committed by psychotic or psychopathic parents who treat the child as an extension of themselves or as an object with which to satisfy their desires. Lesser effects ensue from intermittent parental cruelty and indifference. (Shengold 1989: 2–3)

Means used to accomplish soul murder include physical and sexual abuse, emotional and physical deprivation, and physical and mental torture. The most pernicious aspect of this is that because children are totally dependent upon their carers they need to maintain their support and approval in the face of the terror they face. Thus they continue to see their carers as 'good'. In their powerlessness, they identify with the powerful abuser, seeing themselves as bad while their still-needed parents remain good – the perverse reasoning being that the child's self must be bad if 'good' parents are so unkind.

This sado-masochistic mentality whereby individuals see themselves as powerless, inferior and needing to conform is perpetuated when such people find themselves in positions of power and authority, as when they themselves have children. Often, they become dissociated from their own feelings and bodies in the attempt to escape from overwhelming feelings of panic and pain.

Shengold recounts a case of soul murder taking place. A small boy was given some Christmas presents by his parents who then took them away again to give to poor children:

The cruelty of the giving and then taking away was denied; the boy identified with the aggressor, his conscience taking over his father's inhumanity. He, the boy, was unworthy . . . He idealized his tormentor and suppressed the torment . . . He was effectively deprived of his feelings, memory and identity and became his parents' creature: the Good Boy, a pseudo-identity marked by mechanical dutifulness and a cheerless, loveless existence . . . Underneath lurked murder and suicide; yet A functioned and he achieved. (Shengold 1989:12)

The processes of soul murder are hidden, unarticulated and denied in families where it takes place. Nonetheless, as Shengold shows by drawing on the lives and writings of Charles Dickens, Rudyard Kipling, George Orwell and others, it is not an uncommon experience. It is difficult to imagine that the victims of soul murder, whose selves and persons have been systematically violated and abused, do not often have a sense of chronic shame.

Closely related to Shengold's perceptions about soul murder are Alice Miller's notions of 'poisonous pedagogy'. Miller started professional life as a psychoanalyst but abandoned this perspective when she began to explore her own experience of being abused as a child. She conducted a study of the development of the narcissistically disturbed personality. This led her to believe that children were systematically taught to deny and disvalue themselves (Miller 1987a). Here she observed that many very 'successful', gifted adults who came to her as clients appeared on closer inspection to have a very fragile sense of self. Behind public success and the acclamation that accompanied it lay feelings of emptiness, self-alienation and meaninglessness:

These dark feelings will come to the fore as soon as the drug of grandiosity fails, as soon as they are not 'on top', not definitely the 'superstar', or whenever they suddenly get the feeling they failed to live up to some ideal image they think they must adhere to. Then they are plagued by anxiety or deep feelings of guilt and shame. (Miller 1987a: 20)

Miller discovered that these troubled, shamed people believed themselves to have had happy childhoods, though 'there is a complete absence of real emotional understanding or serious appreciation of their own childhood vicissitudes, and no conception of their own true needs – beyond the need for achievement. The internalization of the original drama has been so complete that the illusion of a good childhood can be maintained' (Miller 1987a: 20–1).

Miller initially accounted for these people who had over-compensated for the rejection of their childhood needs and feelings in terms of narcissistic disorder and false self engendered by parental neglect of various kinds. Later she became more aware of her own experience of childhood abuse. She identified the 'rules' of poisonous pedagogy whereby many children, not just the gifted, are prevented from gaining a proper sense of their own value, selfhood, self-expression and self-esteem (Miller 1987b: 59). Poisonous pedagogy achieves the repression and denial of the child by shame-producing methods such as duplicity, lying, manipulation, withdrawal of love, isolation, distrust, humiliation and disgrace, ridicule and coercion. The child is also invited to internalise a set of false beliefs. These include: a feeling of duty produces love; hatred can be dispensed with by forbidding it; parents deserve respect because they are parents while children do not deserve respect because they are children; obedience makes a child strong while a high degree of self-esteem or pride is harmful; low self-esteem makes a person altruistic while tenderness is indulgent and harmful; responding to children's needs is wrong and does not fit them for adult life; the way you behave is more important than the way you really are; the body is dirty and disgusting; strong feelings are damaging; parents are always right (compare Miller 1987b: 59–60).

Children who are recipients of poisonous pedagogy are beaten, humiliated, lied to, deceived and essentially betrayed. They are likely to develop a profound and habituated sense of self-contempt, defilement, unlovability and inferiority. However, this is hidden beneath passivity, compliance, outward grandiose achievement (which attracts parental approval) and depression (which is more acceptable to adults than outward emotional expression of aggressive feelings). The victims of poisonous pedagogy develop the foundations for a chronic sense of personality shame. The totality of themselves as autonomous selves is fundamentally violated, dishonoured and rejected – like excrement. Adopting the oppressor's point of view, they often view themselves as well as others with contempt (Miller 1987a: 85ff.).

What Shengold calls 'soul murder' and Miller calls 'poisonous pedagogy' is what many would simply call child abuse and neglect. Child abuse and neglect are common in Western society (Walker 1992; O'Hagan 1993). The implication of this is that the conditions that are necessary for chronic shame to develop in individuals are common (Andrews 1998b). In any situation where children find themselves and their needs regularly or systematically ignored, neglected, humiliated, dishonoured, betrayed, objectified, disregarded or overwhelmed there are the seeds of powerlessness, inferiority, weakness, defilement and unlovability that constitute chronic shame.

Some theorists postulate that it is common for whole families to be oriented around shame and the desire to deny and ignore its effects. These family systems support and exacerbate the mechanisms of chronic shame production.

Fossum and Mason, two family therapists, argue that there are shame-bound families whose functioning is fundamentally shaped by the need to deal with shame:

A shame-bound family is a group of people, all of whom feel alone together. To the individuals in the family, shame feels unique and lonely . . . The shame that feels so peculiar to the self paradoxically is a product not of the individual . . . but of the system. Within the family secrecy is rampant and relationships are thin and brittle (Fossum and Mason 1986: 19).

Shame-bound families are different from respectful families. In respectful families, violation of values leads to guilt not shame, people have a better sense of their own individuality, communication is more open, and individuals are accepted as they are, not as they 'should be'. The shame-bound family is oriented towards avoiding the kind of vulnerability that would produce shame (Fossum and Mason 1986: 19ff.). Paradoxically, the attempt to avoid and circumvent shame ensures that shame is unaddressed and perpetuated. Shame-bound families 'don't support a sense of personhood; rather, they undermine the faith that "I am a person" and inhibit the growth of a self-accepting outlook' (Fossum and Mason 1986: 87).

Some 'rules' or habits of interaction seem to operate in shame-bound families. These include the need to control, perfectionism, blaming others, denial of feelings, unreliability, incompleteness, lack of communication and the disqualification of others (Fossum and Mason 1986: 86–7). Fossum and Mason claim that these rules 'would serve as effective guidelines for developing a dehumanizing, shame-bound regime in any human system'. Bradshaw adds to this list of 'rules' the denial of the freedoms to think, perceive, feel, want, choose and imagine, in the interests of maintaining a false, conformist self (Bradshaw 1988: 32).

The child who is born into a shame-bound family has little chance of failing to develop a sense of chronic shame. Whatever else happens, she is unlikely to be loved and appreciated for what she is in and of herself. She is likely to be required to act out some role in the family that helps that system to avoid confronting its shame, such as being scapegoat (being a focus for all the bad feelings that are around), good child (avoiding unwanted negative attention by adopting a conformist personality), or star (Bradshaw 1988: 29). There will be no role models within the family whereby he or she can learn a sense of self-respect and more about his or her own boundaries. Shame is passed down the generations by the inevitable replication of family systems through unarticulated secrets, mysteries and myths over time (Fossum and Mason 1986: 44ff.).

Once individuals attain adolescence or adulthood, the foundations of chronic or personality shame may well have already been firmly laid in their lives. Nonetheless, it is still possible for events, institutions and phenomena to induce or exacerbate a sense of chronic shame.

Factors pertaining to later childhood, adolescence and adulthood
Once one looks wider than the parent–infant relationship and the family, there are many factors that may cause and foster shame.

In the first place, social institutions such as schools and churches can help to produce a sense of chronic shame. Many people have some of their most painful acute experiences of shame at school. A mixture of high expectations, perfectionism, competition and group normativity ensures that many children feel ashamed of themselves intellectually, physically, or emotionally by the time they finish full-time education. This institutionalised, passive shaming may be supplemented by active bullying, belittling, and humiliation from other students as well as teachers. Many adults brought up before 1970 in Britain will also have endured the traditional shaming practice of public corporal punishment (Gibson 1978; Greven 1992). This, too, has long-lasting effects on the personality.

Outside specific social institutions, events may occur in people's lives that leave them feeling chronically shamed and defiled. Various kinds of physical and mental assault – for example, rape – often induce a chronic sense of shame that affects all parts of a person's life and personality. Innocent victims of crimes frequently feel ashamed and afraid to disclose what has happened to them (Lamb 1996). Perhaps it is the sense of lack of agency and power to prevent the invasion of personal boundaries that precisely induces this tragic sense of long-lasting shame.

The same kind of shame also seems to be internalised as part of the personality by individuals and groups who endure lasting oppression. Thus concentration camp victims and others who live under regimes where they are constantly disrespected, violated and not allowed to exercise much autonomy (for example, total institutions like asylums and prisons) also seem to gain a sense of passivity, inferiority and non-personhood that is similar to that found in chronic shame (Goffman 1968a; Bettelheim 1986). As with small children, the state of shamed non-personhood seems in part a survival strategy that allows conformity and a certain amount of invisibility. Similarly, this strategy is an expensive one in terms of repression and the incapacity to recover a real sense of responsible, responsive, feeling self.

Social expectations can be just as efficient in producing people who are essentially chronically shamed. Kaufman points out that in North

American society people are supposed to compete for success, to be
independent and self-sufficient, and to be socially popular and conformist (Kaufman 1993: 29ff.). If they have internalised these ideals or norms,
they may well feel a sense of shame if they fail to conform to them. This
sense may become chronic if they continue to aspire towards them and
fail.

Such is the plight of some people who become unemployed and feel
themselves to be so rejected, such failures and so inferior that they fall
into the slough of chronic shame. Poverty is also often described as a
deeply shame-bound experience that does much to exacerbate a sense
of poor self-esteem, inferiority and powerlessness (Forrester 1997: 98).
Any experience of powerlessness, failure in one's vocation, rejection in
relationships, and even of growing older and so failing to meet social
ideals of youthfulness may eventually nurture a sense of inner chronic
shame.

It is not only in infancy that people's attitudes towards themselves are
shaped by social relationships. We are what others make us, and expect
us to be. It is easy to fall into chronic shame if one's own sense of intrinsic personal and social worth and belonging is not well-founded and
reinforced.

Conclusion

Any experiences that induce a sense of persistent inferiority, worthlessness, abandonment, weakness, abjection, unwantedness, violation,
defilement, stigmatisation, unlovability and social exclusion are likely to
be generative of chronic shame. Perhaps the lowest common denominator in all the factors outlined here is the experience of human individuals being dishonoured, disrespected or objectified. It is this kind of
experience, from infancy onwards, that engenders people whose personalities, characters and attitudes are fundamentally shaped by chronic
shame.

Wherever chronic shame or shame proneness is encountered, the
individuals concerned have probably endured much that is difficult and
destructive in their lives, whether or not they are conscious of this. Many
chronically shamed people can neither name their attitude to self and
others as one of shame, nor are they aware of the causes of this in their
lives. If one knows no other way of being, has repressed the horror and
pain that attaches to the origins of shame, such as experiences of
shaming and rejection in infancy, and has no hope that one's internal

state might ever be different, then shame exercises its influence in automatic and pervasive ways. The lessons of shame are often taught very early in life. If a human being is taught early on that she is worthless, unlovable and excluded, like the proverbial medieval leper, she is likely to have subsequent experiences that reinforce shame-bound responses (Kaufman 1993: 97ff.). The self-rejecting person who has internalised a sense of shame will find it difficult to trust and integrate herself within human relationships. However, it is these very relationships that are ultimately the only means to overcoming shame.

Chronic shame is a paradoxical trap. It is difficult for those without much sense of efficacy, self-esteem or inner personal worth and value to escape from it. Nonetheless, if humans remain learning creatures, capable of change and development throughout life, remedying or changing personality traits and characteristics must be a possibility. The prevention of the conditions that produce chronic shame may be the best way of mitigating this painful condition. However, there may be ways in which those who experience the disentitlement (Goldberg 1991: 86), abjection (Kristeva 1982), defilement and rejection that shame represents can be helped and healed. These are considered in chapter 6 below. In the next chapter, however, I look at the implications and effects of shame, particularly chronic shame, in individuals, relationships and groups.

CHAPTER FIVE

Some effects and implications of chronic shame

Chronic shame leaves a very distinctive mark upon individuals and groups in adult life. Those whose lives have been moulded by shame and reactions to it are unlikely to have a good, well-founded sense of worth and self-esteem (Mruk 1999). They may also be unclear about their own and others' personal boundaries. Individuals who are shame-prone, shame-vulnerable or chronically shamed in terms of their identity and personality often perceive themselves to be weak, inferior, ineffective, defiled, defective, unlovable, diminished, depleted failures. Frequently, they will base their reactions, assumptions, or 'scripts' about life upon these perceptions.

In examining the effects of shame here, 'effect' is used in a loose, soft way, not as the strict correlate of 'cause'. If shame is conceived as a socially constructed phenomenon in a variety of discourses rather than realistically as an 'objective' condition like a germ or a lesion, it is more appropriate to think of it as being bound up with certain other phenomena in an associational way. For the sake of clarity, however, it is helpful to describe these associated phenomena in terms of effects or reactions.

The first part of this chapter considers common defences and reactions to shame, recognising that individuals' shame reactions and scripts may vary considerably. In the second part, I shall briefly outline the kinds of pathology in which shame is widely thought to be involved. Finally, I shall consider the implications and effects of chronic shame upon ethics and morality. Shame, like guilt, is often associated with morality and moral standards (Taylor 1985). Here I suggest that chronic shame is likely to have a deleterious effect upon social relations and ethics.

Reactions to chronic shame

The experience of shame, with its sense of exposure, inferiority, confusion and weakness, is such a painful one that individuals learn to defend against it to avoid experiencing it: 'almost any affect feels better than shame' (Nathanson 1992: 312). The notion of 'defensive scripts' helps to describe the way in which people develop habitual ways of thinking and behaving so that they can avoid shame (Kaufman 1993: 113ff.). These scripts are 'performed' or activated when shame threatens.

Nathanson suggests that there are four basic defensive scripts against shame. These are construed as 'the compass of shame' (Nathanson 1992: 303ff.). At the north point of the compass, Nathanson places withdrawal, while at the south is avoidance. At the eastern point lies the defence of 'attack self'. This is opposed at the western point by 'attack other'.

Withdrawal. Withdrawal can be literal and physical and/or psychological and internal. When shame-arousing memories are aroused, or shame is anticipated, a person seeks to defend themselves from the experience by withdrawing to safety. This occurs on a spectrum that ranges from momentary gaze avoidance to prolonged isolation and depression. The duration and intensity of withdrawal varies according to individuals and circumstances. The withdrawal response is often accompanied by distress and fear which is interpreted as depression (Nathanson 1992: 324). People who habitually act out the withdrawal script of adaptation to shame may appear to be depressed rather than chronically shamed. They can be very difficult to help and relate to.

Attack self. Like withdrawal, attack self can be a useful and healthy response to shame if it is only briefly and mildly in evidence (Nathanson 1992: 326ff.). A little self-attacking can be seen as a sign of appropriate deference, conformity, self-effacement, or modesty. It can enhance social relationships and affinity. If this response becomes habitual, however, it is destructive. It is distressing to see someone ritually humiliating themselves or constantly putting themselves down. This can cut individuals off from wider social relations.

The chronic attack self response to shame can be related to fundamental masochism. Masochism is not to be understood as love of pain for its own sake, nor as a sexual perversion (Chancer 1992). It is a creative solution to the infantile problem of trying to relate to a needed and powerful other. It represents the attempt to retain attachment to hostile or persecutory objects (Montgomery and Greif 1989). Masochism, which may be understood as the acting out of the attack self script, is 'the need, usually compulsive, to seek suffering and pain in order to obtain love and respect, and to sabotage one's chances and success. . . .' (Wurmser 1995: xviii).

Traumatised and unloved children, faced with their own power-lessness and their need for parental care, identify with the powerful aggressive parent. Pain is the way in which the infant experiences nec-essary parental intimacy. The child introjects the critical, hostile, pun-ishing parent into its own psyche, creating a grandiose ego-ideal and a totalitarian super-ego against which it measures itself and finds itself wanting. It attempts intimacy, love and respect through internal identification with the hostile or indifferent parent, creating a paradox-ical inner world in which 'it is good to feel bad' (Nathanson 1992: 334). This way of trying to attain and retain love and respect alleviates the shame of powerlessness and insignificance. Furthermore, self-humilia-tion and masochism actually pre-empt external humiliation, depriving others of the power to humiliate.

This strategy for avoiding shame often repeats itself in self-defeating ways throughout life. The person constantly seeks to be in the position of suffering victim; you are never powerless, alone and abandoned so long as you are a victim, the unconscious script runs. Surveying research findings on masochism, Montgomery notes, 'For some individuals it appeared that a masochistic life, however costly, represented their best possible effort at creating and maintaining a separate and autonomous sense of self. Their suffering salvaged for them a modicum of satisfac-tion, security, and self-esteem . . .' (Montgomery 1989: xiii).

The means used to attack self include self-ridicule, putting oneself down all the time, and being perpetually angry with oneself. The over-whelming experience of total shame is exchanged for a more manage-able diet of constant self-aggression (Nathanson 1992: 329).

The attack self script is associated with feelings of disgust and dissmell about the self. The self cannot stand itself, rejecting itself as funda-mentally disgusting, smelly and undesirable. This chimes well with reli-gious notions of self-abasement, ontological badness, and sin.

I remember as a fervently religious child of around twelve years of age being urged to help beat up the class's scapegoat boy. I refused, where-upon the whole class decided to spit on me. At the time I felt satisfied with my behaviour and indifferent to this abuse from my peers. I was sus-tained by the example of Jesus and the early Christian martyrs. Subsequently, I have realised that I was also sustained by a fundamental sense of self-hatred and masochism, learned from hostile adults at home and school. This meant that when I was being beaten or abused I actu-ally felt quite happy (I was being attended to not ignored) and that I was getting what I deserved! The outward physical attacks of others were pale imitations of the sticks with which I had already decided to beat myself inwardly. In a way, I was powerful and in control of the aggression directed towards myself.

It is costly to relinquish the attack self script. The masochistic person has to give up the hostile inner object to which she has become attached. 'Giving up chronic masochism means giving up the shaming parent, which implies feeling abandonment . . .' (Nathanson 1992: 334). Many are unwilling to undertake this, fearing the sense of the shame-related feelings of abandonment, powerlessness, unlovability and emptiness that may result. That is why many people are lifelong self-attackers and victims. Furthermore, retaining the attack self script has the advantage that one cannot be surprised or shamed by unflattering or hostile external revelations about the self.

Avoidance. The avoidance script involves various ways of deceiving self and others as to the real nature of the defective self (Nathanson 1992: 336ff.). The roots of avoidance lie in the experience of children who exchange the reality of defective parents for a sense of the self as defective. If parents are unloving and unaccepting, the perverse logic runs, then the child feels that it must be defective or in the wrong. Thereafter, it tries in various ways to avoid or compensate for a sense of defect or shame.

A number of strategies can be used to compensate for and to hide the painfully shamed, defective self. One set of avoidance strategies is to seek perfection. The perfect self obviously cannot be defective. A similar self-aggrandising strategy is employed by those who display their achievements in order to deflect attention from a defective self. Some people try to borrow pride, power, worth and significance by identifying with the achievements and characteristics of an admired other, for example, God. All these strategies are very similar to the characteristics that self psychologists attribute to the grandiose, narcissistic self (Broucek 1991; Morrison 1989). Because they involve performance and denial, they are psychologically costly, demanding a lot of energy so that the self is presented in a well-defended, good light.

Other strategies of avoidance are equally demanding. Some people deceive themselves as to their own inner feelings about themselves. They may be tempted to lie to others about things in order to maintain face, or to develop a false, compliant, conformist self that is supposed to be acceptable to others: 'There are . . . people whose very identity is a lie, who live with a sense of self so false that they may be seen as imposters' (Nathanson 1992: 350). In my own case, I think I became a clergyman partly to avoid a sense of inner chaos and worthlessness and to become an acceptable 'somebody'.

Further strategies of avoidance may involve flight and the attempt to forget. Thus people may resort to addictive substances that help them avoid the pain of negative self-consciousness. The pursuit of pleasure can deaden pain and fill the void of emptiness and depletion. Sexual activity and conquest can also produce a sense of self-efficacy and power that makes the bad self feel at least temporarily 'good', acceptable and powerful.

Some shamed people deal with their sense of inner emptiness and depletion by seeking to care for others. They may attempt to gain a sense of worth while anaesthetising painful self-awareness by identifying with a higher cause and being altruistic: 'One thinks here of people who work very hard at worthy and meaningful tasks – large and small – losing themselves completely in a higher cause. Such people often cannot admit that their noble service increases their sense of self-worth considerably' (Jacoby 1994: 40).

People like this may objectify others and be covertly dependent upon them: 'Helpers are dependent on those they help, without whom they would fall into the bottomless abyss of their sense of worthlessness and meaninglessness. And this can turn their willingness to help into its opposite' (Jacoby 1994: 51; cf. Fossum and Mason 1986: 145). These are sobering words for people like me who adopted caring roles early in their lives to meet their own needs in the needs of others. Depleted selves fleeing their own insignificance often make poor, resentful carers who are uninterested in others' real needs.

Attack other. This group of shame avoidance scripts is perhaps the most important and obvious (Nathanson 1992: 360ff.). Some people avoid their own sense of painful shame by externalising their discomfort. They push uncomfortable feelings outwards on to others. Scripts in this category can have costly results as relationships may be sacrificed. Nonetheless, many people employ them much of the time. They attempt to reproduce a sense of shame in those whom they attack.

Words by which you might describe these attacks include . . . Bully, blackmail, slander, put-down, ridicule, disdain, sarcasm, scorn, derision, mockery, satire, burlesque, haughtiness, criticism, censure, superciliousness, scoffing, sneering, slurs, vituperation, caustic, asperity, venom, virulence, viciousness, spite, petulance, cynicism, scathing, harsh, malevolent, malignant, hateful, insulting, excoriating, abusive, corroding, surly, and contemptuous. (Nathanson 1992: 367)

Underlying the words and behaviours constituting attack other scripts are a range of feelings and responses. The first of these is rage, an affect that is often associated with shame. Shamed people often feel angry and wounded by the experiences of shame caused by the failure of intimate others in relationships (Lewis 1971: 41ff., 193). While this shame-rage reaction may be bypassed or unrecognised it may still be acted out (Lewis 1971: 198ff., 323ff.). Shame-rage spirals are perpetuated and amplified in relationships over time (Scheff 1997: 147ff.). Active or passive aggression may be aimed at disappointing or humiliating others who are treated as if they have hurt or damaged the shamed/enraged self.

The rage associated with shame can pervade families, groups, and even whole societies, poisoning relationships (Scheff 1997; Retzinger 1987, 1991, 1995, 1997). The origins of the First World War may lie in the humiliation of Germany by other nations. This led to the creation of a social shame-rage spiral that was eventually acted out in actual warfare against the humiliators (Scheff 1997: 115ff.).

A related response to the direct expression of rage is that of scapegoating (Douglas 1995). Here, the shamed person or group finds someone else who shares similar shame traits upon whom to project their own shame and humiliation (Morrison 1989: 104ff.): '[T]he subject projects his shame 'into' the object (the container), treats the object with contempt and haughty disdain, and thus distances himself from his own shame, while continuing to interact with it through the interpersonal relationship with the object' (Morrison 1989: 106). The scapegoat introjects shame and humiliation, accepting it as his or her own. In this sense, she 'borrows' it from others (Broucek 1991: 72–3). She is then likely to try and 'lend' it to someone else, perpetuating the externalisation of shame over generations and throughout social groups such as families.

Closely associated with this is self-contempt. Despising the self can become a habitual script. Often, this is coped with by projection so that others become the objects of contempt. Outwardly contemptuous people are often shamed people who desperately want to place these uncomfortable feelings outside themselves.

Blaming others is another way of avoiding confronting and owning shame in the unsatisfactory self (Gough 1990; Lamb 1996). If others 'outside' can be accused of internally felt shortcomings, then the shamed person can feel relieved of responsibility, blame and stain. This strategy also legitimates the open expression of anger or rage that shamed people often experience. I have noticed in myself a tendency to want to blame others when things go wrong for me and I feel powerless. Often the church and other 'powerful' corporate bodies have been the objects of my blame and contempt.

Envy forms the core of another externalising script that arises in response to an inner sense of shame (Morrison 1989: 107ff.; cf. Berke

1987, Lansky 1997). Shame is often fuelled by a degree of comparison with others or an ideal state. Envy is the product of seeing others as having more than the self and longing for what they have (Klein 1988b). The shamed person turns from their own inner sense of inadequacy towards the full, powerful object that is the focus of envy. Envy then distracts self and others from the reality of inner depletion even if it is also accompanied by powerful feelings of anger and rage against the envied object. Better and safer, perhaps, to be angry with some enviable, powerful external object than to have to face shame or anger against the depleted, fragile self.

Contempt, blame and envy can coalesce in externalising scripts for shamed people. They may then, for example, have very strong negative feelings towards authority figures such as parents or work managers who are perceived as deserving of rage and anger. This may protect the individual or group from having to face up to painful feelings of shame, powerlessness and inadequacy.

Nathanson's 'compass of shame' provides a structure for discussing possible habitual patterns or scripts that embody reactions to shame. Other writers offer supplementary insights into the effects of chronic shame from their own perspectives.

Like Nathanson, Kaufman uses the language of scripts to describe the defences deployed to predict and avoid shame. These he characterises as those of rage, contempt, striving for perfection to eliminate the inner sense of blemish, striving for power and control to avoid powerlessness and unexpected shame, transferring blame outside the self, internal withdrawal, humour (which diminishes and dissipates the sense of painful exposure) and straight denial of shame (Kaufman 1993: 100ff.). In addition to these defensive scripts he identifies three distinctive identity scripts that are shaped as a response to shame and which shape a negative self-identity. These are self-blame, comparison making, and self-contempt, all of which tend to turn the self against itself (Kaufman 1993: 104ff.).

Bradshaw points up the sense of inner alienation, isolation and self-rejection that shamed people experience and manifest (Bradshaw 1988: 13–14). He highlights the sense of what he designates 'spiritual bankruptcy'. This is characterised by a sense of dehumanisation, having no inner life and needing to receive external validation all the time, being hopeless, powerless and passive (Bradshaw 1988: 22–23). For Bradshaw, a sense of inner depletion and the projection of all goodness and power outside the self is a central feature of co-dependent shame reactions that

are essential to internalised shame (Bradshaw 1988: 14). God often occupies the slot of idealised, all-good other here. From my own experience,
I know that it is easy to see God as good and active while one regards
oneself as passive and bad, needing God's action to rescue one.

Broucek points up the way in which chronically shamed people objectify both themselves and others. They fail to respect the humanity and
autonomy that pertains to the human condition in the desire to avoid
shame or to displace it on to others (Broucek 1991: 59).

Fossum and Mason's 'rules' for the avoidance of shame in families and
social systems are in effect scripts for shame avoidance. They go on usefully to draw attention to the kinds of co-dependency in relationships
that are fostered by shame. In the first kind, the self is 'given away' to
accommodate the interests and needs of others and to gain acceptance
and affection. A second style of co-dependence occurs amongst people
who 'need to be needed' while being unwilling to accept love and help
themselves. This creates a sense of inferiority and powerlessness in
others. Finally, there are those who have no sense of personal and emotional barriers who simply fuse their own feelings and personalities with
others (Fossum and Mason 1986: 144–5). For my own part, I spent much
of my adolescence and early adulthood trying to lose myself in service
to others through church and other voluntary caring work. At the time,
I was continually regretful, indeed repentant, that my self refused to be
lost and I seemed incapable of selfless action and devotion.

Goldberg suggests that individuals respond to chronic shame with a
sense of negative and depleted personal identity. They experience themselves as passive. Furthermore, they lack a sense of humanity and legitimate entitlement:

People who are highly prone to pathological shame have grown up believing
that they are not fully human. They have been treated by significant people in
their lives as if their 'true' self and their judgment of what is right and wrong
were defective and flawed. This deprives them of feelings of personal power
and entitlement to proper treatment from others . . . (Goldberg 1991: 19–20)

This helps to illuminate my own experience. As a child, I felt that I
should have no possessions and if I did have any I should give them away
to 'others less fortunate than myself'. When I did not do this, I felt selfish,
greedy and uncomfortable. If I was having a deprived or difficult time,
however, I felt I was getting what I deserved.

Jacoby emphasises the relationship between the so-called 'inferiority
complex' and shame (Jacoby 1994: 61ff.). He suggests that a sense of
shame comes from comparing oneself unfavourably with fantasised

others. Reactions or strategies of avoidance here include idealising others (so they are so large that one cannot be compared with them), perfectionism, grandiosity, withdrawal, pre-emptive self-condemnation to avoid the pain of attack and unfavourable comparison, and excessive self-control and self-surveillance to avoid and hide inferiority. Some people compensate for their sense of inferiority by being brash and grandiose, while others project into others their own sense of critical gaze.

Both Block Lewis (1971) and Michael Lewis (1992) offer material on the place of anger and rage in shame, especially when it is bypassed or unrecognised. For Michael Lewis, shame is avoided by adopting unrealistic standards, blaming others, claiming success that is out of proportion to group norms or trying to control events and standards (Lewis 1992: 165f.). If shame is not avoided narcissistic and multiple personality disorders are the result (Lewis 1992: 163ff.).

Susan Miller highlights the importance of self-hatred in people who experience shame: 'Periodic shifts from painful shame into self-hate were observed in several research subjects. Others showed ongoing enthusiasm for aggressive self-attack which seemed to leave them minimally susceptible to shame. . . . The move into self-hate is a move from flailing about helplessly to vigorous, steady hammering' (Miller 1985: 136–7). Some people seem to shame themselves as a way of attending to self and calling for help and support from others: 'In Frank's case, it appears that the repeated act of shaming himself corresponds to an overall tendency to attend closely to the self as a parent may attend to a child. The shame also calls out to the listener as a plea for support' (Miller 1985: 150). She also notes the propensity of shamed people to adopt omnipotent, grandiose attitudes as defences (Miller 1985: 139).

In his exploration of the relationship between narcissism and shame, Kinston (1987) notes a number of methods for coping with shame that by now will be familiar. These include incognisance (that is, denial, refusing to recognise that one is shamed), dishonesty, hypocrisy, hiding, and withdrawal. He also highlights the significance of mortification, whereby attempts are made to subdue, control and perfect the self by the use of methods such as self-denial and self-control (Kinston 1987: 235). Mortification, literally the process of deadening or putting down the self, aims to kill the offending, inadequate self and thus to kill shame. It can literally result in the death of a person through suicide or other self-destructive behaviours (Morrison 1987: 287). Mortification has considerable resonance within the religious world which provides ready-made strategies and ideologies which support subduing the self.

A less morbid strategy for dealing with shame is that of humour and laughter (Retzinger 1987). Laughter is one of the main ways in which shame can be dissipated or released. It relieves the individual of self-consciousness and the sense of objectification. However, laughter can also be a defence against shame in instances where people direct laughter either at themselves or others as a way of controlling or deflecting shame. Comedians, for example, can hold themselves up to ridicule and, by attacking self, control the amount of shame that is directed at them, retaining a measure of efficacy and power over self and others (Nathanson 1992: 16ff., 378ff.). Nathanson asserts that '[s]hame can power all forms of humor' (Nathanson 1992: 19). Jokes are essentially attempts to play with the different scripts of attack self, attack other, and withdrawal (Nathanson 1992: 386). Because of their proximity to shame experience, they can easily be used to humiliate others and to increase the toxicity of shame. Nathanson points out that people who are prone to shame may also find it very difficult to accept praise with equanimity. This is because praise often uses the same exaggerated language often used in ridicule. The shame-prone person who is praised may be fearful that she is about to experience a personal, shaming attack. Ironic parents who tease their children may well foster this fear of praise that sets the individual up for a fall (Nathanson 1992: 378ff.).

This selective account of some of the ways in which people react to shame shows just how pervasive and varied are the implications of this condition. From laughter to despair, from hiding to grandiosity, shame has enormous implications for the ways in which people think about themselves and others. It also affects their behaviour. One must beware of associating all the woes and defensive reactions of humans everywhere with chronic shame. However, it seems that the influence of the condition of chronic or personality shame is considerable amongst Western personality types.

Ingrained shame reactions and defences also play an important part in how people relate to others and to organisations and society. Grandiose selves, for example, may ignore the real, separate existence of others and their needs. Those who are consistently protectively cynical or self-attacking may exercise a corrosive influence on those around them. Furthermore, it may be possible for institutions or even whole societies to become bound up with shame-associated defences such as projecting aggressiveness and blame outwards on to others. Perhaps widespread anti-Semitism, or the so-called 'culture of contempt' nurtured by the British government in the 1980s in which people were treated as if they did not matter, are examples of corporate shame-associated reactions. They produce a sense of shame, insignificance, low self-esteem and sometimes rage in those who have to experience them.

Part of the usefulness of identifying the reactive scripts and actions that people adopt is that it can help to make visible the existence of shame in everyday life. While few people may describe themselves overtly as chronically shamed, many exhibit behaviour and attitudes such as consistently blaming others, being passive, deprecating themselves and their achievements, or ridiculing self and others. All these may be seen as possible indicators of fundamental personal and social alienation. If they are recognised as such, it may be possible to begin to deal directly with the underlying condition of the shamed person.

Individuals react in very different ways to the experience of chronic shame. In differing situations and over time they may adapt and adopt a range of scripts and reactions. Broucek notes that while some people adopt an unequivocal idealised, grandiose self and others consistently devalue themselves and idealise others, there are people who swing between these positions. These 'turbulent selves' are labile and inconsistent, sometimes appearing as selfish bullies, sometimes as craven, passive weaklings (Broucek 1991: 59ff.).

From my own experience, I can testify to resorting to different strategies for dealing with shame in different contexts. Sometimes it has seemed expedient to blame and attack others to avoid the feeling of shame and gain a sense of power. The church and other parental organisations and figures are often good targets for such blaming. At other times, it has seemed more appropriate to attack or control my self, to aspire to perfection or to ridicule myself to alleviate a sense of personal inadequacy and badness.

At this point, I want to look briefly at some of the more pathogenic effects and associations with chronic shame.

Shame, pathology and health

The associational links between shame and many kinds of individual and social pathology are as real, non-specific and elusive as those between shame, character and behaviour. Links between shame and a wide variety of mental and other pathologies are widely held to be important. Unfortunately, there is often little understanding of the precise connections between them.

Shame, being a condition of low self-esteem and sometimes of active self-attack and self-hatred, has been strongly implicated in depression by many researchers (Lewis 1987c). Indeed, some have argued that shame forms 'the cornerstone in depressed patients of all types' (Lewis 1987c: 39). The sole supremacy of shame and low self-esteem as the main affective components and important causal factors has not always been acknowledged by other researchers. However, there is little disagreement within the literature on shame, whether clinically or experimentally based, that shame and depression are often integrally and intrinsically linked.

Some researchers argue that guilt has a more important role than is sometimes allowed by the protagonists of shame (Harder 1995). However, others believe that guilt, properly understood and distinguished from shame, has little to do with depression. This develops from failure to handle the anger that emerges from shame constructively (Price Tangney, Burggraf and Wagner 1995). It is not appropriate here to try and resolve this debate, or the exact ways in which shame may contribute to, or be the product of, depression.

Block Lewis and her colleagues arraign shame as a significant factor within schizophrenia, female obesity and dysfunctional marital family relationships, noting that women seem to be more prone both to shame and to depression than men (Lewis 1987a). This list of shame-related pathologies has been extended by Harder to include: 'alcoholism and its sequelae, abuse of other substances, antisocial personality, borderline personality, depression, eating disorders, pathological narcissism, pychoanalytic neuroses (hysteria and obsessive compulsiveness, paranoia), post-traumatic stress disorders, sexual dysfunctions and paraphilias, excessive shyness, suicide, and violence' (Harder 1995: 369; cf. Tantam 1998: 169f.).

Kaufman identifies eight general classes of syndromes that are shame-bound, that is organised around shame, though in conjunction with other affects (Kaufman 1993: 113ff.).

The first class is that of compulsive syndromes in which repetitive re-enactment has become magnified. These syndromes include physical and sexual abuse. Secondly, Kaufman identifies addictive disorders such as alcoholism, gambling and drug-taking. These represent attempts at escape from the painful experience of shame. Eating disorders such as anorexia and bulimia form a third class of shame-related pathology. Here, shame about food deflects attention from a more fundamental shame about the self. In various phobic syndromes such as agoraphobia, Kaufman suggests that fear provides a mask for the experience of shame, while in sexual dysfunction syndromes such as impotence, the acute self-consciousness that is part of the experience of shame may prevent satisfactory sexual performance. Kaufman believes that shame can be causal in splitting syndromes such as borderline, narcissistic and multiple personality disorders. Here boundaries between self and other and relations with the sense of self are problematic. Shame is also active in sociopathic and psychopathic syndromes where people have failed to identify with others and with society. Finally, Kaufman points out that shame is often an important ingredient in dysfunctional family systems.

Before leaving the broad arena of shame and social and mental health, however, I do want to consider further the factors that may come into play to turn shame into addiction, not least because religious rituals and practices can become addictive and a refuge for shame-bound persons (Bradshaw 1988: 104; Linn, Fabricant Linn and Linn 1995).

For Bradshaw, a former priest and a former alcoholic, compulsive addictive behaviours of all kinds are a main effect of shame. They arise because people seek to alter their moods and to escape from the feeling of shame, grief and pain. Bradshaw identifies a number of different addictions. First, there are ingestive addictions focussed upon substances such as food, alcohol and drugs. Secondly, there are feeling addictions such as rage, sadness, joy, guilt, or even shame itself. Thereafter, he identifies thought addictions, activity addictions, addictions to one's own will, and re-enactment addictions whereby people continue to act out past experiences of victimhood, criminality or phobic attacks (Bradshaw 1988: 95ff.).

It is helpful in trying to understand the nature of the relationship of shame to addictions to grasp the nature of the shame-bound cycle of control and release. The argument runs thus. To hide from shame and a sense of inner chaos, people often pursue a strategy of self-control. This can lead to compulsive or addictive behaviours such as dieting, over-work, cleaning, religiosity, miserliness, and helping others, as well as to personality traits such as being overly critical, self-righteous, rigid, blaming, pleasing and placating (Fossum and Mason 1986: 107). The problem is that the more vigorously one controls, the more compensating release becomes necessary.

In the release phase of the cycle, people act out abusively and self-destructively with substances such as alcohol and drugs, as well as sex, money and food. Physical, sexual, and verbal abuse may also form part of the release phase, as well as the manifestation of personal traits such as lack of self-control, self-centredness, unpredictability and self-indulgence. However, the more abandoned the person is in the release phase, the more shame will be felt. The need for ever-stricter control will therefore assert itself, thus starting the cycle all over again (Fossum and Mason 1986: 106).

The cycle of shame-bound control and release goes a long way to explaining the paradoxical-seeming behaviour of some people who seem to veer unhappily between being addicted to control and addicted to abuse. Some of these may use religiously provided rules and practices to try and attain personal control, only to lapse into occasional but severe abandonment, such as binge drinking or sexual or physical abuse.

The splitting that occurs in the control-release cycle is complemented by Bradshaw's notion of the 'Compulsive/Addictive Cycle Fuelled by and Regenerating Shame' (Bradshaw 1988: 16). Bradshaw suggests that shame is the core and fuel of all addiction. His cycle starts with the belief that 'I am a flawed and defective human being. I am a mistake.' This leads to distorted thinking: 'No one could love me as I am. I need something outside to be whole and okay.' This leads people to seek mood alteration using things from outside the self. Thus people fall into a cycle of ritual acting out, such as binge eating or drinking. This increases their sense of shame as well as bringing about other life-damaging consequences. So, for example, heavy drinkers may lose their jobs or their life partners. This closes the circle, reinforcing the false belief that 'I am a flawed and defective human being. I am a mistake.'

The control-release cycle identified by Fossum and Mason and the compulsive-addictive cycle described by Bradshaw are two ways of understanding how a sense of chronic shame based on a negative sense of self can impact severely on physical and mental health and relationships, particularly with relation to addictive behaviours. However, it is not just in the realm of physical and mental health that shame has a serious impact. It also has important implications for ethics and morality.

Shame, ethics and morals

Shame is often associated with morality. It clearly has a role in making clear and upholding certain values and standards. However, I will argue here that often its effects are ambiguous or baleful, particularly in the case of people who suffer from chronic shame. In a way, such people have not yet really joined the moral community. They are trapped in themselves, cut off and excluded from society and relationships. They may have a strong sense of other people's opinions and may be super-sensitive about the effect of other people's attitudes and actions upon themselves. However, they are not other-regarding and moral in the sense of being able to take properly defined and limited responsibility for their own actions and then being able to execute them. Chronically shamed people are pre-social and pre-moral. Only when they have joined society and been recognised as efficacious persons by self and others will they be in a position to take real responsibility and to experience and incur the appropriate guilt that goes with taking such responsibility. Until that time, while they may often behave in socially acceptable and conformist ways, they will not really be capable of exercising reliable moral judgment and responsibility.

This rather harsh-sounding judgment needs to be explored and unpacked. First, however, I would like to exemplify what I am talking about from my own experience. Some years ago, I was a curate in an affluent Church of England parish. At the same time, I was very committed, at least in theory, to social justice and equality. For a long time I had been a keen socialist and I was very concerned about the plight of poor people and the inequalities which blighted their lives. I had always seen things from the victim's point of view, feeling very angry on their behalf against people like me who I perceived to be over-privileged and too well endowed with resources and opportunities. As time went on, I read more and more Latin American liberation theology. This suggests that Christian people should make a preferential option for the poor and should help to change the structures of exploitation that kept poor people poor and rich people like me in considerable comfort (Pattison 1997a). I concluded that if I were to play my part in helping the oppressed to liberate themselves I should join an extreme Marxist political party. But I did not do this. The reason was that I lacked the courage of my moral convictions. I could not face the thought of people in my wealthy parish discovering that I had joined a group of left-wing activists and perhaps despising me. Nor could I face the thought of the contempt that might come at me from party workers because of my job and professional role. The 'poor' were thus (fortunately?) deprived of my efforts and I have felt ashamed of my lack of moral fibre ever since.

Shame impinges on this narrative about possible moral action in several ways. In the first place, it may be that it was my own unexplored experience of shame and victimisation that made me identify with the poor and oppressed in the first place (Pattison 1998). Perhaps it was the experience of envy and rage that sometimes accompanies shame that made me keen to 'put down the mighty from their seats' so that the humble and meek might obtain justice. In this sense I was objectifying oppressed people and making them objects of my own needs and imagination, using them as a vehicle for my own envious and angry feelings about people who have more than others.

It was also my experience of shame that stopped me from acting in ways that might have really helped oppressed people. I lacked a sense of my own power and efficacy, despite believing myself to be one of the powerful, privileged members of society. More than this, my sense of shame meant that I badly wanted to be approved of by other people, to gain affirmation from outside myself, and, if I am honest, not to ruin my chances of gratifying my grandiose needs for external recognition and valuation in the church. Having shied away from what I felt to be a morally right way of acting, I then felt further ashamed because I had demonstrated to myself failure in living up to my ideals and fulfilling my own shame-related desire to be perfect and always to do the right thing. Thus, at all points, and in several different ways, shame responses obscured what I needed to do, prevented me from doing it and left me with a sense of enhanced personal badness and further shame.

In the event, perhaps my failure to act on my moral convictions was not a bad thing – oppressed people had not asked me to work with them. But the point is that it was not the real interests of other people that weighed with me. Rather, my judgment and actions were clouded by shame. It is this kind of experience that has led me to believe that shame has far more serious and pervasive moral implications than is often recognised in a context where most people think of guilt as the main element that is involved.

Shame drastically limits or curtails the scope of concern, involvement and action with regard to other people. Both shame and guilt involve negative judgments and assessments of the self. These include the judgment that the self is in some way defective or 'bad'. However, the psychological implications and predispositions to action implied in each state are rather different.

Some psychological researchers argue that while guilt is a moral emotion insofar as it tends to be externally oriented, other-directed, empathic, and oriented to reparative action, shame has many of the opposite features. It focusses attention acutely upon the global self and its own self-consciousness, not upon particular acts or possible courses of action. It blocks out awareness of other people and their feelings and needs, except insofar as these impinge upon the self. It inhibits empathy

because the self is too engaged in its own internal processes and particularly its own sense of feeling bad. Finally, and as a consequence, shame
actually induces a sense of powerlessness and paralysis. Thus any action
that might be taken to remedy offence, to effect reparation, or to improve
the situation of others, is not taken.

This implies that, far from being a useful moral emotion and a tool
for moral education, shame can actually be morally counter-productive.
Its effect is to produce people who are, paradoxically, a-moral, self-
preoccupied and incapable of acting as agents. They may be unable to
take responsibility for acting, to recognise that they have some control
over things, or to empathise with others. Thus they might fail to honour
personal and moral commitments.

Lindsay-Hartz et al. write:

Comparing shame with guilt, we can see that the opportunity for empathy is
much reduced during experiences of shame. While ashamed, one focuses on
the painful experience of being a negative self. Beyond a conviction that others
view one negatively, one is not likely to be thinking much about any feelings that
others may be experiencing. Consequently, we would predict that shame-prone
people may evidence less empathy than guilt-prone people, and that people who
evidence greater ability to empathize may experience more guilt than shame.
. . . What is clear is that guilt and empathy are likely to be found together, and
that shame, low empathy, and high self-preoccupation are likely to be found
together. (Lindsay-Hartz et al. 1995: 296)

This line of thought is supported by the empirical work of Price
Tangney and colleagues:

[B]oth shame and guilt are negative affective experiences that involve self-rele-
vant negative evaluations . . . In shame, the focus of the negative evaluation is
on the entire self. Following some transgresssion or failure, the entire self is painfully scrutinized and found lacking. With this painful self-scrutiny come a sense
of shrinking, a feeling of being small, and a sense of worthlessness and powerlessness. Shame also involves the imagery of being exposed before a real or
imagined disapproving audience . . . the shame experience is often accompanied by a desire to hide – to sink into the floor and disappear.

They continue,

Guilt . . . is a less global and devastating emotion than shame. Guilt arises from
a negative evaluation of a specific behavior, somewhat apart from the global
self; this specific behavior is found to be immoral, lacking, or otherwise defective. The global self, however, remains intact. With this focus on behavior
(rather than the self) comes a sense of tension, remorse, and regret . . . But
because a behavior – not the self – is the object of approbation, the self remains
mobilized and ready to take reparative action to the extent that circumstances
allow. (Price Tangney, Burggraf and Wagner 1995: 344)

All of which may help to explain why people whose characters are shaped by shame reactions and who feel bad about themselves, often describing this as feeling 'guilty', appear so little able to do anything to show real concern for others. It may also account for their inability to act to help others and why they act in such a powerless and self-protective manner when it comes to doing the 'right thing'. In their subjection to shame, they are trapped in a pre-moral, a-moral, a-social solipsistic state of paralysis that does not allow them to act altruistically.

Indeed, far from being able to act morally and altruistically, shame-bound or chronically shamed people may act in very anti-social and immoral ways, not merely failing to do good, but doing harm to self and others. Many of the effects of shame noted above exemplify attitudes or behaviours that have often traditionally been associated with the seven deadly sins or vices of anger, envy, greed, lust, pride, gluttony and sloth (Schimmel 1997).

Anger and rage, which is uncontrolled anger, have frequently been seen as reactions that are often intrinsic to shame. These aggressive reactions associated with scripts of attacking the other, while they can have constructive aspects to them, are often deeply corrosive of the respectful, trusting relationships between people and in society as a whole. Envy and greed may be products of a perception of the self as inferior, depleted, inadequate and lacking in relationship to others who appear to have more (Berke 1987; Wurmser 1997a). Addictions of various kinds, including eating disorders and sexual addiction, are often a product of shame whereby people seek to find control or comfort outside themselves. In some ways, these correspond to the vices of lust and gluttony in which desires are uncontrolled or immoderately gratified. Passivity and a sense of hopeless, melancholy despair often accompanies shame. These things correspond to sloth and inactivity in terms of traditional vices (cf. Bringle 1990). Finally, contempt towards self and others, objectification, grandiosity, haughtiness, arrogance, disdain, putting others down, and self-preoccupation and indifference to others, all common reactions to shame, correspond to the greatest of the sins, that of pride.

The language of sin and vice may seem anachronistic here. However, I am trying to suggest that shame may be seen to induce, at least in part, many of the attitudes and behaviours in society that are commonly recognised as harmful and individually and socially disruptive.

Some shamed people lack a sense of personal worth and value. This means that they may act compliantly and in such a way as to attract approval from outside themselves rather than being concerned to do the right thing, or what is best for others. The need to be acceptable may also cause shamed people to lie or to be dishonest. The cumulative effect of the need for approval and the need to avoid shame may mean that they function as unreliable hypocrites who act the part of doing right but cannot be relied on to act as they say they will. This unwillingness may be reinforced by a sense of lack of agency and a pervasive passivity that leads to feeble or non-existent moral performances.

A general problem for shame-prone people is that they may radically over- or underestimate their place in relationships and events. Being self-preoccupied and isolated, they cannot see themselves in perspective. Because an attribution of shame involves the whole self, a small amount of displeasure from others may convince a shamed person that they are entirely in the wrong and wholly bad. A person may be as mortified over a small or trivial offence as they are over a major offence. This distorts their moral judgment and sense of responsibility and agency. It may render them unable to distinguish the real nature and significance of offences and wrongdoings, let alone to rectify or act appropriately in relation to them. Some people become so preoccupied with their own sense of badness and the fear of global self-disapproval caused by their minor peccadillos that they become incapable of discerning the trivial from the vital. Thus shame may help major evils to prosper while people's attention is fixed upon themselves and their internal ontological badness.

The need to appear perfect and to control the world may lead to a certain moral rigidity and legalism on the part of chronically shamed people. They may also derive an unattractive sense of moral superiority and worth from strict adherence to a set of rules (Bradshaw 1988: 89f.). Such people may be very unsympathetic to the foibles and exigencies of others because they need to reinforce their own sense of goodness and value. Shamed people who attack others may be overtly humiliating and destructive. Those who attack themselves may be a drain on the resources of the society and groups to which they belong insofar as they may require health and other kinds of care. Like those who attack themselves, shamed people who withdraw from social contact may become a liability to others. They may also fail to make their proper contribution to the community.

There is much scope for shamed people with a variety of scripts to become involved in overtly destructive sado-masochistic relationships in which power and manipulation play a central role (Chancer 1992; Montgomery and Greif 1989). While these relationships may meet needs for attachment and significance, there are considerable dangers of objectification and destructive behaviours coming into play.

Some shamed people may resort to heroic helping relationships to establish their own significance and worth and to meet their own needs in others (Jacoby 1994). Here again, objectification and failing to recognise and respect the autonomy and needs of others are real dangers. One can only speculate about how much physical abuse in helping relationships, caring and parental relationships is affected by the distortions of chronic shame.

The condition of shame, particularly chronic or habitual shame, has an important effect on moral life and relationships. While guilt may have a very constructive role in creating and maintaining social relationships and moral responsibilities, shame has a much more dubious effect. Insofar as shame is a condition of exclusion, isolation and self-preoccupation, it is likely to exercise a negative rather than a positive effect, diminishing possibilities for effective responsibility and action.

This should be borne firmly in mind in the context of cries for more shame and shaming in society. In reality, what is needed is probably a greater sense of guilt with its associated notions of responsibility and efficacy. Shame should be seen as a more primitive, a-social condition than guilt. It needs to be superseded by guilt if people are to live together in a way that enhances mutual life and well-being. What is required for society to be more moral, in the sense of being more respectful and other-regarding, is more guilt and less shame. It is entirely unhelpful that these concepts and conditions are so confused that the significance of both is misunderstood and so relatively ignored. It is also unfortunate that the role of shame in morality has been neglected. This has impeded the development of understanding useful social guilt, while the labelling of shame as guilt has impeded the recognition of shame.

The nature of moral reality and responsibility is of great interest within the religious sphere. Later on, I shall consider ways in which, perhaps, self-preoccupying chronic shame might be minimised so that other-regarding guilt might have a more prominent place. The starting point here must be bringing individuals into the moral and social community from a position of solipsistic isolation and defilement – this in the belief that chronic shame is generally socially and morally destructive in its effects, as well as being personally painful and limiting.

Conclusion

In this chapter, I have tried to show that the condition understood as chronic shame in Western society appears to be associated with a significant number of different types of negative reactions and phenomena. It appears to be embroiled with many unpleasant, unhelpful conditions of the self, causing people to adopt costly and destructive strategies or scripts to avoid personal pain. Shame also appears to be centrally involved in a wide variety of pathological conditions, having a considerable, if unmeasurable, effect upon the general mental and physical health of many members of the population. In moral and ethical life, shame is significantly implicated in attitudes and behaviours that may be very unconstructive and socially and personally subversive.

Overall, the reactions and behaviours associated with chronic shame exercise extensive, profound, and baleful effects on persons and communities. These are costly in terms of personal well-being and relationships, societal functioning, and, probably, in terms of health and social care provision. It is very difficult to attribute any positive, useful role to chronic shame. It seems to maintain people in a state of social isolation and diminished social and personal existence.

In the chapter after next I shall look at some of the ways in which individual and group shame might be healed so that integration occurs. First, however, it is important to give some more detailed attention to corporate and social aspects of shame.

CHAPTER SIX

Aspects of the socio-historical significance of shame

[M]en do not usually define the troubles they endure in terms of historical change and institutional contradiction. The well-being they enjoy, they do not usually impute to the big ups and downs of the societies in which they live . . . The sociological imagination enables its possessor to understand the larger historical scene in terms of its meaning for the inner life and the external career of a variety of individuals . . . The sociological imagination enables us to grasp history and biography and the relations between the two in society.

(Wright Mills 1970: 9–12)

Shame may well be the most socially significant of all the phenomena that are commonly conceived as emotions. It is a socio-cultural phenomenon that reflects and refracts wider social trends and relationships. It helps to define social boundaries, norms and behaviours and signals the state of social bonds (Scheff 1997), as well as providing a powerful tool of social conformity and control. Thus shame is an indispensable and necessary part of the socio-emotional architecture of any social order. This does not prevent it from being a painful, difficult and alienating experience for some individuals and groups in society. Nor does it prevent the exploitation of shame for purposes of power and control by other individuals and groups.

There is a close reciprocal relationship between various kinds of social structure and organisation and different kinds of individual personality structure and disorder (Western 1984). Personalities and intimate relationships are shaped by, as well as shaping, macro-social structures (Wright Mills 1970; Scheff 1990). The incidence and experience of shame is, therefore, intimately linked to social and political structures and variables that change over time. However, it is not always easy to see precisely how particular forms of shame and shame reaction emerge and are products of specific social and institutional arrangements and evolutions. This, in turn, makes it difficult to suggest ways in which those structures might be changed, much less how to do this.

In this chapter, I want to focus on some of the social and historical aspects of shame and approaches to them. This will consolidate these aspects as an important horizon within which shame must be understood. It will also broaden discourse about this topic well beyond the customary contemporary boundaries of the person and the individual psyche. I also want to sketch the process whereby shame has gradually evolved from being understood primarily as a social condition extrinsic to the personality in pre-modern societies to being a psychological condition located in the disourse about the self in modern industrialised societies. Finally, I want critically to consider some of the ways in which shame has been, and continues to be, a means of social control.

In the first part of the chapter, I shall attempt a very broad historical overview of the social evolution of shame in Western society. The second part of the chapter looks at the rise and use of shame and its relationship with power and authority within the context of industrial society. The third section considers the social place and function of shame in relation to the 'reflexive self' of contemporary society. Finally, I shall consider the case for the deliberate, overt use of shame as a tool of social control at the present time.

There is no single authoritative source for considering the socio-historical aspects of shame in Western society, nor has there been an attempt hitherto to create a coherent sociology of shame. In the historical and sociological works I have consulted, approaches to understandings of shame, together with its definition, functions and implications, are various. Thus I make no claim to comprehensiveness or coherence here.

Historical aspects of the evolution of shame in Western society

Shame has been part of the ordering of Western societies since the Greeks and Hebrews, and perhaps beyond (Dodds 1951; Williams 1993). It has been suggested that 'shame-based' cultures, that is, cultures based on conformity to unwritten rules, the maintenance of honour and appearance, and the avoidance of pollution, preceded the evolution of 'guilt-based' cultures, those based upon juridical rules and procedures, internalised conscience and the notion of harmful offence with correlative punishment (Dodds 1951: 28ff.; Benedict 1954: 222ff.). However, the absolute division that is made between the two types of culture and the idea that one necessarily succeeds and supplants the other has been questioned (Parker 1983; Cairns 1993). Furthermore, the assumption that shame has become less important as a tool of social control as Western civilisation has developed now seems problematic (Elias 1994; Giddens 1991). Much of the confusion surrounding historical under-standings of the social nature, role and function of shame stems from differential usage of concepts that continues to confuse.

The nearest thing to a coherent socio-historical account of shame covering a long period of time is sociologist Norbert Elias' *The Civilizing Process* (Elias 1994), first published in 1939. This can be supplemented in a fragmentary way from material in a number of sources such as Schneider (1987a), Wurmser (1995) and Nathanson (1992). *The Civilizing Process* comprises two connected works, *A History of Manners* and *State Formation and Civilization*. Elias was extensively influenced by Freud's notions of the socio-genesis of personality and emotions (Elias 1994: 249). He was not at all influenced by the concepts of shame, shame culture, and guilt culture popularised by Benedict in *The Chrysanthemum and the Sword*, a book which was first published in 1946 (Benedict 1954). Benedict, in turn, reveals no knowledge of Elias' theorising in her work.

Elias never defines shame precisely in his historical study. This takes in the rise of modern Western society from around the year 1000 CE to around the turn of the twentieth century. In it, Elias traces the changing nature of the state and human relationships and the concomitant implications for human manners, behaviour, emotions and relationships generally. Broadly speaking, he confirms Freud's hypothesis that emo-tions and desires have to be repressed and contained within the individ-ual the more complex, intricate and interdependent social relationships become.

In feudal societies, Elias suggests, individuals were inclined to act out their emotions of love and hatred in physical acts such as spontaneous violence and killing. However, the civilising process, with its growth of manners and customs, required that physical action and force should be relinquished. The general impulse was to a highly co-ordinated, inter-dependent social order that was not controlled by external factors such as overt violence, but by internal, personal control. Individuals came to monitor and control their own emotions in a society where only the state was legitimately allowed to administer physical force. Even the state eventually moved from physical force and threats of rather basic kinds towards more psychological controls (Foucault 1979; Rose 1989).

The civilising process was accompanied by the rise and development of the individual who came to be seen as having consciousness, human rights, and so on. The locus of social control increasingly moved from external coercion to internal discipline, control or repression. It is here that Elias situates shame as the means used to effect the internalisation of standards of taste and disgust. So, for example, the use of the fork rather than the hands for eating and the growing revulsion and shame at the latter mode symbolises a whole new way of behaving in society and controlling the self: 'The fork is nothing other than the embodiment of a specific standard of emotions and a specific level of revulsion. Behind the change in eating techniques between the Middle Ages and modern times appears . . . a change in the structure of drives and emotions (Elias 1994: 103).'

Thresholds of shame have been 'raised' as society has evolved. Shame-fear and anxiety has been one of the main ways in which increasingly self-conscious and self-aware individuals have learned to internalise the norms of behaviour and manners that were expected of them (Elias 1994: 104). Experiences of shame and embarrassment in childhood have thus been used to teach people to act 'spontaneously' yet automatically in a civilised, conformist manner (Elias 1994: 105):

The prohibitions supported by social sanctions are reproduced in the individual as self-controls. The pressure to restrain his impulses and the sociogenetic shame surrounding them – these are turned so completely into habits that we cannot resist them even when alone, in the intimate sphere . . . the social code of conduct so imprints itself in one form or another on the human being that it becomes a constituent element of his individual self. And this element, the superego, . . . necessarily changes constantly with the social code of behavior and the structure of society. (Elias 1994: 156)

Elias points out that there is a 'continuous correspondence between the social structure and the structure of personality' (Elias 1994: 156). Furthermore, 'the sociohistorical process of centuries . . . is reenacted in abbreviated form in the life of the individual human being' (Elias 1994: 105).

The civilising process becomes located more within the sphere of the private, the personality and individual self-control in developing societies. At the same time, chains of dependence become closer and longer. People come to experience more inner fears and anxieties rather than outside threats. They observe themselves and others more closely and there is greater sensitivity to shades and nuances of conduct. Inner conflict and self-judgment replace external danger, producing a pronounced sense of personal and affective shame. This replaces shame that is related to the external governance of society, formal social position or recognition, and the maintenance of external conventions of respect and honour:

[I]nner fears grow in proportion to the decrease of outer ones – the fears of one sector of the personality for another . . . Now a major part of the tensions which were earlier discharged directly in the combat between man and man, must be resolved as an inner tension in the struggle of the individual with himself . . . In a sense, the danger zone now passes through the self of every individual . . . The direct fear inspired in men by men has diminished, and the inner fear mediated through the eye and through the super-ego is rising proportionately. (Elias 1994: 497)

In this context, shame-fear and anxiety become radically individual, inward, private experiences. They are no longer accompanied by external public opprobrium and disgrace as they were in more traditional, less individuated societies (Elias 1994: 493). External restraints and events are converted into self-restraints by the development and exploitation of a sense of personal shame in highly individuated persons. These people have a strongly developed sense of inner feelings, self-consciousness, and the need for self-control: 'Both rationalization and the advance of the shame and repugnance thresholds are expressions of a reduction in the direct physical fear of other beings, and of a consolidation of the automatic inner anxieties, the compulsions which the individual now exerts on himself' (Elias 1994: 493).

Elias convincingly shows that the objects of shame, the experience of shame, and the uses to which shame is put, evolve over time as personalities are shaped by social arrangements. One vital continuity remains. Shame, whether internally or externally experienced, is one of the supreme means of ensuring social order, social control and individual conformity.

Elias' research is dated. It perhaps leans too heavily on Freudian notions of self and society. It fails adequately to define and discuss the precise nature of shame (which Elias seems to understand, after Freud, as a kind of anxiety). However, it offers considerable insight into the historical evolution and function of shame and discourse about shame. It shows that while a shame response may be deemed innate to humanity in all kinds of societies, modern notions of individualised shame anxiety that creates a split or battle within the self-conscious self have only arisen within a particular social order. Psychologically experienced and understood shame anxiety exists in a highly individuated psyche in a complex, highly interdependent, differentiated society where social control is mostly internalised within the self.

This important, credible insight helps to explain how so-called 'shame cultures' seem to have little place for shame as individual internal discomfort, concentrating instead on notions of external visibility and offence against the honour attaching to a particular social position (Malina 1996).

Elias' account of the gradual psychologisation, individualisation, and privatisation of shame is tangentially supported by the sociological insights into the history of privacy and personality of some other authors. Berger, Berger and Kellner, for example, argue that Western society has been transformed from one in which honour attaching to external role and social position was central to one in which dignity resides in the person independent of institutional roles. Thus, 'in a world of honour the individual *is* the social symbols emblazoned on his escutcheon. The true self of the knight is revealed as he rides out to do battle in the full regalia of his role; by comparison, the naked man in bed with a woman represents a lesser ideal of the self (Berger et al. 1973: 84). Modern social organisation has evolved from being based on hierarchy and honour to being based on individualism and dignity (Gergen 1991, 1994; Lukes 1973; Morris 1973; Taylor 1989). Thus, the understanding of self, identity, and personal value is now different:

In a world of honour, the individual discovers his true identity in his roles, and to turn away from the roles is to turn away from himself . . . In a world of dignity, the individual can only discover his true identity by emancipating himself from his socially imposed roles – the latter are only masks, entangling him in illusion, 'alienation' and 'bad faith' (Berger et al. 1973: 84).

In this context, the nature of shame as an indicator of social bonds has changed from being focussed upon external social roles and relationships to a more psychological focus on the relationships between 'psychological' selves who enjoy a sense of intrinsic value, dignity and personal depth. There is a shift from the structural to the personal in which the condition known as shame transmutes. From being a relatively objectively assessable condition brought about by failure to meet mutual social obligations of honour and respect pertaining to clearly defined roles, it moves towards being a feeling state and into psychological discourse about the self (Danziger 1997). Under the aegis of evolving individualism, the physical alienation and ostracism that attached to shame in pre-modern societies is transformed into personal discomfort located at the core of the person.

Sennett also adds tangentially to Elias' view that shame has become steadily more individualised, subjectivised, psychologised and individualised. In *The Fall of Public Man* (1986), Sennett argues that up until the eighteenth century people dealt with each other mainly on the basis of conventional public roles signified by, for example, particular clothing and language. The inner essence of the individual, his or her character, was not of relevance or interest within the public realm. What was required was the efficient discharge of a publicly defined and recognised role. Public disgrace and dishonour did not primarily reflect upon an individual's character. It related to failure in discharge of a social role extrinsic to the personality.

Sennett compares this situation of more external, objective, social shame related to role failure in public to that of the present day. Now public life is perfused with apparent intimacy and the cult of the individual personality. Defects of character and failures in personal relations can become as much, if not more, the objects of scrutiny and disapprobation as failures in public duty and policy, as the careers of a number of recent American Presidents show. The kind of shame that is demanded in modern society goes to the roots of the personality and is based in inner feelings. This intimate, personal shame would have found no place in the newspapers of the eighteenth century where shame was related more to public status and observable role performance.

The historic shame attaching to public disgrace and the contemporary shame that is associated with personal lapse can both equally be socially shaped and sanctioned performances on the part of social actors. However, they are performances that are substantially different in the view that they give of self, society, and shame.

One of the very few specific historical studies of the changing nature and function of shame in a particular Western community that has been conducted is John Demos' investigation into shame and guilt in early New England (Demos 1996).

Demos argues that, during the period 1650–1750, New England Puritans were notably shame-prone. The 'heavy work of morality' was done by shame rather than guilt. That is to say issues of appearance, exposure, scorn, social isolation, the threat of abandonment, rejection, inferiority, dignity, and fear of failure to meet ideals were to the fore in creating the psychological climate of the times. In this kind of society,

people like the fictional adulteress Hester Prynne in Nathaniel
Hawthorne's *The Scarlet Letter* (1903) were publicly punished and shamed
for their offences – in Hester's case by having to wear the scarlet letter
'A' around her neck to witness to her offence to all in the community.

Demos describes the character type of an average eighteenth-century
Puritan as one who was acutely aware of the opinions of others and was
heteronomous and conformist in his social and moral attitudes:

> There is . . . a concern for reputation, an instinct for face saving, that reaches
> right to the centre of personality. The New England Puritan . . . was not a weak
> person; he could act effectively when the occasion required. But often he was
> reluctant to claim the motives of action as his own. He preferred to picture
> himself as responding to external influences, especially when his conduct might
> be open to reproach . . . His world was characterized less by stark confrontation
> with self and more by intense face-to-face contacts with a variety of significant
> others. (Demos 1996: 82)

New England Puritans had a sense of being observed or watched, by self,
by others in the community, and above all, by God. The self had become
transparent as the object of observation and scrutiny (Demos 1996:
79–80). With regard to status and the notion of comparison that is so
much a part of modern psychological understandings of shame, Demos
notes that '[a]nother recurrent element of Puritan religious discourse
was the imagery of height' (Demos 1996: 80).

This kind of shame culture was not entirely supplanted by the beginning of the nineteenth century. However, by then, a perceptibly different
guilt culture had come to dominate in New England. Here the emphasis was upon morality, internalised moral norms rather than appearance
and public conformity, offence and harm rather than honour and repu-
tation, punishment rather than abandonment, hatred rather than scorn.

Demos makes a good case for seeing a fairly dramatic change in psychology and character type in New England between 1750 and 1800.
However, he does not explain the social and other factors that led to the
prevalence of the shame culture that spawned and shaped the watchful
Puritans. Nor does he explain how and why it was replaced by an ostensibly more guilt-oriented culture. Nonetheless, insofar as Calvinist
culture has crucially informed and shaped Western individual
consciousness (Weber 1976), it might be argued that Demos has uncovered some of the roots of modern, psychological shame in complex
industrial society. Indeed, one might speculate that Demos' over-self-
conscious, self-watchful, heteronomous Puritans form a crucial stage in
the internalisation of shame and its evolution as a feature of individual,

psychologically based self-control instead of being part of an essentially public response to the violation of proper external relationships of honour and respect.

Shame and authority in industrial society

Moving closer to the modern world, Richard Sennett has explored some aspects of the social use and definition of shame in relation to authority in the industrialised society of nineteenth- and twentieth-century North America. In his sociological study, *Authority* (1993), Sennett explores the ways in which authority is created and emotionally legitimised in industrial societies. Here, the traditional roles, attachments and obligations that pertained in pre-modern, essentially rural societies have been destroyed. In this context, authority is not a static entity or thing. It is an interpretation of power, 'a matter of defining and interpreting differences in strength' (Sennett 1993: 126).

In the insecure conditions of dependency created by industrialisation, people seek to create strong authority figures to ward off their own sense of powerlessness, dependence and, indeed, shame. This produces various kinds of omnipotent authority which are then feared. The first of these is paternalism, an authority of false love that draws on the notion of family roles to legitimate authority outside the family – for example, in the factory. Another form is autonomy, a more recently evolved type of authority characterised as an authority without love because the person who exercises it cares for himself but appears to be in no way dependent upon others.

The creation of strong authority is understandable, but dysfunctional and alienating. Individuals and groups become bound to illegitimate strong authority figures and structures by emotional 'bonds of rejection' such as disobedient dependence, idealisation, and fantasies of disappearance of the authority figure. These leave them and the authority figures firmly locked into the status quo.

Within this broad perspective, Sennett understands shame to be the perception of unacceptable inferiority produced by a sense of dependence upon one's employers or superiors in industrial society. It is both a creation of, and a response to, the weakness and inferiority that is created by arbitrary personal dependence on strong others, 'masters'. While there had always been dynamics of superiority, inferiority and weakness in more traditional society, this was, Sennett suggests, not shame-productive in a personal sense. Superiors and inferiors were fixed in their social positions by reciprocal obligations and factors perceived to be outside themselves: 'In aristocratic or other traditional societies, weakness was not *per se* a shameful fact. One inherited one's weakness in society; it was not of one's own making. The master, too, inherited his strengths; they too were impersonal' (Sennett 1993: 46).

Following Elias, Sennett asserts that physical violence as a tool of social control and punishment gradually declined and came to be regarded as uncivilised in the nineteenth century. However: 'The erosion of physical violence in the past century is not a sign of the lessening of coercion. It is a sign of a new set of controls like shame appearing, controls less palpable than physical pain but equal in their subduing effect' (Sennett 1993: 94). Thus, '[s]hame has taken the place of violence as a *routine* form of punishment in Western societies', becoming 'an everyday tool of discipline' (Sennett 1993: 95, 93).

Thus, shame and its exploitation were integral to the exercise of paternalistic authority, an authority of false love (Sennett 1993: 71). This was exacerbated with the rise of autonomous authority, which Sennett defines as authority without love. Autonomous authority figures present the illusion of being wholly independent, disinterested and free (Sennett 1993: 192). The autonomous authority, the person 'who has marshalled his or her resources, who is therefore self-controlled', can discipline others by making them feel ashamed (Sennett 1993: 92ff.). This kind of person, typical of the modern corporate manager, uses shame to exercise implicit control by means of indifference:

Rather than the employer explicitly saying 'You are dirt' or 'Look how much better I am,' all he needs to do is his job – exercise his skill or deploy his calm and indifference. His powers are fixed in his position, they are static attributes, qualities of what he is. It is not so much abrupt moments of humiliation as month after month of disregarding his employees, of not taking them seriously, which establishes his dominion . . . The grinding down of his employees' sense of self-worth is not part of his discourse with them; it is the silent erosion of their sense of self-worth which will wear them down. (Sennett 1993: 95)

This shame-based discipline of indifference creates the dynamics of master and hopeless victim, bound together with 'bonds of rejection'. While resentful, the victims of this process internalise a sense of inevitable victimhood. They enter a tacit sado-masochistic contract with authority that prevents liberation and fundamental change (Sennett 1993: 152). Defensive attempts to negate authority in order to overcome ambivalence about dependency, vulnerability and exposure employing the negative bonds of rejection do nothing to bring about the fall of strong authority. Instead, shame about being weak strengthens the bonds of shame and makes people more anxious to create strong authorities to ward off the unpleasant feelings of shame (Sennett 1993: 46).

In this context, some people attempt to adopt a mask of detachment, a detached, ironic, inner 'real' self. This helps to avoid the experience of shame and to give a sense of autonomy and self-respect. Unfortunately, this distancing response, a familiar one that often occurs in relation to humiliation and shame, also leads to a kind of passivity that maintains the authoritarian status quo: 'The separation between an outer, obedient figure and an inner observer can also lead to passivity . . . The outer self goes through the motions. The inner self disbelieves all that the outer self performs – this 'real' self becomes a source of negation, but also a permanent region of indifference' (Sennett 1993: 137).

While the roots of dependence and its correlative shame may lie in the nineteenth century, they form a living legacy to the present:

Shame about being dependent is the legacy of 19th Century industrial society to our own . . . Studies of poor, urban American blacks, for instance, testify to their belief that to be on welfare, to be dependent upon people who are judging your weakness in order to decide how much you need, is an intensely humiliating experience. For all that these blacks know that the deck may be stacked against them, the internalizing of dependence as shame occurs. There is evidence, again, that similar feelings are experienced by French and English workers on relief. (Sennett 1993: 47)

Sennett goes on to review ways in which the apparently insuperable sado-masochistic relationship between power and weakness as expressed in correlative relations of strong authority and shame-dependent victimisation might be challenged. He advocates the adoption of an 'ethics of recognition', based on mutual acknowledgment, sympathy, sensitivity and modesty about the self as an antidote to shame-producing indifference (Sennett 1993: 129).

I shall return to the means for unmasking strong authority and reducing correlative socially induced victimhood in the next chapter when I consider the task of personal and social integration as the task of dealing with shame. Here it is enough to note the service that Sennett has done in pointing up the evolution and usage of some kinds of shame as a significant mechanism of control in industrial society over the last two hundred years. Socially engendered shame is shamelessly used emotionally to manipulate and control individuals and groups in many situations in modern society.

Further insights into contemporary understandings and uses of

shame in Western society are to be found in the work of social and cultural critics like Giddens and Lasch, to which I now turn.

Shame in the era of the reflexive self

Sennett's work forms a preface to the ways in which shame has continued to be used as a means of social control in the twentieth century. So,
for example, Goffman and others have explored the ways in which the
inhabitants of 'total institutions' such as mental hospitals, military
establishments, monasteries and boarding schools are ritually humiliated and stripped of former identities in order to assume a new identity
based on obedience and conformity (Goffman 1968a). The same sorts of
practices have been found in concentration camps and institutions
where brainwashing occurs. Here, shaming techniques are systematically used to break the will and identity of individuals so they become
compliant, dependent and malleable (Bettelheim 1986; Orwell 1954).

Similar humiliating practices have been more recently identified in the
more intimate spheres of the home and the family. We have already considered the victimising shaming that is used in the physical, psychological
and sexual abuse of children, for example (Andrews 1988b; Lewis 1998;
Miller 1987a, 1987b, 1991; O'Hagan 1993; Shengold 1989; Walker 1992).
Spouse and other kinds of abuse that employ and produce shame within
the domestic sphere are common, if often hidden and denied (Retzinger
1991; Scheff 1997). This litany of overt shame and humiliation would
perhaps justify the characterisation of the present era as an 'age of
shame' in which social factors conspire to make shame one of the main
tools that is used in subduing and dominating others (cf. Hilton 1988).

The present era perhaps deserves the description of being an 'age of
shame' for less direct reasons. If some modern sociological theorists are
correct, we are living in the age of the self-conscious, reflexive self. In
this context, individuals conceive of themselves as being detached from
traditional structures and relationships. When traditional roles, expectations and norms, together with the practices and rituals that support
them, have fallen away, guilt associated with conforming to static, widely
understood rules becomes less significant than the shame that accompanies uncertainty about the self in an ever-changing world.

Giddens (1991) argues that modern society is now post-traditional.
The stabilities of tradition and habit that surrounded the more static,
stable order of pre-modern society have been supplanted by uncertainty,
doubt, and risk (Beck 1992; Furedi 1997).

In traditional society, people's lives were often fairly stable and pre-dictable in an order where roles, rules and expectations were well under-stood. Modern society, by contrast, provides individuals with little stability. They are likely to move around to gain or keep employment. They may leave their families and communities of origin completely behind them, play many different roles in many different places, have a number of partners, as well as having constantly to renegotiate their social roles and responsibilities. All this creates a climate of anxiety, insecurity, doubt and uncertainty.

Within this overall picture the modern individual self is not a fixed, constant entity but a reflexive project. Due to continuous change and mobility, all the individual has to hang on to is her own sense of self as she changes places, jobs and intimate relationships throughout life. It may not be possible to develop a sense of fundamental trust in reality, others, or the self. The individual has the task of constantly reinventing the self, creating and re-creating a life narrative or 'trajectory' that holds the self together to provide coherence and a sense of identity (Giddens 1991: 70ff.). This plunges people into intense self-observation and self-absorption. No longer are individuals provided with external clothing which denotes exactly what their role or status is in society, as they might have been in medieval times. Instead, in clothes, as in manners, behav-iour and attitudes, individuals can choose from a wide range of possibil-ities how to present themselves to others from hour to hour and audience to audience.

The possibility of presentational metamorphosis allows freedom and self-expression for individuals. However, it also creates anxiety as people worry about whether their 'face fits'. The modern self is constantly on a stage, under the eyes of a critical audience, trying to improvise the correct performance of a role. All are actors seeking to present them-selves credibly on the stage of social expectation. However, they lack clarity as to what social roles and expectations might be in an unstable environment. This creates anxiety, strain and tension (Goffman 1971a: 63–4).

The stakes are high. Individuals are required to provide public per-formances that appear to reveal their 'authentic' selves (Hochschild 1983). As in the real theatre, if there is a failure to perform adequately, shame is an ever-present danger lurking in the wings and cutting to the centre of personal esteem and identity. In this context, it is not surpris-ing that personal therapy may take a crucial role as over-exposed selves try to overcome the depredations of shame. However, therapy has a more fundamental role as the 'routine art of self-observation' that allows the construction of the narrative of the self and enhances self-control (Giddens 1991:75f., 180; Giddens 1992: 108; cf. McLeod 1997).

Shame enters centrally into this depiction of the predicament or project of the modern self. In the first place, it arises as a condition because of a failure to establish a sense of basic trust and relationship with family, community or society (Erikson 1965). This leads to personal alienation.

Secondly, shame is related to the difficulty of trying to find coherent ideals by which to live in a fragmented, pluralistic society: 'Lack of coherence in ideals, or the difficulty of finding worthwhile ideals to pursue, may be as important in relation to shame anxiety as circumstances in which goals are too demanding to be attained' (Giddens 1991: 69).

Thirdly, Giddens suggests, against Freud's dictum that 'the price we pay for our advance in civilisation is a loss of happiness through the heightening of [a] sense of guilt', that shame has, in many ways, replaced guilt on the level of individual experience: 'The characteristic movement of modernity, on the level of individual experience, is away from guilt' (Giddens 1991: 155). The certainties of an external moral order mediated into social control through a sense of individual guilt have been dissipated in favour of greater inner referentiality (Giddens 1991: 155). The modern shame- rather than guilt-directed individual self is more concerned with inward perceptions about the success of the self in living up to its own ideals about itself than it is about the transgression of clear, externally defined rules and standards: 'The more self-identity becomes internally referential, the more shame comes to play a fundamental role in the adult personality. The individual no longer lives primarily by extrinsic moral precepts but by means of the reflexive organisation of the self' (Giddens 1991: 153). Thus, '[s]ocial bonds and engagements increasingly . . . recede in favour of an endless and obsessive preoccupation with social identity' based on personality and personal experience (Giddens 1991: 171).

The modern individualised self is 'frail, brittle, fractured, fragmented' (Giddens 1991: 169). Not only made anxious about issues of basic trust, identity and belonging, it is self-observing and acutely aware of the observation and opinions of others. It is narcissistic and inherently shame-prone.

According to critics like Sennett (1993) and Lasch (1984, 1991), the narcissistic personality has become a dominant personality type in modern capitalist American society:

Narcissism is a defence against infantile rage, an attempt to compensate with omnipotent fantasies of the privileged self. The narcissistic personality has only a shadowy understanding of the needs of others, and feelings of grandiosity jostle with sentiments of emptiness and inauthenticity. Lacking full engagement with others, the narcissist depends on continual infusion of admiration and approval to bolster an uncertain sense of self-worth. (Giddens 1991: 172)

The narcissistic, shame-prone personality plays an important part in the present social order. Narcissists without ties and with chronic needs for approval and compensatory importance make for a good, compliant workforce:

[T]he narcissist has many traits that make for success in bureaucratic institutions, which put a premium on the manipulation of interpersonal relations, discourage the formation of deep personal attachments, and at the same time provide the narcissist with the approval he needs to validate his self-esteem . . . The management of personal impressions comes naturally to him . . . As the 'organization man' . . . the narcissist comes into his own. (Lasch 1991: 43–4)

They are also excellent consumers of goods and services, seeking significance and fulfilment through conspicuous individual consumption: 'Consumption addresses the alienated qualities of modern social life and claims to be their solution: it promises the very things the narcissist desires – attractiveness, beauty and personal popularity – through the consumption of the "right" kinds of goods and services' (Giddens 1991: 172). Lasch notes that: 'Commodity production and consumerism . . . create a world of mirrors, insubstantial images, illusions increasingly indistinguishable from reality . . . The consumer lives surrounded not so much by things as by fantasies. He lives in a world that has no objective or independent existence . . .' (Lasch 1984: 30). Here there is the implication that those empty, alienated selves who fail to perform or consume appropriately in consumerist, mirror society may experience the emptiness, alienation and rejection of intense personal shame.

One further shame-relevant theme emerging from *Modernity and Self-Identity* is that of surveillance. This is a kind of 'institutional reflexivity' that attains 'control of social activity by social means' (Giddens 1991: 149). Surveillance is 'the supervisory control of subject populations, whether this takes the form of "visible" supervision in Foucault's sense, or the use of information to coordinate social activities' (Giddens 1991: 15). While both senses of this term may be relevant to shame, it is the former that is most resonant with it. On a daily basis, people are aware of public optical surveillance from closed circuit television systems. Foucault's 'panopticism', whereby inmates were constantly subjected to the view of authority in prisons and asylums, has become part of everyday life (Foucault 1979). Inspection by 'authority' extends beyond what is physically visible to practices like the systematic examination of accounts and financial affairs by credit agencies or governmental authorities. Beyond this many theoretical and practical disciplines help assay and control individuals and groups.

Rose (1989) argues that the management and control of the individual self have become priorities in modern society. While subjectivity may feel an entirely personal, private matter to individuals, thoughts, feelings and actions are 'socially organized and managed in minute particulars' (Rose 1989: 1). In the quest for governmentality, the quest for knowledge and control of individual subjectivity has become 'a central task of the modern organization' (Rose 1989: 2). This has engendered new theoretical and applied disciplines that provide 'an expertise of subjectivity' (Rose 1989: 2).

'Engineers of the human soul' or human subjectivity, such as psychologists, social workers, personnel managers, counsellors and therapists draw upon the theoretical knowledge of psychology and other disciplines (often gained through observation and even mass surveillance) to help people understand, control, and if necessary restructure themselves and their self-perceptions. All of which allows a greater measure of calculation and control (Rose 1989: 8). So, for example, child psychology and industrial psychology have arisen as ways of understanding and being able to manage or control the individual in the home or the workplace.

Rose does not allude directly to shame. However, in a society where people's personalities are open to scrutiny and are subject to external surveillance and measurement, there must be a constant vulnerability to the experience of shame:

Through self-inspection, self-problematization, self-monitoring, and confession, we evaluate ourselves according to the criteria provided by others . . . The government of the soul depends upon our recognition of ourselves as ideally and potentially certain sorts of person, the unease generated by a normative judgement of what we are and could become, and the incitement offered to overcome this discrepancy by following the advice of experts in the management of the self. (Rose 1989: 11)

This vulnerability to shame is 'private', internal, implicit or tacit, unlike the shame that results from ritual external humiliation in one of Goffman's asylums or Demos' New England Puritan townships. This does not mean that it is any less potent. Shame may have become internalised within the 'depths' of the personality as the psychological self has emerged (Danziger 1997). However, it is still important in gaining and maintaining social conformity and control. Indeed, internalisation may have increased its power rather than diminishing it from the times when people displayed the signs of their public shame openly on their bodies through the wearing of scarlet letters, or the presence of a judicially inflicted brand (Goffman 1968b; Hawthorne 1903). Shame now penetrates the boundaries of the body into the quick of the soul. In the surveillance society of personalised shame it may seem that there is nowhere to hide.

Shame may be differently formulated, construed and exploited now than it was in the past. However, it still forms an important part of social life and of social control. In highly individualised capitalist societies, people may be less subject to external humiliation and extrinsic social shame. However, factors such as the reflexive nature of the self, internal referentiality and the nature of narcissism, together with the prevalence of various kinds of surveillance, mean that individuals can easily be exposed to a sense of psychological shame and inadequacy. Internal disciplines such as close self-observation can combine with factors like surveillance from outside to produce a situation in which persons are likely to feel acutely self-conscious, isolated, and in danger of failing to meet performance expectations.

The shame-prone individual may be seen as a personality type that is socially shaped and appropriate to modern socio-political conditions. He or she may be in an ideal position to exploit and control the conditions and institutions that pertain in the late capitalist social and economic order. However, he or she is vulnerable to being controlled and exploited by them. The vulnerability maintained by fear of shame can be deployed directly and indirectly to influence individual psychology, attitudes and behaviour. Shame and the fear of shame thus play an important part in shaping and controlling individual behaviour and social relations in contemporary society. However, the role, form, and understanding and experience of shame have changed considerably as a modern, mobile, pluralistic social order populated by 'psychological selves' has emerged from a more stable, communal, traditional one.

The deliberate use of shame in society

Shame is an important part of the socio-emotional architecture of the present order. Its use and presence, while real, is often ignored, denied, disguised or totally concealed. Shame is perhaps at its most potent as a means of social influence and control when its presence and use are unacknowledged.

In recent years, however, shame has received a certain amount of positive attention as a means for effecting desired social change and for maintaining or improving standards in individuals, institutions or communities. Thus, the British government in the 1990s began to discuss 'naming and shaming' failing schools and other institutions. This idea encapsulated the notion of inspection followed by publication and exposure of the findings so that members of the public would be aware of institutional shortcomings and those in charge would change their ways.

Deliberate, planned shaming has also been mooted as a way of preventing and remedying individual criminal behaviour in the community. One of the main protagonists of this approach is John Braithwaite, an Australian criminologist (Braithwaite 1989).

Braithwaite observes that in societies like Japan where shaming rather than punishment is used as a way of maintaining social conformity, crime rates are lower. Furthermore, people are less likely to become hardened criminals whose identity revolves around being a member of a deviant group. Braithwaite notes the signal failure of many modern Western societies to prevent crime and deviant careers with the administration of expensive *post hoc* punishment using formal judicial means administered by a distant, impersonal state. He argues that it might be more effective if communities used the more immediate, informal, cheap methods of shaming such as gossip and disapproval. This he calls 'reintegrative shaming':

Reintegrative shaming is shaming which is followed by efforts to reintegrate the offender back into the community of law-abiding or respectable citizens through words or gestures of forgiveness or ceremonies to decertify the offender as deviant. Shaming and reintegration do not occur simultaneously but sequentially, with reintegration occurring before deviance becomes a master status. (Braithwaite 1989: 100–1)

This kind of shame harnesses the power of shame in face-to-face, interdependent relationships to prevent crime, to punish it quickly when it occurs, and to reintegrate offenders who repent into the community. Appropriate shaming must be limited in time, specific to particular actions, warm and firm, non-excluding, 'intolerant and understanding' (Braithwaite 1989: 166): 'reintegrative shaming demands routine non-punitiveness and routine control by communitarian disapproval underwritten by occasional state shame-based punishment in which stigmatization is minimized' (Braithwaite 1989: 140).

It is important that there should be rituals of integration that end any period of shaming. As a model for this, Braithwaite cites the 'loving family': 'Family life teaches us that shaming and punishment are possible while maintaining bonds of respect' (Braithwaite 1989: 56). Using shame thus should produce mature internal control in all individuals living in a particular community (Braithwaite 1989: 172).

Reintegrative shaming is carefully distinguished from stigmatising shaming, which is socially dysfunctional:

Stigmatization is disintegrative shaming in which no effort is made to reconcile the offender with the community. The offender is outcast, her deviance is allowed to become a master status, degradation ceremonies are not followed by ceremonies to decertify deviance. (Braithwaite 1989: 101)

A number of critical points can be made about Braithwaite's positive view of the appropriate use of essentially moral shame. (Braithwaite is not interested in the psychology of shame and basically conflates it with personal guilt as a means of bringing about social conformity and rehabilitation.)

First, the effective use of reintegrative shame implies the prior existence of closely knit communities bound together with bonds of personal, face-to-face interdependence. Despite the voluble advocacy of communitarian theorists like Braithwaite and Etzioni (1995), in many places in Western society such communities no longer exist. Even if they were to exist, it is not clear that they would be desirable. Bauman, for example, points up the potential limits, arbitrariness and unregulated totalitarianism that can prevail in close communities (Bauman 1993: 44ff.).

Without the existence of interdependent communities, it is doubtful whether reintegrative shaming is a real possibility. However, if such communities were to exist, there are substantial dangers with the application of shame to social deviance and control. Braithwaite acknowledges that many individuals and groups may not be competent shamers:

They will 'natter' rather than use shame to confront and follow through on misbehavior, they will forget to temper shame with praise, they will administer shame and praise non-contingently, they will neglect to monitor behavior . . . they will simultaneously shame and reinforce behavior . . . and they will neglect to explain the reasons for the conduct being disapproved. (Braithwaite 1989: 168)

If the shaming process is complex and maladministered, it might lead to the very stigmatisation that Braithwaite wants to avoid. Braithwaite likens effective shaming to the notion of loving the sinner and hating the sin as practised in families and religious communities. However, it is very difficult to reach and maintain a balance here outside the context of very intimate relationships. Often sinners feel that it is they who are hated and excluded, not just their 'sins' (Pattison 1990).

Braithwaite admits that shaming is a 'rough and ready' tool of justice (Braithwaite 1989: 161). Its immediacy and informality is part of its attraction as an instrument of social control. However, it can become a blunt instrument of tyranny and oppression of the majority against a minority:

By increasing the power of societies to shame, we will increase the extent to which the power of shaming can be harnessed for both good and ill. Shaming can be used to stultify diversity which is the stuff of intellectual, political, and artistic debate and progress, or simply to oppress diversity which is harmless. Shaming can become the principal weapon of the tyranny of the majority. (Braithwaite 1989:157–8)

Because no external, formal process is required to administer shame, people may misunderstand individuals and situations so that the innocent suffer. Braithwaite cites the example of a young man in a Prisoner of War Camp who was 'sent to Coventry' by his comrades for stealing, though it was later found that he was innocent. 'The experience of his mates shunning conversation with him emotionally destroyed him; broken, his health deteriorated rapidly . . . A few months later the young man died' (Braithwaite 1989: 157). If shame can kill the innocent, its use must be judicious and cautious. Even if shame does not actually lead to the physical death of individuals, its effects can be devastating in terms of lowering morale and inducing a sense of hopelessness and passivity. This suggests that shame is not the easy, clean, unproblematic method of social integration that it first appears to be.

The criminal justice system is stigmatising, humiliating and demoralising as well as being of doubtful effectiveness in rehabilitating offenders and reducing crime. However, the notion of due process protects people from arbitrary physical or social death at the hands of the shamers. In the light of Braithwaite's discussion of reintegrative shame it is difficult to will to return to the world of the kind of everyday communal shame fostered in the tiny communities of seventeenth-century New England. Shame too easily leads to the kind of humiliation and stigmatisation that most people would be too inexpert to avoid.

At best, the use of shaming as a deliberately fostered tool of social control, even if it were in some ways possible and desirable, is likely to be ambivalent in its administration and effects. It may be very destructive. This applies not only to individuals but also to institutions. Staff and users of British institutions that have been 'named and shamed' bear witness to the demoralising, depressing effect that this can have on everyone involved. Often, they feel that there is no hope and no limit to their humiliation once it has been imposed. 'Shamers' often forget to formulate and implement rituals of reintegration.

Shaming is difficult to control and administer justly because of its informal, personal nature. Its public use, underwritten by official sanction, may also inadvertently support and legitimate shaming in arenas where it might be harmful – for example, in shame-bound, abusing families and abused individuals. While the communal conditions that would make reintegrative shaming possible do not presently exist widely, the dissemination of this concept contributes to the popularisation and legitimation of shame of all kinds as a tool of social regulation and control. This may have considerable unforeseen and undesirable social and individual consequences.

Conclusion

Notwithstanding the somewhat disparate and patchy approach to the socio-historical implications of shame evidenced in this chapter and occasioned mainly by the inconsistent and partial nature of the sources consulted, it is possible to adduce some tentative general conclusions.

First, it is clear that shame, however understood and exploited, has always had a significant role in human societies and relationships since known history began.

Secondly, the nature, understanding and use of shame have changed over time and in different social circumstances that have shaped notions of the self as well as those of social order. In general, it seems that shame has changed from being an external, objective social phenomenon attaching mainly to group membership and role performance to being something far more individual, personal and psychological. There has been a broad movement from 'social' shame to 'psychological' shame. The emergence of a 'psychological' or reflexive self which can be inwardly shamed rather than externally disgraced is itself a social phenomenon integrally related to social changes and developments.

An important implication of the changing nature, locus, understanding and usage of shame is that it is difficult for us to understand
how shame was experienced by our forebears:

[T]he very word shame has represented quite different inner [and external –
SP] experiences over time. If it is difficult to know exactly what one of our contemporaries means when using emotion labels, it is even more difficult to know
what those labels meant in an era characterized by a vastly different realm of
daily experience and accumulated history. (Nathanson 1992: 433)

This is an important point to bear in mind when consulting any kind of
historical text or tradition, including religious texts and traditions
(Malina 1996).

A third conclusion that can be drawn is that shame is inextricably
bound up with issues of social control and conformity in society. All societies and groups need to curb and control the attitudes and behaviours
of their members so order can prevail. Shame is one important, necessary mechanism by which this is accomplished.

Different societies use shame in different ways. Sometimes it is more
extrinsic and formal, sometimes more internal and informal. In some
communities social control by shame rather than guilt is deliberately
preferred and officially fostered. In others, shame may not be so important and its use may be covert. However, it is usual for societies and
groups of all kinds to use shame of some kind to attain individual and
social control.

In modern Western society, shame is an intensely personal feeling of
psychological rejection. Even the most isolated reflexive self who has
rejected conventional rules and morality needs to feel some kind of
belonging and acceptance, if only to the self. Shame used as a method
in social control is perhaps all the more effective for not being recognised
as shame.

One common denominator that may unite experiences and uses of
shame down the centuries is the fact that to those who are shamed it is
an unpleasant, unwanted state of alienation and rejection. This remains
a powerful means of exacting social conformity even amongst those
whose ideology includes the ideal of not conforming to ideals.

The fourth conclusion to emerge is that shame is a powerful but
ambivalent tool for social control. While the deliberate or unwitting
deployment of shame may be very effective in exacting individual and
group conformity, this can also be very damaging and destructive.
Braithwaite's soldier experiencing 'psychological' shame and Sophocles'
King Oedipus experiencing 'social' shame through objective defilement

and role failure both experience a deep sense of alienation and unwantedness (cf. Sophocles 1947). This may lead to the experience of social or
physical death, a searing fate for any human being given the social
nature of our existence. The implication of this is that the deployment
of shame should be undertaken with caution, reflection and skill.
Otherwise, the effects on individuals and groups may be as devastating
as they are unforeseen.

Finally, a word about discourse. Shame experience down the centuries
can only be known about through the words of those who have lived in
the past. It seems clear that discourse and meanings surrounding shame
have changed radically over time. While the word 'shame' has a long
history, its very different usage in different contexts implies enormous
changes in its basic meaning and the experience that it both reflects and
shapes. This may help to account for the confusion of usage that has
appeared in this chapter.

In this chapter, I have considered some of the social and historical
background to the use and understanding of shame to relativise and
contextualise modern, mostly individualist, accounts of this phenomenon. It is now time to turn again directly to contemporary experience to
ask what might be done to alleviate or eliminate unwanted or destructive experiences of shame.

CHAPTER 7

Dealing with shame: the task of integration

The punishing actions of shaming usually consist in exposing the person even more, holding him up in the pillory to the mockery of the public. Every bit of his shamefulness and ignominy is dragged into the light of day and exposed to public derision because 'laughter kills'. . . .

The second step is to send the person into hiding. The humilated one is shunned. He is sent into solitude, outside human intercourse, discarded from the communality of civilized society . . .

Thus one can expiate the sin of exposure of weakness by open degradation and subsequent disappearance . . . This hiding is brought about by denial and repression or, more radically, by suicide, running away, or intoxication.

(Wurmser 1995: 82)

Shame can be understood as a condition that denotes alienation, isolation, defilement, depletion and pain, both individual and social. It is not simply a psychological condition with its origins within the individual. In many ways, shame signals a state of social relationships, whether past or present. The impress of chronic shame upon individual character or personality is socially created and exploited in micro- and macro-relationships. Its consequences can be drastic: 'Shame . . . provides a powerful means of social control . . . The potency of shame in mediating relationships with others may be one reason that, when it goes wrong, it is often associated with severe psychological disturbance' (Tantam 1998: 172).

Chronic shame casts a baleful shadow across individuals, families, groups and whole societies. The effects and implications of chronic, habitual shame reactions are mostly negative and destructive. The lives of the victims and scapegoats with whom the experience of shame is most frequently associated bear eloquent witness to this. It is, therefore, important to address the issue of dealing constructively with such shame so that its effects are alleviated. This must not be conceived only as a matter of personal therapy or individual healing. Shame is a condition of alienation that has social and therefore political dimensions revolving around the use of power and social control. These dimensions must also be addressed.

The use of the word 'integration' is proposed as a way of indicating that the task of dissipating or eliminating dysfunctional, chronic shame extends beyond particular individuals. Within present understandings of self and society in the West, what might be required for optimal well-being is a situation where individuals and groups are recognised and respected by themselves and others as *distinct*, but also as *belonging* within the community (Thrane 1979: 336). When individuals experience the 'too-littleness' of isolation they may experience shame. But they may also experience it if their individuality and its boundaries are overwhelmed by social incursion, as in the surveillance societies of the former Communist East (Kundera 1984; Sennett 1993: 95ff.). The dual causation of shame by too much isolation or too much social attention may be compared with Shengold's observation that the shame-related condition of individual soul murder is the product of either deprivation, or of trauma in which a person is over-stimulated and overwhelmed (Shengold 1989: 1). The end that is sought, then, appears to be that of persons in society who have been adequately respected and honoured as individuals and valued as members of some kind of community by those around them.

In this chapter the overall work of integration will be presented as consisting of two main tasks. The first is to overcome or transcend the sense of chronic or personality shame in individuals. The second is to address the social and political factors that create and exploit an unhelpful sense of shame and alienation on the level of institutions and communities.

THE TASK OF OVERCOMING SHAME IN INDIVIDUALS

Shame manifests itself in individuals as a painful sense of self-consciousness, self-alienation, depletion, defectiveness, defilement, weakness, inferiority, and inarticulacy. Individuals feel thrust back into themselves, unwanted and unwantable, both by others and themselves. They defend against the sense of shame by developing habitual scripts and defences which can then become fixed reactions or personality traits, determining relations with self and the rest of the world over a

whole lifetime. Chronically shamed individuals, whose lives are fundamentally shaped in the shadow of shame, live a diminished, alienated
existence as 'outcasts from life's feast' (Joyce 1956: 114). They often fail to
develop their full individual and social potential and may find it hard or
impossible truly to be present to themselves or to others. To pursue the
visual metaphors that pervade the discourse surrounding shame, they
may find they cannot face themselves or other people. The task of
integration here is therefore to help people escape isolation, to find a new
'face' that symbolises self-respect and respect from those around them.

In this part of the chapter, I shall consider some of the ways in which
individuals might move from a situation of self- and social alienation to
one of greater integration and acceptance using essentially personal and
therapeutic means.

Chronic personality shame is not easy to live with, to transcend, or to
heal. There are no easy solutions or infallible techniques that can be
applied. The condition of chronic shame is a hard one to ameliorate
because individually and socially alienated people are, by definition,
fundamentally cut off from the individuals and communities who might
help them. With defences against further humiliation and rejection in
place, any attempt to build interpersonal or social bridges may itself be
perceived and treated as a threat to such sense of personhood and self-
respect that an individual may still possess. Thus, attempts to enhance
integration may be futile at best and reinforce shame at worst.
Nonetheless, there is some knowledge as to how people might begin to
move forward on the stony road that might lead towards a more integrated and fulfilling life.

Recognising shame

It is not possible to address shame in individuals if its presence is
unrecognised. Shame is a condition that is closely associated with the
wish to hide or to conceal oneself in the face of unbearable psychological pain. The experience of shame, because it is so painful, is often
avoided, denied or defended against. Thus the individual experiencing
it is not necessarily aware that they are in fact experiencing shame.
Furthermore, people who are chronically shamed, as well as those who
try to help them, may themselves understand their condition to be one
fundamentally of depression, anger, guilt, or just 'feeling bad' (Gordon
1996). Thus, shame can be misinterpreted, bypassed, unacknowledged
or ignored. A range of defensive scripts ranging from self-hatred to

contempt for others can disguise or overlay shame experience. It may not be possible to suppress or ignore the signs and symptoms of acute shame, such as blushing, or casting one's eyes or head downwards to avoid the gaze of others. The signs and symptoms of chronic personality shame that has become persistent within the person may, however, be more difficult to identify.

Goldberg suggests that, in a clinical setting, shame-bound persons can be recognised by a variety of different 'signs and symptoms'. These include visual clues such as whether the person looks as if they do not trust and have rapport with the therapist. Verbal responses to the therapist can also be indicative:

I listen for constriction in the free expression of feelings and for passive statements about self that seem bound with secrets and well-concealed fantasy lives implied in their metaphors. Shame-bound people frequently speak about themselves in *allusions* rather than make direct personal statements . . . they speak from an *acquaintance* with themselves, rather than a knowledge from within. They make references to themselves and significant aspects of their lives as 'it', rather than conveying the centrality of these events . . . from a personal identity that is experienced as 'me'. Often there are . . . many *impersonal pronouns* used in their accounts of the events in their lives . . . There is also an overabundance of *power* words like 'must,' 'have to' and 'can't' contained in their speech. (Goldberg 1991: 258)

Goldberg's insights are complemented by those of Kaufman (1993: 178f.) and Retzinger (1991, 1995). Retzinger is a psychologist who has conducted research on relations between couples. She has uncovered indirectly apparent traits, attitudes and behaviours that may indicate the presence of shame.

Retzinger acknowledges the importance of recognising the conventional physical responses to shame in overt, undifferentiated, unacknowledged shame. Here shame is relatively easily recognised through its manifestation in external bodily markers that can occur separately or in combination. These include the hand covering the face, licking or biting the lips or tongue, gaze aversion, blushing, forehead wrinkling and false smiling (Retzinger 1987: 171). She has also developed context-related markers for shame that occur linguistically and paralinguistically.

Among the words that may be used by those experiencing unacknowledged shame are those relating to the feeling of alienation, such as dumped, estranged, deserted, rejected, rebuffed. Another set of words may relate to a sense of confusion – stunned, empty, lost, aloof. Words that relate to feeling ridiculous include foolish, absurd, stupid, bizarre.

The feeling of inadequacy associated with bypassed shame is marked by the use of words like helpless, weak, small, failure, worthless, impotent and oppressed. Associated with a sense of being uncomfortable are verbal markers such as tense, uneasy, nervous and restless. Hurt may be indicated by the use of words like wounded, tortured, dejected and defeated. Other verbal markers for shame include '[m]itigation (to make appear less severe or painful); oblique, suppressed reference, eg, 'they,' 'it,' 'you,'; vagueness; denial; defensiveness; verbal withdrawal (lack of response); indifference' (Retzinger 1997: 301–2).

Beyond verbal or linguistic markers for shame, Retzinger suggests that there are paralinguistic markers. These include vocal withdrawal and hiding behaviours and/or thought disorganisation, for example, speaking over-softly, irregular speech rhythms, hesitation, self-interruption representing self-censorship, filled pauses (-uh-), long pauses, silences, stammering, fragmented speech, rapid speech, condensed words, mumbling, breathiness, incoherence or lax articulation, laughed words, and speaking in a monotone.

A combination of visual, linguistic and paralinguistic markers is required for underlying shame to be diagnosed. The more markers are constellated together, the stronger is the evidence for shame. These markers are contextual and depend upon relationships between self and others. Thus it is no use seizing upon the use of one or two words and assuming that a person is experiencing shame, or is habitually shamed. Nonetheless, the persistent presence of markers such as these may allow the inference of shame even outside a clinical setting.

Having identified some of the ways in which shame in individuals might be discerned and recognised, I want now to look at ways in which it might be transcended or dissolved.

Informal solvents of shame

Until very recently, there have been few means that could consciously and deliberately be applied to the relief or elimination of shame. Means for dissipating or transcending shame were informal, unsystematic, spontaneous and somewhat haphazard.

There appear to be two broad groupings of informal strategies that may dissipate shame and might thereby facilitate integration. First, those that are to do with escaping from shame. Secondly, those that are mainly to do with transcending shame.

Escaping from shame

A variety of means may help individuals and groups to escape the shadow of shame. The lowest common denominator of all of them is that they remove individuals from a sense of negative self-consciousness and/or integrate them into a wider group or community; they take people 'out of themselves' and may join them to others.

One set of mechanisms revolves around avoiding the recognition of shame in the self. Various defensive strategies such as attacking the self, attacking the other, withdrawal, and avoidance may allow individuals to avoid facing up to the reality of their own sense of shame. While these strategies may not be constructive, they allow individuals to escape from shame rather than being entirely annihilated by it.

A second, somewhat casual, means of escaping from shame is simply to let the feeling of shame dissipate spontaneously (Lewis 1992: 127ff.). Waiting for the spontaneous dissipation of shame is probably most appropriate to acute reactive shame which is likely only to last with intensity for a short time. In the case of chronic or personality shame, the feeling of uncomfortable negative self-consciousness is unlikely to move quickly or spontaneously. Nonetheless, chronically shamed people may seek to escape their melancholy condition by trying to find distractions that interrupt the noise of self-consciousness. Such distractions might include entertainment, addiction, work or hobbies. At best, distraction provides only transient escape and release from chronic shame. This may be welcome while it lasts.

A third means of escaping shame may be to identify with an idealised group or individual in such a way that the shamed self is silenced or forgotten. By joining a close, admired, powerful group a shamed person may find belonging, significance, and a sense of honour. Merger allows a sense of group self to supplant the painful sense of inadequate individual self. This kind of group identification has prominent elements of idealisation and grandiosity which perhaps lie behind the fanatical attachment people can display towards sports teams, political parties, or national identity. Many of the psychological factors that lead to the emergence of authoritarian personalities susceptible to mass fascism and nationalism are exactly the same as those that lead to shame:

[A] basically hierarchical, authoritarian, exploitive parent–child relationship is apt to carry over into a power-oriented, exploitively dependent attitude towards one's sex partner and one's God and may well culminate in a political philosophy and social outlook which has no room for anything but a desperate clinging to what appears to be strong and a disdainful rejection for whatever is relegated to the bottom. (Adorno et al. 1969: 971)

'It is interesting that authoritarian movements are often preoccupied with notions of moral pollution and defilement, elements closely related to shame' (Sennett 1993: 159).

Ritual may also be an informal means of dissipating or escaping shame. Sociologically, ritual is the 'focussed marshalling of symbols redolent with arrays of meaning' (Mitchell 1970: 158). Through it, individuals and groups are connected to the social order: 'The troubled mind, disturbed relations between people and nature, between individuals and groups may be rectified by constructions of order through ritual' (Mitchell 1970: 158). Rituals such as eating or worshipping together, whether formal or informal, often have the effect of binding individuals and groups closer together. In creating a sense of group solidarity and well-being, they help people to de-objectify themselves and to forget their sense of shame (Ford 1999).

Turner argues that in traditional societies rituals help to transform shame into beauty: 'Sacrifice transforms a shameful act – the public killing of a living being or its substitute – through collective acknowledgement of our condition and recognition of the nature of the universe, into an experience of beauty' (Turner 1995: 1063). This kind of transformation seems equally possible on the individual level in the modern world. I can testify to the shame-reducing effects of becoming immersed in corporate liturgy and, particularly, in singing.

Rituals do not invariably reduce or alleviate shame. Some rituals may heighten alienation and exclusion. It is possible to feel very much isolated, alone and self-conscious if everybody else seems to join in a song, but one does not oneself know the words or understand their meaning. Similarly, even formal rituals of reconciliation and repentance such as the practice of formal confession can actually lead to greater self-consciousness and shame (Lewis 1992: 131). In early New England, religious rituals were consciously used to demarcate an in-group and an out-group, with 'sinners' like Hester Prynne feeling the full weight of shame brought about by formal exclusion and ritual scapegoating (Demos 1996; Hawthorne 1903; cf. Douglas 1995).

A final informal means of escaping shame is that of humour and laughter (Lynd 1958; Nathanson 1992; Retzinger 1987; Scheff 1987). When people laugh, it is argued, self-consciousness is left behind and shame is dissolved, producing a sense of self-unification and solidarity with others, at least temporarily:

At the very core of the process of reconciliation lies good-humored laughter, especially laughter at oneself. The affectionate admission of one's own foibles in a way that leads to spontaneous laughter signals the completion of the shame response cycle and the possibility, therefore, of reconciliation not only with others, but with one's true self, the suffering, foolish, awkward, impossible animal that is the human being. At this moment, the pretension, ambition, greed, and bitterness that interfere with simple cooperation and mutual aid turn to dust . . . laughter may be a path toward survival. (Scheff 1987:148)

Scheff argues that shame-spirals are interrupted by laughter. Furthermore, 'chronic shame is most effectively dispelled by good-humored laughter' (Scheff 1990: 175). He goes on to suggest that high self-esteem and creativity depend on being free of chronic shame.

A similar point relating specifically to the therapeutic context is made by Nathanson:

All of us who spend our lives doing psychotherapy have watched with pleasure when a patient learns to laugh gently about some once-hidden subject, something that once caused searing pain. There is a laughter of love, a laughter that shows the sudden pleasure of self accompanying healthy new self-recognition. (Nathanson 1992: 394)

Considering humour and comedy as a whole, Nathanson suggests that, '[i]f love is the balm that heals the pain of individuals, comedy is the solace, consolation, and relief for entire tribes' (Nathanson 1992: 379).

This mention of comedy raises a cautionary note in relation to laughter as a spontaneous solvent for shame. Lynd suggests that laughter can actually be a defence against shame (Lynd 1958: 96). Jokes and laughter can denote self-hatred, self-objectification and contempt for self and others as well as acceptance (Nathanson 1992). The use of humour can deepen the sense of shame and self-consciousness that individuals can feel, particularly if jokes are made at their expense and with a view to excluding them from 'in-groups': 'laughter kills' (Wurmser 1995: 82). Laughter may be joyous, accepting, cynical, contemptuous and many other things besides (Gilhus 1997; Screech 1997). It is profoundly ambivalent in its meaning and effects and is far from being an unequivocal balm (Pattison 1993). Nor is it easy to prescribe or 'manage' it in such a way that it necessarily promotes individual healing and integration. It is, therefore, important not to over-estimate or romanticise the therapeutic effects of laughter. However, it certainly has a significant part to play in the informal, spontaneous dissipation of shame.

There may well be many other informal, spontaneous aspects and means of escaping shame. Probably the most important informal means of dissipating individual shame and attaining integration arise from aspects of ordinary, everyday human relationships such as respect and love. The importance of these relationships will be obliquely covered when the deliberate healing of shame is considered below. Now I turn from escape to the 'transcendence' of shame.

Transcending shame

To transcend shame is not necessarily to escape from or to cure shame, but rather to use and transform it, to make something of it, either consciously or unconsciously. Here art and creativity may play an important part.

Wurmser (1995) suggests that the trauma of basic unlovability, woundedness, grief and despair that underlie shame can be 'heroically transcended' by means of creativity, self-loyalty and masking. The creative response is illustrated by Beethoven, a man who blended woundedness, idealisation and aggression together with controlled theatophilic and delophilic drives (the unconscious drives to see and be seen) to create gripping art that inspires and moves others. Beethoven transcended and sublimated shame through monumental creativity that did not remove his hurt and woundedness but put them to very positive use (Wurmser 1995: 294ff.).

A second heroically transcendent response to shame is that of authenticity or self-loyalty. Here Wurmser instances Ibsen, another victim of deep childhood unhappiness and neglect who coined the term 'soul murder'. Ibsen was, in his writings and personal life, prepared to violate or go against conventional social norms and assumptions in order to be true to what lay within him. This loyalty to the self can lead to being aggressive and ruthless towards both self and others, defending the island of self by 'rage, shame and contempt'. 'Thus, in a deeper sense the creative person does not mourn – he scorns, destroys, throws away' (Wurmser 1995: 301). Nonetheless, Wurmser is able to conclude of Ibsen, Beethoven and their like: 'The real miracle . . . is that in some of us this horror of the self and this violation of the other is so gloriously, so splendidly outweighed and transformed that it serves other suffering persons as a redeeming token of humanity. Yet at what cost!' (Wurmser 1995: 302)

The final example of creative transcendence is that of masking. The adoption of a mask at festivals in traditional societies allows the masked one to behave shamelessly, to mock the feared and the sacred, such as the feared spirits of the ancestors or even death itself. The masked person's visage is fixed, counterfeiting the face as it would be in death. The petrified becomes the petrifier and faces the feared thing down (Wurmser 1995: 307). Fear is abolished or reduced by impersonating or identifying with its source or object:

The mask changes the shamefully exposed into the shameless exhibitor, one who fears to be seen as weak into one who is seen and feared as strong. It is the *glorification of transformation,* of metamorphosis – the transcendence of individuality by turning it into a universal symbol . . . It changes what is usually hidden by the guardian of shame – inner reality – into powerfully fascinating images, gestures, and music. It is the victory of archaic forms of showing and seeing and the defeat of shame. (Wurmser 1995: 306)

Creativity and the powers of life within humanity win out over social convention and death in masking as in artistic creation and self-loyalty. However, here, as with other informal, spontaneous methods, there is ambivalence. Masking can simply be an avoidance of shame, as well as providing opportunities to shame others without personal cost or consequence.

Creativity, self-loyalty and masking are all possible transcendent responses to shame. They are not, however, inevitable. For every Ibsen or Beethoven there must be thousands of people who live lives that are simply stifled by shame. For them, creativity of any kind is a wishful dream. Thus, the transcendence of shame and unlovability is no way systematically and deliberately to heal chronic shame. Turner argues that '[o]ur dignity as human beings, paradoxically, depends upon the acceptance of our shame' (Turner 1995: 1073). We must, therefore, 'find out how to accept and dissolve our shame in ritual, laughter, art, and insight' (Turner 1995: 1072). Be that as it may, I will now move on from informal, spontaneous, and traditional methods of escaping from or transcending shame to the systematic, deliberate work of therapy.

Therapeutic responses to shame

Two main therapeutic approaches to the alleviation of chronic shame will be distinguished here; self-help and informal approaches, and formal psychological and clinical approaches to the therapy of shame. I do not attempt a complete guide to healing shame.

Self-help approaches to relieving chronic shame
The most comprehensive self-help guide to overcoming shame that I have come across is John Bradshaw's book, *Healing the Shame that Binds You*

(1988). In this volume, Bradshaw advocates a number of different but related strategies for healing chronic or personality shame. These mostly relate to improving self-respect and self-esteem and to reducing depression. In this regard, Bradshaw's work is very similar in content and tone to books that have nothing in themselves to do directly with shame (Burns 1990; Rowe 1983; Sanford and Donovan 1993).

Bradshaw first suggests that shame and shamed persons need to come out of hiding. Only if shame is brought out into the open, recognised and accepted, can people begin to be healed of it. The process of coming to terms with shame in this way is designated 'externalisation' (Bradshaw 1988: 115f.). The techniques then outlined are geared to bringing externalisation about.

Bradshaw's first suggestion for externalisation is to find and join a group of people who will engage in honest, non-judgmental and non-shaming relationships. Here all emotions can be exposed and talked about. Since the roots of shame often lie in unsatisfactory human relationships which did not mirror adequately the child's needs and self, an important therapeutic first step is to re-engage with the human race. This step is difficult, risky, and essential (Bradshaw 1988: 119ff.). One way of engaging with such a group is to follow a twelve-step programme such as that followed by groups like Alcoholics Anonymous (Bradshaw 1988: 125ff.).

Subsequently, Bradshaw advocates making contact with the vulnerable, child part of the self that was abused and rejected. This is accomplished by exploring original feelings of pain, coming to terms with grief, and meditating upon 'embracing [the] lost inner child' (Bradshaw 1988: 140). The next task is to recognise and integrate disowned parts of the self, feelings and needs that have been denied or shame-bound in growing up. This is brought about by voice dialogue with the self, meditating on the different 'parts' of the self, and by integrating and interpreting one's dreams. 'Toxic shame's greatest enemy is the statement I love myself' (Bradshaw 1988: 157). Choosing to love oneself is, therefore, important. It is accomplished through accepting oneself unconditionally in such a way that one regards oneself as neither more nor less than an imperfect, fallible human being. Next, Bradshaw suggests that people must attempt to heal their memories and to change their self-image. Here Neuro-Linguistic Programming techniques can be applied to change historic scripts of thinking and behaving. Self and body image can be changed by using a variety of meditational techniques (Bradshaw 1988: 167ff.).

Shamed people often feel that they experience a kind of negative inner voice that makes unrelenting disparaging and critical comments about the self. This inner voice, which represents a fantasy bond with the 'good', idealised but persecutory inner parent, must be confronted and changed. Bradshaw suggests various strategies such as externalising the inner voice – for example, by writing down what it says and replying to it, learning how to stop obsessive shaming thoughts, and making positive affirmations about the self (Bradshaw 1988: 183ff.).

Toxic shame crucially affects relationships with other people which may be characterised by co-dependency and sado-masochistic elements as people are dominated by a fear of intimacy together with an equal need for attachment. The therapeutic work here consists in giving up and grieving one's empty, false self. This allows the development of a more authentic self that can enter more fully into healthy, non-victimising relationships with others (Bradshaw 1988: 203ff.).

Bradshaw concludes that 'the work of transforming toxic shame into healthy shame leads directly to spirituality' (Bradshaw 1988: 217). Spirituality and the religious disciplines that accompany it can themselves be obsessive and prevent the externalisation of toxic shame (Bradshaw 1988: 219). However, ultimately Bradshaw believes that it is vital, 'through prayer and meditation to create an inner place of silence wherein we are centred and grounded in a personally valued Higher Power' (Bradshaw 1988: 116).

It is difficult to evaluate the effectiveness of Bradshaw's approach to healing toxic or chronic shame. He brings to it much enthusiasm and commitment, together with the assurance that the techniques he advocates have worked for him and for others whom he has helped (Bradshaw 1988: 116). However, it is tempting to think that, like many self-help book authors, Bradshaw sells more hope than experience. In the case of shame in particular, re-establishing effective relationships with self and others probably needs more than a good deal of commitment to self-improvement. Shamed selves are unlikely to be highly motivated to escape from the solipsistic rut of despair into which they are sunk. To begin on a self-help programme requires a degree of self-respect and a sense of efficacy that is likely to be lacking. If the programme fails to 'work' it may reinforce a sense of incapacity and hopelessness, and therefore amplify chronic shame.

Questions might also be raised about the place of God or a Higher Power in Bradshaw's therapeutic schema. This might be seen to reinforce the sense of personal helplessness and passivity that often accompanies shame. Above all, the programme that Bradshaw commends does not really solve the problem of isolation and self-confinement. Shamed people may have great difficulty in trusting and meeting the people they may need to be healed of shame. Reading a self-help book is unlikely to be an adequate solvent to shame and isolation. For this reason, some people deliberately seek out another person who might be able to help, a counsellor or a therapist.

Approaches to healing shame in individual therapy

The literature relating to the healing of shame in individual therapy is extensive. However, it is much stronger on the diagnosis of shame in therapeutic encounters and on the obstacles and problems that arise in trying to treat it than it is on actual techniques that are of proven effectiveness in dealing with it. The assumption seems to be that the usual mixture of listening to, and accepting the feelings and projections of, shamed people may, given a lot of patience and understanding, lead to changes in attitudes towards self and others.

All therapeutic theorists agree either implicitly or explicitly that shame is a difficult condition to recognise and diagnose. It can easily be bypassed or unacknowledged (Lewis 1971). It is a hidden condition which, almost by definition, may not be foremost in therapeutic encounters.

Often, shame is concealed by conditions such as depression, anger or sadness (Lewis 1992: 138ff.). Thus clients are often unaware of their shame. Part of the work of therapy may be to help them dismantle the defences that they have erected against recognising the shame that they suffer. Many theorists point out, however, that shame is a difficult emotion to accept in others: 'there is a tendency for the observer of another's shame to turn away from it' (Lewis 1971: 16). There may therefore be a real desire in the therapist to avoid recognising and acknowledging shame (Kaufman 1993: 227–32). The therapist's own shame may be aroused by a feeling of not being able really to help the client and by the sense of shame that may come from being invasive of another's privacy (Broucek 1991: 96). If shame is not diagnosed, it may interfere with other aspects of therapy. Furthermore, shame-related symptoms may actually be exacerbated by lack of diagnosis (Lewis 1971: 348). This means that people may get worse rather than better through attending therapy.

It is commonly agreed that shame must be acknowledged and owned if it is to be healed. Without insight and knowledge into the nature of shame a person will be unable to get rid of, or dissipate it (Lewis 1992: 127ff.). The therapist must recognise and interpret the client's shame without exposing them in such a way that shame is amplified and the client seeks further hiding and inner veiling. This is not easy to do because the whole situation of therapy is one that can easily bring about an increase in shame (Broucek 1991: 79ff.). The client can feel awkward and ashamed about seeking therapeutic help. Furthermore, there may be a perceived inequality in status and expertise between client and therapist which produces feelings of inferiority and shame. Beyond this, the asymmetrical contract between client and therapist means that the former is exposed to the latter, but the latter does not usually reciprocate in kind: 'The contrast between the imperturbable, benign listener who has adopted an almost saintly acceptance of the patient, and the patient himself, with all his guilty, "irrational" thoughts and feelings, particularly evokes shame on the part of the patient' (Lewis 1971: 15).

If a positive transference develops towards the therapist, this brings about the possibility of unrequited love which immediately opens the client up to the possibility of the shame of inferiority and rejection. In some kinds of therapy clients lie down while their therapists sit in a chair and can literally oversee them at a time when the client cannot see the therapist's face. Perhaps lack of facial contact and recognition, together with a certain taciturnity on the part of some therapists, may produce a sense in the client that he or she is objectified, inferior, unwanted or unaccepted, the very feelings that may have brought him or her into therapy in the first place (Lewis 1991: 481). It can certainly help to ensure that shame is bypassed or unacknowledged (Broucek 1991: 86). Finally, therapists can fail to respond adequately to the exposure of their clients, thus producing a sense of rage, guilt and increased shame in them (Broucek 1991: 79ff.). Broucek arraigns the whole traditional practice of psychoanalysis as inherently shame-producing and -amplifying. It provides enormous scope for clients to be humiliated by therapists who adopt a professional role that allows them to 'remain on the scene as analyst while fleeing the scene as person' (Broucek 1991: 87).

In treating shamed individuals, it is vital to build a relationship of basic trust between therapist and client. This is likely to be difficult. Chronically shamed people are inherently mistrustful of human relationships and of exposing themselves to others. It may, therefore, take a very long time for a relationship to build up in which it is possible to begin to work on the roots of shame. Some writers caution against moving too quickly towards interpretation of the client's feelings and condition. Others suggest that, in order to create a trustworthy, non-shaming relationship, it is important to extend a more equal kind of friendship to clients than would be normal in working with other types

and conditions (Kaufman 1993: 226ff.). Goldberg advocates being available to patients outside consulting hours and taking a genuinely friendly
and to some extent mutual interest in their lives (Goldberg 1991: 288).
This may help to reduce the distance between client and therapist which
may feel to the former like shame-generative rejection, hostility or
indifference.

A key part of undertaking psychodynamic work with clients is to work
with the transference in which the client projects their feelings on to the
therapist. With shamed people, therapists may have to endure a good
deal of scorn and humiliation from their clients without retaliation
(Lewis 1971: 454). Some clients may try to avoid a sense of shame by
being more analytical than the therapist, beating him or her to the
analytical interpretation and so objectifying themselves while establishing their own superiority (Broucek 1991: 93). Others may never move
from a position of idealising the therapist and adopting a position of
helpless inferiority. From the perspective of working with narcissistic
clients, Morrison suggests that in successful therapy for shame where the
client is accurately mirrored, people will move from a position of shame
to one of grandiosity, then gradually to contempt and de-idealisation of
the therapist (Morrison 1989: 89). It is always possible for people to get
stuck at any point in this process. Furthermore, therapists themselves
may fail to deal properly with their own negative counter-transference
on to their clients (Retzinger 1998). The therapeutic process is a
demanding one for all involved.

Shamed individuals who seek change through therapy must be prepared to give up their previous identity and the self-narratives around
which they have shaped their lives (Kaufman 1993: 201; McLeod 1997).
Surrendering what might be termed 'false self' may well feel like death,
for a false self is all that an individual has (Richards 1996). Letting go
and grieving this false self is a costly, lengthy process that requires giving
up a whole way of looking at and living one's life. Many people do not
feel able to do this.

Not only must the 'false self' with its connections to the idealised
'parent' be abandoned, but the individual must then seek to build a new
sense of self-esteem and self-regard, indeed a sense of pride: 'The self
must learn to affirm the self from within. This . . . translates into having
esteem for self, valuing of self, respect for self, pride in self' (Kaufman
1993: 224). This pride may be understood as 'enjoyment/excitement
invested in the self, or in accomplishments by the self' (Kaufman 1993:

225; cf. Nathanson 1987a: 186). Working towards restoring the 'interpersonal bridge' between the self and the self, and the self and others, involves recovering the primal interpersonally based scenes of shame (Kaufman 1993: 177ff.). In the process of identity regrowth and healing shame, the client identifies with the empathic, mirroring therapist and can thus internalise and learn a new, shame-free way of being. He or she may experience a 'transmuting internalisation' that permits real change (Morrison 1989: 182). As time goes on, clients may learn to change foundational narratives, metaphors and scripts so that they relate to self and others in life-enhancing, active ways, transcending the role of voiceless, passive, alienated victim (Kaufman 1993; McLeod 1997; Wurmser 1995).

There are no sure, certain, or quick ways of healing shame. Goldberg acknowledges that 'the treatment of shame, at the present time, is not an exact science. At best, it is a creative and compassionate art' (Goldberg 1991: 257). Change, if it occurs at all, is incremental. People must learn a vocabulary about their feelings of shame and gain the confidence to share these feelings (Macdonald 1998). The process of creating a language for shame and then integrating it in wider social narratives might be seen as the most important way in which individuals become integrated within themselves by becoming integrated in wider stories and metaphors (McLeod 1997: 96–8; cf. Cox and Theilgaard 1997; Frank 1995). A language of self-knowledge helps to locate individuals within known social experience rather than outside it. Thus many child abuse victims, for example, have found personal healing in discovering that their experience is not unique and unspeakable, a condition of 'abomination' that cannot be named or verbalised (Stout 1988: 145–62). The use of language therefore creates a sense of personal efficacy as well as one of belonging to self and others (Frank 1995).

The therapeutic process is likely to be lengthy and the outcomes may be uncertain. Case studies of the treatment of shame often show mixed results, with clients often leaving therapy before they have overcome a sense of chronic shame (Lewis 1971; Goldberg 1991; Miller 1985). As far as I know, no outcome studies of the effectiveness of psychotherapeutic treatment of shame have been undertaken. Many theorists about the therapy of shame are modest in their claims about its effects. Wurmser, for example, suggests that the promise of the psychotherapeutic process is creative 'mutative insight', that is, recognition that brings about (non-specific) change:

Insight in all its specificity, integration, and aptness . . . becomes a feat of seeing without being afflicted by guilt and especially by shame for that observing, a victory prompted by, and overcoming, at least signal shame and signal guilt, a feat neither Teiresias nor Oedipus not any other figure in tragedy was able to achieve . . . It is, in short, a victory of curiosity over shame. (Wurmser 1995: 286)

Morrison believes that shame cannot be eliminated by therapy, but people may be helped better to live with it:

How does one learn to accept potential shame through life, to live with it without experiencing self-devastation, despair, and mortification? . . . First of all, we can consider the energy investing in secrets – in hiding and concealing facts and feelings about self – which might be modified. It need not be so terrible . . . to reveal certain secrets to selective others. Second it is possible to turn more frequently inward, to oneself and to affirming selfobjects, for the nod of approval or acceptance about ourself or our efforts – to grant less judgmental and critical power to the public, viewing audience. Finally, through that inward gaze, we can attempt to transform the harshness and severity of the ego ideal into a more accepting, attainable ideal self. (Morrison 1989: 182–3)

Most psychotherapeutic treatments of chronic shame are costly, lengthy, demanding, and unpredictable. Perhaps the main things that 'talking therapies' achieve are a growth of trust that facilitates the possibility of articulating and understanding the condition of shame. This in itself is an individually and socially integrating experience. Ultimately, however, no complete cure may be possible. Treatment itself may even exacerbate the condition of the shamed (Lewis 1971). Thus, even formal treatments for shame offer little more hope for the chronically shamed than the self-help methods or spontaneous and informal means of escape considered earlier. Chronically shamed individuals may, therefore, easily be stuck for life in a condition of alienation, isolation and self-denigration, with all the unhappiness that that implies.

On this regrettably pessimistic note, I turn now to the issue of dealing with shame in society. Is it possible that there may be effective ways and means of alleviating and eliminating dysfunctional social shame so that individuals and groups may be released from alienation and become more fully integrated into the social order from which they are isolated?

THE TASK OF OVERCOMING DYSFUNCTIONAL SHAME IN SOCIETY

From the expulsion of undesirable family members from the home, through group scapegoating and ritual bullying in institutions, to national governments treating their employees and populations with contempt, and international conflicts that find their roots in national humiliation (Scheff 1997), shame plays an enormous part in shaping social life and maintaining social control.

Often, the social use of shame is not consciously planned or executed, nor is it well articulated or understood. While it may be generally accepted that shame has a significant and sometimes very positive role to play within national and corporate life, there is little conscious understanding of what shame is, what kinds of shame are desirable or undesirable, or how shame might be used appropriately, even creatively. Consequently shame may be unleashed in groups, organisations and societies in a very destructive and unhelpful way. Building upon and amplifying individuals' sense of shame, socially generated and sanctioned shame can create widespread despair, alienation and humiliation.

Here I want to point up some of the ways in which shame impinges dysfunctionally upon social and organisational life. Becoming aware of this is an important preliminary to the social integration that must accompany and reinforce individual integration. It may then be possible to infer some ways in which integrating structures and practices might be shaped.

Recognising dysfunctional shame in society

Eastern societies like Japan are often designated 'shame cultures' while Western societies are often called 'guilt cultures' (Benedict 1954). Unfortunately, this crude distinction blinds Westerners to the extent to which shame – informal social exclusion from primary reference groups, or the threat of such exclusion – is an important but ungoverned part of social control in their own culture.

Here, I will briefly note some of the ways in which shame and humiliation are used both deliberately and unwittingly to maintain and manipulate the social order. Mostly I regard the phenomena that I am about to describe as negative and dysfunctional. This is a value judgment. It all depends from whose perspective one is looking as to whether the generation and use of shame in society and social organisation is to be regarded as positive or negative. I would argue, however, that being uncritical and unaware of the ways in which shame is created and deployed is almost bound to have substantial dysfunctional and negative implications because shame is allowed to be uncontrolled and arbitrary in its effects.

Shame helps to define and defend the boundaries of groups. Those who are excluded from the membership, respect and good opinion of groups or individuals upon whom they depend are likely to experience and internalise the sense of rejection, inferiority, alienation and dejection associated with the word 'shame'. The experience of being socially shamed can be undermining for individuals and groups, particularly if they are stigmatised and denigrated at the same time (Lewis 1998). The reality, or threat, of socially induced shame forms a powerful incentive to conformity.

The more particularly or closely a group or individual is dependent upon another individual or group, the more powerful shame will be as a threat to identity and well-being. In closely knit groups or societies, exclusion can certainly bring about social death. This may, in turn, bring about physical death insofar as personhood and worthwhile human existence are socially sustained – 'face' is bestowed upon us by others.

Shame is thus a powerful, if little examined and understood, tool of social control. It is a particularly attractive weapon or strategy when there are significant differentials of social power and status, for example, in situations of extreme dependency. It is also useful when a powerful minority wishes to subdue or contain a greater dependent majority. Systematically shamed people tend to be depressed, passive, dependent victims. Sometimes, it is very much in the interests of powerful minority groups that they should stay this way.

There are occasions upon which groups and individuals may set out to shame and alienate others in a quite conscious and deliberate way. However, the use and manipulation of social shaming is perhaps more often an unconscious, hidden process. Those who are engaged in the social diminishment of others are often consciously unaware of what they are doing.

Having set out this assumptive framework, it is now time to exemplify social shaming in action. My first example demonstrates how shaming may be deliberately used to control and manipulate a group in business. The chief executive of the Pepsi corporation, John Sculley, used shaming to gain worker compliance and to get the results that he sought:

> Through rigid codes (e.g., dressing), and through carefully orchestrated rituals ('public hangings' for poor performance), discipline and conformity at Pepsi were tightly maintained. According to Sculley, executives willingly subordinated their working lives to a strict logic of winning market share. Friendship, family, and other interests were pushed to the margins. This corporate hegemony was so strong that no sign of complaints, doubts or questioning was tolerated. (Alvesson and Willmott 1996: 199)

Frequently shame is produced and exploited more subtly (Sennett 1993). So, for example, calling people who work in an organisation 'human resources' rather than 'people' objectifies individuals. This may help to produce a sense of shame. Similarly, various methods of evaluative surveillance and appraisal can engender or build upon a sense of individual shame (Pattison 1997b: 107ff.).

Shame can also be associated with work practices such as making people unemployed. Many of those who become unemployed feel that they lose identity and a sense of self-esteem and social purpose through what seems like a 'humiliating event' (Brown 1996: 39–41). Some may become depressed or even commit suicide because of this sense of shame (Smith 1987). Others may deny their unemployment to avoid the personal and social diminishment that may accompany it. Unemployment may be seen as individual tragedy. However, in a society where having a job is seen as a key to full citizenship, those who provide jobs can use the threat of the shame of unemployment to discipline and order their workforces.

Shaming methods have deliberately been deployed down the centuries. So, for example, colonists, slave owners, prison camp guards, torturers, child abusers and pimps have used humiliation and shame, as well as direct violence, as ways of putting and keeping others down in obedient compliance (Bettelheim 1986; Pattison 1997a; Walker 1992). Shame has the advantage of subverting people psychologically from within. They are not then able to assert themselves against their oppressors. An important step in gaining a sense of autonomy and respect, therefore, has been for the oppressed and shamed to reshape and claim their own inner identity. Thus US Black activists in the 1960s declared that 'Black is Beautiful' over against three hundred years of denial of this. In Africa, Frantz Fanon pointed up the mental disorders that arose from Black people having to live in a society ideologically constructed around White assumptions and interests in a book, significantly entitled *Black Skin, White Masks* (Caute 1970; Gendzier 1973). Gays, abuse survivors and people who have survived mental health problems have similarly tried to slough off the stigma that can surround an identity shaped by shaming experiences to assert their basic acceptability and goodness to themselves and others (Cotter 1997; Goffman 1968b; Read and Reynolds 1996; Walker 1992).

Turning away from deliberately used and inflicted shame, many institutions and organisations unwittingly use shaming and humiliation as a means of social control. Scapegoating, for example, is a common feature of many groups and organisations. Douglas (1995) argues that scapegoating is a way of transferring blame on to a victim in situations where the self or the group may be exposed and found wanting. Identifying a widespread tendency towards 'strategic scapegoating' in public life, Douglas points out that this itself may be shame-driven:

The driving force behind a great deal of public scapegoating in modern times seems to be related to the possibility of exposure, a fear of being found out, a fear that the public image so assiduously created and probably not rooted in the actual person, will be destroyed. Hence the powerful need to dissemble, to deny with as much authority as possible, to deflect and so look for others to take the blame. (Douglas 1995: 47)

Blaming and scapegoating is widespread in contemporary society. Many parts of British public service foster a 'blame' culture. Here relatively powerless individuals end up taking total responsibility for things for which they can only be at most partly to blame (Malby and Pattison 1999; Pattison, Malby and Manning 1999). Those who have the courage to point out things that are wrong and 'whistleblow' frequently find themselves being scapegoated, victimised and excluded as others attempt to deflect the shame associated with potential exposure. Hunt (1995: 154ff.) lists being sent to Coventry, labelled a troublemaker, spied upon, ground down, pre-emptively 'disciplined', fired, and having one's character assassinated as ways in which whistleblowers are shamed and victimised in the National Health Service. Similar practices are found elsewhere. Part of the subtlety of scapegoating and humiliating shaming is that it does not officially occur and is not officially sanctioned.

Similar shaming and bullying can be found in many groups and institutions. It is still common in British schools, for example, for teachers to call students names, to be rude to them, and to ridicule them publicly. The *Guardian* newspaper of 9 December 1998 tells the story of a boy at a school in Manchester who was allegedly punished by an experienced teacher for chattering in class by having the word 'prat' written upon his forehead. This represents the tip of an iceberg of unthinking shaming and humiliation integral to the life of many institutions where one group has power over another. Hospitals, particularly mental health institutions, are another place where individuals may find themselves being ridiculed or humiliated (Goffman 1968a; Pattison, 1997a).

Psychologist Tom Kitwood (1997) has made a systematic study of the factors that depersonalise and humiliate individuals in care settings, particularly in relation to people who have dementia. Their condition is exacerbated by depersonalising 'malignant social psychology' (Kitwood 1997). The principles of this psychology are deployed by institutions and care workers. They include treachery, disempowerment, infantilisation, intimidation, labelling, stigmatisation, invalidation of the person, banishment, objectification, ignoring, imposition, withholding, accusation, mockery and disparagement (Kitwood 1997: 46–7). These principles are applicable more generally than to people with dementia in institutional settings. Anyone attempting to humiliate, shame, or depersonalise others would find them of great utility.

The deliberate, as well as the accidental, use of shame and humiliation is an important part of everyday social life in advanced Western civilisations. Shame and humiliation continue to form some of the most powerful tools of social influence and control, all the more effective because they are often hidden, unarticulated and unexamined.

It is my contention that socially generated and manipulated shame often builds upon individual propensities to shame. Furthermore, it heightens and reinforces susceptibility to shame in all areas of life. The informal use and prevalence of social shame amplifies and legitimises the use of shame in family and individual relationships. It cannot be surprising that there are many individuals in society with a strong or chronic sense of shame when so many important social institutions foster this condition. Shamed people, like depressed people, may be unhappy but they are also malleable, quiescent and biddable. There are, then, considerable advantages from some perspectives to the social promotion of group and individual shame.

The implication here is that individual integration cannot be divorced from social integration. How, then, can socially dysfunctional shame and shaming be minimised so that integration can occur?

Overcoming chronic shame and humiliation in society

Robert Solomon argues that 'there isn't nearly enough shame' in our society (Solomon 1992: 223). He means that often organisations and their members fail to live up to the ideals and responsibilities to which they should aspire. I agree. However, in some ways there is too much shame in our society. Humiliation, bullying, uncontrolled shaming and scapegoating make many lives miserable. They reinforce the dynamics of social exclusion and victimisation. They create and amplify a sense of chronic shame in groups and individuals that prevents them attaining inner freedom and full social participation.

If shame promotes social responsibility, moral conformity and cohesion, it may be deemed a positive and creative force. If, however, it diminishes individual and group self-esteem and self-respect, it can be seen as destructive. Shame and shaming are powerful but ambivalent and largely uncontrollable, unmanageable forces in social life.

I believe that shame and shaming cannot be eliminated from societies and groups. Wherever persons have any kind of social identity, there will always be the possibility of shame as the dynamics of inclusion and exclusion unfold. The experience of shame as a measure of the social bond between individuals and groups is an unpleasant one when it occurs. However, it is normal, inevitable and even desirable if it alerts people to threats to the state of the social bonds between them (Scheff 1990: 15). There is, then, a kind of functional or healthy social shame in all societies and groups.

This kind of 'healthy', normal shame must be distinguished from the kind of shame that is created and manipulated to control others. A main distinguishing feature between these two types or uses of shame is that the latter is characterised by elements of humiliation, whether or not this is conscious or planned. Humiliating shame permanently alienates people from themselves and from society. It fosters and amplifies chronic individual and corporate shame amongst stigmatised groups like Jews, Black people, and people with mental health problems. It is humiliating shame that should be eliminated from all levels of society if personal and social integration are to occur.

Margalit argues for the importance of creating and maintaining the 'decent society', one 'whose institutions do not humiliate people' (Margalit 1996: 1). This macro-ethical concept supplements the micro-ethical concept of the 'civilized society' 'whose members do not humiliate one another' (Margalit 1996: 1).

I want to advocate respectful social and individual relationships that are both decent and civilised. This would allow individuals to be part of society and also to be respected as individual persons. They would not have to endure the shame of isolation, nor yet the shame of total incorporation. Relationships would be based upon mutual respect. An implication of this is that individuals and groups would need to eschew the use of humiliation and humiliating shaming to gain or maintain control.

There are no easy routes to the non-humiliating, integrating society. As far as I know, although many people have aspired towards social relationships characterised by respect, and many others have noted the nature of oppression and humiliation in a variety of social contexts, no-one has so far systematically set out an analysis or programme that puts the elimination of humiliating shame at the centre. Here, I can only set down a few fragmentary clues as to how one might proceed.

The first task here might be to gain a much better understanding of the causes, prevalence and use of humiliating shame in society. Here the work of those exploring structures and mechanisms of abuse in particular institutions and groups is relevant (Goffman 1968a; Kitwood 1997; Walker 1992).

We still do not know enough about how and why humiliation occurs to prevent it effectively. Thus incidents of bullying, humiliation and abuse remain common. It is difficult to prevent structures of shaming and humiliation from being created ever anew in different institutions such as government, industry, health and educational services, and families. Better 'thick' descriptions of the ecology and context of shame and humiliation are still needed. We also need more knowledge about how to create circumstances in which such ecologies will not arise. This will involve complex analysis of how social institutions, social policies, economic factors, gender relations, individual interests, organisational norms and contemporary beliefs and attitudes work together to make shame and humiliation main mechanisms of social control. Such a complex analysis cannot be undertaken here. However, there is a great deal of case material arising from psychiatric hospitals, children's homes, prisons, schools and family abuse that already exists to inform analysis of this kind (Pattison 1997a).

Humiliating structures and practices are unlikely quickly to be eliminated. What, then, can individuals and groups do to facilitate their own transcendence of humiliation? One important practical contemporary response to humiliation is that of liberation, recovering a sense of pride and identity. Questioning norms and assumptions forced upon them by dominant cultures and institutions such as patriarchal society and the medical establishment, women, Blacks, gays, people with mental health problems, child abuse survivors and others have sought to find their own voices and stories. They have created solidarity with those in a similar position and sloughed off or inverted the shaming, stigmatised identities historically allotted to them. Such liberation movements are too numerous to list or describe here. Their principles are now likely to be familiar (Pattison 1997a). Unfortunately, the real progress made by those who have traditionally been victimised and put down has not so far eliminated the mechanisms of humiliating shaming that still pervade many social structures.

Close to the liberationist project as a response to shame and humiliation is Sennett's pursuit of the 'ethics of recognition' (Sennett 1993: 129ff.). Sennett is critical of the kind of authority that is exercised in modern society, but also of the responses towards it. Authority depends upon the use of the shame of autonomy. This is colluded with by the dysfunctional responses of the shamed and subordinated whose psychological condition resembles what Freudians might call identifying with the aggressor (Young-Bruehl 1991: 210ff.). It perpetuates a relationship of servitude and domination.

The solution is for shamed and oppressed people to undertake a journey of recognition. This involves acknowledging the slave and master within (Sennett 1993: 151). Once individuals can recognise their own part in continued submission and oppression, they can go on to challenge the legitimacy and nature of authority. The dynamics of domination and submission are made overt and so can be transcended as autonomy and freedom are attained (Sennett 1993: 125ff.). It is here that the possibility of creating a society based on mutual 'recognition' begins.

It does not end with the individual. Sennett suggests that people who have power and wield authority, together with their subordinates, must endeavour to create authority that is fundamentally democratic because it is 'visible' and 'legible' (Sennett 1993: 165ff.). Instead of being seen as invincible and omnipotent, authority must be limited and honest in its claims.

Moving away from what people can do for themselves to challenge humiliating, shaming practices, Kitwood outlines principles for implicitly non-shaming work with other people. While mainly concerned with people suffering from dementia, his ideas are generally applicable.

Kitwood suggests that the psychological needs of people with dementia, like those of all people, are those of attachment, comfort, identity, occupation and inclusion (Kitwood 1997: 82). People with dementia often have difficulty in ensuring that these needs are met. The result is personal diminishment and depersonalisation. To restore and maintain the person, care workers have to discard the features of malignant social psychology, described earlier. Instead, they must try to offer recognition, negotiation, collaboration, play, timalation (sensual experience), celebration, relaxation, validation, holding and facilitation (Kitwood 1997: 119–20). They also need to be able to receive from the person cared for whatever is offered. Thus personhood, 'face' and social belonging are maintained and people do not fall into the abjection of depersonalisation and exclusion.

These are precisely the qualities of respectful, shame-free, non-humiliating relating that need to prevail in all human relationships and organisations. Significantly, Kitwood does not believe that this kind of relating can occur in certain kinds of settings. Homes for demented people that are run in such a way that the manager is remote and authoritarian, status divisions amongst staff are large and rigid, clients have the lowest status of all groups, communication is one-way and impersonal, and power differentials are high, cannot foster respectful person care (Kitwood 1997: 103ff.). Social context, organisation, and politics thus have a crucial effect upon personhood and possibilities for health or humiliation.

Some organisations do not run on the basis of depersonalising shaming and humiliation, though many still do. Some may even be able to enhance the personhood of others through respectful care and relationships. This provides some hope with which to conclude this consideration of healing socially generated, excluding shame.

The elimination of humiliating shame is probably necessary if one is to aspire towards a 'decent', 'civilised' society where people acknowledge each other's humanity and individuality and treat each other with respect.

There is no natural law that determines that human beings should live within social arrangements and organisations that persistently humiliate them and encourage them to humiliate others. Life structured by an ethic of personal and social recognition and respect is not unimaginable or unattainable. It will, however, be hard to realise. Many people are so entrapped by their internalisation of shame and humiliation that malignant social structures and assumptions seem inevitable rather than contingent. Here again, then, it is apparent that individual and social integration and change go hand in hand. It will not be possible to produce a society in which structures of shame and humiliation are curbed or eliminated without individuals and groups who have the courage and confidence to challenge the status quo. At the same time, it will not be easy for such individuals or groups to emerge if humiliating, shaming structures remain firmly implanted in everyday life.

Conclusion

In this chapter I have reviewed various methods that might be used to overcome or eliminate the kind of chronic dysfunctional shame that diminishes and blights the lives of individuals and groups. The task here is one of individual and social integration, for persons and social structures are integrally linked. Without acting in both the social and the individual spheres, the alienation represented by dysfunctional shame cannot be healed or prevented.

Structures of shaming and humiliation are firmly entrenched, often in quite a low-key, everyday way in many parts of society. There are, however, possibilities for creating 'decent', 'civilised' societies and groups. The road towards producing a situation in which individuals feel integrated with themselves and with one another in respectful relationships within society is a long one. However, chronic, diminishing shame is not inevitable or wholly incurable in either individuals or the social structures of which they are a part. Recognising that shame is present and understanding its nature and function better is, perhaps, the first step towards integration on many levels. It allows the possibility of addressing more directly the nature and effects of chronic shame as a signifier of personal and social alienation.

Summary: towards a working understanding of shame

The quest to understand shame has been a journey into increasing complexity. It has become clear that there is no one way of approaching or understanding shame, no one 'reality' that underlies all experiences of shame, no simple 'lowest common denominator' that links all uses of the term 'shame' together. Furthermore, there is no 'master narrative' that satisfactorily accounts for all, or most, aspects of the phenomenon of shame. All that is available is a range of different discourses in which shame is variously situated and understood. Sometimes these discourses are complementary, at other times they may be contradictory. Nonetheless, some important points have emerged.

In the first place, a number of significant distinctions can be made about usages of the term 'shame' which allow the identification of 'types' of shame. However, it is important to emphasise that the differences identified may be primarily those of discourse and usage. No claim is being made here for difference anchored in 'objective reality'.

One type or usage of shame that can be distinguished is ontological shame. This may be characterised as shame that relates to being human and finding oneself to be limited and mortal. The state of being human, finite, mortal, embodied, dependent on others and so on involves fundamental shame (Hans 1991). This state of ontological shame is not unlike the ontological guilt described by Tillich (1962b). It can be destructive in its effects, However, there is little that can be done to alleviate this existential shame beyond recognising and accepting it. It is an inevitable part of human being and destiny.

Another type of shame can be described as normal or healthy shame (Scheff 1997). It seems to be the case that most, if not all, humans have a capacity for shame in some circumstances and this can be normal and functional. Sometimes this kind of shame is akin to awe or reverence (Schneider 1987a). It helps to mark and maintain the boundaries of respect for self and others. This kind of shame often does not require alleviation or elimination because it helps to maintain social order and relationships.

A further distinction of type or usage is that between acute and chronic shame. Acute shame is short-lived and may be highly functional as a warning or communication to self and others. However, chronic shame can often be very dysfunctional, in many different ways, both for individuals and for the communities in which they live. It is chronic shame that I have suggested needs to be eliminated or alleviated.

Finally, a useful distinction can be made between social and psychological shame. All shame is socially shaped and much shame may be socially engendered. There is a difference between shame perceived as an objective social condition or state and shame experienced as a condition of individual psychological emotion. In the modern world both social and psychological shame continue to exist alongside each other. However, the locus of shame has now become the self-consciousness of the reflexive individual and it is usually understood to be mainly an internal psychological emotion. Shame often feels primarily like internal personal badness rather than an objective social state. People today take shame personally and psychologically. Groups of stigmatised and unwanted individuals can, however, also experience a profound sense of shame and unwantedness.

I now want to propose a personal and tentative working understanding of shame. This does something to encompass many of the negative meanings of shame that are the main concern of this book. I suggest that, for present purposes, shame can best be understood as toxic unwantedness. This understanding owes much tangentially to Douglas' definition of dirt or uncleanness as 'matter out of place' (Douglas 1969: 40). However, the contemporary notion of dirt has to be intensified in the case of shame. It is not just a matter of inert unwantedness – dirt lying around the place has no value but is mostly ignored. Shame appears to have a quality of active revulsion and danger. This is the same sort of feeling that is associated with germs and disease which people perceive as dangerous and to be actively avoided. In this context, the notion of miasma, intimately associated with pollution in ancient Greek thought, comes to our help (Parker 1983; cf. Corbin 1986). Miasma denotes dangerous, toxic dirt that actively threatens the order and safety of individuals and communities until it is dealt with by purification. That which is dirty, dangerous and unwanted is excluded from the community, expelled or ignored. It is a kind of wordless horror that people shut out from experience, understanding and language. Shame is thus well characterised as a state of abjection (Kristeva 1982), abomination (Stout 1988), abnegation, or affliction (Weil 1959). Like disease bacteria, it is often revealingly perceived to be contagious (Lewis 1971: 15; Lewis 1998).

Groups and individuals who fall into a state of long-term toxic unwantedness, abomination and abjection find themselves the objects of inarticulate stigma and rejection to others and often to themselves. They inhabit a state which is beyond words, outside humanly defined and recognised reality, in a wasteland of uncleanness. They may become social and psychological lepers, objects of fear and loathing from whom others avert their gaze. Sharing the same values as others, they may not even be able to look themselves in the eye, literally or metaphorically. Like the polluted and shamed Oedipus, they become despised and hated outsiders to others and to themselves with no 'face' or sense of wanted, valued selfhood (Sophocles 1947). Their identity is spoiled and fundamentally devalued at its roots, however well this may be disguised (Goffman 1968b).

The person who experiences shame does not want or value him- or herself. If this condition is prolonged or becomes habitual, shamed persons and groups become toxic nobodies. The society that shames groups or individuals does not value or want them. Indeed, shamed, defiled or stigmatised individuals and groups may be positively feared and actively rejected. Perhaps more damagingly, they may just be confined to a realm of wordless invisibility in which they are unacknowledged. While the reasons for entering into shame may sometimes be valid and functional, any person or group that is habitually shamed will be dehumanised. Shame is an important marker of the bounds of human community and belonging. Those who live beyond the shame boundary inhabit the realm of the unclean and inhuman. They may be less valuable to self and others than domestic pets.

Toxic unwantedness may be consciously perceived, clearly articulated and deeply felt, or it may be unconsciously maintained, unarticulated, and essentially ignored. Whatever its state of visibility and recognition, the sense of polluting unwantedness, of shame, has important effects upon groups and individuals. For social creatures such as human beings are, a fundamental feeling of shame or unwantedness represents social and personal alienation. To be excluded, unwanted, treated as defiled, and shamed by self and/or others is to risk death – social, psychological, personal, or even physical. It is this sense and reality of unwantedness that needs to be addressed and overcome if people are to live full, socially and individually integrated lives. Spoiled, soiled identity must be restored and people must be given face by and within the human community if they are to live full and responsible lives. If shame and stigma are conferred by human beings, human beings are the only means of acceptance and valuing for the shamed. In the restoration of face, one might hope that Christianity has an important part to play.

PART III

Shame and Christianity

Introduction: bringing Christianity into the picture

At the beginning of this volume, I outlined a method for a practical theological approach to shame. I suggested there that working towards a practical theology of shame requires a critical conversation between what is known of the condition described as shame and religious beliefs and practices.

The first two Parts of this book were devoted metaphorically to 'listening' to contemporary understandings of shame drawn from non-theological, non-religious disciplines and practices. This was not an easy task, because there is an enormous variety of perspectives upon the nature of what are called emotions in general and upon shame in particular. In the first Part of this book, therefore, some of the problems involved in trying to understand and define shame as a phenomenon from a multi-disciplinary perspective were considered.

This was followed in the second Part by a consideration of the experience of shame, particularly the kind of chronic or habitual shame reaction that appears to diminish and blight the lives of individuals or groups. On the face of it, it appears to be the case that chronic shame represents a significant negative condition in our society. It is a condition of polluting, defiling unwantedness that alienates people and groups from themselves and from society. Dealing with chronic shame by means of strategies for social and individual integration is complex. There are no easy solutions, not least because we do not have a complete, coherent understanding of the underlying factors and implications inherent in shame. It remains a condition that is somewhat hidden, obscure, ill-defined and poorly understood, despite the efforts of many different theorists, researchers and clinicians.

Having established a reasonable working understanding of some important aspects of what the condition known as chronic shame appears to be and do within various discourses in Western societies, it is now time to turn to the second part of the practical theological activity proposed. This is to examine how Christian ideas and practices intersect with shame in individuals and groups.

In chapter 8, I shall give an account of how some twentieth-century theologians and pastoral care theorists have approached shame. It will be seen that contemporary Christian thinkers have largely failed to recognise and respond adequately to chronic shame. More than this, Christianity has failed to recognise the ways in which its own ideology and practices may have contributed to the production and exploitation of dysfunctional shame. Chapter 9 explores some of the ways in which this has happened with a view to inviting the contemporary Christian practitioners and theologians to respond in a more appropriate way to shame. Moving beyond this, the final chapter of the book suggests some positive ways in which Christians might begin to change their attitudes and practices in relation to shame. I do not provide any quick or infallible solutions here, only starting points for possible change.

CHAPTER EIGHT

Modern Christian responses to shame

Anoint and cheer our soiled face
With the abundance of thy grace
(*Veni, creator Spiritus*)

This chapter critically reviews some of the main theological and practical responses to the phenomenon of shame from within the Christian community in the twentieth century. Few theologians have taken shame as a central category for theological analysis and understanding. However, on the level of pastoral theory, there is a growing body of literature that refers to the understanding and pastoral treatment of dysfunctional shame. Much of this emanates from North America where shame has become a major psychological category for understanding the ills of the self. Even here, though, there are a limited number of understandings of shame and its implications. A number of theorists claim to provide theologically and religiously informed understandings and approaches to shame. However, there is little of substance that the Christian community has to offer to those who suffer the alienation and unwantedness of dysfunctional shame. Those who claim expertise often derive this from secular, mostly psychological, theorists who are themselves often defeated by the dynamics of chronic personal and social shame.

My purpose here is to reveal the nature and limits of Christian religious and theological activity in relation to shame. This represents an attempt to be honest about the limits of understanding, knowledge and concern. It is only by recognising and accepting limits and gaps that we may gradually get into a position where appropriate religious understandings and responses to shame can be formulated. Many theorists and theologians obscure the complexity and problematic nature of shame with over-simplistic responses. The beginning of wisdom lies with the acknowledgment of ignorance and the acceptance of practical impotence and inadequacy.

In the first part of the chapter I will chart some of the pitifully few straightforwardly theological responses to shame. I shall then consider the ways in which specifically pastoral theologians have attempted to address shame, both in theory and in practice. Nearly all of these responses have been limited in scope and repetitive in content. Often, they are unsupported by good-quality empirical and experiential data.

This is probably symptomatic of several things. First, shame has only recently emerged as a perceived pathological condition requiring a specific response in its own right. Secondly, there is a general lack of knowledge and expertise in our society about how to deal with dysfunctional shame on any level, whether individual or social; religious thinkers and workers participate in this general ignorance. Thirdly, religious practitioners and theorists find the whole issue of shame just as difficult to deal with in all its complexity and incorrigibility as any other group of people who wish to promote human well-being. They may feel ashamed of their lack of expertise, competence and effectiveness in this area and so seek to avoid its very practical challenges.

Recent theological responses to shame

The 'western Christian tradition has spoken chiefly in terms of sin and guilt, and has seen salvation principally as the forgiveness of sins . . .' (McKeating 1970: 45). This generalised judgment is confirmed by others (Gorringe 1996; McGrath 1986). There are important strands in the Western Christian tradition of salvation and atonement that emphasise themes of healing and redemption from bondage. However, most theologians have devoted their attention to notions of guilt, offence and forgiveness in trying to understand the nature of human alienation from neighbour and the divine. This bias has continued almost unchallenged until very recently. A number of important recent British theological books that have heralded a revival of interest in atonement, Gunton (1988), Fiddes (1989) and Bradley (1995), find no space for shame as a category for thought and analysis. The word is not even mentioned in the indexes of these books.

For most theologians, shame has not been a significant phenomenon as part of human experience or as a feature of the relationship between humans and God. It has received a negligible amount of sustained theological attention in the twentieth century.

The Protestant theological 'giants' of the century either ignore shame altogether or deal with it in a brief, incidental, or desultory manner. In *The Nature and Destiny of Man* (1964), Reinhold Niebuhr does not index shame as a category at all, though pride and sin receive considerable coverage. Karl Barth mentions shame and being ashamed on four occasions in his *Ethics* (1981), mainly in the context of discussing the divine call to human beings in their sexual distinctiveness. Following Genesis 2.25 which notes that 'the man and his wife were both naked, and were not ashamed', Barth argues that men and women are not ashamed before each other when each recognises the other's distinctive nature and mutual dependence (Barth 1981: 182). He suggests that when this distinctiveness and mutuality is brought into question, people will be ashamed because they bring into question their own humanity and creatureliness. In this context they may blush and be exposed to 'the evil laughter with which male and female should not laugh' (Barth 1981: 182). The role of shame here and elsewhere in *Ethics* is essentially social and moral, with little theological significance. It is only casually mentioned while forensic notions of sin and guilt, by contrast, receive greater and more systematic attention.

Van Deusen Hunsinger outlines further aspects of Barth's thought on shame as contained in the *Church Dogmatics* where a mere three direct references to shame are indexed (Barth 1961: 671, 674, 675; cf. van Deusen Hunsinger 1995: 198ff.). It appears that Barth almost incidentally identifies a number of different kinds of theologically significant shame in the pursuit of the more central theme of sin. In the first place, humans find themselves in the objective position of being shamed before God because they are sinners. This shame is removed by God's entering into the shamefulness of sin in the life and death of Jesus. Thus a new status is given to Christians. They are accorded honour because of God's acceptance and love. However, they also experience a new kind of non-debilitating subjective shame. This comes from awareness of God's merciful goodness in overcoming sin coupled with the awareness of the humility of Jesus in taking sin upon himself. Barth makes little use of psychological or sociological notions about shame in constructing his theology. His sketchy notions of shame are undeveloped and of little use in trying to create a well-informed, comprehensive, Christian response to dysfunctional shame.

An important twentieth-century theological treatment of shame is to be found in Bonhoeffer's *Ethics* (1964). Bonhoeffer regards shame as having social and moral significance in marking out interpersonal boundaries and helping to define the social and moral order (Bonhoeffer 1964: 184). However, he also allows shame some direct and overt theological significance in the relationship between human beings and God. Shame is the condition that prevails as a marker of the ontological condition of being no longer united with God. It is a mark of separation, differentiation and disunity that is inevitably experienced by all human beings simply by virtue of their humanity:

Man perceives himself in his disunion with God and with men. He perceives that he is naked. Lacking the protection, the covering, which God and his fellow-man afforded him, he finds himself laid bare. Hence there arises shame. Shame is man's ineffaceable recollection of his estrangement from the origin; it is grief for this estrangement, and the powerless longing to return to unity with the origin. (Bonhoeffer 1964: 20)

While people experience remorse in response to some kind of fault, they feel shame because they sense a basic lack of something: 'Shame is more original than remorse' (Bonhoeffer 1964: 20). So profound is the feeling of shame that emerges from the sense of disunion and loss that man 'covers himself, conceals himself from man and from God' (Bonhoeffer 1964: 21). This covering acts as a memorial of original loss and disunion. It is also an important protection that creates a sense of necessary privacy and secrecy. Shame, which is 'the memory of the disunion from the Creator, and of the robbery from the Creator' (Bonhoeffer 1964: 22–3) is characterised by a dialectic of concealment and exposure. It can only be finally disposed of in an 'act of final shaming' or exposure when human sin is laid bare through confession before God and other human beings. This opens the way for 'the restoration of fellowship with God and men' (Bonhoeffer 1964: 23).

Bonhoeffer's comments upon shame are tantalisingly brief. While suggestive and intriguing, they are unclear and unsystematic. Without the benefit of much modern psychological thinking about shame, Bonhoeffer's concept of this phenomenon seems to be based on a couple of verses in Genesis 3 in which humans recognise themselves to be naked and then cover themselves. This biblical image is amplified by some acquaintance with Nietzsche's thought about shame and religion. However, Bonhoeffer strips Nietzsche's notion of shame of all its sense of anger, envy, inferiority and resentment towards God (cf. Hans 1991; Schneider 1987a; Wurmser 1997a). The element of stain and defilement that is so prominent in much modern thinking about shame is absent. There is, instead, an emphasis on shame as a kind of covering, almost a badge of the ontological state of shame. Only the important ingredients

of loss, concealment, secrecy and the need for public exposure and reconciliation to effect an overcoming of the alienation of disunion with
God and other humans remain.

Perhaps the most important missing element from Bonhoeffer's somewhat undifferentiated concept of shame is the sense of personal, psychological pain and unwantedness that many chronically shamed people
experience. For Bonhoeffer shame is an inevitable, ontological part of
the human condition. Indeed, it signifies the condition of being human,
finite and lost. This is certainly one important aspect of understanding
and giving appropriate theological importance to shame. However, it
hardly engages with the painful reality and specificity of contemporary
human alienation and defilement represented by chronic, dysfunctional
shame.

Bonhoeffer gives some theological significance to shame. This is more
than most other theologians do. In the space of a few pages, he has made
one of the most complete, comprehensive statements about shame of
any major twentieth-century theologian. This emphasises the invisibility and insignificance of the topic on the theological stage.

The elements of hatred and protest against an all-seeing, all-knowing,
all-powerful and so abusive and invasive, shaming God that were so crippling for Nietzsche and for others like Martin Luther are brought back
into the theological frame by Paul Tillich in one of his published sermons
(1962a). In 'The Escape from God', Tillich takes as his text Psalm 139.
This begins, 'O Lord, thou hast searched me out and known me. Thou
knowest my downsitting and mine uprising, Thou understandest my
thought afar off' (Tillich 1962a: 46). Tillich rightly suggests that the
notion of God suggested here as a person who is omnipresent and omniscient is a 'text of terror' (Trible 1984) for many. They would wish to avoid
'the horror of the all-reflecting mirror and of the never-sleeping Witness'
that reflects and amplifies a sense of individual shame, imperfection and
inadequacy (Tillich 1962a: 56). Tillich cites Nietzsche approvingly as one
who 'knew more about the power of the idea of God than many faithful
Christians' (Tillich 1962a: 50). In Nietzsche's story of the Ugliest Man
(Nietzsche 1969: 275–9), the Ugliest Man murders God because he 'looks
with eyes that see everything; He peers into man's ground and depth, into
his hidden shame and ugliness' (Tillich 1962a: 50).

Having acknowledged the offensiveness of an inescapable God with
the very angry and negative feelings that this can elicit in individuals
(such as Martin Luther, who acknowledged that he hated God (cf.
Erikson 1962)), Tillich tries to reinterpret the meaning of omniscience

and omnipresence to be less threatening. He suggests that these concepts refer not so much to a person but more to the inevitable nature of human existence: 'Omniscience means that our mystery is manifest. Omnipresence means that our privacy is public' (Tillich 1962a: 53). Another way of reconciling ourselves to an omnipresent God, suggested by the psalmist, is to recognise that God is the friendly ground of our being and to allow 'admiration of the Divine Wisdom' to overcome 'the horror of the Divine presence' (Tillich 1962a: 54). Ultimately, the will to flee God and the will to be equal with God have to be contained within the tension between being seen in all our darkness and in 'a height of a fullness which surpasses our highest vision'. The unavoidable presence of God as the witness in the centre of an individual's life 'implies both a radical attack on his existence, and the ultimate meaning of his existence' (Tillich 1962a: 57).

Tillich's sermon is not primarily a treatise on, or analysis of, shame. Nonetheless, it is illuminating for this topic. Tillich is very successful at catching the horror that may be induced in fundamentally shamed individuals by the theological notion of an omniscient, omnipresent personal God. It seems that for Tillich, as for Bonhoeffer, Nietzsche is his main teacher here rather than the biblical tradition. This has much in it about shame that is mostly ignored by modern theologians, not least perhaps because it is often God who directly humiliates and shames people.

While Tillich catches the reality of the horror of shame for individuals in a world under perpetual divine surveillance, I am not sure that his sermon really deals with this reality satisfactorily. Strangely for a thinker with Tillich's knowledge of psychology and psychoanalysis (cf. Tillich 1984), it does not seem to occur to him to introduce the notion of projection to explain the sense of being under a constant critical gaze. For many people, the God who is ever-present and watching is what psychoanalysts might call a 'hostile introject' (Klein 1988b: 61ff.). In this perspective, God is a psychological object upon which people project their inner feelings and beliefs.

A psychodynamic perspective on the God from whose presence people want to escape would also allow for the notion that people might need active therapeutic help to redeem their projections on to the divine object. Trying to understand concepts in different ways and extracting different meanings from them may be transformative for individuals. However, it is unlikely that fear and terror can be ministered to effectively by word play. In the end, Tillich's exhortation to live with the tension of being grounded within a witnessing gaze that sees both the good and the bad within the person does not take seriously enough the reality of fear and terror felt by individuals in the face of the omnipresent, omniscient God object. Tillich's reflections on trying, ultimately ineffectively, to escape from God have less use and application to toxic shame than one might like. Ultimately he rejects the sharp and difficult challenge embodied in this quotation from Nietzsche: '"Is it true God is present everywhere?" a little girl asked her mother; "I think that's indecent" . . .' (Nietzsche 1974: 38). Tillich is thus better at diagnosis than cure, though he deserves credit for tackling this topic at all.

More recently, and from a different direction and background, two British-based theologians situate a theological discussion of the significance of shame within a wider vision of theology based on praise. Hardy and Ford (1984) argue that the basic form of Christian existence is praise in recognition of the reality of divine existence and creation. This leads to a general attitude of 'recognition, honouring, and delight' that finds an important place for respect for human dignity (Hardy and Ford 1984: 73). Hardy and Ford argue that the logic of overflow in praise is counterposed and counterfeited by a logic of overflow of evil that leads to the negation of all activity and life. A prominent feature of this kind of negation occurs in the phenomenon of shame which they understand to be 'the perversion of the movement of respect' that accompanies praise-based existence (Hardy and Ford 1984: 89).

Hardy and Ford distinguish two kinds of shame. Right shame is measured by God's judgment on us and is the recognition before God of 'being in some wrong relationship or false position' (Hardy and Ford 1984: 90). Confession and repentance of this will eliminate this kind of shame and joy will eventuate. Wrong shame is the infliction of shame and humiliation on others. Here it is not only Stalin and Hitler who are arraigned as promoters of shame: 'the most insidious forms of wrong shame are religious or quasi-religious' (Hardy and Ford 1984: 93).

Jesus Christ plays a crucial part in overcoming shame. By taking upon himself and embodying both right and wrong shame, Jesus, in his suffering and death, overcomes and redefines shame, inaugurating possibilities of respect for self and others, and for praise. He opens the way to a 'new ecology of blessing, laughter, mutuality and praise'. This goes far beyond therapeutic, psychological and Stoic responses to shame that simply allow people to cope better with shame (Hardy and Ford 1984: 96). Through enduring shame of all kinds, Jesus opens the way to a new order. By faith, trust and identification with Christ, Christians make this new order their own reality, 'irresistibly rejoicing in freedom from shame before God, others and ourselves' (Hardy and Ford 1984: 98). Posing the question of whether God should be ashamed because of the rule of evil, hatred, suffering and death upon earth, Hardy and Ford maintain that God is vindicated by the death and resurrection of Christ in which the old order is transcended and transformed into something new and different (Hardy and Ford 1984: 103ff.).

Hardy and Ford's approach to shame is an original, positive one. They give shame as a lived human experience a prominent place at the centre of their theological work, making it a test case and example for their theological assertions. They also evince a nuanced, differentiated account of different types of shame, though this does not really match any of the typologies to be found in the psychological literature. Rather than drawing on Nietzsche and contemporary social scientists, the points of reference upon which Hardy and Ford draw are contemporary experience and parts of the biblical tradition, mostly ignored by other systematic theologians. They are then in a position to make direct, theologically based proposals for dealing with the evil that they perceive to exist when shame abounds.

Hardy and Ford's theological approach to shame has many attractive aspects. However, some critical points need to be made about it.

First, I am not sure that they really take the reality of toxic shame seriously enough. Of course, it would be good if those who live in the valley of the shadow of deathly shame could transcend this through becoming part of a praising community. However, it is not clear that this is always possible for individuals, however faithful they might be. Overcoming isolation and alienation is a task as well as a vision. Hardy and Ford may be too quick to dismiss the insights of psychologists and others in trying to understand the condition of shamed people. If so, the optimistic project that they outline may be wishful thinking for many committed Christians. Building communities of faith and praise takes hard, practical work, not just enlivening visions and metaphors. Furthermore, as Hardy and Ford implicitly acknowledge in discussing the perversion of religion and religious institutions, such communities may be places where shame is denied rather than transcended. It is particularly oppressive for shamed people to have to pretend to be joyous or happy to avoid stigmatisation and rejection. It does them no good if they remain fundamentally shamed, alienated and inwardly oppressed while having to parrot the rhetoric of joy and praise in public for the sake of acceptance and conformity.

Hardy and Ford provide a positive, Christocentric, distinctively religious and theological framework and vision for understanding and overcoming shame. It is far more advanced than that produced by any other contemporary theologian. However, without some more practical bridges between vision and reality shamed individuals and groups may continue to perish. Finally, in common with the other theological approaches considered above, Hardy and Ford reject or ignore the Nietzschean insight which would be supported by thinkers like Klein (1988b) and Rizzuto (1979) that the notion of God might in and of itself contribute to the generation or exploitation of shame.

Perhaps the best future prospects for new theologies of shame that take human relationships and insights from social sciences seriously lie with feminist theologians. In a now classic article published in 1960, Valerie Saiving (1979) suggested that the then prevalent notions of sin, love and salvation were not universal. They reflected the situation and preoccupations of men with an emphasis on 'anxiety, estrangement . . . the conflict between necessity and freedom . . . identification of sin with pride, will-to-power, exploitation, self-assertiveness, and the treatment of others as objects rather than persons [and] its conception of redemption as restoring to man what he fundamentally lacks . . .' (Saiving 1979: 35). These issues, Saiving suggested, were not women's issues. For them, sin, salvation, love and temptation had to be differently construed:

[S]pecifically feminine forms of sin . . . are better suggested by such items as triviality, distractability, and diffuseness; lack of . . . focus; dependence on others for one's own self-definition; tolerance at the expense of standards of excellence; inability to respect the boundaries of privacy; sentimentality, gossipy sociability, and mistrust of reason – in short, underdevelopment or negation of the self. (Saiving 1979: 37.)

With these words, Saiving helped to initiate a rereading of the Christian theological tradition which, in principle, is much more open to taking shame seriously with its concerns about the underdevelopment, under-assertion and negation of the self. Redeeming shame is different from redeeming guilt. For women and other shamed people, redemption from sin might mean far more positive self-assertion, self-affirmation and action rather than more repentance, passivity, and ceasing to act in a definite, harmful way. Saiving's perceptions have been amplified and developed by others who have questioned traditional pictures of sin and salvation by asking 'what sin is for those who have little pride or sense of self' (Brock 1988: 2; Grey 1989).

Much of the work of feminist theologians has been to create a critique of the categories and priorities of the kinds of theology referred to above. It will be important to refer to this critique in subsequent chapters. In the meanwhile, it can be concluded that, with the possible exception of Hardy and Ford's work, the response of Christian theologians to the contemporary experience of shame has been weak and patchy.

Recent pastoral and pastoral theological responses to shame

There has been a flurry of interest in the topic of shame in the broad field of pastoral and practical theology over the last two decades, particularly in the USA. There shame has been an important cultural and psychological category for understanding the individual condition in late capitalist society. I will now consider some of the more significant contributions to thinking about and dealing with shame that have been made by pastoral theologians.

The work of John Patton

John Patton has long been interested in shame (Patton 1997). From his experience as a pastoral counsellor and academic, he has written what is, I believe, the most sensitive, scholarly, practical, and theologically well-informed work on this subject – a book somewhat misleadingly entitled *Is Human Forgiveness Possible?* (1985).

Patton argues that some people, particularly within families, seem unable to forgive those who have offended them. Such people suffer from a sense of shame that complements the guilt that may be felt by those who have wounded them. Shame is a condition that provokes people to defend against it, often by maintaining a sense of power, such as the power to forgive, or by an assertion of righteousness. Patton believes that these defensive strategies must be overcome if people are to be able to forgive those who have offended them. They will have to give up the defences of the power of forgiveness and of righteousness if they are to attain full reconciliation and communion with themselves and their fellows.

Within the religious environment there is an emphasis on the deliberate action of forgiveness. Against this, Patton argues that people only retrospectively discover that they have forgiven others when they have actually given up any claim to have the ability to do so: 'human forgiveness is not doing something but discovering something – that I am more like those who have hurt me than different from them. I am able to forgive when I discover that I am in no position to forgive' (Patton 1985: 16).

Enabling forgiveness requires understanding the nature of shame and acting to reduce its effects. However, the road to comprehension and action is obscured within the Christian tradition by an emphasis on guilt (Patton 1985: 39). While shame is more personal and relational, guilt is more rational and objective. Patton argues that Christianity and pastoral carers have a vested interest in maintaining the primacy of guilt because it is easier to understand, can be dealt with at a cognitive level, seems to require an immediate, quick, verbal response such as confession or catharsis, and allows pastors to feel some measure of power and control. They can do something instantly like pronouncing absolution instead of feeling powerless, even ashamed (Patton 1985: 89f., 126f.). Traditional Christian practices of penitence and forgiveness may well hide shame and the need for a more profound, personal and relational forgiveness that is accomplished by an individual person themselves finding the capacity to do this.

Patton turns to Kohut's (1971) self psychology to gain understanding of the origins and nature of shame within the context of the narcissistic personality. Shame is basically a response to a narcissistic wound. When a person has been wounded, they may defend against this shame with the responses of rage and power (including retaining the power to forgive or to withhold forgiveness), or of righteousness (i.e. being right). When these defences are used, there is no possibility of re-establishing full relations with others. The self is cut off.

The way forward is for people to accept and experience their own shame (Patton 1985: 186). This enables them to surrender their defences of rage, power and righteousness to discover the mutuality of forgiveness in healed relationships. They can then take responsibility for their lives and the real guilt that accompanies living. Often, the church and its representatives have felt that it is enough to emphasise the outward forms of forgiveness and formal words. However, such words are secondary and may even be irrelevant. The real pastoral task is to get alongside people who have sustained narcissistic wounds and cannot forgive because of the bonds of shame defences: 'pastoral caring is helping persons not with forgiveness but with the pain of being themselves' (Patton 1985: 186). By entering into sensitive, long-term relationships, pastoral workers may be able to help people to develop a sense of empathy for their own 'impoverished self' and surrender their sense of righteousness and the power to forgive. The 'function of the church and the ministry is not to supervise acts of forgiveness, but to provide relationships in which genuine humanity, including the possibility that I am forgiving, can be discovered' (Patton 1985: 186).

Patton briefly reviews, and takes creatively into account, most of the relevant theological literature pertaining to shame from the Bible onwards. From the biblical notion of righteousness, for example, he re-sites obedience and forgiveness within the context of fulfilling the demands of human relationships rather than performing specific acts or obeying particular laws. Patton's vision of the possibility of human forgiveness and overcoming shame is underwritten by the notion of the Kingdom of God as the context for forgiveness. Human forgiveness between persons functions as 'a witness that God's reconciliation has taken effect' (Patton 1985: 148). Because reconciliation is part of the life of the Kingdom it cannot be commanded, predicted or bidden, only dis-covered. Sometimes the church community can bear witness to and manifest such reconciliation. Pastoral carers, too, can help to point up the discovery of the Kingdom and of reconciliation if and when this occurs. However, Patton is realistic about the fallible, unpredictable nature of both the church and pastoral care (Patton 1985: 166). The process of helping people to come to terms with the pain of being them-selves does not carry with it guarantees of a successful outcome. It is a lengthy one, requiring much 'prayer and fasting' as people attempt to address deep narcissistic injuries (Patton 1985: 110).

Patton's book has many strengths. It is critical of traditional Christian views of forgiveness and presents a wider vision of reconciliation that takes seriously the personal problems that people may have in moving towards forgiveness. Patton makes no claims for the infallible therapeu-tic efficacy or benefits of Christian community or pastoral care. He is modest and practical in his suggestions for pastoral practice, acknowl-edging the problems of healing that exist for narcissistically wounded people who have to overcome much shame to discover the possibility of community and forgiveness. If it is mainly focussed on individuals and psychological understandings of shame, leaning heavily on the para-digm of self psychology, this is a feature of many other books also.

I do, however, have some reservations about Patton's approach. First, he appears to place the onus of change upon those who have been nar-cissistically injured by the offence or neglect of others, past or present. While it may be that ultimately forgiveness cannot be accomplished without shamed people overcoming their defences, this stance appears to leave no role for change on the part of those who wound and offend in the first place. Thus Patton's approach is potentially victim-blaming; it places responsibility for change and forgiveness with those who have had to bear most in the first place and may have least inner resources for effecting reconciliation. It would have been good if Patton had done something to sketch in the situation and responsibility of 'offenders' rather than 'victims', not least because some of the former might themselves be extensively afflicted by shame (Lamb 1996). Perhaps the Christian tradition would support the notions of victims changing to be reconciled with their offenders quite vigorously. However, this seems to ignore the politics and power relations that characterise oppressive, injurious relationships. These are more apparent now that child abuse has become prominent than they were when Patton wrote his book.

Secondly, I applaud Patton's rather modest claims for pastoral care and counselling as a ministry of support and discernment which does not make people 'better' but rather assists them as they try to discover the reality of forgiveness and the presence of 'good news' where it exists. However, while I agree that Christian pastoral care may have a lot to be modest about in relation to healing shame, I suspect Patton avoids the practical questions of how Christian thought and practice might beneficially intersect with shame and shamed people. It is not good enough to stand aside from issues of structure, organisation, theology and outcomes in pastoral care in favour of a role of simply witnessing to, and possibly articulating, the presence of reconciliation if it comes to be present. Christian ministry and practice must impact on shame and narcissism, albeit that its influence may be marginal. If such activity has any effect at all, more should be done to maximise its powers to heal narcissistic wounds and to minimise any injurious effects it might have. To this extent, the reconciliation figured by the Kingdom of God might become more tangible and less arbitrary. The quest for understanding and informed intervention does not necessarily deliver pastoral care into becoming a kind of psychological technology rather than an effective enterprise of theologically informed witness.

My final reservation has to do with Patton's assertion that the power to forgive must be surrendered if reconciliation is to take place. Patton argues that the power to forgive is a shame-based defence, extending his critique to the church which maintains a sense of its own power by retaining its power to pronounce forgiveness on people. If Patton is right here, as I believe he is, then it is plausible to argue that he should be more critical of the notion of God that he employs. If God has the power to forgive and reconcile, should this perhaps also be seen as a kind of distortion and defence that sets God apart or alienates God from creation? In which case, does our understanding of God need fundamental reconstruction to acknowledge that God's saving work is ultimately a relinquishing of the power to forgive?

This radical implication of Patton's thought is consonant with, and extends, some modern theological notions of God as surrendering God's power in an act of *kenosis* that makes Godself powerless, a 'crucified God' (Moltmann 1974). A God who is powerless, even to forgive or effect reconciliation, puts the responsibility for reconciliation squarely on the shoulders of living humanity. This is a daunting picture, but one that may be appropriate in the contemporary world since it overcomes the problem of ontological shame whereby people feel inferior and defiled before an omnipotent, omniscient other. The trouble is that it totally undermines traditional atonement theory. It also threatens the ontology of divine forgiveness and reconciliation that underlies Patton's book. A powerless God shares the reality of contemporary powerlessness. There is no underlying divine action into which human beings can sometimes insert themselves. There is just the hard work of continuing to effect reconciliation and forgiveness as a human activity that may be inspired by the generative image of a helpless God who wholly shares the condition of powerless and powerful humanity. This adds a new urgency to the need for human beings to take responsibility for their lives and to find ways of living with the guilt that living inevitably incurs.

The work of Donald Capps

Donald Capps, a leading North American pastoral theologian, has returned to shame in various works over the last two decades, approaching it from different directions in connection with other themes. So, for example, he has written at least two essays that bear upon the significance of understanding shame and narcissism in relation to St Augustine (Capps 1990a, 1990b). Here I shall briefly review his contributions to understanding shame in the modern world, particularly in relation to pastoral work.

In the course of discussing pastoral care throughout the life-cycle and its life-stages (Erikson 1965), Capps identifies the role of the pastor as personal comforter in relation to the pain of shame as being one of considerable significance (Capps 1983: 81ff.). In this context, Capps understands shame to be a 'psychological condition' that has its roots early on in childhood, comprising 'the first major threat to the growing child's newly won sense of being "at home" in the world' (Capps 1983: 81). Drawing mainly on the work of Lynd (1958), Capps describes the phenomenological experience of shame, the personal effects of shame (for example, its capacity to erode trust in self, others and world), and the effects of shame on the world view of individuals in exposing the tragic dimension of relations between parents and children and making people aware of the difficulties of communication and the pain of isolation.

Shame represents a wound to the self and a threat to identity. Instead of avoiding shame, the Christian response to this condition should be one of exposing one's shameful self 'again and again' to God; 'the core of Christian identity is to be "exposed before God"' (Capps 1983: 89). Following the example of St Augustine who exposed himself to God and so found God no longer to be hidden or absent, Christians should open themselves up to God in self-disclosive prayer. This will allow them to gain God's view on their shameful experience, facilitating self-acceptance and allowing individuals to experience connection instead of isolation. The job of pastoral carers as personal comforters is not to smooth over the wound of shame. Ignoring the 'official theology' of the church which has concentrated on guilt to the exclusion of shame, they are to facilitate the kind of self-exposure that allows individuals to accept their shame so that they can then end their isolation from God and from other people: 'Jesus' experience on the cross is the paradigmatic shame experience for Christians. For him the cross entailed self-exposure and incongruity, threat to trust and total self-involvement, tragedy and isolation' (Capps 1983: 92). By exposing, facing up to, and embracing their shame, Christians identify themselves with Jesus' experience of shame which was of the 'most excruciating kind'. To embrace our shameful selves is 'to identify with Jesus and thereby to experience God as no longer hidden' (Capps 1983: 92).

In *The Depleted Self* (1993), shame is situated within a discussion of narcissistic depletion based on the work of self psychologists like Kohut (1971) and Morrison (1989). Capps argues that the notion of sin needs to be reinterpreted because shame appears to have replaced guilt as the main category for exploring the sense of human 'wrongfulness' in selves that are often fundamentally shaped by narcissism (Capps 1993: 4ff.). He goes on to explore the nature and emergence of narcissistic selves in contemporary society, drawing on thinkers like Lasch (1991, 1984) and Sennett (1993), emphasising that this kind of self is, in Morrison's (1989) terminology, a 'shameful self', a self that is depleted, hollow and hungry (Capps 1993: 33).

Christian theology and practice has not taken shame and the narcissistic, shameful self seriously even though many Christians may themselves experience emotional privations that lead to personal shame and self-contempt: 'Christian theology has well-developed theologies of guilt, while the majority of its constituency is struggling with the debilitating,

demoralizing, and even dehumanizing effects of shame' (Capps 1993: 35).
The emphasis upon guilt and the dangers of 'selfishness' means that little
attention has been paid within the religious community to the depradations and prevalence of shame. Furthermore, Christians may even be
encouraged to renounce the desire and need to be mirrored in such a way
as to attain a proper sense of selfhood, thus denying the benevolence and
necessity of divine mirroring which is suggested by, for example, the
words of the Aaronic blessing (Num. 6.24–6).

Capps suggests that Christians need to experience good mirroring
that responds to the need to 'affirm a brighter world than we had known'
(Capps 1993: 68). This affirmation or 'reliable mirroring', which comes
from God but is refracted through pastoral relationships, is not a
grandiose fantasy, but the necessary assurance that 'we are the gleam in
God's eye, that we are God's beloved, in whom God is well pleased'
(Capps 1993: 69).

A whole chapter of *The Depleted Self* is devoted to looking at the place
of sin in a shame-based theology, arguing that shame demands a theological response. Predictably, Capps considers shame to be a psychological condition, the self-owned experience of deficiency and failure to live
up one's own ideals (Capps 1993: 72). Once again he draws on Lynd
(1958) to characterise shame experience as self-involving, self-constrict-
ing and estranging. It is within this context that he believes theology
should be a 'source of therapeutic wisdom' (Capps 1993: 84). However,
to move towards a theology of shame requires the displacement of the
distorting prominence of guilt. Furthermore, theology must take into
account three important 'problematics of the self'.

First, the divided nature of the self between true and false self,
grandiose and idealising self, must be taken into account. Secondly, the
defensive or victimised self must be considered, remembering that
victimised selves are not necessarily innocent or unoffending. Thirdly,
the condition of the depleted self as the victim of long-term shaming
must be taken into account. In connection with the depleted self in particular, Capps again invokes the importance of Christ's death:

A theology of shame will not focus on a quality that marked Christ's radical
difference from us – his guiltlessness – but on an experience he shared with us:
the sense of failure, the dejection of defeat, and the realization that one cannot
remedy the failure. This is the deepest meaning of Gethsemane from the perspective of a theology of shame. The story of the cross is a story of the depleted
self. For Jesus, it was not primarily the public humiliation that made this a
shameful event, but the inner awareness, the self realization, that, from his own
perspective, his life had failed. (Capps 1993: 99)

In the light of this contentious and evidentially unsupported judgment, it is suggested that if the object for the theology of guilt is the sin of pride (that is, an inflated sense of self), the corresponding object for a theology of shame should be *acedia* or despair that frustrates the work of self-repair (cf. Bringle 1990).

Capps moves towards creating a theology of shame by suggesting a number of biblical stories and images that would seem to provide theologically based therapeutic insight and wisdom for the shamed and depleted. Surprisingly, however, he omits reference to texts which overtly treat of shame, for example, the story of Adam and Eve in Genesis.

The story of Jonah gives insight into the narcissistic condition. It describes the experience of a man, initially divided, depleted and defensive, dealing with a God who acts as an autonomous, shaming authority in Sennett's (1993) terms. Capps suggests that this story should be seen as an exploration of the narcissistic self in a kind of dream about false self and a false God. Jonah has to wake up from this dream in order to be able to take charge of his life, to gain a proper sense of autonomy, and to create satisfactory relations with others and with God.

Capps argues that the story of the woman who anointed Jesus' feet with precious ointment, in which Jesus appreciates and defends her action, is a paradigm example of mutual self-trust that produces affirmation. Jesus was able to accept rather than humiliating the woman because of his own youthful experiences 'in which his own belief in himself was graciously, powerfully affirmed' (Capps 1993: 164). This kind of response, based on the bond of love, provides Christian warrant for individuals developing and having faith in themselves.

Next, Capps cites the story of Jesus telling his mother Mary and his beloved disciple at the crucifixion that they should behold each other as mother and son (John 19.26–7). This is to be regarded as the beginning of a new era in which the bond of shame is replaced by the bond of love, positive mirroring occurs, and authority and relationship is not based on shame and shaming. 'God is the one who authorizes and underwrites our mutual beholdings' (Capps 1993: 166–7). This story, which illustrates God's way with humanity, provides religious grounds for the overcoming of relationships of shame.

Capps' book concludes with the moral imperative of self-care and self-affirmation based on the example of Jesus. He suggests that the stories from the New Testament that he has cited 'make clear that the central concern of Jesus in face-to-face encounters was to focus attention on the self and its heroic struggle to survive' (Capps 1993: 167). Capps arbitratily asserts that: 'Aware that, in his younger years, he had been an endangered self, Jesus was conscious of the dangers of self-loss. He was unusually responsive to those who were seeking ways to discover and affirm their true selves . . . (Capps 1993: 167). Thus the example of Jesus supports the struggle against 'the unbearable prejudice against the self' (Capps 1993: 169).

Shame next appears in *Agents of Hope* (1995). In the context of arguing that what pastoral workers and carers most have to offer to others is the gift of hope, Capps cites shame, together with apathy and despair, as one of the major threats to hope (Capps 1995b: 98ff.). Shame occurs when individuals find that the future does not turn out as they had fantasised and predicted. This induces a sense of failure, as well as the suspicion of self-delusion, corollary doubt about the self, and a diminished sense of trust in self and the future. If we invest ourselves in a future that turns out to be different from what is predicted and expected, the reality exposes us baldly as failures.

From this basis, Capps goes on briefly to explore shame and the bipolar self, drawing on the work of Kohut. He also considers the defensive strategies adopted against shame described by Kaufman (1985) and then recommends Kaufman's therapeutic methods as very helpful in pastoral work. Turning again to the woman who anointed the feet of Jesus with oil, Capps reaffirms the importance of engendering and encouraging self-affirmation in people (Capps 1995b: 133ff.). He also returns to the notion of exposure as the way out of shame, following Michael Lewis' suggestion that confession to others can help in coming to terms with shame (Lewis 1992). Confession allows people to re-enact their shame, to objectify themselves, and to look at themselves dispassionately. Intensification of shame is one way of facing it. Pastoral workers can help by becoming informal and occasional confessors to shamed people who need the liberation of exposure.

Capps' work highlights shame as a phenomenon requiring a practical and theological response. It also expands the interdisciplinary understanding of shame, introducing theologians to some of the main ways of interpreting shame, including some that imply a social context, causes and effects. Capps has argued powerfully for a theology of shame that counterbalances the traditional priority given to guilt, as well as advancing some theological motifs that might contribute to it. Furthermore, he has suggested ways in which people might be helped to recover from shame by various pastoral methods. However, his work also has limitations.

First, Capps completely ignores the important work of fellow pastoral theologian John Patton which draws on much the same sources as his own. This is unfortunate, for Patton's practical and theological concerns are very similar to those of Capps. Capps' discussion would also have been greatly enriched by some consideration of the work of Barth, Bonhoeffer and others on shame.

Secondly, while Capps displays some awareness of the social and cultural factors and context involved in narcissism and shame, his analysis and response to this condition is basically confined to the psychological and individual.

Thirdly, although Capps has written about shame over a number of years, his basic understanding and thinking about shame, especially about its pastoral treatment, have not been much developed or refined. So, for example, some kind of exposure to God and others is still the solution for dysfunctional shame in both his first (1983) and last (1995) works. While the range of Capps' references has increased somewhat, this does not seem to have much expanded Capps' range of possible response. Two, more fundamental, criticisms remain.

The first relates to the project of constructing a theology of shame. Capps (1993) has many useful things to say about the need for a theology of shame. However, his own attempt to create a theology that is a resource of 'therapeutic wisdom' turns out to be a rather dubious fig leaf. Capps suggests that the use of biblical stories and material such as the life of Jonah, the experience of Jesus, and stories from his life can be mined to provide illuminating theological material and a basis for tackling shame. However, ultimately he provides little such material and it does not add much of substance to understandings and treatments of shame. Furthermore, close examination shows his approach to be as much fanciful as imaginative in terms of selection and interpretation.

In the case of the story of Jonah, Capps' interpretation that it is a kind of narcissistic dream is an interesting one that might cast light on the text in an imaginative way. However, this does not cast much light on to contemporary experiences of shame. Moving to the more normative New Testament material, here again it is not clear what Capps' interpretations really add to understandings and approaches to shame other than sketchily to legitimise the importance of taking shame seriously.

I have castigated Capps elsewhere for his somewhat haphazard, eisegetical approach to biblical texts (Pattison 1993). This seems to reach a kind of apotheosis in relation to shame. The problem arises because Capps appears to want to legitimate contemporary approaches on the basis of an appeal to the historical Jesus and his experience. While appearing to be scholarly and objective, Capps allows himself to be casual and pietistic here. So, for example, Capps suggests that in Jesus' encounter with the woman who anointed his feet Jesus took a non-shaming approach of mutual affirmation. This may or may not be true. We do not know what approach Jesus thought he was taking. Nor do we know what he thought about the self or shame. We do not know what his experience of shame was. Nor do we know whether Jesus felt that his life and ministry were a failure when he was crucified, or that he felt a sense of personal shame.

One hard-bitten, non-confessional New Testament scholar surprisingly allows that Jesus may have 'died disappointed' (Sanders 1995: 276). It is possible to argue from lack of evidence that Jesus actually sought and in some sense welcomed his death which formed a deliberate culmination to his ministry (Harvey 1985; Klassen 1996). Another recent scholarly book on the life of Jesus has no place in its index for the self-consciousness or self-awareness of Jesus (Theissen and Merz 1998). An authoritative book about Jesus by a devout evangelical biblical scholar summarises the problem with a reference in the index: 'psychology of [Jesus] (inaccessible to us)' (Wright 1996: 739). It is not clear that the individual personality structure or selfhood of Jesus would have been self-perceived in the same way that a modern Western individual would perceive it, nor, therefore, that his understanding of shame, living in a more corporate 'we-conscious' society, would be the same (Malina 1983, 1996; Moxnes 1988).

The difficulty of establishing what the man Jesus thought, felt, or experienced becomes clearer if the issue of his guilt or sinlessness is considered. Ludemann suggests that '[i]f we consider Jesus as a human being we must grant that he was neither sinless nor without error' (Ludemann 1997: xxii). Nineham argues that one cannot infer truths about the historical Jesus from a lack of evidence: 'To prove an historical negative, such as the sinlessness of Jesus, is notoriously difficult to the point of impossibility' (Nineham 1977: 188). Discussing Jesus' experience of guilt or sin, Nineham suggests that

because of the cultural gulf which separates us from Jesus and his times, what moral perfection, or 'being the man for others', would have meant for him and his contemporaries might well be significantly different from what such phrases imply for us. We must therefore recognize that if the historical Jesus were to walk into the room . . . the first disturbing impression might be not so much his greatness as his strangeness. (Nineham 1977: 195)

Capps ignores this cultural gulf, basing his theology of shame on a simplistic reading of the New Testament. A biblically based theology worthy of the name would need to be much more critical and discerning than this in the interests of being truthful not only about the past but about the present with the continuities and radical discontinuities that exist between two worlds and two texts (Pattison 1993; Ludemann 1997). Capps therefore stands accused of a kind of imagistic, tokenistic use of biblical images and stories that is opportunistic and devotional rather than critical. The effect is drastically to reduce the value and putative power of the 'therapeutic wisdom' that he claims to supply.

Readers should probably also be wary of the practical approaches and techniques that Capps suggests for dealing with shame. It will be recalled that he argues that the way to diminish shame is to enable exposure to others and to God, either through personal prayer (1983) or through informal confession to others. These suggestions are limited in scope. This approach does little to tackle such practical difficulties as the trust and time that might be needed before exposure seems possible to a shamed person. It also presupposes that exposure to God or one's co-religionists will be a positive, therapeutic experience. One's internalised image of God may be a persecutory, hostile introject (Rizzuto 1979; Klein 1988b). One's co-religionists may find it very difficult to cope with another's sense of shame.

Personally, I have often found that it is difficult to be totally honest in prayer (one has internal defences) and that being so may simply exacerbate feelings of inferiority, defilement, alienation etc. Similarly, it has often been my impression that pastors and others do not want to know about the things that I feel ashamed of – they have defences, too. Capps takes no account of religious factors and church communities actually engendering or exacerbating shame through their words and actions. It is doubtful that his suggestions would have real value for many deeply shamed people, even if his ultimate aim of helpful exposure might be laudable.The kind of gradual, personally supportive approach adopted by Patton, which might eventually allow the surrendering of shame-bound responses and defences, seems a good deal more realistic and less invasive.

Capps' approach to shame is important and suggestive. However, it is more impressive from a distance than it is on close examination, being both fragmented and fairly repetitive. In particular, while Capps' eloquent call for a practical theology of shame is valid, his own positive response to this is flimsy and poorly supported by the theological method which he deploys in using biblical texts. It seems perverse in this connection that he ignores most of the biblical texts that overtly treat of shame. Furthermore, the practical responses that Capps suggests seem partial and inadequate at best, possibly harmful and unrealistic at worst. Capps thus signally fails in the task of creating a practical pastoral theology and approach to shame. This failure is made more conspicuous by the subtlety and comprehensiveness of Patton's work upon which Capps inexplicably fails to draw.

The work of Lewis Smedes

Lewis Smedes' *Shame and Grace* (1993) is a short, accessible book from an evangelical perspective. It is heavily illustrated with stories and anecdotes, some taken from Smedes' own experience, that illustrate shame and responses to it. It seems to be a kind of self-help manual that enables Christian believers to recognise and come to terms with their own shame by accepting grace.

Smedes sees shame as a 'heavy feeling' of not measuring up that can easily lead to a feeling of self-disgust and fundamental unacceptability (Smedes 1993: 5): 'Shame is a vague, undefined heaviness that presses on our spirit, dampens our gratitude for the goodness of life, and slackens the free flow of joy' (Smedes 1993: 9). Having distinguished shame from cognate conditions such as guilt, embarrassment, depression and frustration, Smedes identifies types of people who may be shame-prone. These include those who are overly responsible, obsessive moralisers, approval addicts, the 'never-deserving', and people condemned by their dream memories (Smedes 1993: 17ff.).

Smedes identifies four varieties of shame. Healthy shame arises when there is conflict between the individual's true, inner self – the ideal self that is patterned on Jesus and God's call – and the false self. Such shame informs the individual that something is wrong and nudges him or her in the direction of the true, ideal self amidst the vagaries of the actual and the false self (Smedes 1993: 31ff.). Unhealthy shame is based on deceit and untrue perceptions arising from the false self. These distort a person's perception of themselves so that, for example, they may see themselves as perfect or wholly defiled. Among the sources of the deceptive, inauthentic false self are culture, graceless religion, and unaccepting parents, all of which can set up ideals that people cannot meet (Smedes 1993: 37ff.). Spiritual shame is evoked by seeing or being seen by God and feeling unworthy and humbled. Smedes feels this shame is real and appropriate. Its painfulness is moderated by the experience of God as loving presence rather than simply judge or king (Smedes 1993: 45ff.). Finally, social shame occurs when various kinds of social rejection occur that pertain either to groups or to individuals (Smedes 1993: 52ff.). Smedes concludes this part of the book with a consideration of the value of the individual's sense of shame, arguing along with Schneider (1987a) that shame can act as the necessary preserver of personal mystery and privacy (Smedes 1993: 61ff.).

Turning to sources of unhealthy shame, Smedes argues that this can be engendered by parents who disown their children and do not take pride and interest in them (Smedes 1993: 69ff.). In addition, churches can exacerbate or feed shame in various ways – for example, by perfectionism, emphasising duty and the unworthiness of human beings, and failing to provide a sense of affirmation and acceptance (Smedes 1993: 77ff.). People can fan their own shame by, for example, discounting their positive features, judging themselves against perfectionist ideals, and transforming criticism of what they might do into fundamental criticism of what they are (Smedes 1993: 83ff.). In trying to escape from shame, people adopt various responses such as doing good, doing evil, embracing and revelling in shame, or becoming legalistic and self-righteous (Smedes 1993: 91ff.).

For Smedes, the healing of unhealthy shame, 'the shame we don't deserve', lies not in the inadequate 'secular' methods of lowering ideals to a manageable level, living up to ideals, or accepting oneself as one is, but rather with 'a spiritual experience of grace' (Smedes 1993: 105). Grace in this context is 'the experience of being accepted before we become acceptable' (Smedes 1993: 107). It represents the work of God in pardoning, accepting, providing spiritual energy and producing a sense of gratitude in the shamed individual. This enables them to recover a sense of the inner child which is accepted for what it is, not because it is judged deserving, worthy, or acceptable (Smedes 1993: 108ff.). Grace works to remove the fear of rejection that lies at the heart of shame. It recognises the worth in persons that allows them gradually to accept themselves and to come to terms with shame (Smedes 1993: 119). Grace is not a magical cure-all. Although it can be experienced by individuals directly within themselves on their own, traces of grace are also to be found in a very concrete form in the accepting attitudes of other people such as friends, and within religious communities such as churches.

The 'lightness of grace' that overcomes the inner fear of rejection enables individuals to come to terms with those who have shamed them by forgiving them. It also helps them gradually to accept themselves and to move towards being the true self that God intends them to be, though this may take a long time to complete. A sense of grace-based pride or elation should emerge that is accompanied by joy and gratitude rather than arrogance as individuals move toward realising Christ as their true inner self (Smedes 1993: 155). In this process, false self and unhealthy shame are disposed of in favour of discovering the true, Christ-based self and the healthy shame that continues to prompt movement towards this condition of the self. Joy, therefore, returns (Smedes 1993: 159ff.).

Smedes' book is clear, well expressed and interestingly illustrated with stories about experiences of shame. Unlike most authors, Smedes is overt about his own experience of this condition. This lends much credibility and practical wisdom to his approach as he actually follows the advice that many give which is to expose and share shame instead of allowing it to be hidden away. Smedes is almost unique among theologians in being specifically critical of the part that religious communities and ideas can play in engendering or exploiting shame. Furthermore, he allows for some measure of social causation and expectation in the emergence of shame. Smedes has a realistic sense of the time that healing undeserved shame might take and acknowledges the importance of human relationships in healing shame as well as creating it. His approach is thus in many ways a sensible, practical, specific and humane one, not an exercise in high-flown generalisation.

Nonetheless, Smedes' approach presents some critical problems. The downside of writing a popular, accessible book is that he often does not attribute the sources of his theoretical views of shame. Despite some awareness of social context, judging from the sources he cites in his bibliography, he draws mainly upon psychological views of shame from a typical range of authorities such as Kaufman and Block Lewis. His approach is therefore fundamentally individualistic.

Curiously, although he lists a representative selection of the psychological literature on shame, psychological and therapeutic methods for dealing with shame hardly make any appearance in the book. Although Smedes seems to set great store by grace coming through other people, he deliberately excludes humanistic methods for coming to terms with shame, such as modifying ideals or accepting ourselves as we are, in favour of having a direct experience of divine grace. This opens up a practical hole in his strategy for helping self and others. There is no infallible way of ensuring that people do gain an appropriate experience of divine grace, nor that they can be healed by religious experience and methods on their own. Possibly this shows the measure of Smedes' faith in direct divine intervention. However, it does not provide much of a ladder for many people, particularly non-believers, to come to terms with unhealthy shame. It is difficult to see why Smedes should not see the need to use 'human' wisdom and knowledge to resolve shame when he uses such wisdom to understand the condition.

It is equally difficult to understand and give content to Smedes' view of human being. Smedes suggests that people may experience themselves as false self, actual self, and ideal or real self, the last category being a religious category based upon personal life in Christ. However, he fails to spell out what the essence of the real self might consist of, and what its nature and implications might be. He also opens up a potentially damaging split between ideal and reality that might exacerbate shame in individuals who perceive themselves to be shamed and inadequate in the face of too many vague ideals. He admits that the notion of finding a life in Christ is open to the abuse of individuals engaging in grandiose fantasies and over-identification with an omnipotent other that might distort the true nature of the personality (Smedes 1993: 155).

Finally, like Patton, Smedes' prescriptions for dealing with shame mostly involve change in the shamed individual who has to forgive not only him- or herself but also those who have shamed him or her. It is important that shamed individuals should not become trapped in the past. Forgiving self and others may be part of moving beyond it. Nonetheless, this restricts the possibility of others changing and of structuring rules and behaviours so that shame is not induced in the future. The prospect of victim blaming here inadvertently rides again. The crucial importance of forgiveness in Smedes' approach may come from having to give a prominent place to a traditional theological concept that has been of huge significance in Protestant thought. Unfortunately, relating all the ills of the human condition to offence and its correlative forgiveness means that other aspects of considering and removing the stain of shame are ignored or distorted.

In conclusion, then, while Smedes' approach is broad, accessible, experiential and humane, it is less useful, well explained, and exhaustive than it appears on first sight. Smedes' humanistically derived insights into the nature of shame are vitiated by the importance he gives to a particular view of providence, faith and atonement. This prevents him from being as practical as he might be about how unhealthy shame might be countered and tackled in both Christian believers and in non-believers. Not everyone will have the faith to overcome shame by overtly religious means. Even very faithful people may find that faith does not heal chronic unhealthy shame, just as it does not heal every physical disease. The onus is on Christian theorists who believe in God's purposes for all people, therefore, to take seriously the gap between disorder and cure and to either account for it in a way that preserves God's love and benevolence, or to bridge it in practical terms using whatever means are to hand. If this is not tackled, Christian hope for the world is in danger of becoming pious delusion for some individuals.

The work of James Fowler

One of the most substantial recent contributions to the practical theology of shame is to be found in James Fowler's *Faithful Change* (1996). Here, five chapters are devoted to personal and social shame. This is seen as a good example of the need for emotional healing and reconstructive change for individuals who need to grow while facing the realities of postmodern life in the light of faith (Fowler 1996:10). Without facing the challenge of shame, there will be no possibility of recovering 'spiritual aliveness and integrity' (Fowler 1996: 93).

Fowler acknowledges the ubiquity yet hiddenness of shame in modern society (Fowler 1996: 91). He defines shame as an emotion of self-assessment and draws upon an undifferentiated synthesis of psychological and neuropsychological material from authorities such as Schneider, Erikson, Lynd and Block Lewis to understand it. Following Tomkins and Nathanson, Fowler argues that shame has an innate basis in human physiology as an auxiliary affect that is matched by the auxiliary affect of confidence-pride (Fowler 1996: 97ff.). In a subsequent discussion of shame, guilt and conscience, Fowler follows Schneider in arguing for the importance of discretion shame as a custodian of personal worthiness. This type of shame is distinguished from 'disgrace' shame that arises when the whole self is found to be defective (Fowler 1996: 104ff.). Next, Fowler rather idiosyncratically defines five different types of shame that comprise the 'spectrum of shame' (Fowler 1996: 113ff.). These are: healthy shame that protects relationships between people; perfectionist shame that is based on the false self; shame due to enforced minority status, such as being Black in a discriminatory society; toxic shame that comes from having to create a false, public self in order to survive a dysfunctional family; and shamelessness, that is, the absence of shame in people who have not learned how to trust others.

Finally, Fowler considers the relationship between shame and grace, arguing that the story of Adam and Eve in Genesis is about shame, not about pride and lust that lead to guilt. Fowler believes that the story is essentially about the 'fall' into self-consciousness, separation, and responsibility that all humans experience as children growing up and entering a relational world with other people who are different. In this psychodynamically and theologically insightful context, 'shame is not the act of sin'.

Rather, it is the subjective amplification of the objective fact of the potential for separation or destruction of relation involved in the sinful act. Shame provisionally interrupts the pursuit of sin in order to provide a time for self-aware evaluation for the sake of avoiding a more serious breach. (Fowler 1996: 136)

This view of shame as part of human evolution and growth rather than 'fall' from perfection supports an Irenaean view of redemption rather than that of Augustine (Hick 1966). Fowler moves on then to look at Nietzsche's view of Christianity, countering the sense of alienation, anger and *ressentiment* that Nietzsche displayed towards the oppressive character of the religion of his birth with the life of Jesus himself. This demonstrates acceptance for people who are shamed and excluded, such as the woman taken in adultery or the Gerasene demoniac: 'Jesus offers a quality of really seeing each of the persons and conveying such acceptance and regard that they find a new relation to him, to God, and to the communities of which they are a part' (Fowler 1996: 144). If only Nietzsche had been able to accept the kind of grace that was apparent in Jesus' life and work instead of finding it threatening in his solitude, Fowler laments, 'who can know what so fertile a mind and so sensitive a soul might have offered' (Fowler 1996: 144). On this rather inconclusive note, Fowler concludes his discussion of shame.

I am disappointed in Fowler's treatment of shame. Although his concluding theological perceptions about the nature of the fall of Adam and Eve are interesting and to some extent original (though they draw heavily on Bonhoeffer's *Ethics*), there is little of originality in this work. Fowler's account of shame is derivative and uncritical of its psychological sources so that a kind of haphazard, idiosyncratic synthesis occurs (Pattison 1986). His narrative and discussion are fragmentary, and to some extent incoherent. Ultimately, Fowler makes no creative proposals for concrete, practical, theological or therapeutic responses to shame. It is thus difficult to see how his work helps in any direct way to meet its self-avowed goal of meeting the spiritual challenge of shame.

The work of Simon Robinson

One of the fullest, most interesting and most specific responses to shame from a pastoral theologian comes from Simon Robinson (1998). Robinson argues that many clients who seek counselling, particularly those who have experienced child abuse, inhabit a moral world that is 'characterized by sin and bound together by shame'. The marks of sin that he recognises include distortion of reality, denial and distortion of moral responsibility, a fragmented world in which the person is alienated from self, others and God, the denial of hope in others and in God, and the denial of responsibility for self, thoughts, feelings, actions, and for moving on (Robinson 1998: 32). This condition of sin is maintained by the presence of toxic shame that is basically acquired through failure to establish satisfactory relationships in early childhood. Shame-bound persons are unable to change their negative perceptions of the self and to move on or behave differently.

The solvent for this condition is to establish a pastoral counselling relationship built upon agapeic person-centredness. Such a relationship is characterised by honesty or veracity, and by fidelity. Within it, the interpersonal bridge may be re-established through mutuality. Internalised shame is returned to its origins so that the client's story comes out into the open and she is able to own and take responsibility for it. Finally, an internal healing process takes place in the relationship as the client learns to mourn the unsatisfactory parents of the past. The client is then freed to explore new identities, meanings and behaviours in life – she becomes a creator as well as an interpreter of her own moral experience. The result is a person who can take responsibility 'for understanding values and virtues and, indeed, responsibility for understanding her own sinful nature and moving forward' (Robinson 1998: 43).

I have much sympathy for Robinson's vision and proposals. Establishing relationships is essential to alleviating shame, and the alleviation of shame is vital if people are to move into more satisfactory relationships with self and others, as well as into taking more realistic responsibility of various kinds. However, Robinson's approach must also come under critical scrutiny. This will show that, perhaps, he bases his assertions more on hope than experience.

It should be said first that Robinson has consulted only a limited range of sources on the nature and treatment of shame, principally Fowler (1996) and one of Kaufman's early works. This delivers him into a very particular, psychological approach to shame and healing shame, notwithstanding the assertion that '[s]hame is a complex phenomenon with no simple, agreed typology' (Robinson 1998: 33). One of the effects of pursuing individualistic, therapeutic and psychological models in this way may be to raise, once again, the possibility of victim blaming in which it is up to the shamed person to change and forgive rather than the shaming victimisers.

More seriously, Robinson's definition of sin seems to be somewhat arbitrary and it is not clear from whence it is drawn. Furthermore, he does not define exactly what *agape* is, or how this might be different from the unconditional positive regard that people might expect to find in almost any counselling relationship, whether religious or non-religious. It is thus difficult to know what real difference *agape* might make. Robinson asserts that agapeistic counselling relationships need to be undergirded by a community that 'embodies agape' (Robinson 1998: 43). But what would communities embodying *agape* look like? One might hope that Christian communities are full of other-respecting love and fidelity. Unfortunately, this is often not the case in practice.

This poses a further problem: where are agapeic pastoral counsellors to be found? Many pastoral workers are poor at counselling and rela-tionships, perhaps needing agapeic pastoral counselling themselves. How are such persons to be helped to develop agapeistic skills? Perhaps all this talk of *agape* is not significant anyway. Ultimately, Robinson uses Kaufman's thoroughly non-religious categories and understandings to structure the counselling task and process.

Further issues arise in relation to the empirical validity of Robinson's processes. Robinson claims to base his understandings upon 'work with survivors of child abuse'. He does not make it clear whether this work is his own or that of others. Neither does he suggest how long a person might need to be in counselling, or how often, for *agape* to do its work. Nor, more significantly, does he really show how agapeistic work with such people really works by using examples or statistics.

Although on a first reading Robinson's work appears specific and practical, it proves, like many other pastoral theological approaches, to be more in the realm of pious hope than in that of empirical experience. It is difficult not to conclude that Robinson, like many other pastoral theologians, radically underestimates the difficulty of helping people to escape from toxic personality shame. The therapeutic literature, reviewed above, showed that healing shame is a long, difficult process. It is doubtful whether non-specific *agape* is the panacea that can swiftly heal the pain of shame.

Other contributions to the pastoral care and pastoral theology of shame
Many books and articles contribute in various ways to an understanding of shame. Here, I note the general nature of some of these contributions and what they add to pastoral understandings and practices.

Whitehead and Whitehead (1994) consider shame in the context of advocating the need for Christians to befriend negative emotions. Shame and guilt are emotions that monitor the boundaries of belonging. Drawing on a standard selection of modern psychological authors, but also on Jung, Williams (1993), and the New Testament notion of honour, the Whiteheads discuss the nature of healthy shame. It is ambivalent and 'a dangerous dynamic in the process of socialization' (Whitehead and Whitehead 1994: 109f.). Shame can facilitate both conformity and resistance in social relationships. It promotes necessary virtues such as humility, and dignity which is an enduring awareness of one's own worth. Shame is distinguished from guilt by the fact that it addresses worth while guilt addresses correctness.

Uniquely, the Whiteheads devote a whole chapter to social shame and the quest for honour and dignity in society which can use shame to exclude and stigmatise: 'Religion plays a highly ambiguous role in the realm of shame and belonging' (Whitehead and Whitehead 1994: 153). Ultimately, social shame is transformed and healed by individuals appropriating a sense of their worth and acceptance in God's sight. Thus they escape the quest for social acceptability, respectability and conformity. The naked, unashamed, crucified Jesus who maintains his sense of worth in the sight of God transforms the nature of shame and belonging, allowing people to see God face to face (Whitehead and Whitehead 1994: 156). The Whiteheads use a wide range of sources and have interesting ideas to contribute about the nature of shame and ways of dealing with it. Unfortunately, many of these are only briefly set out.

In *The Image of God* (1995), Howe briefly outlines how theological concepts might affect the way in which shamed people might be dealt with in pastoral care. While preserving an important place for healthy shame, he suggests that 'shame is a cry of disbelief that God believes in us' (Howe 1995: 156). Howe juxtaposes various kinds of dysfunctional shame experience under the heading of certain biblical ideas and texts. He does not, however, demonstrate any practical techniques that might help people to see themselves through the affirming gaze of God's eyes with the lenses of faith beyond suggesting non-specific pastoral counselling and the kind of twelve-step programme advocated by Bradshaw (1988).

A much more grounded, practical approach to shame is to be found in Ramsay (1991). This brief article is packed with practical wisdom about working with women who have been shamed through child and sexual abuse. Ramsay recognises that this destroys basic trust and that helping people means spending much time with them. 'Hearing into speech' abused people who have to overcome habitual denial to see themselves as victims and then survivors is a delicate, arduous process. It demands patience, courage and strength from pastoral carers. Ramsay is critical of traditional Christian attitudes to bodies and sexuality. She suggests that traditional images of God as powerful and protective may be unhelpful to abuse victims. Furthermore, rather than putting all the responsibility for healing exposure upon victims, she suggests that education and advocacy should occur in Christian communities so that shaming and victimising structures of abuse are exposed, made public and thus neutralised. Ramsay's approach contains little appeal to theology or scripture. It is, however, refreshingly realistic about the practicalities of trying to overcome obstacles to helping people who have suffered shaming abuse. Her findings and recommendations could be applied to all who have experienced serious, persistent, corrosive shame.

A final contribution to the pastoral theological literature about shame comes in van Deusen Hunsinger's study, *Theology and Pastoral Care* (1995). Here the case of a person who suffers from depression due to humiliation and shaming in childhood exemplifies the importance of adopting both psychological and theological languages and approaches in pastoral counselling. She first interprets this case psychologically (van Deusen Hunsinger 1995: 172ff.). Kaufman's notion of shame-based identity is used to explore the interpersonal origins of shame, the internalisation of shame and the way it intersects with the evolution of identity, defending against shame and disowning the self, and restoring the interpersonal bridge. In this person's case, the interpersonal bridge was restored and a new identity was created in the pastoral counselling relationship through nurture, affirmation and identification.

However, the process of psychological understanding and healing is then interpreted within an overarching Barthian theological perspective.

From this viewpoint, the depressed woman has a distorted view of God because she cannot see that God as seen in Christ, unlike her parents, is not punitive or an enemy. She needs to recognise the fundamental mercy of God that pervades even God's righteousness. Justification by faith means that she has to grasp the notion of her own 'worth beyond price' which will give her access to forgiveness and life in Christ, moving beyond neurotic guilt and distorted projections on to God (van Deusen Hunsinger 1995: 193). Following Barth, van Deusen Hunsinger argues that because God has entered into the shame of sin in Jesus, human beings now share the objective honour and worthiness that God gives to Jesus (van Deusen Hunsinger 1995: 198f.). Debilitating shame is transformed so that the only sort of shame that is left is that which pertains to witnessing God's own humility in Christ. This is a shame of proper reverence and respect.

This approach provides a theological narrative and understanding that religiously undergirds, locates and explains what is going on in the therapeutic process without being reductionist or dismissive of psychological ideas and interpretations. Van Deusen Hunsinger situates therapy for shame within a broader context of God's acceptance, love and grace offered to sinners. Precisely what this adds to the therapeutic process in practical or theoretical terms is unclear. However, it provides broad legitimation for the making real of acceptance and the striving to help people feel respected. Van Deusen Hunsinger may not take seriously enough the shame-creating and -perpetuating aspects of God, images of God, and religious ideas and practices. Here it is enough to note that she is one of the few people to have made a determined attempt to relate the modern theological tradition to the practical task of assisting people who are shame-bound in some way. Her attempt underlines the poverty of that tradition in trying to understand and relate to contemporary experiences of shame.

Evaluating pastoral and pastoral theological responses to shame

Shame is an increasingly important theme within pastoral care and pastoral theology. All the sources examined give prominence to shame and its treatment. Moreover, most agree that shame has been inadequately considered within the Christian tradition which has focussed upon guilt. Some would point to the urgent need for evolving a theology or theologies of shame with a view to better informing pastoral practice in relation to shame. Overwhelmingly, there is a general sense that Christianity should gain a more discriminating understanding of shame. All the authors considered find a positive place for the kind of 'healthy' shame that embodies appropriate respect and reverence for others in society and for God. Equally, they all seem to assent to the notion that there are some kinds of shame that are destructive and alienating for individuals. In the latter case, Christianity should be willing and able to work towards healing. The theological basis for this lies in the love and acceptance of God as manifested and exemplified in the ministry of Jesus who welcomed the alienated and transformed shame by his death.

Beyond these observations on broad consensus, however, a number of less positive critical observations can be made. First, although the literature on the pastoral significance of shame is growing, it is fragmented, inconsistent theologically and psychologically, and thus far, less coherent and illuminating than it might be.

The theological material that is adduced in relation to shame tends to be rather basic, general and unspecific, revolving around notions of divine acceptance, the life and work of Jesus and, sometimes, the story of Adam and Eve. However, little attempt has been made to attend to the phenomenon of shame within the religious tradition although the Bible is full of references to it. Only Schneider (1987a) and Patton (1985) give this any consistent attention and even their findings are inconclusive. Some 'secular' writers such as Lynd (1958) and Hans (1991) seem more interested in exploring the religious roots and connotations of shame than many pastoral theologians.

The effects of this lack of interest are threefold. First, there is a failure clearly to understand the historical meanings of shame in the Christian tradition and in different cultural settings with all the distinctions and ambivalences that might be implied in these. Secondly, direct and tangential theological themes and insights that might inform understandings of shame have not been brought to light. Thirdly, the Christian theological tradition, whether biblical or non-biblical, largely fails to provide any real 'therapeutic wisdom' that aids dealing with shame. What pastoral theologians and carers have to say about shame is largely informed by contemporary therapeutic resources. Where this kind of therapeutic wisdom is ignored, for example by Capps and Smedes, the practical response that is suggested seems trite and unrealistic.

It is to the credit of many pastoral theologians that they are prepared to learn about shame from outwith the theological tradition because it seems to yield so little wisdom and insight. However, only a limited number of resources and understandings are deployed. Generally, theorists fail to grasp the pluriformity, disparity and dissonance of theories and understandings of shame. Mostly, it is understood as a psychological condition and the insights of a limited range of psychologists such as Kaufman and Kohut are used to understand it. The contested and pluriform nature of meanings of shame goes unnoticed, together with knowledge of cultural significances and implications. The social and political context and significance of shame is often ignored and it is treated as an individual problem. Rich themes with social as well as theological resonances such as that of stigma (Goffman 1968b) are passed by.

Although a few writers allow for some notion of social shame, social shaming, and social causation of shame (Capps 1993; Whitehead and Whitehead 1994), these elements are marginal to pastoral and theological concern. Only Whitehead and Whitehead (1994) display any acquaintance with the idea of shame as a social construction. This blindness to the social aspects of shame perhaps explains why pastoral theorists are so uncurious about the rise and prominence of shame and narcissism at the present time in North America. American pastoral theology has always had an individualistic focus (Pattison 1993). Individualist, psychological understandings of shame mean that pastoral theorists have no concept of the prevention of shame, or of mitigating shame at a social and institutional level. This is inadequate because abusive relationships and family patterns are often at the root of the production of chronic, dysfunctional shame. Only Ramsay (1991) seems to take this into account.

A third shortcoming lies in the general failure of pastoral theologians to recognise the part religious thought and practice may play in engendering and exploiting shame. This role is acknowledged by Ramsay (1991) together with Whitehead and Whitehead (1994) *en passant*, and by Smedes (1993) at greater length. However, on the whole Christianity seems to be tacitly regarded as being of unequivocal and real benefit to those who suffer dysfunctional or chronic shame. Nearly all the stories related by pastoral theologians about shamed people who receive pastoral care or partake in religious communities end in those people experiencing some kind of 'improvement'. There are few tales of people whose shame is unalleviated or whose condition is worsened by their religious encounters.

There are no records of those who are not helped, and no outcome studies are available as to the effects of religion and pastoral care on shamed people. It is, therefore, impossible to judge the impact of these things amidst an aura of general optimism about the grace of God and the church that goes far beyond the modest claims of secular psychotherapists. I suspect that many people are actually not helped to come to terms with shame by Christianity. Here, though, let it be noted that Christian pastoral theologians are largely uncritical of the effects and benefits of Christianity as it impacts on different people and different kinds of shame.

Pastoral theologians also seem uninterested in exploring how ideas, images, rituals and liturgies might fund the imaginations of shamed people for good or ill. Perhaps tellingly, all Christian writers on shame, with the exception of Smedes, discuss it as if it is a condition that applies to others, not to themselves. This amplifies a sense of protective distance and perhaps a desire for power and control over shameful impotence that may disguise the prevalence of shame within the Christian community. Possibly this may help to account for the fact that not one single pastoral theologian discussed here, with the partial exception of John Patton (1985), seems to have any awareness of how the dynamics of shame can affect helping relationships, producing compulsive dominant carers who meet their own needs for significance and reassurance by trying to rescue others (Jacoby 1994).

Overall, pastoral theology is still ignorant and uninformed about the nature and complexities of shame. This seems to be true in relation to the theological tradition, social and cultural history, and contemporary social reality, as well as in relation to religious thought and practice. Above all, pastoral theology has little to offer in the way of proven effective methods for helping integrate shame individually and socially. The Christian pastoral theology that I have described and discussed here stands arraigned of not taking shame seriously enough, despite its own considerable best efforts. In particular, it has not come to terms theologically or practically with the negativity and intractability of chronic shame.

Perhaps it is a symptom of the incapacity to deal with this kind of devastating shame that pastoral theology mostly fails to recognise the existence or insights of shamed people except as 'objects' of compassion. In fact, church history is full of examples of 'outsiders', people who have felt shamed and rejected in one way or another but who have provided fundamental, energising insights into the nature of faith. Such people might include Theresa of Avila, Martin Luther and, more recently, Søren Kierkegaard, Simone Weil and Friedrich Nietzsche. Often these outsiders provide searing and uncomfortable critiques of conventional

Christian faith and practice at the cost of leading lonely and unhappy lives. Thus Simone Weil, a woman who was profoundly narcissistically wounded and felt herself to be a permanent outsider (Plant 1996), describes Christianity as a religion of slaves and herself as a slave (Weil 1959: 33f.). She goes on to describe her experience of God as one of 'affliction', a shame-like experience of desolation and rejection in which 'all the scorn, revulsion and hatred are turned inwards' (Weil 1959: 81). Despite her attraction to the church, Weil insisted on maintaining her distance from it because of its exclusivity and a desire on her part to side with outsiders within the universal compassion of God (Weil 1959: 41).

A more robust critic of the complacency and small-mindedness of Christianity was Friedrich Nietzsche. Nietzsche was deeply injured by his upbringing in a religious household (Fowler 1996), but arguably he retained a real care and concern for Christianity in the midst of pointing out its many faults and dangers (Tanner 1994: 37). Unfortunately, many Christian theologians, pastoral and other, just omit any reference to the voluminous work of Friedrich Nietzsche on shame. If his thought is cited, it is then effectively dismissed as somehow wrong-headed (Tillich 1962a; Fowler 1996; Schneider 1987a). Ultimately, Nietzsche seems to be regarded as a hopeless case, someone who got it wrong and failed to understand the 'true', benevolent and liberating nature of Christianity. He was a man consumed by his own shame and resentment (Wurmser 1997a). He therefore alienated himself from divine grace and human community. Together with Sartre, he is consigned, with apparently little regret, to a kind of outer darkness of inner loneliness and social isolation that is essentially tragic and unredeemable (Schneider 1987a: 130ff.).

It is understandable that theologians find Nietzsche's critique of Christianity as a shame-engendering and -reinforcing force in the world difficult. Nietzsche's writing is unrelenting both in its force and its over-weening, lip-curling contempt and hatred for the religion in which he was brought up (Nietzsche 1974, 1989; Kaufmann 1976). He invariably exaggerates his arguments so that sensible, unexceptional points are mixed in with others that are outrageous. The effect on the Christian reader is one of consuming a rich, poisonous cake that is often over-whelming, upsetting and depressing. Here is a short extract to give a sense of its timbre:

In Christianity the instincts of the subjugated and oppressed come to the fore: here the lowest classes seek their salvation. The casuistry of sin, self-criticism, the inquisition of the conscience, are pursued as a pastime, as a remedy for boredom . . . Christian too is a certain sense of cruelty against oneself and

against others; hatred of all who think differently; the will to persecute . . .
Christian, finally, is the hatred of the spirit, of pride, courage, freedom, liberty
of the spirit; Christian is the hatred of the senses, of joy in the senses, of joy
itself. (Kaufmann 1976: 588–9)

Nietzsche problematises two important assumptions that undergird the
legitimacy of Christianity. First, he questions the benevolence and
beneficial human effects of Christianity. This is difficult for a religion
that claims to save humanity. Secondly, Nietzsche's unrelenting nihilism
suggests that there are limits to the grace of God. Again, this is a difficult
issue for a religion that claims to witness to universal salvation. That
Nietzsche died an atheist as well as being insane makes it relatively easy
to dismiss or water down what he had to say without much danger of
challenge from within the religious community. Thus Tillich (1962a)
quotes Nietzsche's thoughts about the appallingness of always being
seen by God but then moves on implicitly to suggest that Nietzsche is just
plain wrong in interpreting his own religious experience in the way that
he does. But this kind of patronising, desultory response is inadequate.

Nietzsche's extensive thought about shame deserves to be taken far
more seriously by Christian theorists and practitioners. In the first place,
Nietzsche is one of the very few thinkers to have ever given extensive
thought to the experience of shame and what brings this about and sus-
tains it. Secondly, beneath a degree of bombastic hyperbole, Nietzsche
is a perceptive psychologist who is honest about his own experience. To
reject his analysis is to reject an authentic source of insight into shame.
Thirdly, while the ultimate tragedy of Nietzsche's life and experience
must be recognised, it could be argued that Nietzsche managed, at
enormous personal cost, heroically to transcend shame in his thinking
and writing (Wurmser 1995). He deserves some honour for this.
Fourthly, it is unlikely that Nietzsche's experience of shame, despair and
ressentiment was unique. Many people have experienced the same kind of
upbringing and religious formation that he did (Miller 1987a, 1987b). I
can testify from my own experience that it is perfectly possible to feel
the kind of loneliness and resentment that he did, even if one does not
utterly despair of divine grace and the Christian religion. Thus,
Nietzsche as a kind of extreme limit case of human existence provides
data and experience about shame that may be illuminative for others.
Finally, if Nietzsche's thought and experience are dismissed this suggests that Christian thought and practice may not be able to cope with
the reality of extreme, toxic shame and the sense of resentment towards
the divinity that it can produce. Similarly, it often cannot cope with

other conditions such as the diminishments of dementia or the extremes of embittered anger (Campbell 1986; Pattison 1989a).

The incapacity to acknowledge and embrace difficult situations and the fact that not all those who turn to Christ are healed is a perennial problem in a Christianity that witnesses to the universal benevolence and healing power of God (Pattison 1989b). However, there is nothing to be gained by dishonesty here. Denial contributes to a sense that Christianity is ideological and literally incredible. This is a faithless response. It colludes with the suppression and denial of shame, particularly chronic shame. Christianity cannot gain strength or credibility from the denial of reality by dumbing down the sharpness of shame and alienation as it is found in Nietzsche's writings and experiences. To put the point sharply and rhetorically, to damn, ignore and dismiss Nietzsche and people who share his human condition is ultimately to damn Christianity itself – and in a far more profound way than Nietzsche himself was able to accomplish. When theology can listen to and appreciate Nietzsche, it will be able to cope with the reality of lived chronic shame.

Conclusion

The result of this survey of recent Christian theological and pastoral responses to shame is a disappointing one. Within the theological arena, shame has not been a major discrete category for analysis and understanding, even in the context of discussions about atonement. Theologians use the word shame *en passant*, but most direct theological attention has been focussed upon guilt and offence as the main constituents of sin and alienation from God and humanity. A number of theologians do allow some significance to shame in their writings. However, often their understandings of shame are partial, arbitrary or desultory. Shame has yet to receive the comprehensive theological examination that it deserves.

Within the sphere of pastoral responses to shame, things are a little brighter. Particularly in North America, pastoral theorists have become increasingly aware of the significance of shame. Many books on pastoral care now recognise the importance of shame, especially its negative, toxic effects upon individuals. However, there are limits to the pastoral and practical understandings and responses that are outlined. Almost all treatments of the phenomenon of shame considered here are brief and superficial. Authors often unquestioningly adopt a psychological, individualistic understanding of shame. They omit to deal effectively with its social context, construction and usage. Frequently, theorists fail to grasp the disparity and dissonance of theories of shame, opting for one basic idea or theorist and orchestrating other sources around it. Mostly, pastoral theorists fail to correlate shame with specific theological ideas or religious practices. Where they attempt this, they often do not get beyond broad theological themes and generalisations. There is some awareness that religious ideas and practices may generate, exacerbate or exploit feelings of shame in individuals and groups. However, this is not explored by many theorists. Finally, while most pastoral theorists are clear that Christian belief and practice should alleviate and heal toxic and chronic shame, none of them have any real idea of how this might be done except in the most commonsensical, general terms.

Contemporary Christian belief and practice, while committed to the alleviation and healing of individual toxic shame, has relatively little of demonstrable use to offer to the process of individual and social integration. Such wisdom and technique that is retailed by pastoral theologians is mostly culled and recycled from a limited range of secular psychologies, often in an uncritical way.

I do not want to suggest that Christianity should provide all the answers or techniques that are necessary for reducing the individual and social alienation represented by chronic shame. It is probably more important that Christian theological and practical responses should become more hesitant, humble, questioning and receptive than they have been hitherto. There is an urgent need for a greater acknowledgment of the diversity and complexity of understandings of shame. This should be matched by a recognition that dysfunctional or toxic shame is pervasive and difficult to alleviate. Chronically shamed individuals cannot be integrated into fullness of personal and communal life by the simple existence of religious communities or of pastoral workers, nor by the ritual invocation of theological concepts such as *agape* and grace. What is required here, then, is hard work to grasp better understandings of shame and how dysfunctional shame may be dealt with in the light of theological understanding.

We are at the beginning of a very long process of education into understanding the discourses and concepts that surround the phenomenon known as shame. There are no easy theological answers and no quick religious fixes to shame. Starting from this low point may, however, allow the evolution of more sensitive, robust and effective religious responses to dysfunctional shame in individuals and groups.

There is a positive side to the apparent lack of experience and theorising about shame in the present context. The way lies open for Christians to develop new and more sophisticated, complex theories of theology and action around shame. This is not an option that is so readily available in regard to other phenomena like guilt whose understanding and treatment are well trammelled by theologians and religious functionaries (Coate 1994; McGreal 1994; McKeating 1970; Tournier 1962). The possibility exists here for making new 'tyres' – theologies, theories and religious practices – rather than for re-treading old ones. This is, however, dependent upon a certain openness to the complexity and apparent incorrigibility of dysfunctional shame.

CHAPTER NINE

Shame in Christianity

Shame is unquestionably a condition that society shamelessly manipulates for its own ends, and it disseminates the spores of the abject to as many locations as possible to guarantee greater control over the lives of its constituents.

(Hans 1991: 137)

You have taught me to worship a god who is like you, who shares your thinking exactly, who is going to slap me one if I don't straighten out fast. I am very uneasy every Sunday, which is cloudy and deathly still, and filled with silent accusing whispers.

(Keillor 1985: 254)

In the last chapter, I suggested that contemporary Christian responses to shame, especially chronic shame, have been limited and inadequate. Here I propose to explore some of the factors intrinsic to Christian ideology and practice that may actually produce and exploit shame. My working hypothesis is that Christianity, like other social institutions, engenders and promotes shame, often to enhance order and control. Shame can be used as a very effective means of manipulating people into obedience and compliance in the interests of the powerful who identify those interests with the will of God.

The ambivalent relationship between Christianity and dysfunctional shame

The relationship between shame and Christian thought and practice is complex and ambivalent, as is the relationship between Christianity and human well-being generally (Batson et al. 1993). Christianity can create, exploit and deny shame in groups and individuals. However, it can also diminish and alleviate shame, enhancing worth, efficacy and esteem.

I possess a series of letters from self-identified shamed people. For some of them, Christianity as they experienced it in early life helped to create a sense of shame and oppression. For others, their religious training and upbringing had no perceptible effect upon their sense of self-hood and shame. For a third group, Christian ideas and practices helped them to survive, develop and grow as happy autonomous people. Lastly, there is a group of people for whom Christianity acts as both an oppressive and a liberating force in relation to their sense of shame.

This picture is confirmed in literature. James Joyce's Catholicism fuelled his imagination with shame and fear so that he spent the rest of his life denouncing and trying to escape from it (Joyce 1968): 'There is no heresy or no philosophy that is so abhorrent to the church as a human being . . .' (Ellmann 1982: 107). Depictions of religiously funded fear and humiliation emerge in the biography of the twentieth-century Irish Catholic, Frank McCourt (1997), as well as in Edmund Gosse's (1949) account of a Protestant childhood in nineteenth-century England. However, Gerard Hughes, a Scottish Jesuit priest, records no sense of humiliation or shame arising from his early, fairly intense religious upbringing, though he did feel very guilty about masturbation (Hughes 1997). Stories of positive growth and development out of shame due to the influence of Christianity can be found in many evangelical auto-biographies, as well as in books like the Linns' *Healing Religious Addiction* (1995). Accounts of people for whom their Christian involvement may have caused or exacerbated shame, but also may have ultimately helped them to develop and become freer, may be found in autobiographical books by Grace Sheppard (1995) and American theologian Roberta Bondi (1995). Sheppard was crushed by a sense that she should be perfect and could not be so, while Bondi was disabled by feeling unacceptable to both her earthly and heavenly fathers.

A similar range of experiences and reactions between Christianity and various groups can also be postulated. For many gays their experience of Christian belief and practice is humiliating, denigrating and objectifying. For many Black and other oppressed peoples, however, Christianity has provided a means to worth, dignity and hope as the Black theology and various theologies of liberation bear witness. In many situations, Christian ideas and practices may function in an ambivalent fashion in relation to individual and group shame.

Having acknowledged the reality of an ambivalent and complex relationship between human shame experience and aspects of the Christian tradition, I want now to claim the privileges of an autoethnographic author to state that my own early experience of Christian ideas and practices did little to dissipate my own sense of shame and defilement and much to reinforce it. It is from this biassed, selective perspective that

I will give some account of the ways in which Christianity might engender, exacerbate, exploit and ignore shame.

This solipsistic stance allows others entirely to disagree with, or to reinterpret, the material presented here. What may be shaming in one person's eyes in one context might not be so in differing circumstances for other people. It also permits me to be selective in a vast topic area. I recognise that other people will interact with Christian ideas and practices differently. However, I want to suggest that many of these practices and ideas have a potential for shame arousal and reinforcement. This needs to be recognised if Christianity is to become an ally of those who are chronically shamed and defiled. By seeing how Christian ideologies and practices have affected me, readers may be led to reflect on their own experiences of shame and shaming in the religious context and what has led to them. I assume that my experiences are not so unique that my contemporaries will be unable to understand them, even if their own experiences are different.

The first part of this chapter examines the ways in which certain aspects of Christian ideology or theology can intersect with personal experience to generate or maintain a sense of shame or defilement. The second looks at some of the ways in which the practices of the Christian community may reflect, amplify and confirm the dynamics of chronic shame or defilement in individuals and in groups.

THEOLOGICAL IDEAS AND IMAGES AND SHAME

I will now consider some of the ways in which Christian ideology in the form of theological ideas and images might engender and promote shame, relating these to my own experience as a 'shamed self'. I will particularly consider the mainstream Christian ideas and images that surround the themes of the nature and doctrine of God, sin and guilt, pride and humility, and the nature of the person or the self. It is my broad contention that if such ideas and images are encountered in particular ways, they can engender or reinforce a sense of shame. They can blind people to the realities of shame in themselves and others. The implication is that Christian theologians may need radically to reinterpret or change aspects of their discourse if they want to render shame visible and to help to overcome the depradations of a sense of unwantedness and defilement.

First, however, I need to make some preliminary remarks about my understanding of theology in this context.

Some preliminary remarks on theological ideas and images

Theology is a set of polysemic images, metaphors, similes, narratives and myths (McFague 1983; Soskice 1985). Theological images and ideas can therefore be variously interpreted according to context and culture. They do not have a stable, fixed meaning. Understandings of theological ideas are not static either and can be very various. Where one person finds an image that appears to create or perpetuate shame, another finds the opposite, or notices nothing at all. This makes it very difficult to comment on the functionality or dysfunctionality of any particular image or concept. Van Deusen Hunsinger, commenting on Rizzuto (1979) notes:

[O]ne cannot legitimately make . . . generalized statements about any image's dysfunctionality. For one person an image of God as Father could be very functional, where for example there was a positive, mature relationship with the person's father. In another person, however, such a father-image would only exact high costs in stress and anxiety, where for example the father was more authoritarian and unyielding . . . (van Deusen Hunsinger 1995: 140–1)

Often, within the Christian tradition there are apparently contradictory or counterbalancing ideas or images. So, for example, God loves people exactly as they are – but God also wants them to repent and change; the creation is good because it is made by God – but it is evil insofar as it does not follow God's plans and precepts. Usually, there is not one single understanding or voice on any issue. Thus, there is much scope for creative or destructive understanding and misunderstanding of the tradition. In many ways, Christian theology as a whole functions as a myth insofar as it may effectively unify and attempt to overcome contradictions (Lévi-Strauss 1972: 229). However, those contradictions can be concretised in the lives and minds of individuals and groups.

Because Christian ideas and images are polyvocal, pluralistic and susceptible to many interpretations there is seldom one absolutely 'correct' interpretation. Nor can the authors or originators of ideas and images be held entirely responsible for interpretations of their products. Certain concepts or practices may have the capacity to shame or frighten individuals or groups in a particular context. But this does not mean that they were consciously intended to do so, either by their originators or by their contemporary interpreters. However, it may not be possible to ensure that people receive ideas in such a way that they are not shamed or frightened.

Theological images and ideas are human artefacts that emerge from a particular socio-political and historical milieu (Pattison 1997a). There are three implications to this. First, such ideas and images often reveal more about the human beings who constructed them and their world view and assumptions than they necessarily do about the nature and being of God. Secondly, these images and ideas reflect a particular social order and world view. Thus, if a set of theological concepts or doctrines emerges from a context in which shame-associated phenomena are prominent or are exploited, it is feasible that these ideas will embody, or at least be consonant and compatible with, a shame-based view of the world. Thirdly, liberation theologians, amongst others, have done much to show that dominant images, ideas and texts are often created and sustained by dominant social groups, the 'victors' or the 'powerful'. They therefore wittingly or unwittingly help to sustain the power and influence of these groups and their world views (Pattison 1997a). Since shame is a powerful tool of social manipulation and control, some theological ideas and images might almost overtly set out to engender and maintain shame amongst ordinary believers in society. It therefore behoves theologians to employ the 'hermeneutics of suspicion' (Tracy 1987) when approaching classic theological ideas and texts. They need consciously to look for the influence and ideology of particular social and political groups. In this socio-political context, too, theologians must take some critical responsibility for the effects of their ideas and images.

Within this discussion, I regard 'God' as an object or symbol along the lines of psychodynamic or literary understandings of the term 'object'. Rycroft defines an object as being:

That towards which action or desire is directed; that which the subject requires in order to achieve instinctual satisfaction; that to which the subject relates himself. In psycho-analytical writings, objects are nearly always persons, parts of persons, or symbols of one or the other. (Rycroft 1972: 100)

Whether or not God is a 'real' subject and has an existence independent of human beings is not an issue here. The point is that people believe God, or aspects of God, to be real; they are affected by this: 'God is real since he produces real effects' (James 1960: 491). It follows that the images and ideas surrounding the idea of God that are utilised may have differing influences on people. It is the effects of ideas and images of God and the way they correlate with phenomena like shame that concern me presently.

Pursuing this a little further, it should also be pointed out that people formulate their own internalised God objects and internalised images of

God early in their lives (Rizzuto 1979; cf. Jacobs 1993; Jones 1991). Sometimes these correspond and resonate closely with God images and ideas in the Christian tradition. Often they may be wholly or partially different. There may therefore be a dynamic interaction between Christian God images and ideas and people's own internal images.

A similar kind of rather unclear and ungovernable interaction and partial correspondence between images of God and social structures has been observed by Nicholls (1989). This kind of interaction, whether psychological or social, may help to explain why some 'official', public and conscious religious ideas are received and accepted, while others are rejected. The analysis below is mainly concerned with the way in which ideas are assimilated and used by people who may themselves have unconscious images of a psychological God object, not with the ultimate truth of articulated religious ideas and doctrines.

To sum up: theological images and ideas from the Christian theological tradition may interact with people's conscious and unconscious beliefs and internalised objects to affect their attitudes and behaviours in relation to shame. This inevitable process helps to shape people's views of themselves and of their world. It takes place within a socio-political context and has social and political implications. Within this assumptive framework, I can now examine the ways in which some Christian images may help to engender and sustain human shame.

Images of the invisible God

'No man hath seen God at any time,' declares the evangelist (John 1.18 AV). Had he read the Hebrew scriptures more carefully, John would have known that this was not strictly true, for there it is claimed that Moses and Jacob amongst others had seen God face to face (Gen. 32.31, Deut. 34.10). Nonetheless, John's perception is broadly true in terms of Christian theology. Here it is claimed that God is beyond human knowledge and perception except through the medium of God's own self-disclosure. The fact that the Christian God cannot be known in Godself, that God is immaterial, transcendent, spirit, has not prevented theologians from trying to understand God through the media of words and concepts, metaphors and images (McFague 1983, 1987; Soskice 1985).

These images and concepts have reflected and shaped people's understandings of themselves and of God (Saussy 1991). They have become fixed in scriptures, creeds, philosophies, liturgies and theologies. Like many others of my generation I first encountered them as a child in school assemblies, Sunday schools, and in my home.

Here I will critically and selectively examine some of the images and concepts of God drawn from Judaeo-Christian tradition to show how they may help to generate and maintain human shame.

The evolution of Christian ideas about God can be crudely divided into two phases. First, there are the words and images of God provided by the Jewish tradition and contained in the Hebrew or Old Testament scriptures. This was followed by the distinctively Christian elaboration of theology which was heavily influenced by Greek thought. One essential model or fundamental understanding of God has dominated the Judaeo-Christian tradition in its biblical and post-biblical development. This is the monarchical model of God:

> The monarchical model of God as King was developed systematically, both in Jewish thought (God as Lord and King of the Universe), in medieval Christian thought (with its emphasis on divine omnipotence), and in the Reformation (especially in Calvin's insistence on God's sovereignty) . . . the dominant western historical model has been that of an absolute monarch ruling over his kingdom (McFague 1987: 63).

McFague describes this dominant model of God as both psychologically powerful and dangerous. While it makes us feel good about God and ourselves and inspires 'strong emotions of awe, gratitude and trust toward God', it also inspires 'abject fear and humiliation'; 'in this picture, God can be God only if we are nothing' (McFague 1987: 64).

The monarchical God is distant from the world, relates only to the human world, and controls the world through a mixture of domination and benevolence. McFague (1987) therefore proposes different metaphors and models of God as Mother, Lover and Friend. These, she thinks, are more suitable for theology in an ecological, nuclear age. Maybe so, but most people alive today who have been exposed to the Christian religious tradition have encountered God through the images and concepts of the dominant monarchical tradition as contained in the scriptures, creeds, liturgies and prayers of the historic churches. These in many ways mirror and reinforce the practice of monarchical parenthood that has led to so much narcissistic disorder and shaming of children (Miller 1987b). Aspects of this tradition have helped to shape and perpetuate human shame and it is these that are explored here.

The ascent of the monarchical deity and the rise of human shame are almost contemporaneous in Judaeo-Christian mythology. In Genesis 3, Adam and Eve disobey the commands of the creator-ruler God and shame makes its first appearance as they are exposed before the critical gaze of their maker. God himself does not appear to experience shame in the literature of the Old Testament, unless his people dishonour him and bring him into a position of disrepute and apparent contempt. However, he is very good at creating shame in human beings. If he hides his face, that is, his presence (Moore 1996: 90), from creation it perishes or experiences annihilation (Ps. 104.29). If his people displease him, he covers them in shame and scorn (Ps. 44.9ff.). As for God's enemies, he laughs them to scorn and treats them with contempt, that is, he shames them utterly: 'He that sitteth in the heavens shall laugh: the Lord shall have them in derision' (Ps. 2.4 AV).

For those like Nathanson (1992) who see laughter as the great solvent of shame, and others who want to portray Christian laughter as a positive, healing force (Kuschel 1994), it is worth noting that the roots of the Judaeo-Christian tradition tap a very bitter stream of derision and contempt: 'Divine laughter in the Old Testament is mocking laughter' (Gilhus 1997: 22; cf. Screech 1997). The hallmark of divine laughter is of aggressive mocking, scorn and ridicule, not that of merriment and joy. This shame-producing laughter from a contemptuous, shameless God is not an encouraging starting point for those who would wish theological ideas and images to address, reduce and alleviate human shame rather than to exacerbate it.

The God of the Old Testament is a kind of all-too-human oriental despot who overtly exploits shame in the interests of bolstering his own power and control. It may be more difficult to see how more abstract and spiritual images and attributes of God affected by Greek thought might engender and exacerbate human shame. However, ideas and images that do not directly address or mention shame may help to inculcate it in the human psyche, funding the imaginations of shame-prone people to produce or exacerbate the elements of humiliation, unlovableness, unwantedness, inferiority and defilement that characterise shame (Brueggemann 1993).

– *God is wholly different from human beings.* This notion of deity creates a fundamental disidentification between humans and their God. As we have seen, the way in which people acquire identity and personhood is to be recognised, honoured and communicated with by other human beings who attune themselves to the person's needs and interests (Lewis

1992; Stern 1985). Although human terms are used to describe God in the Christian tradition, he is clearly not human. It is difficult to see how this kind of entity might provide adequate 'mirroring' for human development. This may contribute to individuals devaluing their own embodied humanity in favour of the 'spiritual'.

– *God does not have a body.* Although recent attempts have been made to ascribe a body of some kind to God (McFague 1993), the majority Christian tradition, following in the steps of Platonic philosophy, clearly sees God as disembodied. This creates disidentification between God and humanity, which is firmly enfleshed. The body is often the seat of shame, concerned as it is with earthy matters of sexual reproduction, ingestion, digestion and excretion (Hans 1991). The ideal of the disembodied spirit which has often informed Christian theology and spirituality fails to mirror the reality of the human condition and may lead to its implicit disparagement and shaming, for 'if God is found beyond the body, anything can be done to the body' (Alves 1986: 9).

– *God is pure and holy.* Not only is the divinity not embodied, it is not defiled, smeared and besmirched by excretions such as faeces, urine, semen and blood, so often the causes of shame in human beings. Furthermore, the holy God cannot look upon or tolerate that which is evil, shamed or defiled. A commentary on the implications of this for shamed people can be found in Kundera: 'I, as a child, grasped the incompatability of God and shit and thus came to question the basic thesis . . . that man was created in God's image . . . either man was created in God's image – and God has intestines! – or God lacks intestines and man is not like Him.' He goes on, 'The objection to shit is a metaphysical one. The daily defecation session is daily proof of the unacceptability of Creation . . . either shit is acceptable (in which case don't lock yourself in the bathroom!) or we are created in an unacceptable manner' (Kundera 1984: 239, 241). As a child who suffered from a condition known as encopresis (which basically means defecating in the wrong place at the wrong time (Mainprice 1974)), I was all too aware of the shameful physical distance created between the all-pure disembodied God without bowels and people like me. Metaphorical or psychological defilement, for example because of sexual orientation, is equally painful and shameful in the face of a holy and pure God. Christian ideas and images of God as holy and pure may, therefore, increase a personal sense of alienation from self and the divine. The associated quest for reconciling purification with the divine can also foster some most unpleasant human attitudes and vices such as self-righteousness, exclusivism, and contempt for others:

> If we are polluted by original sin . . . God – the only pure site in the world – can help us to deal with our abject lot by providing rituals of cleanliness that mark off our difference from others and thereby demonstrate how our purity places us above the unclean other . . . God gives us the cleanliness we need in order to overcome our feelings of shame by demanding that we give up the world of the body to which our shame is first attached. And in turn He corrupts us by making us feel that we are superior to those who have not so denied the body and thereby remain unclean. (Hans 1991: 186)

– *God requires people to be holy and obedient to his will.* Far from mirroring human feelings and desires and meeting their needs, God requires humans to change themselves to become as he wants them to be. Despite the rhetoric of God's service being perfect freedom and people finding their 'true' selves in him, Christian discourse advocates conformity to God's needs and will. Effectively, people must learn to mirror God. The call to become as God wants one to be, to obedience and to conformity, can help to crush people's sense of their own goodness and the appropriateness of their being. The Christian tradition may encourage a kind of shameful heteronomy and conformity that leaves people feeling profoundly discontented with themselves as they are. In this way, it may foster the acquisition of an outwardly conforming 'false self' (Richards 1996).

– *God is perfect. God is good and complete in Godself.* The implication is that human beings should aspire to perfection: 'Be ye therefore perfect, even as your Father which is in heaven is perfect,' Jesus says to his followers (Matt. 5.48 AV). This saying has been heard as a summons to be perfect in character and behaviour. It thus sets up an impossible ideal of which most humans are bound to fall short. They will then experience profound shameful dissatisfaction. As a child, one of my aunts gave me a book of lives of the saints. 'I think I might like to be a saint,' I later told her. It took me years to realise that the aspiration to perfection is pernicious and persecutory for shamed selves.

– *God is rational and does not have feelings or desires.* Human beings, on the other hand, are all too aware of their desires and feelings that are often based in the body (Pattison in press). The awareness of disparity between an ideal, self-controlled, passionless God and the realities of being passion-tossed as a human being can again create a painful feeling of shame and inadequacy. Subduing or denying the passions can then become an ideal of living, particularly as it is modelled by Christian religious (Miles 1988, 1992). Those who cannot overcome their bodily based emotions may then regard themselves as bad and inferior. Witness here the Puritan divines of early New England who struggled vainly and self-reproachfully with their ungovernable sexual urges (Rubin 1994), or myself as a religious teenager desperately wishing that I did not have a body, or a penis with a mind of its own!

– *God is omnipotent*. This means that, in an ultimate sense, God reserves all initiative and action to himself. The corollary is that human beings are relatively powerless and completely dependent upon the action of God to make his grace and power available to them. The notion of an active, omnipotent God may play into human shame by emphasising elements of passivity and lack of autonomy – 'we have no power of ourselves to help ourselves', as the *Book of Common Prayer* collect for the second Sunday in Lent has it. It certainly does little to make people feel that their actions and wills are of significance.

– *God is unbiddable and often absent*. Although people are exhorted to think of God as a loving, attentive parent who is constantly seeking the best for his 'children' it is also made clear that God's ways are not our ways. Thus there are many occasions upon which mortals are left to muse on the absence or arbitrariness of the creator, depriving people of loved ones or failing to prevent natural disasters. Insofar as God does not appear to be present or to respond to human prayers and needs, people may be inclined to think that this means they are themselves misguided, bad, or even evil. God's unbiddability and inscrutability may reinforce a sense of human badness and powerlessness, rather as an abusive or neglectful parent may elicit a sense of ontological badness and fundamental flaw in a child. This increases a destructive sense of worthlessness, impotence and unwantedness.

– *God is omnipresent*. If God's unaccountable absence can be painful and traumatic for believers, God's presence may be persecutory and tormenting. 'Whither shall I go from thy spirit? or whither shall I flee from thy presence?' writes the psalmist. 'If I ascend up into heaven, thou art there: if I make my bed in hell, behold, thou art there' (Ps. 139.7–8 AV). This testimony to God's presence everywhere is comforting to many. As a shamed child, however, I found it to be a 'text of terror' (Trible 1984) along with the collect for purity in the eucharist that invoked God as one 'from whom no secrets were hidden'. It suggests that one is perpetually under a kind of divine surveillance. There are no doors or boundaries that can shield one from the gaze of an omniscient and probably disapproving deity who respects no boundaries or privacy.

One of the main features of the development from polytheism to monotheism in the ancient world was the concentration of moral watchfulness and shaming gaze in one single source. This provided a greater sense of security. However,

The trade-off that Western civilization made when it moved away from the polytheism of the body toward the monotheism of the mind has been clear to us for quite some time: we traded the uncertainty and fluidity of polyvalent looks for the gaze of the . . . *invisible* Other with the omnipresent stare . . . (Hans 1991: 125)

The shaming sense of being unable to escape the all-seeing divine 'eye in the sky' and the sense of wretchedness and defilement it can evoke is expressed by Luther:

He [the infant] is put to sin and shame before God . . . this means that there is no corner or hole in the whole of creation into which a man might creep, not even in hell, but he must let himself be exposed to the gaze of the whole creation, and stand in the open with all his shame . . . (Erikson 1962: 256)

– God does not need anything from humans – humans do not actually deserve anything from God. Much of the Christian theological tradition emphasises the profound difference and asymmetrical relationship between God and the creation. God is complete in and of Godself; the divine does not actually need what human beings have to offer. This compounds a sense of impotence and worthlessness, for to avoid shame people need to feel that they can actually do and offer something useful to others (Goldberg 1991: 139). It is also necessary in obviating the sense of shame to have some sense of entitlement to proper treatment (Goldberg 1991: 19f.). This is abnegated if people are brought up in the belief that they are not actually entitled to anything from life except that which is given to them on the whim of some erratic powerful other. The price of developing a sense of absolute gratitude to and dependence upon God may be the acquisition of a diminished view of the power and value of the self. This may foster shame.

– God punishes wickedness and sin. Even in the ministry of Jesus there is the threat of punishment and damnation for those who fail to obey and respect the will of the Almighty (Pfister 1948: 210ff.). This notion was later elaborated into doctrines of hell and purgatory that for centuries helped to keep ordinary Christian people in a state of fear and subjection (Fenn 1995; Nineham 1993). If people feel envious or resentful of God, or are tempted to disobey the deity, the threat of punishment acts as a deterrent against questioning the way things are. Enduring

one's lot may result in heavenly reward. Failing to do so will definitely bring punishment in its wake, either in this life or the next. This prospect does much to engender a sense of fatalism and passivity as well as reinforcing the belief in ontological badness in the shamed believer. It thus easily amplifies shame.

In many ways, the God of the majority orthodox tradition, with whose images I was confronted as a child, is a shame-generating monster. Moore describes the biblical God as 'a projection of male narcissism', 'the supreme embodiment of hegemonic hypermasculinity, and as such the object of universal adoration' (Moore 1996: 139). The relationship that exists between this God and his creation is fundamentally one of domination-submission that propagates sado-masochistic relationships as the price for divinely guaranteed security and favour (Moore 1996: 123; Wink 1992). Schüssler Fiorenza notes in relation to Western mysticism that 'men, like women, have taken up the "feminine" position of receptivity and surrender with respect to G*d, conforming to a masculine G*d's desire for the feminine while at the same time sustaining masculine practices of control and superiority with respect to the world' (Schüssler Fiorenza 1994: 39). To live in the presence of this kind of God is to exist in a state of almost permanent chronic shame and abjection. It is to feel at all times acutely self-conscious and inadequate, that one is perpetually weighed in the balance and found desperately wanting.

The idealised God of Christian orthodoxy, immortal, invisible, omnipresent, all-powerful, rational, disembodied and unbiddable can be powerfully attractive to the shamed and narcissistically wounded who wish to be healed, enselfed and made significant within a loving parental gaze: 'Of all the needs . . . a lonely child has, the one that must be satisfied . . . is the unshaking need for an unshakeable God' (Angelou 1984: 23). Unfortunately, the kind of God imaged in the orthodox tradition in its continuing use of scripture, creeds and liturgy is unlikely to meet the real needs of many shamed people. Rather, they may be encouraged to see themselves as bad, powerless, defiled and unworthy before the face of an all-good creator.

The kinds of characteristics and relationships of the traditional monarchical God upon which I have been reflecting here mirror, buttress, and amplify the kind of beliefs implicit in 'poisonous pedagogy' that Miller arraigns for producing abused, narcissistically wounded, and shamed children:

(1) A feeling of duty produces love.
(2) Hatred can be done away with by forbidding it.
(3) Parents deserve respect simply because they are parents.

ildren are undeserving of respect simply because they are chil-
en.
bedience makes a child strong.
high degree of self-esteem is harmful.

(7) A low degree of self-esteem makes a person altruistic.
(8) Tenderness (doting) is harmful.
(9) Responding to a child's need is wrong.
(10) Severity and coldness are a good preparation for life.
(11) A pretence of gratitude is better than honest ingratitude.
(12) The way you behave is more important than the way you really are.
(13) Neither parents nor God would survive being offended.
(14) The body is something dirty and disgusting.
(15) Strong feelings are harmful.
(16) Parents are creatures free of drives and guilt.
(17) Parents are always right. (Miller 1987b: 59–60)

A moment's comparison of these belief characteristics and those that I earlier ascribed to the Christian God will reveal a worrying degree of similarity and resonance. The Christian God as imaged in the majority tradition and still described, discussed and worshipped is in many ways a guarantor and contributor to abusive parenting. This God continues to be the 'official' deity of Christianity, ever to be worshipped, honoured and adored, even by the most shamed members of the human race.

In this account, I have demonstrated some ways in which interpretations of Christian ideas and images of God may intersect with the experience of shame-prone people, particularly children, legitimating and amplifying a sense of shame. Not all people who encounter such ideas find them shaming. However, religious images and ideas can have a baleful effect upon the minds of people who are receptive to them, perhaps because of previous shameful experiences or persecutory internalised objects. For them, these images can be persistently tormenting (Capps 1995a: 51).

If people form their God images unconsciously, long before they are susceptible to the articulate suggestions of a verbalised religious tradition (Rizzuto 1979), then it could be argued that there is little point in amending that tradition. People will make of it what they can and will. If they find in it confirmation of, say, the sado-masochistic nature of relationships between parents and children, this is just a way of making explicit what they already experience and believe at a deep level. In this sense, religious ideas and images may be useful indicators and articulations of some people's psychological state. They cannot be changed until people have different infantile experiences that are characterised more by attunement and care than by domination and neglect.

There may be truth in this argument. However, I suggest that the uncritical propagation of images and ideas that can harmfully fund and reinforce the shamed imagination as well as legitimating shaming practices and attitudes in families and wider society cannot simply be uncritically accepted.

Sin and guilt

Traditional ideas and images of God may contribute to the generation and propagation of shame. The main contribution of the Christian tradition of sin and guilt has probably been to hide shame from view and to distort the uses to which it is put. This is a somewhat perplexing assertion, because shame-like experiences of awe matched with a sense of defilement often seem central to theistic religious experience (Otto 1950; Ricoeur 1967).

Reflecting upon the experiences of the prophet Isaiah and of the apostle Peter, who spontaneously define themselves as unclean in relation to the experience of the numinous, Otto suggests that this sense 'does not spring from the consciousness of some committed transgression, but rather is an immediate datum given with the feeling of the numen: it proceeds to "disvalue" together with the self the tribe to which the person belongs, and . . . all existence in general' (Otto 1950: 50). This sense of defilement and disvalue can be co-opted into a moral world view, providing numinous cathexis for social and ethical standards:

Mere 'unlawfulness' only becomes 'sin', 'impiety', 'sacrilege', when the character of *numinous unworthiness* or *disvalue* goes on to be transferred to and centred in *moral* delinquency. And only when the mind feels it as 'sin' does the transgression of law become a matter of such dreadful gravity for the conscience . . . (Otto 1950: 52)

The transvaluation of religious feeling into a sense of moral sin and offence preserves and exploits the sense of shame-like experience. Shame is made to lend its power and authority to the law. However, shame itself is effectively hidden so that it cannot be directly considered or addressed. Religious experience, and especially the experience of alienation and difference from the divine, comes to be understood primarily in terms of moral offence and disobedience rather than in terms of uncleanness, inferiority and unworthiness. Thus, these important elements of human experience may be hidden and ignored.

The picture of the moralisation and unacknowledged exploitation and hiding of shame seems to correspond reasonably well with the evolution of Christianity. Western Christianity, and Protestant Christianity in particular, has as a central tenet the fundamental sinfulness and guilt of human beings in relation to the divine. Sin has been variously understood and defined. However, the main thrust of this tradition has been that an ontological state of fallen sinfulness of will is made manifest in specific immoral acts and offences against God. In a process that parallels a similar religious moralisation of illness as a divine punishment for misbehaviour (Pattison 1989b), the woes experienced by humankind were found to have their cause in disobedience and offence and their cure in conscious confession, repentance and forgiveness. The moral nature of sin and alienation from God was concretised in practices such as aural confession where sins were articulated and elaborated (Delumeau 1990; Dudley and Rowell 1990; Hepworth and Turner 1982; Tambling 1990). It has also been one of the main determinants of atonement theory.

Atonement theory has many strands and facets (Aulen 1931; Gunton 1988; Fiddes 1989; Young 1975). However, a dominant image has been the forensic one of offence against the laws of a just God (McGrath 1986; Pruyser 1991; Gorringe 1996). For this offence, humanity is liable to punishment. In the theory known as substitutionary atonement, still popular amongst Protestant groups, it is held that the redeeming or atoning work of Christ consists primarily in taking upon himself the punishment due to humankind. By dying on the cross, Jesus accepted and endured the punishment due to humanity. This effected their liberation from sin. It opened the way to reconciliation and reunification between God and God's creatures, making available the grace of God to those who believe and trust in Christ.

Manifestations of the dominance of the forensic and guilt traditions abound throughout the mainstream Western Christian tradition (Milton 1969). The Anglican *Book of Common Prayer*, which helped to shape my own views of my self in relation to God, requires worshippers repeatedly to define themselves as offenders and to confess the sins and offences that contribute to a general sense of unworthiness:

We have erred and strayed from thy ways like lost sheep. We have followed too much the devices and desires of our own hearts. We have offended against thy holy laws. We have left undone those things that we ought to have done, and we have done those things that we ought not to have done; And there is no health in us.

This general sense of criminality is not confined to Protestantism (Joyce 1968). Describing the mentality of youthful Catholics in the 1950s, Lodge writes:

There were two types of sin, venial and mortal. Venial sins were little sins which only slightly retarded your progress across the board. Mortal sins were huge snakes that sent you slithering back to square one, because if you died in a state of mortal sin, you went to Hell. If, however, you confessed your sins and received absolution through the sacrament of Penance, you shot up the ladder of grace to your original position on the board, though carrying a penalty – a certain amount of punishment awaiting you in the next world. For few Catholics expected that they would have reached the heavenly finishing line by the time they died. (Lodge 1981: 7)

The dominance of guilt and offence as the main understandings for sin and alienation from God has downgraded the importance of the notion of alienation as a sense of stain and defilement. At the same time, playing on the sense of ontological badness and inferiority has been exploited in the interests of maintaining order and control in church and society. It amplifies and gives power to the notion of guilt:

All authoritarian regimes are based on the manipulation of human feelings of shame, and those regimes begin with God and the paternalistic world of which He is a part. God/the Father takes the shame that exists within any human and trains it to be shame in the face of God/the Father . . . God/the Father then promises the abject child to eliminate the shame through the simple expedient of obedience: one feels shame because one is not right with the Lord, or is not consonant with the wishes of the Father, and so one only needs to subscribe to the regime of the Lord or the Father in order to escape from the shame that projects His fierce gaze so unrelentingly upon us. The promise of God/the Father is always the same: the end of our shame through total self-denial. (Hans 1991: 186)

The outworking of this kind of tacit exploitation is a system of confession and penitence fuelled by shame but articulated as guilt. This is infinitely self-perpetuating. It is unable to foster either integration or forgiveness because often it fails properly to address either shame or guilt. While guilty people need forgiveness, shamed people need a sense of valued self.

The confusion of shame and guilt ensures that many groups and individuals conform to ecclesiastical mores. They hope that one day their sacrifices, confessions and obedience will effect a real appropriation of deliverance from a non-specific sense of worthlessness and badness. Human unhappiness may be a small price to pay for the power that goes with the illusion that an individual or group may be able to make real salvation and the fantasy of acceptability and worth. Thus Christianity 'promises so much triumph but requires a lifetime of self sacrifice' (Fenn 1991: 31).

Recently, the centrality of forensic and judicial theories of atonement with their emphasis on individual human guilt and offence against moral conscience has come into question. One line of attack comes from modern political theologians. They have pointed up the predominantly social nature of sin and evil that oppresses people. They argue that much of what passes for individual guilt is trivial and in any case socially conditioned in a world where oppression and liberation need to be understood in global terms (Pattison 1997a). A second approach is that of more systematic theologians, especially those influenced by feminism. These thinkers have begun to reinterpret the death of Christ not so much in terms of historical once-for-all justification and atonement for sin as in terms of metaphor or example that elicits positive contemporary responses (Bradley 1995; Brock 1988; Carlson Brown and Bohn 1989; Grey 1989). From this perspective, salvation becomes broader and more diverse than simply overcoming sin.

Historical scholars are also now questioning the Augustinian-Lutheran interpretation of Christian tradition that has emphasised individual guilt as the fundamental concern of Christianity from Jesus onwards. Stendahl (1976) questions whether Paul suffered from an acute sense of introspective individual conscience. He argues that this kind of conscience and the interpretation of justification that goes with it was an invention of St Augustine: 'Paul was equipped with what in our eyes must be called a rather "robust" conscience . . . there is no indication that he had any difficulty in fulfilling the Law' (Stendahl 1976: 80). Stendahl notes that 'Paul never urges Jews to find in Christ the answer to the anguish of a plagued conscience (Stendahl 1976: 61).

The displacement of individual guilt as the key to Pauline and subsequent Christian theology has been developed by others. Sanders (1991) suggests that Paul's soteriology was not based on the primacy of sin or systematic theological and psychological reflection on the human condition, but rather on reflection upon his experience of life in Christ.

Augustinian-Lutheran lenses have been arraigned for distorting interpretations of Pauline texts that see them and their account of 'justification by faith' as being mainly concerned with resolving matters of individual guilt. Stowers (1994), for example, examines the rhetorical structure of Romans and concludes that Paul was concerned with the plight of whole peoples, not with the Fall or with individual guilt. In trying to see past the Augustinian interpretative preoccupation with individual sin and guilt, he writes: 'Paul's letters reveal a kind of Christianity that existed before Christianity became a religion of intrinsically sick human nature and its cure' (Stowers 1994: 329). Similarly, Paul's conversion has been reinterpreted not as a realisation of sin and forgiveness, but more as a story that conforms to the genre of the call and commissioning of a prophet (Bailey and Vander Broek 1992: 144ff.).

Revision of interpretations of the concerns and work of Jesus is also under way. A leading authority on the historical Jesus argues that although repentance may be a dominant theme in religion and Jesus was a perfectionist (Sanders 1995: 204), he was not predominantly concerned with individual sin and repentance in his ministry. 'It is not that Jesus disliked repentance and thought that people should never feel remorse and pray for forgiveness' (Sanders 1995: 232). However, Jesus was 'not a repentance-minded reformer'; '"change now or be destroyed" was not his message, it was John's. Jesus' was, "God loves you"' (Sanders 1995: 233). Jesus emphasised good news about God, not the value of repentance.

It may be possible to interpret the Christian tradition in ways that do not make individual sin and guilt central to religious commitment and experience (Jantzen 1998). If this emphasis were to be changed, and there is no intrinsic reason why it should not be, it is perhaps possible that the indiscriminate exploitation of guilt and shame in Christianity might be curbed. Perhaps a message such as 'God loves you' could come to supplant and take precedence over the blunt, crude message 'you are guilty, sinful, stained'. This might enable people more easily to explore their sense of worth before having their worthlessness and shame reinforced.

'Le pécheur est au coeur même de chrétienté . . .', writes Charles Péguy (Greene 1971: viii). The sinner may indeed be at the very centre of Western Christianity. However, while this sinner might feel abnegated, inferior, unwanted, defiled and powerless, in the light of the Western Christian tradition he is perhaps more likely to ascribe the sense of badness to some offence or disobedience rather than to fundamental shame and worthlessness. Gordon (1996) argues that personal guilt is an inner attribution of badness that can be caused by offence, lack of acceptance, or by abuse. I believe that the effects of the latter two causes of a badness attribution are better described and dealt with as shame.

The Christian tradition recognises and has means of dealing with guilt practically and theologically. However, it has little to offer to the condition of shame (Pruyser 1991). Shame is confused and conflated with guilt. This prevents the fundamentally a-moral sense of shame from being recognised and addressed. It also means that guilt-relieving methods such as confession, repentance and forgiveness are unlikely to be effective in alleviating the 'sinner's' condition, particularly over the long term. They might, however, provide some kind of temporary relief if shame can be successfully reconstrued as guilt. Within the Western tradition of interpreting a sense of badness as guilt, many people may be mired in unrelieved and unrelievable shame. This situation will not change until Christianity turns more directly towards the strands in human alienation that may be characterised as shame. Christian theology may therefore have to repent, turn around, and change its focus of attention quite radically – for example in relation to atonement – to make shame and defilement much more directly visible and redeemable.

Pride and humility

A further theological idea that may contribute both to the neglect and propagation of shame is that of pride. Pride may be defined as 'exaggerating our worth and power, and feeling superior to others' (Schimmel 1997: 29). It is closely associated with arrogance, contempt for others, and over-reaching proper personal and human limits – denoted by the term *hubris* in Greek philosophy.

Within the Christian tradition, pride has connotations of direct rebellion and disobedience against God, turning away from the Almighty to become *incurvatus*, and the failure to recognise one's proper place as a human dependant. Pride is the first and most deadly of human sins. It is the fountainhead of all sin within Augustinian and medieval theology, fundamentally corrupting the will and nature of humanity. Ascribing the transgression and fall of Adam to pride, the result of original sin (Augustine 1991: 82), Augustine writes,

For 'pride is the start of every kind of sin.' And what is pride except a longing for a perverse kind of exaltation . . . This happens when a man is too pleased with himself: and a man is self-complacent when he deserts that changeless Good in which, rather than in himself, he ought to have found his satisfaction. This desertion is voluntary . . . (Augustine 1972: 571–2).

'Pride comes before a fall.' This saying highlights the perception, common to Greek and Hebrew culture in the ancient world, that self-assertion and a lack of proper respect for the order of things brings with it inevitable punishment either from God, gods, or Fate. Within this overall tradition Milton's Satan in *Paradise Lost* is the best icon of the dangers of pride (Milton 1969). Pride has remained an important theological category for understanding the fallen nature of humanity up till the present day (Niebuhr 1964 (I): 186ff.).

The counterbalancing virtue to pride is humility. This concept exalts a basic reversal of the world's values by suggesting that it is the humble and meek who are important and significant to God rather than the rich and powerful (Wengst 1988; Oppenheimer 1986): 'He hath put down the mighty from their seats, and exalted them of low degree' (Luke 1.52 AV). Jesus, the anointed messiah of God, is characterised as a humble servant both in the words that are ascribed to him in the gospels and in Paul's epistles: '. . . being found in fashion as a man, he humbled himself, and became obedient unto death, even death on the cross' (Phil. 2.8 AV). Significantly, perhaps, accompanying all the exhortation in the New Testament and other Christian writings to humility, serving others, looking to the interests of others before one's own, and resisting attempts to exalt oneself or boast, there is a parallel theme. This kind of earthly humility will bring eventual triumph and glory with Jesus in the Kingdom of God (Perkins 1995): 'God also hath highly exalted [Jesus], and given him a name which is above every name: That at the name of Jesus every knee should bow, of things in heaven, and things in earth, and things under the earth (Phil. 2.9–10 AV).

There might seem to be little wrong with advocating the wickedness of pride and the rightness of humility. However, this is a classic case where theological ideas may produce secondary effects and interpretations in relation to shame that may not have been intended by their authors and perpetuators.

One effect of the Christian tradition's perceived 'horror of pride' (Oppenheimer 1986) and corresponding exaltation of humility is that it prevents any kind of nuanced, positive evaluation of pride in individuals. If pride is automatically assumed to designate egotism, inordinate self-esteem, and contempt for others, then it is indeed a deeply unattractive and destructive vice. However, Oppenheimer (1986) points out that some of the opposites of pride, like small-mindedness, are just as unattractive as pride itself.

Within the literature of psychology, pride may be reconceptualised not as *hubris*, but as a kind of necessary sense of confidence, self-esteem and competence experienced by the successful self: 'Pride is enjoyment/excitement invested in self, or in accomplishments by self'

(Kaufman 1993: 225). This sense of simple, appropriate, subjective plea-sure occasioned by experiences and actions is close to the sense of joy. It is far removed from the desire to destroy or domineer over others. It actually allows the self to experience itself silently and builds up a sense of expansiveness, efficacy, entitlement and necessary self-esteem.

Lewis believes that pride should be defined as the specific attribution of success to the self in relation to a particular action or event (Lewis 1992: 75). *Hubris*, by contrast, is exaggerated pride, over-confidence, or conceit based on a global over-valuation of the self as a whole rather than upon specific attributes or acts. It is the concomitant of narcissistic wounding and self-abnegation that leads to compensatory grandiosity, self-obsession, arrogance and contempt for others. The implication is that what is often uncritically condemned as pride by theologians using traditional categories is, in fact, a symptom of shame.

The remedy for *hubris* based on shame, according to the psychologists, is the development of a proper sense of self-esteem, self-efficacy and self-respect: 'Central to the resolution of shame is the development of a self-affirming capacity within the client. The self must learn to affirm the self from within' (Kaufman 1993: 224).

So tainted has the notion of pride with connotations of arrogance, conceit and selfishness become, that this different way of understanding it is concealed: 'Individuals are generally socialized to avoid the appear-ance of conceit, arrogance, or superiority. In an effort to banish these particular qualities from children and adults, pride itself has become bound by shame' (Kaufman 1993: 225). Thus, shamed individuals and groups who manifest the symptoms of narcissistic wounding in the form of *hubris*-associated attitudes and behaviours are likely to condemn themselves and to be condemned by others. They will then not receive the kind of understanding and help that they really need in order to develop a proper sense of self and sober self-estimation (Rom. 12.3). Thus Christian ideas about pride may reinforce shame and its correla-tive *hubris* rather than dissipating or healing narcissistic wounds.

Unnuanced, uncritical notions of humility can be just as destructive. The exhortation to be humble can be taken as an instruction to abandon all sense of autonomy and agency. It may amplify shame-induced passiv-ity and depression, as well as actually increasing self-obsession: 'True humility excludes self-consciousness, but false humility intensifies our awareness of ourselves to such a point that we are crippled, and can no longer make any movement or perform any action without putting to work a whole complex mechanism of apologies and formulas of self accusation' (Merton 1972: 147). Forcing an unnuanced view of humility upon people who are engaged in self-hatred, depression and shame amplifies humiliation. It affirms their lack of selfhood and may feed into sado-masochistic relationships with self, others, and God.

Shame and humiliation, rather than humility, can often lead to aggression and contempt towards others as well as towards the self. Perhaps it was this kind of dynamic that helped occasion Nietzsche's contempt for religious 'slave' or 'worm' morality. This was ostensibly based on humility but in fact founded on *ressentiment* leading to denied envy, hatred, and spite together with fantasies of revenge, reward, triumph and destruction (Greven 1992):

While every noble morality develops from a triumphant affirmation of itself, slave morality says No to what is 'outside,' what is 'different,' what is 'not itself': and *this* No is its creative deed. This inversion of the value positing eye – this *need* to direct one's view outward instead of back to oneself – is of the essence of *ressentiment*: in order to exist, slave morality always first needs a hostile external world . . . its action is fundamentally reaction. (Nietzsche 1989: 36–7)

Humility based on humiliation and shame rather than love and acceptance produces hatred, self-righteousness and rigidity, not change and reconciliation.

Traditional Christian attitudes of condemnation of pride and exaltation of humility have inspired some fine religious lives and have helped to define the identity of this religion. Unfortunately, the way in which these ideas have been received and interpreted can also stand in the way of understanding pride, shame and humility in the modern world, forming a kind of ideological fog. So afraid have Christians been that they may fall into pride and fail to attain humility, they have tended to interpret the tradition about pride and humility to mean that any act or attempt at self-assertion is in itself sinful or wicked. Children of my generation were led to believe (by not disinterested adults!) in church, school and home that any attempt to assert themselves or to follow their own wills and desires might well be the fruit of pride, and therefore a dangerous sin.

This notion of prideful over-assertion with its accompanying danger of inevitable punishment prevents many Christians from discriminating between a proper sense of selfhood and autonomy and overweening egotism. Humiliation of children and subordinates by teaching them that they should not enjoy their own subjectivity or assert themselves, that they should eschew pride and seek humility, is often accompanied by the kinds of practices on the part of envious, narcissistically wounded adults and superiors that are designed to break the will (Miller 1987b). Paradoxically, it is precisely this kind of mental and physical environment that produces narcissistically wounded individuals. They may then exhibit the worst symptoms of compensatory *hubris* – arrogance, contempt of others, grandiosity and so on. Hitler himself can be seen as the apotheosis of arrogance and a terrible product of humiliating, will-breaking, anti-hubristic child-rearing (Miller 1987b). If Hitler's ambitions to rule the world and children's enjoyments of their small everyday accomplishments are both characterised as pride, and so condemned, there is little chance that *hubris* and shame can be healed or that proper humility based on sober self-assessment and other-regard can be promoted.

Rereading and reinterpreting the Christian tradition on pride and humility may have an important role in producing circumstances in which there is a better chance that true humility and self-acceptance or pride will have a proper place. This, however, presupposes that self-acceptance is not a bad thing. And here again there is a problem because the Christian tradition has often appeared to provide blanket condemnation not only of pride, but also of the self.

The problematic self

If pride of any kind has been equated with sin, arrogance and contempt of all kinds in the Christian tradition, the notion of individual self often enjoys a similar kind of disapprobation and disregard. This prevents Christian believers from having a nuanced view of persons and reality.

My own childhood was haunted by this memorable quotation from the lips of Jesus Christ: 'Whosoever will come after me, let him deny himself, and take up his cross, and follow me. For whosoever will save his life shall lose it; but whosoever shall lose his life for my sake and the gospel's, the same shall save it' (Mark 8.35–6 AV). I took this to be a daunting command not to think about myself and my own 'selfish' needs and desires, but rather to think of those of others and of God to the absolute exclusion of my own.

This kind of interpretation was reinforced by exhortations in school, home and family not to be so selfish, to be generous to others, to share what I had selflessly, and to think of the needs and interests of others rather than my own. This made me feel bad about having any possessions, and I gave a lot of them away, realising as I did so that this was not enough: 'We are unprofitable servants: we have done that which was our duty to do' (Luke 17.10 AV). Insofar as I withheld anything and indulged

my own needs and desires, I identified with the rich young ma[n]
gospels who 'went away sorrowful', being unable to obey Jesus'
tion, 'If thou wilt be perfect, go and sell that thou hast, and give
poor . . . and come and follow me' (Matt. 19.21 AV). Not surprisi[ng]
felt ashamed and guilty that I could not do better for Jesus' sake, particu-
ularly since I actually resented giving things away out of what I would
now see as a well of emotional inner emptiness. I weighed my nine-year-
old self in a balance against a man who had given his own life up for the
sake of his friends, indeed for the life of the whole of humanity, and
found myself sadly wanting.

I now view this interpretation as a symptom of shamed selfhood. I
lacked a sense of selfhood, self-acceptance and entitlement that would
allow me to enjoy myself as I was, and to experience my real wishes and
desires as I felt them. Instead, I desperately tried to create an idealised
or perfect 'false self' that would be acceptable to others and to my fantasised ideal God (Richards 1996; Saussy 1991). While I was trying to die
to my unacceptable 'selfish' self, that self would not die! So I found
myself in a constant state of mortal combat with it as I tried to control
it in the name of Christ.

I recount this experience here to show how elements of Christian theology and teaching, from the Bible and elsewhere, mingled with my
psychological disposition to produce a very unsatisfactory and negative
view of the self. The self, especially the desirous, embodied self, was to
be curbed, deprived, controlled and disciplined at all points lest it fall
into sin and further enmity with God. Paradoxically, focussing upon the
self as the locus of sin and failure before God actually reinforces self-
consciousness, self-awareness and even self-centredness. The individual
soul becomes the scene of an intriguing and vital drama in which the
forces of good and evil fight it out, as in some medieval morality play
about Everyman. The apparently contradictory attitudes of simultaneously focussing upon the individual self while deprecating or ignoring it
have their roots deep in the Christian tradition.

The roots of ignoring what we would now call the individual, psychological self may be found in the New Testament. Malina, a biblical
scholar who uses the insights and methods of cultural anthropology, suggests (1996: 35ff.) that there was no such thing as the atomised individual autonomous self in New Testament times. All selves were 'we' selves.
These selves only existed and had identity in relation to particular families or groups. They would therefore put the interests and needs of those
groups before their own.

Addressing Jesus' call to 'deny self', Malina suggests that this was a call to potential disciples not to deny their own personal needs and emotions, but rather to leave behind their old identities and in this sense to become non-selves, or rather new selves in a new community (Malina 1996: 67ff.). The sacrifice of self, in this reading, would represent death as a social reality. This was to die as an 'individual', too, as one was excluded from the social group where one was recognised to be a member person. Contemporaries of Jesus would not have recognised themselves as possessing a strong inner-directed and self-aware psychology which should take precedence over social needs and identity. It is this kind of fundamental group over against individual identity that led to the morality of the early Christian church, as expressed in the texts of the New Testament, being heavily corporatist and altruistic (Goulder 1994; Pagels 1982).

There is very little in the New Testament with its heavy emphasis on the corporate Kingdom of God and the church community as the locus for Christian living that would lend support to modern personalist notions of authenticity, self-realisation, and individual self-acceptance. Individual consciousness and conscience had not yet been born (Stendahl 1976). At least, they did not have the same form and significance that they do in the modern Western world. Furthermore, a strong emphasis on the importance of inspiration by the Holy Spirit, conversion, 'putting on Christ' and being completely transformed suggests that the 'self' as it is in its natural state is not so much to be accepted as to be fought and fundamentally changed.

It is important, however, to acknowledge the ways in which Christianity has nurtured the emergence and value of the individual self. Charles Taylor and others see the Christian tradition as one of the well-springs of modern psychological individualism (Taylor 1989, 1991; cf. McFadyen 1990; Morris 1972; White 1996). In the first place, Christianity offers the example of a single man, Jesus, whose life and death have the power to change the world and start a new community. Paul, too, appears to have influence as a historically significant individual, albeit that it may be a mistake to attribute to him a modern kind of psychological consciousness.

It is with Augustine, the first known autobiographer, that reflexive individual consciousness decisively starts to develop in the West (Augustine 1991; Freeman 1993; Taylor 1989): 'I have become a problem to myself,' Augustine confides to his God and his readers (Augustine 1991: 208). 'It is hardly an exaggeration to say that it was Augustine who introduced the inwardness of radical reflexivity and bequeathed it to the Western tradition of thought' (Taylor 1989: 131).

Augustine introduced the first person viewpoint into consciousness because he believed the light of God was to be found inwards, within the rationality of the person. Light was not the only thing that Augustine found within. Original sin was the mark lying upon the soul of each human being. Thus while the individual was in one way godlike and worthy of respect, he or she was also the locus of sin and evil. Distrust and potential contempt of the corrupt self were thus introduced at the moment when significant importance was being attached to the individual. I am reminded here of Peter Brown's comment upon Pauline views of the body that might equally be applied with relevant modification to Augustine's view of the human person or self: 'we are presented with the human body as in a photograph taken against the sun: it is a jet-black shape whose edges are suffused with light' (Brown 1989: 47).

An ambivalent, and somewhat pessimistic, view of the fallen individual self has pervaded Christianity from Augustine to the present. This provides a poor basis for constructing a positive view of the self, self-esteem or personal pride. Indeed, it continues to provide a critique of these modern phenomena (McGrath and McGrath 1992).

The result of the ambivalent tradition about self and personhood, at least in the Protestant West, has been that, on the whole, Christians cannot look on the good and bad aspects of individual selfhood with detachment or equanimity. At any time, battle may break out between that which is evil and that which is godly in the self. The self is in a position of permanent siege and temptation and it is guarded only by a corrupt and weak will. In these circumstances, external rescue and salvation by the direct agency of God is the only hope. The self has no power of itself to help itself. The self thus remains a kind of unregarded skeleton in Christianity's cupboard that inspires distrust, strong feelings and anxieties. Believers in all ages have been advised to overcome or ignore it in the interests of obeying God's will. Of course this particular injunction allows those in power and authority in both church and society to gain assent and compliance from those in their thrall or care.

There are those within the Christian community who rail against the implicit and explicit denigration and ignoring of the individual, psychological self. Sebastian Moore, for example, defines sin as self-disesteem (Moore 1980). He goes on to argue that self-disesteem is 'the root of all evil', the basis of what might be called original sin, and he acknowledges that '[r]eligion has done much harm by endorsing people's wretched ideas of themselves, whereas it is precisely religion's job to cure people of this sin of self-negation' (Moore 1980: 68–9).

Feminists, too, have argued that the Christian tradition has spent far too much time worrying about the sin of pride and over-assertion when a problem that many women face is not being assertive enough on account of not having a fully developed, properly individuated sense of self (Saiving 1979). Similar arguments about the depersonalising, objectifying, disempowering and dehumanising effects of Christian thought and practice have also been put by Black and liberation theologians in relation to whole peoples and groups. This does not stop traditional Christianity from continuing to distrust and condemn the self at regular intervals and in unnuanced, indiscriminate ways. This in the face of the wise comments of shamed people like John Bradshaw, who writes: 'Shame-based people are egocentric. I compare it to having chronic toothache. If your tooth hurts all the time, all you can think of is your tooth. You become tooth centred. Likewise if your self is ruptured and it is painful to experience yourself, you will become self-centred' (Bradshaw 1988: 195). This suggests that the way out of self-obsession and crippling self-consciousness is more likely to emanate from self-acceptance than from some perverse notion of self-denial that ultimately leads to other-denial as well. One of the supreme paradoxes of Christianity must be that it simultaneously manages to denigrate the self while often amplifying self-consciousness, self-examination and self-fixation (Rubin 1994). 'The conscientious religious person is always at risk of deep self-centredness' (Hughes 1997: 61), an observation that is perhaps confirmed by the finding that Christians are seldom more altruistic than non-religious people (Batson et al. 1993).

Conclusion

In this part of the chapter, I have reviewed from a personal viewpoint aspects of Christian thought and belief that may, from some perspectives, help to engender or exacerbate inappropriate, dysfunctional shame in individuals and groups. However, religious images, symbols, myths and narratives are capable of multiple interpretations, interactions and effects. For some people, the images and symbols I have highlighted may be understood in ways that alleviate shame.

The implication of my analysis is that Christians, especially theologians, may, in the interests of reducing unnecessary shame and humiliation, need to think carefully about the symbols and interpretations that they propagate. While many people may be helped by their understandings of the Christian tradition, some may be damaged, particularly when those understandings are introduced to them in childhood.

This kind of danger led Melanie Klein to deplore the introduction of the idea of God to children as a kind of disrespectful, boundary-breaching abuse: the 'idea of an invisible, omnipotent and omniscient deity is overwhelming for the child' (Klein 1988a: 23). I do not share Klein's desire for an absolute embargo on the idea of God in childhood. However, I am deeply aware of the haunting, tormenting power of certain religious ideas in my own childhood. It might be possible for individuals not to be thus adversely affected, just as it is possible for some people to survive child abuse and later to flourish. However, this is not a reason for abusers or ideologues to continue to behave in the same old harmful ways. If symbols, images and beliefs about God can be formulated and propagated that are less likely to induce feelings of defilement, unwantedness, inferiority, unlovability and powerlessness in people, then it is desirable that this should happen. The implication of refusing to engage in such creative reformulation may be that theology and theologians are themselves bound up in maintaining the unholy canopy of shame. Perhaps the canopy covers their own shame by allowing them to shame others.

CHRISTIAN PRACTICE AND SHAME

Christian practice is as important as theology. It is in actions, attitudes and habits that theology is fleshed out and communicated. Here basic stances and behaviours in believers are established. Like theological images, ideas and beliefs, Christian practices are also capable of generating, maintaining and hiding human shame of various kinds. This can prevent Christianity from recognising and responding helpfully to shame, particularly dysfunctional chronic shame.

I want here to establish a *prima facie* case for the possibility that some important Christian practices can, on occasion, foster, promote, exploit and hide shame. I shall then speculate on some of the factors that may lead to the production, exploitation and disguising of shame before looking briefly at some of the effects that shame-bound and shame-promoting religion may have upon its adherents. My account here is informed by my own experience and observation of Christian community life as mediated to me through the established state Anglican Church of England.

Liturgy

Liturgy is crucial in shaping the lives, attitudes and identities of Christians. It is in various services with their mixture of ritual actions and words, spoken and sung, that many people internalise who and what they are in relation to the religious community. They also learn much of their theology here. In the face-to-face relations of liturgy, Christian people learn of their sense of worth and inclusion, or the lack of it (Hardy and Ford 1984; Shuman 1999). The official ideology of liturgy is that it is intended to build up the body of Christ and make manifest God's accepting love. However, there is a considerable ambivalence in the messages that may be implicitly and explicitly communicated in worship. Some of these, like the religious symbols and images examined earlier, may communicate to at least some people a sense of rejection, inferiority, unlovableness, powerlessness, worthlessness and defilement.

Entrance to the Christian community is through the sacrament of baptism, a ritual whose focus is upon cleansing, removing defilement in the form of sin, and acquiring a new 'clean' identity in Christ, sometimes symbolised by the donning of a white robe. For many people, baptism is a joyous experience that achieves exactly what it is supposed to, a sense of worth, new life and belonging. However, the repetition of baptismal ceremonies within the Christian community and the renewal of baptism vows by long-standing church members is a potent reminder of a basic sense of uncleanness and unworthiness. It is the first of many reminders to believers that while they may have put on Christ, words like 'unworthy', 'sinful' and 'unclean' still very much apply to them.

These words are routinely picked up in other liturgical events. Very few services in mainstream denominations ever take place without some kind of acknowledgment of unworthiness, inadequacy and sin. Often these confessions are placed in close juxtaposition to other words that make it clear that God is good, clean and almighty. This happens, for example, in the Communion Service in the *Book of Common Prayer*, upon which I was brought up. Here the Sanctus, where God is lauded as 'Holy, holy, holy', is immediately followed by the prayer of humble access in which the worshippers confess that they 'are not worthy to gather up the crumbs' under the Lord's table.

This kind of contrast between God the great and good King and his humble subjects is explicit in rites of confession. It is also implicit in much of the rest of liturgy. Worshippers even today routinely call God King and Lord, using other titles of royalty and nobility with equal facility. This emphasises a relationship of hierarchy, dominance and submission that is based on an asymmetrical relationship of power between humans and the divinity. The language of sin conjoined with that of hierarchy would seem designed to engender a sense of impotence and defilement. It often succeeds in doing so, particularly in the case of those people who already feel bad about themselves.

The language of inferiority and stain that pervades much liturgy is often amplified and confirmed by factors such as setting and ritual action. The design of many churches, together with the use of ornaments made of precious metals and Roman court clothes as vestments, reflects the fact that much liturgy is inspired by the customs and practices of ancient secular courts such as that of the Roman emperor. Bowing, using incense, separating off the populace from the sacred space, wearing special clothes – all these things owe their provenance to secular practices and hierarchical arrangements that were designed to reveal and maintain power in society. An invisible God now occupies the sanctified space in which the secular ruler might have sat enthroned, but this God is often allotted exactly the same honours and attributes as an earthly royal counterpart. As in medieval royal courts, members of the commonality are encouraged to kneel and bow their heads before the deity, particularly if they are making requests for grace in the form of prayers. This kind of movement explicitly expresses the unequal, dependent relationship that an inferior might have with a patron or superior within a traditional, hierarchical society (Malina 1996). Here again, then, there is the potential for worshippers to find themselves feeling somewhat inferior, fearful, excluded and unwanted as ill-prepared, badly dressed, unclean supplicants at the local throne of heavenly grace.

Christianity may not be a conventional 'cleanliness' cult (Countryman 1989). Nonetheless, it is a community with boundaries defining 'inside' and 'outside', 'clean' and 'unclean' (Malina 1983). Often these boundaries are defined by sexual and other bodily activity rather than by physical boundaries or ritual exclusions. However, the boundaries are real. Part of the purpose of Christianity is to move people from a position of alienation and defilement into 'clean' divine space and corporate belonging and purity (Malina 1983). This process cannot be accomplished without the evocation of dirt and defilement in the first place.

Many apparently incidental, practical factors can also produce or amplify a sense of shame, particularly in outsiders to the community. Often, insiders know the liturgy and its accompanying movements by heart. For outsiders, however, it appears to be an exclusive mystery to which there is no *entrée*. I well remember at about the age of seven going to a church and crying because I could not find my way around the many books that had been handed to me to 'help' me to participate. Another moment of rejection and exclusion arose later in the service when many of the adults present left their pews, and me with the pews, to go and huddle, backs to the rest of us, around the altar to receive communion. This act of solidarity with other community members was an act of rejection and lack of solidarity with outsiders. Inadvertently, it reinforced in me a sense of unwantedness and unworthiness. I should also acknowlege that together with some anger, it raised within me a sense of envy and curiosity, and a fair determination to be included rather than excluded at some time in the future. In retrospect, perhaps this was a somewhat masochistic response. One way and the other, seeing others eating together while I was excluded did not do much for my sense of esteem and value.

There are other aspects of liturgy that might help to engender and promote a sense of shame, feeling bad and inferiority in people. For example, sermons are often oriented in one way or another to informing people that they are not 'good enough'. Hymns, while they may have the capacity to break down a sense of isolation and self-preoccupation because people sing them together, are often composed of lyrics full of the rhetoric of self-hatred and inferiority while they fawn upon the power, goodness and majesty of the Almighty. For many years I sang:

> Let holy charity
> Mine outward vesture be,
> And lowliness become mine inner clothing:
> True lowliness of heart,
> Which takes the humbler part,
> And o'er its own shortcomings weeps with loathing.

The last line had particular meaning and resonance for me.

I do not want to account for all shame-producing and -sustaining aspects of liturgy here, but rather to suggest that it is possible that liturgy can indeed engender and exacerbate shame, particularly in people who are uncertain of their own worth and value in the first place. It should be remembered that often children are routinely exposed to worship of various kinds at tender ages. They may be highly vulnerable to internal-ising a negative view of self, particularly if their background has been neglectful or abusive. The hierarchical, dominant God of much formal Christian liturgy and prayer may seem to promise acceptance and love at the expense of self-negation and sacrifice. In this guise, the deity may mirror and amplify the image of the sadistic or neglectful parent. This may help to create or reinforce an adaptive or false, dependent self amongst worshippers, particularly impressionable, needy, young wor-shippers.

In a book that was influential for several decades, an Anglican bishop wrote of worship:

In worship . . . the worshipper . . . sees himself to be nothing: in worshipping his Redeemer, he knows himself incapable of redeeming even the least of God's creatures. The most he can hope for is that God will deign to use him for the forwarding of His high designs. Worship tells us much good of God, but little good of ourselves, except that we are the work of God's hands . . . it leaves us nothing upon which to pride ourselves. (Kirk 1931: 448)

For persons who have an inadequate sense of self, this sort of experience may amplify a sense of powerlessness, uselessness, defilement and objec-tifying depersonalisation. Despite the passage of time, and attempts by feminists amongst others to modify the language, actions and settings of liturgy so they are less overtly humiliating (Morley 1992; Wren 1988), Kirk's God still lives and is the official deity of choice that is worshipped in the Church of England amongst other denominations. It will be many decades before the language of power, domination, obedience, royalty, submission and humility is replaced by a different kind of reverence, love and praise.

Christian child-rearing and formation

Religious education and the rearing of children within the Christian faith are seen as priorities for religious communities wishing to perpetu-ate their existence. There are different ways of helping children to appropriate and be shaped by the truths and insights of Christian faith. Many of these are benign, self-enhancing and creative. However, for some, religious formation may be an education into shame.

This thought first occurred to me when I read Rubin's *Religious Melancholy and Protestant Experience in America* (1994). This historical study describes the way in which Protestant evangelical pietism, formed as a consequence of the Reformation's individualisation of religious experience and in relation to anxiety about the reality of salvation, seems to be closely associated with melancholy (what moderns might regard as 'depression' (Jackson 1986)). Rubin describes a system of religiosity based upon

(1) Experiential oneness with God; (2) the quest for spiritual perfection through . . . conversion; (3) reliance upon the objective authority of the biblical Word as interpreted by the prepared heart of the new man, himself transformed by the 'ingrafting' of a dynamic, organic relationship between the believer and Christ; and (4) the opposition to . . . the sinful orders of the natural man and the world. (Rubin 1994: 29)

The end of this system was the experience of God's presence within the self as a sense of ecstatic love. This could only be gained by a constant inward battle against sin and impurity, often manifested in the inability to control sexual and other bodily based urges and desires. When believers lost the sense of God's presence, they believed themselves to have fallen into sin. Despair and melancholy then replaced divine communion (Rubin 1994: 132). Remedies such as radical fasting were required to restore a sense of control that might lead to conversion and the restoration of divine presence. A cyclical movement of despair, ascetic action, conversion, ecstatic presence, then a new fall into despair or melancholy seems to have characterised the lives of many pietists. These made up a considerable proportion of the population in North America in the eighteenth and nineteenth centuries. Melancholy and Protestantism appeared inextricable.

Sometimes, no matter how much a person tried to discipline themselves, the divine presence remained clouded or absent. In this situation many devout believers fell into total despair. Some actively committed suicide, while others, like William James' father, died of ascetic practices such as fasting after living for years in depression and gloom. Rubin recounts several cases, from the seventeenth century to the present day, of people who fell into pietistic despair.

One of the most tragic of these is that of Benjamin Noyes. Noyes was a student who committed suicide at the age of nineteen in 1815, having fallen into the belief that he was the hypocritical enemy of God, probably because he could not control his urge to masturbate. Rubin writes:

Noyes emerged from boyhood as an exemplary evangelical personality. His diary entries . . . reveal a youth who actively and warmly embraced the ideals of evangelical Pietism: (1) the mortification of self and surrender to the will of

God; (2) the routine practice of devotional piety in fasting, secret prayer, self-examination [hence the diary – SP], Sabbath keeping and public worship; (3) a tender-hearted personal relationship with God; and (4) a generalized benevolent concern for the salvation of all people . . . (Rubin 1994: 139)

Noyes possessed 'a keen analytic mind, a tender heart open to religious sentiments and affections, and a harsh, exacting conscience' (Rubin 1994: 138). As a product of an evangelical family, he was 'obsessed with feelings of guilt and shame, unable to win the love of his earthly or heavenly fathers' (Rubin 1994: 138). 'Equating self with autonomous agency, he felt compelled to quash [the issue of adult autonomy] by self-torture, self-denying evangelical humiliation, and selfless surrender into the bosom of Christ. Yet, these spiritual exercises led him into desolation and self-destruction' (Rubin 1994: 138).

Noyes' despair was the fruit of a religious upbringing. His father advocated 'will-breaking, filial piety, and obedience' to parents, and suggested that children should be required to display meekness, humility and submission to parental authority (Rubin 1994: 137). The evangelical temperament was formed in children by 'breaking the will of toddlers, crushing their sense of self and autonomy and bringing them into habitual obedience and submission to parental authority and family government . . .' (Rubin 1994: 48).

Children were inducted into obedience, self-control and self-denial which helped to create a continuously active conscience which reflected and censured thought, emotions and conduct. By this means, evangelicals were 'prevented from attaining the developmental goals of basic trust and autonomy' that are the counter-pole of shame. They remained obsessed with narcissistic self-observation and were required to declare war upon the self, directing all their anger inwards (Rubin 1994: 48). 'Evangelicals spent their lives in a futile attempt to prove themselves worthy of parental love through acts of total submission and obedience. At adulthood, submission to God replaced filial obedience and the need to recover God's love became paramount' (Rubin 1994: 49). Not surprisingly, '[e]vangelical selves continually alternated between melancholic and contemplative personae, never achieving integration and autonomy; they were always at war with the self and unable to secure a lasting spiritual comfort in divine contemplation' (Rubin 1994: 49).

To return to the present day, I do not want to suggest that the great majority of children within religious communities are brought up along the lines of classic evangelical piety as described by Rubin. Nonetheless, elements of this kind of anti-child, soul-murdering strategy derived from pietism are not unknown in religious circles today. Whenever ideas and practices are introduced to young children that require of them obedience, submission and self-denial for the sake of God, Jesus or parents, a contribution may be being made to the engendering of shamed, melancholic selves.

Similarly, when children are beaten or physically punished 'for their own good', soul murder may be in progress. It is alarming that many Christians, including the present Archbishop of Canterbury, adhere to the view that smacking children to discipline them is acceptable. Evangelical Christians, in particular, seem keen not to spare the rod and so spoil the child; a number of successful paperbacks advocating corporal punishment have been published in recent years. In a study of the psychological effects of physical punishment in religious communities, Greven points out that there has been an obsession with authority, control and obedience in evangelical churches for centuries (Greven 1992:69). This often finds expression in the call for the use of physical punishment as a reflection of the love and fear of God that children must learn if they are to avoid damnation (Greven: 1992: 63).

The combination of ideological teaching on the importance of obedience, self-denial and submission and physical violence on small children remains a powerful tool for producing conformity long after children have forgotten the blows that fell upon them. It remains an important source of shame, self-hatred, melancholy and depression. Although I was brought up in 1950s England rather than North America, I recognise the combination of shaming 'theological' teaching and physical abuse in the settings of school, home and family that accomplishes the murder of the soul. Individualistic pietism is not confined to Protestantism. Many Catholic practices such as confession and daily prayer help to focus children and young people inwards upon themselves, their faults, and the sources of alienation and offence against God. This helps to create and fix self-conscious souls in their own private hell. The net result can be lifelong melancholy and pervasive shame.

Rubin concludes his book on religious melancholy thus:

[E]vangelical Pietism drew upon the structure of religious experience and selfhood of Augustinian piety. Religious personality, self, and identity were forged in the crucible of redemptive suffering. Many believers freely chose to live inside this prison of ideas ... Others who suffered evangelical nurture and languished in spiritual desolation were trapped ... by the persistent memory of childhood cruelty . . . With life cast as a continual inner warfare and a rejection of the 'natural man,' melancholy reigned. (Rubin 1994: 238)

Wherever this kind of world view prevails, human flourishing and freedom from shame is likely to be diminished. Sadly, children continue to be inducted into it (Miller 1987a, 1987b, 1991; Parkinson 1997; Walker 1992). It is in this light that Rubin believes that the future of religious melancholy (and one could add 'shame') 'unfortunately looks bright' (Rubin 1994: 238). He notes that 'many evangelical Christians today suffer from scrupulosity, depression, anxiety, and fear' (Rubin 1994: 229).

Moral attitudes and teaching

One of the main features pertaining to religious communities in the contemporary world is that they are groups with a distinctive kind of morality. Indeed, often churches are at their most visible publicly when they are making moral stands or judgments on internal or external concerns. However, there are aspects of the way in which this activity is conducted that might be taken to cause or to exacerbate dysfunctional shame.

Much Christian moral teaching is implicitly informed by the twin notions that, first, perfection, purity and moral conformity are required of all believers, and second, that human beings are simply not good enough to attain the standards that are required of them. Church leaders are fond of holding up 'ideals' of behaviour, particularly in relation to sexuality and family life, while often simultaneously acknowledging that these are often not realisable for many individuals. It is here that notions of 'loving the sinner while hating the sin' are invoked to try and narrow the gap between witnesses of perfection and the reality of individual circumstances. Sometimes, this kind of exhortation is followed with statements about the sinful nature and need for forgiveness of all human beings, including those who proclaim the ideal.

This kind of stance may be very appropriate to those who have a robust sense of their own worth and responsibility. In the case of shame-prone people, who may possess an idealised view of how they ought to be together with a sense of personal failure and badness, this kind of idealisation and perfectionism may exacerbate a sense of personal inadequacy, hopelessness and failure. Instead of increasing efficacy, worth and power, idealistic moral exhortation may be crushing. It may fix individuals or groups in a state of entrapment and alienation. Often churches offer no tangible means whereby people might narrow the gap between corporately promulgated ideal and personal reality. This may freeze them into a state where they feel like inadequate frauds or hypocrites because of the perceived, unbridgeable gap between what is and what 'ought' to be. The pernicious, paralysing effects of this kind of idealisation upon shamed people, pointed up in other contexts by psychologists like Winnicott (1990) and Rogers (1967), have yet to be fully recognised within religious communities.

While Christian moral teaching may often be idealistic and perfectionistic it is also, paradoxically, frequently rather non-specific. Christian worshippers are often required to confess their sins. However, it is left to the individual to determine what exactly their sins are. This non-specificity and putting the duty of discernment on to the individual provide much scope for unbounded imagination and scrupulosity. People are invited to feel bad before God, and then to work out what exactly has got them into this state of alienation. For some, this leads to the elaboration of a myriad of offences and faults that then account for a sense of sinfulness and ontological badness. Here again, shame-prone people can be trapped in a slough of non-specific offence that is accounted for in terms of individual sins, but which has very little to do with particular thoughts or actions. Non-specific exhortation on sin plays upon and exacerbates a sense of badness while providing little help for people to identify their real offences and to grapple with these in a realistic way. Thus people are confirmed in the pre- or a-moral state of badness associated with shame and fail to grow towards real efficacy and moral responsibility.

This brings me to the use of shaming within Christian morality. Much of what I have described so far amounts to the use of shaming that makes people feel bad, not about what they have done, but about what they are. To commit specific discrete sins and offences and then to acknowledge these and be forgiven is to be an actor who takes responsibility and sometimes makes mistakes. To be a sinner is to have made a global judgment about the whole self as fundamentally bad, defective and worthy of rejection. While Christian moral teachers may like to think that they are addressing responsible individual actors who sin, a main part of their audience may be shamed people who regard themselves as wholly bad sinners. Thus moral teaching and attitudes may often create and maintain sinners rather than enhancing personal and social responsibility.

This tendency is exacerbated by the fact that often individuals and groups are singled out for condemnation and rejection not because of anything that they have done, but basically because of something that they are. Notoriously, Christianity has been particularly harsh in its attitudes towards gay people and other embodied 'sexual deviants' (amongst whom one could number the whole of womankind!) (Cotter 1997; Davenport-Hines 1990; Nelson and Longfellow 1994; Pattison 1990). While a theoretical distinction is often made between orientation or being and specific acts, the overwhelming witness of Christian practice has been that such people are, at best, second-class citizens whose life and habits need strict regulation, abstinence and control. At worst, they are regarded as an abomination by virtue of their very existence and they should have no place in the Christian community. Such attitudes cannot do anything but nurture a sense of defilement, alienation, unwantedness and unacceptability in the individuals and groups who are their object, and many pastors, moralists, and lay people love to have it so.

Of course, since the incident of Adam and Eve in the Garden of Eden, sexuality and the body have been seen as particularly sensitive sites for shame, particularly amongst young people (Kaufman 1993). The implied, non-specific condemnation of all things bodily and sexual must therefore do much to increase fundamental shame amongst young people who are exposed to Christian morality. Many gay people have had to struggle to put faith together with their knowledge of their sexual orientation and desires. The advent of the AIDS epidemic hardened Christian attitudes towards gay people, turning them, in a burst of unmitigated homophobia, from stigmatised second-class citizens into demonised social 'lepers' (Jantzen 1990). For some, only leaving the community of 'faith' behind has allowed them to discover themselves as valuable in their own eyes and those of God.

Negative, shaming attitudes towards the ontological being of particular persons and groups are not confined to sexual minorities. Black people and women, regarded as physically 'marked' in their own distinctive ways, have also been the butt of much prejudice and rejection by the Christian 'tribe' (Selby 1991). Until recently, for example, women were not allowed to be priests in the Church of England and they are still not allowed to be bishops. Black people, too, have experienced institutionalised discrimination and marginalisation. All of which conspires to do little for a sense of value, significance and worth and much to engender and maintain what might be called a sense of shame and disidentification.

In this context, there is much for established religious communities to

be properly ashamed and guilty about in their supposedly 'moral' and
attitudinal witness. In the only place in the gospels where Jesus speaks
specifically of shame (Mark 8.38), he refers

not to shame at a sinner or a sufferer or an outcast, but shame at the pretended
followers of his who disown the cross and the solidarity with human shame and
suffering it represents . . . Jesus . . . expresses deep shame at those of us who
affirm him as Christ, call ourselves after his name, and yet refuse to follow him
in a vocation of being alongside. (Jantzen 1990: 30)

Christian discipline

One of the places in which the Christian community might be seen to
act most overtly to engender and exploit shame is in the area of church
order and discipline. Here, exclusion and rejection seem often to be the
disciplinary tool of choice. Ever since the apostle Paul called for those
who did not love the Lord Jesus Christ to be 'anathema', i.e. cast out
(1 Cor. 16.22), exclusion has been a preferred mechanism for ordering
the community. Much of church history from its very beginnings, with
its litany of disputes over authority, doctrine, heresy, schism, witness and
practice, can be seen as a debate over who should be regarded as 'clean',
holy and within the community, and who should be regarded as profane
and without (Goulder 1994; Malina 1983; Shaw 1983). This is symbolised in disputes over who should be allowed to participate in the holy
meal of the eucharist. Even today, many Christian communities exclude
members of other churches from the eucharist. This is a potent,
poignant sign of rejection for many. Doubtless, this kind of blanket
exclusion of groups or kinds of others is not meant to stigmatise or to be
taken personally. The trouble is that it does, and it is.

As a young clergyman, I was told that the only real 'power' that priests
have is to excommunicate people from the eucharist. While this may not
be the threat of extinction and total social exclusion that it was in
medieval Christendom, it is significant that this notion of active exclusion survives as at least a theoretical means of church discipline.
Exclusion from a community that often characterises itself as a family
and its corporate meals is a potent way of communicating shame,
defilement, unacceptability and unlovability.

The threat of exclusion, still real in some churches, remains an important way of maintaining conformity and order. For lay people in many
denominations these days, exclusion is more likely to be accomplished
informally by making people uncomfortable about their lifestyle, morals

and general conformity. Thus many gay people and people with marital difficulties have excluded themselves voluntarily from intolerant religious communities over the years. On the whole, those communities have shown remarkably little concern or interest in their fate once they have gone. Another sign of the shame-laden 'abominable' nature of those who lie beyond the pale of the chosen people, perhaps.

The dynamics of formal exclusion apply with greater force in relation to clergy, however. Clergy are often idealised and required to be moral and spiritual exemplars by their denominations. Frequently, 'higher' and more visible standards of behaviour are expected of them. So, for example, the Church of England will not officially tolerate physically active gay relationships amongst clergy while it chooses not to concern itself so directly with the sexual activities of non-ordained people (House of Bishops 1991). The rub here is that if clergy manage to conceal their deviant behaviour, homosexual, heterosexual or criminal, from public attention so that it does not cause 'scandal', they will often remain in their jobs. If, however, their behaviour becomes known and an embarrassment to the church, they are likely to be forcibly and automatically removed from their posts.

This seems to be a clear example of the dynamics of shame whereby appearance is all in a community that is run on dynamics of the preservation of 'face', honour and respect (Malina 1983), rather than on the principles of guilt, repentance and forgiveness. The first casualty of a system in which honesty is punished is honesty itself (Selby 1991: 49). If clergy perceive themselves to be in any way defective, they are likely to conceal this from themselves, their co-religionists and those in authority over them. This traps them in a web of shame and economy with the truth so that they are unable to behave openly, morally and responsibly. As we have seen, defences against fundamental shame of this kind can include self-righteousness, contempt for others and the attempt to project shame on to others. Perhaps this helps to maintain the shaming attitudes that clergy and religious communities so often appear to enjoy placing on those who are perceived to be outsiders. It certainly does little to foster genuine forgiveness, openness to others, and the benevolent rather than the authoritarian exercise of pastoral power.

Exclusion is a means of forcibly removing 'evil', impurity, and problems from the community of faith. It can be seen as the product of communities that are shaped by and exploit the dynamics of shame that are typical of tribal, face-to-face societies (Malina 1983, 1996). The use, or the threat of the use, of exclusion as a means of effecting communal homogeneity and harmony is a symptom of unaddressed shame that stands in the way of developing systems of responsibility, guilt and forgiveness. The shame-laden mechanism of exclusion, whether it is used against individuals or groups, is difficult to limit or control. It is almost bound to create or exacerbate a profound sense of shame in those who are formally or informally excluded.

Christianity and the generation and maintenance of shame: the evidence

Aspects of Christian ideology and practice can generate and exacerbate shame in individuals and groups. I believe this certainly to have been true in my own experience which has largely shaped the foregoing account. However, it is legitimate to ask whether there is any corroborative evidence from other sources to support my interpretation. The answer to this question is that there is some relevant evidence. However, it is less abundant and less clear than might be desirable for two main reasons.

First, where religion is implicated in shame-like states it is not necessarily directly correlated with shame. Thus shame remains hidden, implicit, or entwined in descriptions of other states such as depression or abuse (Gordon 1996). Secondly, there has, until recently, been little empirical research into the relationship specifically between shame and religion. This means that often evidence for a sometimes negative relationship between Christianity and shame must be tangential rather than direct. That said, there seems to be a good deal of material that broadly supports the kind of assertions and relationships explored earlier in this chapter.

Some of the clearest evidence for the deliberate use and abuse of shame in Christianity comes from historical sources. I have already reviewed Rubin's (1994) work on religious melancholy and evangelical pietism in America. This reveals a set of religious beliefs and practices based on non-mirroring child-rearing that induced a character structure beset by narcissistic anxieties and by shame.

Rubin's picture is to some degree complemented by the work of Demos. His study of shame and guilt among the seventeenth-century Puritans of New England (1996) shows an overtly religiously dominated society in which exposure and public humiliation were main tools of social control. The best icon of this era is Hester Prynne, an adulteress who had to wear a scarlet letter in public as a symbol of her sin and shame (Hawthorne 1903). While the worlds and character structures of

New England Puritans and evangelical pietists may have changed, some of the traits revealed there continue to be felt in religious communities, particularly evangelical religious communities. They provide evidence for the fact that, historically, Christianity has been centrally implicated in the inculcation and fostering of shamed personalities and identities, though the exact nature and meaning of shame have varied over time.

This finding is echoed in one of the very few empirical studies ever to have been undertaken of the relationship between psychological shame and religion. Ould (1995) found that there seemed to be a positive correlation between membership of conservative Calvinist churches in the USA and the presence of chronic shame in the personality. Ould seems to suggest that narcissistically damaged, chronically shamed church members are drawn into conservative churches because 'they provide explicit values (and people embodying those values) in which a narcissistic sufferer may find merger with perfection' (Ould 1995: 108). Unfortunately, the demands for perfection, obedience and purity that these churches make are often impossible to achieve. This can lead believers into a position of heightened shame whereby they experience a sense of failure, rejection and alienation from an ideal, perfect God. One possible implication of Ould's thesis, consistent with Rubin's work on evangelical pietism, is that the more committed and determined to be good and perfect one is (perhaps to compensate for unworthiness or narcissistic inadequacy), the more likely one is to end up in a very committed, perfectionist religious group which has unrealistically high standards that may then amplify one's shame.

Ould's findings find some confirmation in letters I have received from English Christians from a variety of religious contexts. While a self-selected group of people aged over 50, most of whom identify themselves as having been shamed as children and who have subsequently had therapy, their testimony about the intermingling of religion and shame is illuminating. One woman writes:

[S]omehow I always felt deeply 'bad' as a person and therefore sought always to stop people finding out what I was really like, since they would certainly not like me if they did. This meant keeping people at a distance . . . I always 'knew' that if anyone seemed to like me, they would eventually find how bad I was and reject me . . . I realise now that what underlay the religious teaching we received was a belief that being human, and especially sexual was intrinsically bad; it would be better if we could get rid of our humanity and become entirely 'spiritual', whatever that is. There is some better theology around in evangelical and charismatic circles these days, but I am not sure that many people truly believe it. Often they profess to, but then they also propound a dualistic approach . . .

Original sin was a firm belief and I remember my father saying about a tiny baby crying, 'How could anyone look at that and not believe in original sin' [St Augustine's exact view – SP]. He said it as a joke, but it represented his beliefs and our brand of Christianity.

This woman believes herself to be recovering from shame. She has managed to maintain a sense of the goodness of God and of the value of faith. So has this man, whose childhood experience, this time in a Catholic family, was equally unsupportive and shaming:

Alone and unworthy of love because one really was unlovable meant that it was simple and true to sing, 'Guilty, vile and helpless we'. We had no idea that this was the way that was consciously selected as a means of family control by the parents to establish the order they desired for the family . . . This parental need for control had its origins in fear. They themselves had a fear, based on kindly, well-intentioned ignorance of themselves needing also to be accepted . . . So one felt internally bad, even before the criticism would come. One felt unworthy as a person . . . One became one's own persecutor, arresting officer, prosecutor, jury, judge and executioner. To want to have a toy or not to let others have mine was to be that appallingly selfish child who wanted to be competitive or even possessive. And the final card, how could there be anything wrong with you compared with your [ill] sibling and all they endured? What are you crying for? You never had as many operations, so many weeks in hospital. And one would slink away, not only feeling full of shame and humiliation but feeling that they were right in their attitude of disgust, because you were disgusting. And you needed to take it to the priest for confession (we were a good Catholic family).

Another person writes:

My experience of shame was a general feeling of not feeling good enough, always needing approval, feeling guilty, ugly awkward, stupid bad, and having to be good . . . My parents were active members of an evangelical Anglican church and we were taken to church and Sunday school. The teaching was salvation by faith and not works but it did not feel like this, there were expectations to be met, things to do, there was no freedom of expression, and no room for feelings, anxieties, doubts and questions. Life there felt performance based, don't rock the boat, keep it safe, there's a right way of doing things, there are those who are 'in' and those who are 'out'. Grace was not shown to people who did criticise, not fit, ask questions. I think that my religious upbringing strengthened my feelings of shame and the Bible and teaching was used to boost the power of my parents.

These vignettes reveal several aspects of the relationship between psychological shame and Christianity as experienced by some people. First, shame generation and amplification is not confined to any one church or religious community. Secondly, the incidence of shaming is

bound up in a complex ecology of personal psychology and circumstances, parental and family attitudes, and religious beliefs and practices.
Thirdly, religion is often not the primary cause of shame. It acts as a but-
tressing phenomenon that fails to challenge shaming child-rearing and
often seems to support and legitimise it with its undifferentiated vocabulary of guilt, shame, humility, disgust and redeeming victimisation
(Pattison 1998). Religion fails to protect children from shaming or to give
them a sense of value and worth. Fourthly, while religious beliefs and
practices may not set out to cause or maintain shame, they have frequently done so. For those trapped in shame-bound, shaming, abusive
and neglectful families as children, Christianity has often contributed to
their sense of being unable to escape from a sense of personal abnegation and alienation.

More tangential, indirect evidence about the relationship between
Christianity and shame can be found in a variety of other sources where
'shame' itself may be a secondary or incidental concept. The literature
of child abuse and neglect is peppered with incidental references to
shame and unworthiness as a symptom in the abused (Walker 1992).
Insofar as such abuse may be caused, sanctioned or ignored by religious
communities and personages, Christian ideology and practice can be
implicated in the causation and maintenance of shame, though shame
may not be perceived to be the primary problem or predicament of
abuse survivors (Blumenthal 1993; Capps 1995a; Parkinson 1997; Poling
1991).

Another oblique source of evidence for the relationship between
Christianity and shame can be found in the literature of mental health.
The relationship between mental health and religion is complex and
ambivalent (Batson et al. 1993). However, shame and narcissistic disorders are closely associated with depression (Lewis 1987c). If Christian
ideas and practices combine to produce a sense of despair or depression
based on 'badness', they may well be implicated in the manufacture of
shame. Cumbee suggests that some depression can be seen directly as an
'ecclesiogenic neurosis' rooted in 'rearing, teaching, preaching and
value-setting that has been propagated by churches and church representatives' (Cumbee 1980: 255). The sources of this depression are

(1) morbid, false or neurotic guilt; (2) despair resulting from the failure of a
works/righteousness life style; (3) a 'worm' theology; (4) the Uriah Syndrome;
and (5) Religious sexism. (Cumbee 1980: 255)

It is unnecessary to have a full understanding of these concepts to see
that, together, they are closely associated with the induction of a sense

of low self-esteem, humiliation and lack of worth that may induce shame as well as depression.

Further sources of insight into the sometimes negative relationship between shame and Christian theology and practice in the form of novels and autobiographies referred to at the beginning of this chapter. There I emphasised the fact that religious ideas and practices do not necessarily have to be interpreted as shame-generating or -maintaining. Christianity is not inevitably pathogenic or 'toxic' (DeBlassie 1992). The ambivalent, potentially positive and changing relationship of shame and Christianity is illustrated here in a further quotation from one of my correspondents:

My faith and Christian commitment were also the means of breaking through the shame I felt. I attended X's teaching on cross cultural counselling of abuse survivors.

The emphasis of his teaching is on the grace and peace of God. It is God's grace that is first . . . we do not change in order to experience grace. God meets us where we are and in his peace our pain can surface and he meets us in our woundedness. Because of God's grace we do not have to conform and perform for acceptance. These aspects of his teaching had a profound effect on me. The pain of wounds surfaced more strongly and I gained a freedom to be who I am without having to perform and pretend. I am not ashamed of being me any more. The process was long, slow and very painful at times. Of course, it is not complete.

It is good that some shamed people eventually discover freedom, worth and self- and other-acceptance within the Christian tradition. How much better it would be, though, if Christian ideas and practices had not helped to fuel their sense of shame in the first place. If this religious tradition is to minimise its collusion in the creation and exploitation of chronic shame, alienation, and associated disorders such as abuse, it must be prepared to face up to the negative implications of some of its ideas and practices.

CHAPTER TEN

Towards more adequate approaches to shame

[I]n my eyes Christianity is catholic by right but not in fact. So many things are outside it, so many things that I love and do not want to give up, so many things that God loves, otherwise they would not be in existence.

(Weil 1959: 41)

[R]eligion not only has a seamy side but has such an extensive one that it needs to be pointed out again and again. 'Thank God,' we should say, 'for the critics of religion.'

(Malony and Spilka 1991: 49)

In the last chapter, I discussed some of the ways in which Christian ideas and practices may impact upon individuals and groups to produce or amplify a sense of dysfunctional shame. It should not be inferred from this that Christian religious thinkers, pastors or communities deliberately set out to inculcate or to propagate shame. Many would be shocked if they thought that one of the consequences of their beliefs and practices was an increase in human alienation. Nonetheless, this may often be the reality, at least for some people.

There may be some Christians who would maintain that shame is an entirely appropriate state for human beings to experience. They might hold that there is not enough sense of shame in the contemporary world and that too much shame, of any kind, is better than not enough. Their hope might be that those who put their faith in God will ultimately be redeemed from sin and shame in such a way that they gain everlasting life. If their psychological health is not all it might be in earthly terms, this is compensated for by eternal salvation which is far more religiously important than ephemeral contemporary happiness or well-being. Such people would not be unduly perturbed by my findings here.

For others, however, religiously engendered and nurtured shame, especially chronic dysfunctional shame with its painful sense of isolation,

275

unlovability, wariness, lack of trust, impotence, passivity and defilement, presents a significant challenge. Dysfunctional, chronic shame is cause and symptom of diminishment of potential in individuals and groups. It is the root of much social and personal alienation, and a major factor in preventing individuals from growing to mature responsibility. It has many of the negative qualities associated with the theological concepts of sin and evil (Robinson 1998). If the purpose of Christianity under the aegis of God's incarnation in Christ is thought to be broadly something like 'the increase of the love of God and neighbour' (Niebuhr 1977: 27ff.), or making and keeping human life human (Lehmann 1976), believers, thinkers and pastoral carers will need directly to face the challenge of shame. If contemporary social and psychological well-being and integration are important aspects of actualising salvation, healing, deliverance and reconciliation, this challenge cannot be ignored.

This chapter offers some provisional suggestions for ways in which the Christian community might cease to do unwitting evil and respond positively to the phenomenon of chronic, dysfunctional shame in individuals and groups. The first suggestion is that the Christian community must become more critically aware of its own use and exploitation of shame. Partly to allow this to happen, it is necessary, secondly, for the religious community to undertake some de-idealisation of itself, its God, and its effects. The third suggestion is that the church should change or modify some of its practices to enhance the possibilities of human flourishing and minimise the possibility that people will become caught up in alienation, self-hatred and shame. The final proposal is similar in its intent. It is that theological ideas and symbols should be critically assessed and changed. This in the interests of helping to realise the vision of human beings fully alive, communicating and communicant in a community of responsibility.

The fundamental, underlying question is, Can and will the Christian community respond positively to the challenge of shame? This question cannot be answered here. The costs of change are high. Failure to change, however, will also bring with it substantial costs, especially for those individuals and groups living in the valley of the shadow of shame.

Assessing the exploitation of shame in the church

The church is not alone in creating and exploiting shame. No social organisation can avoid shame, for it is an important indicator of the nature of human relationships (Scheff 1997). Where two or three people are gathered together in a group, there is always the possibility of shame and exclusion arising as norms, roles and practices are defined in the interests of personal and group identity. Often, shame can be functional, desirable, 'good' shame that helps to preserve appropriate boundaries, standards and relations of respect.

It is not possible for the church to dispense with or to eliminate shame at will. Nor is it feasible for Christian or any other communities completely to command, control or direct shame. Shame is a bit like dry rot or some kind of stain; its incidence and spread may be unexpected and ubiquitous. Its occurrence may often be both unforbiddable and unbiddable. The church cannot avoid engendering shame, therefore, and it would be entirely unhelpful if it were to idealise itself as an organisation that should be shame-free and shame-eliminative.

Within this context, however, greater self-knowledge and discernment of the ways in which shame may be engendered and function might allow a more critical approach in both theory and practice. In particular, it is desirable that Christians should become more aware of the ways in which shame has been used and exploited, often inadvertently, in the interests of communal advantage, profit and survival.

There are at least three areas in which shame and shaming may be wittingly or unwittingly exploited by the church. The most obvious of these is the area of church discipline. However, recruitment and retention of both church members and clergy are further spheres where shame may play an important role.

Shame and church discipline

Like guilt, shame is a potent and natural tool for attaining conformity and order in groups and societies. Shame, or the threat of shaming, with its implications of loss of face, exclusion and so on, is particularly relevant and effective in the context of traditional societies. There social norms are reinforced more by the attitudes of group members on a face-to-face basis than by formal laws and courts (Malina 1983).

After two millennia of existence, the Christian community still has many of the features of a traditional, shame-based society populated by 'we-selves' rather than those of a guilt-based rational society populated by autonomous individuals (Benedict 1954). It is not accidental that churches often liken themselves to families. Many aspects of church life are still run on informal understandings and personal contacts rather than upon formal contracts and rules. Clerical appointments in the Church of England are one example of this. Here clergy are often appointed without formal application; they do not receive a contract but have, instead, a licence from a bishop at whose pleasure they continue to serve. There are undoubted personal and corporate advantages to belonging to and living in a face-to-face community whose emphasis is upon 'we-formation' and character rather than upon individual autonomy and externally imposed rules, as a number of social and ethical thinkers have pointed out (Etzioni 1995; Hauerwas 1981; Wilson 1983: 73ff.).

In a community that is run along the lines of a traditional society, it is not surprising that informal personal pressure, or the threat of exposure and shame, may be preferred as the most appropriate way of preventing or dealing with deviance. This is a manifestation of the kind of 'pastoral power' that Foucault identifies as Christianity's distinctive contribution to technologies of power (Kritzman 1988: 57ff.; Dreyfus and Rabinow 1982: 213ff.).

Pastoral power, developed in the early centuries of the church, is oriented to the salvation of individual souls as well as to that of the whole Christian flock. In this context, individual obedience to the pastor is of vital importance. Significantly, the pastor must have a total knowledge of each of his sheep: 'he must know what goes on in the soul of each one, that is, his secret sins, his progress on the road to sainthood' (Kritzman 1988: 69). Furthermore, 'this form of power cannot be exercised without knowing the inside of people's minds, without exploring their souls, without making them reveal their innermost secrets' (Dreyfus and Rabinow 1982: 214). Self-examination and the guidance of conscience, integral to this kind of pastoral power, eventually coalesced into the widespread practice of sacramental confession which enlarged the scope of pastoral power exercised by the clerical hierarchy (Delumeau 1990; McNeill 1977). After the Reformation, the practice of self-examination became more privatised, but was nonetheless ubiquitous in some groups (Rubin 1994). It was often associated with anxiety, self-doubt, shame and melancholy.

Pastoral power was benevolent in its intentions, panoptic in its scope, and effective in inducing discipline, order and social control for many centuries. It utilised the dynamics of guilt/forgiveness and shame/exclusion to maintain orthodoxy and orthopraxis. Modern pastoral care may be less intrusive. However, the exercise of pastoral and liturgical power still involves the use of elements of guilt and shame, often unconsciously, to maintain obedience together with organisational unity, conformity and purity.

The use of shame and the exploitation of narcissistic damage in persons and groups renders them idealistic, passive and needy of approval (Ould 1995). Shamed people may be somewhat self-obsessed, grandiose, melancholic, and lacking in a sense of initiative and agency. However, they are likely to be malleable, conformist and obedient. In their concern for extrinsic recognition and approval, they may also be the kind of people who are 'concerned to show others, self, and God that [they are the] good, kind, caring – even heroic – [people that their] religion celebrates' (Batson et al. 1993: 333). This makes them unproblematic and useful to the wielders of ecclesiastical power and authority. Like depressed people in psychiatric hospitals (Johnstone 1989: 18f.), shamed people are often quiet and acquiescent, turning their aggression in upon themselves rather than challenging those in power. Whilst somewhat inert and unhappy, such persons do not present a challenge to the status quo. It is not to be expected that those who benefit from this situation, such as clergy and church leaders, will be eager to expose or change the mechanisms that produce and maintain it.

Many religious communities may directly benefit from the exploitation of shame as a tool for producing docile, obedient 'sheep', effectively communities of shamed characters. The advantages of the exploitation of shame must be acknowledged if churches are to exercise discernment and discretion in their assessment of the place and importance of shame.

Shame, evangelism and church maintenance

The second area in which the religious community may benefit from the exploitation of shame is in that of recruiting and retaining church members.

The deployment of the language of shame, defilement and stain may function as an important evangelistic tool amongst the chronically shamed. Insofar as this language is used, it may act as a magnet for people who suffer from a chronic sense of badness and long for deliverance from this. C. H. Sisson suggests that 'the vain, the ambitious and the highly sexed' are the 'natural play of the incarnate Christ' (Ecclestone 1993: 169). Shamed people could be added to this list of those vulnerable to Christianity. Indeed, it may be that the vain, ambitious and highly sexed are themselves products of shaming narcissistic wounding.

Shamed individuals and groups may feel that a community that constantly talks of guilt, shame, and badness must have the key to transcending these conditions. The idealised Christian God who can rescue the passive shamed and provide them with a sense of cleanliness and worth in the context of a community that values and wants them is a powerful attraction to the narcissistically wounded and unwanted, the loveless who would be lovely. It is not a question of condemning religious communities for using the language of shame and belonging or for holding out the hope of deliverance. However, churches should be critically aware of the implications that the exploitation of this kind of language may have for individuals and groups. This will allow an appropriate response to them.

It is one thing to draw people in with apparent promises of healing, reconciliation, purification, love and belonging. It is quite another to deliver on these promises in terms of actually effecting an end to the sense of badness and alienation. The church 'talks dirty', but can it actually cleanse and heal?

It seems to me that often churches fail to move people on from their shamed state (cf. Jacobs 1988: 91ff., 108ff.). This might be because if they attain a state of adequate responsible personhood, worth and self-esteem, they might become non-conforming, independent and critical of the church community; they may fail to contribute to it, or even leave it. A congregation of conforming, hungry, expectant, unresolved, dependent 'children' may not represent a vision of human wholeness or maturity. However, it does comprise a church that has members who will continue to support its work. Too often, pastors and others in conventional churches seem content to exploit the shame and immaturity of their members in the interests of keeping themselves in existence. The hope of relief from shame is infinitely profferred yet permanently deferred in religious communities that lack the determination and the tools to relieve individuals and groups from their painful burden of shame. Thus shame is inadvertently exacerbated and exploited for the supposed benefit of the church.

Shame and the clergy

It is not only lay people whose sense of shame and hope for deliverance may be exploited by Christian communities. Some clergy may be drawn into the ministry because of factors that have much to do with shame. In many denominations, the role of a minister is described in terms of idealised parenthood. Some churches even give their clergy the title 'Father'. For poorly enselfed, shamed people this ideal role may give a sense of identity, power, and grandiose significance (Pattison 1998). Being closely identified with God and set apart may be appealing to people who have an inadequate sense of their own worth and value. Clergy are often given a very distinct set of clothes to wear in a hierarchical role where being selfless and self-sacrificing are approved values. This may help to resolve or defer the need to explore who one is as a human being with needs and desires. In this way, the ministerial role may offer a kind of narcissistically compensatory public selfhood or external image to those who suffer from a lack of self or from possessing a kind of conformist false self (Richards 1996).

A fascinating, if extreme, example of the ministerial role providing self-evading cover for individuals is to be found in Cole (1998). Cole describes a man suffering from Möbius syndrome who was unable to enter into satisfactory relationships with others because none of the muscles in his face had moved since he was an infant (Cole 1998: 115ff.). This man lived in his head, detached from his emotions. He chose a career in ministry so that he had a fixed social role which provided him with a captive audience. The job of a priest gave him an 'offical' face with which to cope with the world. Only since he has given up being an active clergyman has he begun to explore his own real feelings about himself and others, instead of feeling a spectator to his own life: 'I am beginning to realize . . . that worthiness or love is absolute and unconditional . . . It's ironic that I left the Church in terms of the parochial ministry to discover this' (Cole 1998: 130). While the way in which this man acquired a sense of alienation from humanity was undoubtedly unusual, finding a solution for a lack of sense of worth and selfhood, however caused, in priesthood is perhaps less uncommon. It certainly chimes with my own experience (Pattison 1998).

Many clergy do not enter ministry out of a desire to avoid or compensate for a fundamental sense of shame. For them, minstry may be a vehicle for discovering a full sense of accepted and accepting selfhood. However, on the basis of the amount of child abuse, dishonesty, bullying, and authoritarian leadership that is to be found in many denominations, it seems plausible to suggest that shamed individuals as well as shame-exploiting structures are to be found in the ministry. Such individuals may be prone to self-righteousness, perfectionism, envy, blaming others, co-dependent relationships and all the other dysfunctional responses that accompany a sense of deep, chronic shame. The church may benefit from shame if it helps with ministerial recruitment. However, its hopes of promoting reconciliation, worth, and loving relationships may be jeopardised if the ministry is composed of significant numbers of people who have not come to terms with their own shame.

I have suggested three areas in which shame may be exploited by churches and religious communities to their advantage. Others could be mentioned. For example, it seems likely that one of the main ways in which Christian communities maintain distinctive identity and police their boundaries with the world is by using shame or the threat of it. Significantly, this is often evoked in relation to sexual behaviours and relationships (Countryman 1989). Here Christians are expected to maintain certain standards and whole swathes of human desire and bodily activity are hidden from consideration under the blanket category of unspeakable 'abomination' (Stout 1988). Enough has been said here to indicate the extent to which churches may exploit and 'benefit' from the use of shame, whether it is directly or inadvertently deployed.

Far more empirical research could be done to substantiate, refute or complexify the assertions I have made here. However, there is a *prima facie* case for thinking further about the ways in which religious communities use and abuse shame. The cost of recognising the exploitation of shame is considerable. It might also be highly inconvenient because it brings into question certain central and important practices, assumptions and habits. Without a willingness to acknowledge and explore the exploitation of shame by the religious community itself, however, it is doubtful that that community will be able to minister effectively to shamed people and groups. In this connection, it is sobering to note some socio-psychological evidence that suggests that, in general, religious affinity correlates with poorer positive mental health, greater intolerance for people who are different from ourselves, and no greater concern for those in need than non-religious people (Batson et al. 1993: 373).

Aspects of Christian idealisation

One factor that is likely to prevent the acknowledgment of the exploitation of shame within Christianity is this tradition's proneness to idealisation. Idealisation is a psychoanalytic term. It denotes a defensive process whereby ambivalence is overcome by splitting objects and reality into good and bad. On the one hand, an all-good, perfect object may be created whose limitations and shortcomings will then be ignored. On the other, negative idealisation occurs in which evil objects, or persons, are created whose advantages and good points are denied and disregarded. Idealisation creates dependence and subservience rather than emulation and imitation: 'It is a defence against the consequences of recognizing ambivalence and purchases freedom from guilt and depression at the cost of loss of self-esteem' (Rycroft 1972: 67).

The notion of idealisation is closely related to a more theologically familiar term, dualism. Dualistic religions maintain that there are separate principles of light and darkness, life and death, good and evil (Russell 1977: 98ff.). As a monotheistic religion, Christianity disavows this kind of dualism in theory; there is no other creative principle than the one God from whom both good and evil flow. In practice, however, Christianity often acts as if it is at least semi-dualistic, allowing for almost independent evil forces such as Satan and the devil whose work and existence is contrary to the will of God (Russell 1977; Pagels 1996). Significantly, '[t]heological dualisms undergird structures of dominance. Dualisms are reactions to abuse that produce the need for a more rigid, controllable universe. The dualisms split matter from spirit, darkness from light, good from evil, body from soul, feeling from reason, and male from female' (Brock 1988: 16). It might be argued that imaging a wholly good, perfect God in whom there is no evil at all is bound to produce some kind of dualism in theory, in practice, or in both. Otherwise, there is no scope for difference and distinction and there is nothing upon which uncontrollable, inexplicable evil and badness can be blamed and projected.

The resolution to dualism and idealisation lies in integration and the tolerance of ambivalence. However, giving up idealisation has its costs in terms of loss of necessary dependency and defence.

Idealisation is a common phenomenon in people who are psychologically shamed or narcissistically wounded (Kohut 1971). Here, however, it is its presence in the religious community that is of relevance. For reasons too complex to explore here, Christianity adheres to a vision of an idealised God who is all good, who is perfect light without darkness, who encapsulates all virtues and positive qualities, and who is to be unequivocally worshipped, adored and obeyed (cf. Feuerbach 1989: 29f.). This tendency is prominent in the Johannine literature of the New Testament: 'God is light, and in him is no darkness at all' (1 John 1.5 AV). Not only is God regarded as light, purity and goodness, Jesus Christ has the same ideal attributes, being uniquely sinless amongst human beings (Nineham 1977).

The Christian community identifies and often fuses itself with this perfect, all-good God, seeing itself as God's chosen people, filled with and directed by the immediate presence of God's spirit (Pagels 1996: xvii). This means that the church often sees and speaks of itself as effectively part of God, the body of Christ, the direct instrument of the

good God's will. This may be a symptom of defensive fusion in which
control, obedience, authority and domination are affirmed at the
expense of proper respectful relationships of connection between
persons and between persons and God (Brock 1988: 29ff.). Where there
is fusion, relationship is lost and anger is deployed upon changing or
eliminating the 'other' rather than caring for the self (Brock 1988: 30).

In failing to recognise and remember the difference between God and
the church, the latter may fall into the temptation of idealising itself and
seeing itself as perfect. This can have unfortunate consequences in relation to recognising and responding appropriately to shame and shamed
people because idealisation may both actively foster shame and prevent
its recognition and acknowledgment.

The first unhelpful aspect of the church's idealisation of itself and
over-identification with God is represented by a persistent failure to
recognise that it can do harm and damage people, both within and
outside the Christian community. It is symptomatic that churches have
been very slow to recognise that children and others are abused and
exploited within the religious community (Parkinson 1997). Clergy, who
are themselves idealised, are now recognised to be an important source
of abuse. Even so, the need to maintain a sense of basic organisational
goodness has meant that many abuse victims have had their experiences
either denied or ignored by those in the hierarchy. This kind of ideali-
sation-related denial is consonant with a reluctance to acknowledge the
damage that Christianity has done to other races and faith groups in the
past and continues to do in the present (Bowker 1987). On a more trivial
level, it supports a lack of interest in exploring whether ecclesiastically
based activities such as pastoral care actually help people in any perceptible way (Lynch 1999).

The undergirding assumption at all points seems to be that because
the church claims to be united with and guided by a good God's will and
purpose it will inevitably be helpful and positive in its interventions and
practices. This, as many child abuse victims and demonised 'others' in
religious wars know, could often not be further from the truth (Lambert
1998). It is only quite recently that Christians have become more self-
critical. They have begun to see that Christianity can be a 'harmful religion' (Osborn and Walker 1997) that has a considerable shadow side
which is not necessarily wholly beneficent and salvific. Even so, for the
most part, the idealised overall image of the church is carefully maintained in the interests of preserving the goodness and perfection of God
and of keeping up the self-esteem of the Bride of Christ.

Unfortunately, this kind of idealisation and its associated rejecting dualism may have very negative connotations in terms of recognising and responding to shame. It is difficult for an idealising community to recognise that it has a part in creating and maintaining shame. If the church sees itself mainly as an instrument of a reconciling gospel and divine salvation, the fact that it may help to nurture and maintain alienation will be a very hard truth to accept. The temptation may be to reject or ignore this threatening and potentially damaging insight.

The essence of an idealising, dualistic response in which some people regard themselves as being fused with God is either to assimilate or to demonise unwanted difference rather than to accept it for what it is. Hence the dynamics of conversion, scapegoating, or destruction that have often characterised Christian history. Whole theologies and systems of liturgical practice have been built that sustain the fundamental integrity and goodness of God and Christianity on the basis of creating demonic outsider 'Others' such as Jews and Muslims (Walker Bynum 1995: 214ff.).

A distinctive but pernicious aspect of Christianity has been its capacity to find and scapegoat an enemy within – witches, gay people, heretics, liberal theologians – and to demonise and reject that enemy, too (Pagels 1996; Lambert 1998; Ludemann 1997). It is only recently, for example, that the negative role and image of Judas, the diabolical 'enemy' agent within Jesus' own intimate group of disciples, has begun to be re-examined (Klassen 1996), and this has not been without popular Christian criticism and revulsion. Perhaps it is no coincidence that this revision accompanies a critical re-evaluation of institutionalised Christian anti-Semitism that has systematically sustained the Jews as demons outside the realm of salvation for almost two millennia (Carroll 1991; Ludemann 1997).

Ecclesiastical authority, unity and purity have often been maintained by the scapegoating and victimisation of groups or individuals (Pagels 1982; cf. Douglas 1995). This process has been sacralised in theology and liturgy by an implicit belief in the efficacy of 'redemptive violence' (Wink 1992) and a more open exaltation and even romanticisation of victimhood (Gudorf 1992; West 1995). Some theorists argue that victimhood and sacrifice have been decisively exposed and ended by Christ's death on the cross (Girard 1996: 18). Others, however, see the structures of scapegoating and sacrifice as alive and unendingly flourishing within the Christian community, producing an endless stream of victimised groups and individuals who ultimately fail to purify the church (Hans 1991).

Fenn suggests that, in its quest for purity, the church might be seen as 'a school for professional victims' (Fenn 1991: 174), demanding perpetual sacrifice.

If the production of victims, mirrored in the symbolic 'sacrifice' of the eucharist, represents a continuing if unsuccessful effort to remove defilement and stain from the body corporate of the religious community, then that community has still not come to terms with the reality of shame and rejection that is integral to creating and sustaining such victims. It is still trying to dispose of shame and stain in the interests of maintaining corporate idealisation rather than trying to understand and integrate it. If the theology and technology of religion are eliminative rather than integrative, there is little chance that shame and shamed 'victims' will ever be properly acknowledged and integrated. Rather, they will be required to lay down their unhappy lives for the sake of keeping God and the church 'good'. And it should be noted here that the strategy of privileging and inverting the status of victims, beloved of feminists and liberation theologians, is no answer to the problem of ceasing to produce and exploit victimhood in the first place (West 1995; cf. Furedi 1997). Victims, whether exalted or despised, are a product of unhelpful dualistic idealisation.

The cost to the religious community of recognising and responding positively to shame is that of turning from idealising dualism. This is an enormous price to pay in terms of fundamental identity, thought and practice. One cannot therefore be optimistic about its being paid. The implication is that shame and shamed people will continue to live in the kind of darkness that will allow the church and its God to continue to enjoy the sense of dwelling in the effulgence of purity, glory and light; in *chiara* without any *scuro* (Hills 1987: 16).

One main effect of self-idealisation is to block awareness of the negative effects of ecclesial life and practice. Another is to prevent the church from ministering effectively to those who walk in the valley of the shadow of shame. The self-identification of the church with a good, omnipotent God makes it very difficult for that body to recognise its ignorance and limitations (Hull 1985), let alone to find a valued place for honest doubt and other disruptive, but genuine, human experiences (Davidson 1983; Pohier 1985). If God is all-good and all-powerful and the church is equipped with the necessary gifts and powers that it needs to realise God's will on earth, then it is difficult to accept that the religious community may not always be able to help people to attain fullness of life.

This problem arises acutely in the instance of physical illness where some Christians would argue that specifically religious healing methods such as prayer should be the main, and possibly the sole, means of effecting cure (Pattison 1989b). Many would take a more moderate view than this. However, it is indicative of a trend within Christianity to regard itself as perfect, omnicompetent and all-sufficient in its own right. This means that ministers and others may be very reluctant to acquire relevant knowledge and techniques from non-church sources such as psychotherapy and counselling (Symington 1994). It also means that they may be unwilling to acknowledge the limits and failures of belonging to a religious community and using 'religious' methods and techniques.

If, for example, shamed groups or individuals are not healed and integrated by their experience of belonging to a church, this reality may be denied. There may also be a reluctance to acknowledge failure to really help people and to acquire relevant new skills and knowledge. One response to being unable to find appropriate ways of alleviating a particular condition is effectively to deny or ignore the condition as being of no account. This may occur in relation to 'chronic' conditions such as dementia or intractable mental health problems where people are simply abandoned to their fate and their condition is consigned to the realm of 'abomination' that lies outside language, explanation, help, or even acknowledgment (Stout 1988). Shame may often fall into this silent realm because nothing can be done about it. Another response is to attribute the failure to get over or 'heal' shame to the inadequacies, faithlessness or intransigence of the shamed. Thus, the 'victims' may be blamed and have their sense of alienation reinforced while the institution and its officials retain a sense of their own goodness and efficacy despite all evidence to the contrary.

Ecclesiastical self-idealisation and over-identification with God are understandable human responses. They bring some advantages in terms of cohesion and a sense of value and efficacy to the church. Unfortunately, they vitiate attempts to recognise and respond positively to shame, alienation and victimhood, especially when these things are actually present within the church community and that community in some way benefits from them.

Without a shift away from this kind of idealisation, it is unlikely that shamed people and groups will ever gain full access to the sort of integrating help that might be hoped for in the church. However, a move away from idealisation would mean fundamental practical, doctrinal and attitudinal changes in a community that has been to some extent moulded by idealising, shame producing and maintaining structures over two millennia.

In this connection, it might be asked whether the church would be the same body, have the same identity, or attract the same kind of adherents if it changed to a less self-idealising stance. Would the church be the church as we have tended to think of it in the past? If it was not, what would it look like and how would it operate? These are daunting questions that are not susceptible to answer here. They give some indication of the major implications of taking the challenge of shame seriously within the Christian community.

Without some kind of basic acknowledgment of institutional flaws and failings, there is little scope for honesty, growth, responsibility, or healing of shame. Self-delusion and idealisation may be comforting immediate responses. In the long run, however, they leave Christianity dishonest, discredited, partial, and unable to face up to or to cope with profound alienation. Indeed, in practice, alienation and exclusion will be bound to be preferred to integration and reconciliation, whatever the rhetoric of inclusion and healing that is employed.

In a different context, Shaw argues the case for de-idealising the church and its ministry: 'An immediate task before the Christian church is to acknowledge its own unacceptable face' (Shaw 1983: 1). The selective, uncritical, idealising vision of Christianity and church history, still propagated by churches, is misleading and destructive, he suggests:

The cost of obedience in terms of frustration and immaturity is overlooked. The cult of innocence . . . burdens experience with guilt and nostalgia. Above all, the self-assertion of so much religious conviction is neither acknowledged or criticised . . . Thus the Christian is not encouraged to brood too long or too often on those who are outside: the Muslim, the Hindu, or the atheist . . . The sinners and the atheists seldom answer back, and are never allowed the last word. (Shaw 1983: 2–3)

Christians must take responsibility for the ambivalence of their history and tradition if they are to be credible witnesses in the world today:

To be a Christian obviously involves learning to take responsibility for one's own life, acknowledging one's own sins, gaining a new realism about oneself; but being a Christian must also involve taking responsibility for a particular religious tradition, acknowledging its dangers and mistakes and learning from that experience without evasion. (Shaw 1983: 1)

This kind of painful, de-idealising revision and repentance is essential if Christianity is to cease its collusion with the creation of defilement, victims and shame and to exercise a more effective influence in the work of reconciling and reintegrating shamed individuals and groups. The cost of failing to respond to this challenge will be the perpetuation of life-denying, dysfunctional shame and alienation. The illusory purity of a tribal church (Selby 1991) will be maintained at the expense of further exploitation, scapegoating and victimisation of real people and groups.

RESPONDING TO SHAME IN PRACTICE AND THEOLOGY

It is not feasible to set out a systematic, comprehensive approach for responding positively to shame in theology or practice. In the first place, there is still only limited understanding of the nature and function of shame. Secondly, shame is a relative phenomenon that may be caused and understood differently between both individuals and communities. Thirdly, what causes or exacerbates shame in one person or group may not have the same effect on others. Practical and theological responses must therefore be 'local' (Schreiter 1985) and specific if they are to be appropriate and helpful.

We are at a very early stage of having any understanding of a complex, multi-faceted phenomenon and how it might relate to religious ideas, communities and practices. Thus, all that can be offered here are some ideas and questions for theology and practice that might help movement forward in understanding and responding to dysfunctional shame. The points raised below arise mainly from reflection on my own experience. No claim is made for their universal relevance and validity, or for comprehensiveness of scope or depth.

The challenge of shame in Christian practice

There is no aspect of Christian thought or practice that might not engender or exacerbate shame in some individual or group. Shame is often an essentially unmanageable, uncontrollable and unpredictable accompaniment to symbols and actions that is not necessarily intended by their originators. It is, therefore, impossible to identify and commend practices that are totally 'shame-free'. Equally, it is not possible to suggest practices that will be valid in all situations and with all groups and types of people. What can be suggested is a set of considerations and desiderata that might be used to interrogate or frame practices of various kinds. If these are attended to, there may be some chance that Christian practices might be less unwittingly dysfunctionally shaming and more consciously integrative than they are at present.

Perhaps the most important starting point for practical responses to shame is developing awareness of shame and the way that it impinges upon one's own life. Know thyself! Shame is a category of hiddenness, wordlessness, abomination and rejection. It is difficult, and may be literally appalling, to become aware of its presence and effects. However, without this kind of awareness, it is difficult to see how progress can be made. If dysfunctionally or chronically shamed lives are lived out without any conscious knowledge of the effects of shame in them, shame may be passed on to and replicated in others (Miller 1987b, 1991). A first practical response must, therefore, be to make some attempt to understand the shadow of shame in one's own life so that the cycle of abusive and shaming relationships can, if necessary, be questioned and halted. Not passing on or confirming shame in others by virtue of one's contempt, envy or self-righteousness may be the single most important contribution that any individual can make to creating an integrating, accepting community. This is a hard task that is comparable to the work of forgiving others who have hurt us, and not passing on the anger and abuse that have been vented upon us.

Willingness to engage in the task of acknowledging and recognising personal shame will probably require the help and support of others. In concrete terms, it may be necessary to seek the support of therapists and others who are able to help people to accept themselves as they are without self-censorship or denigration. Although it is fashionable in some Christian circles to question and denigrate the knowledge and methods made available by psychology and counselling, it seems likely that pastoral practice has not yet learned all that it could, theoretically or practically, in this area (Symington 1994). Learning to attend to shame and shaming experiences, whether in self or others, is difficult. Counselling and psychotherapy offer some of the insights and disciplines that may be needed here. So the second desideratum for pastoral practice that I want to advance here is that Christians should be prepared to learn about how to understand and work with shame from other disciplines. This will help to prevent either evasion or facile optimism in relation to dysfunctional shame and will deepen an integrative religious response.

Understanding shame within the self and being prepared to learn from the insights and methods of psychology and counselling may open up the way to a third possibility, that of attending to and acknowledging the shame of others. This is likely to involve sensitive observation and listening to individuals and groups. Often, it will be very painful to listen to stories of shame; frequently they will be 'survivor' stories underlined by accounts of abuse and denigration that will be difficult to hear without feeling ashamed oneself (Poling 1991; Blumenthal 1993). The temptation not to want to attend or listen may be quite overwhelming in these circumstances. However, this leaves shamed persons isolated and unhelped.

The ministry of really listening to what people are saying, of attending to their particular stories without trying to generalise, moralise, or theologise, is an important integrative response that Christians can offer in response to chronic shame. Listening of this kind renders speaker and listener as subjects instead of objects. It is a 'hearing into speech' that connects individuals with a community of discourse out of the silence of shame (McLeod 1997). It can begin to develop a sense of worth, respect and belonging in the abject and dishonoured. Ramsay writes:

'Hearing into speech' requires courage, both for the survivor and for those who listen, for the story leads through the valley of the shadow of death. Often it includes the experience of terror, pain, and anger of the victimized child and the anguish and rage of the adult who is now able to voice what she experienced and acknowledge the consequences for her life. Pastors who listen are called on to receive and validate those powerful feelings. Further, they need to be aware of and contain their own sometimes frightening and powerful responses if they are to remain available to the wounded victim. (Ramsay 1991: 116)

Responding to shame is not just a matter of attending to shame in oneself and other individuals. It is also vital that Christian pastoral workers and others should attend to the place and function of shame within groups and communities. It is important to recognise how shame, especially dysfunctional shame, may be generated and exploited within the religious community. Given the way in which sexual behaviour and orientation often form a *cordon sanitaire* or boundary of purity and stigma around the Christian community (Malina 1983; Countryman 1989), one obvious place to begin exploring the effects of shame may be in the arena of sexuality.

Beyond the religious community, groups and societies often engender and nurture shame in relation to issues of social order and control. In this context, it will be relevant to examine which groups and individuals are shamed, in what ways, and to whose advantage or disadvantage. These matters are intimately related to power, justice and inequality, as well as to the well-being of societies and communities as a whole.

Shame is not divorced from social and political structures and uses. To respond appropriately to shame means having an awareness of socio-political dimensions with a view to trying to minimise the manufacture and spread of dysfunctional, chronic shame that unhelpfully severs groups and communities. It might be hoped that Christians would want to identify and assist groups and communities that have been shamed rather than those who shame them. However, the work of integration and reconciliation is a two-way process. There may be a role for mediation and activity with both the 'powerful' shamers and 'powerless' shamed. Shame as social alienation should be as important an aspect of Christian concern and understanding as chronic shame within persons. The two are, in any case, closely related. Frequently social alienation impacts upon the sense of worth and self-image of individuals, as the witness of the Black and gay communities makes clear.

Beyond expanding awareness and understanding of shame in individuals, groups and societies, itself a considerable task, there are a number of other things that might be thought of in relation to Christian practice. If the purpose of Christian existence is in part to nurture human flourishing then there may be ways in which this religious tradition can both cease to do evil, or that which is less than good, and also promote well-being.

In the first place, pastors and others can examine practices, beliefs and symbols with a view to finding out whether or not they tend to generate or exacerbate dysfunctional shame. If it turns out that certain practices, language or attitudes tend in this direction, it is incumbent upon them to cease to use them.

A good example of this need for a change in usage is to be found in the case of sexist language in worship (Wren 1989). For many years, women found themselves and their experience to be invisible and unmirrored in the exclusively masculine language used in liturgy. This damaged their sense of worth and significance. Very gradually, therefore, new language is being introduced which might do more to enhance their self-esteem (Morley 1992). Some traditionalists argue that sexist, patriarchal language is inclusive or neutral. This is not the experience of many women who have found traditional language diminishing. It is therefore quite right that ancient practices have been re-examined and, where necessary, changed.

A similar process may be required in the instance of practices, languages and images that systematically foster alienation and worthlessness in local congregations. It is no argument to suggest that just because things have always been done in a particular way this should continue whatever the cost in shame and diminishment to particular groups or individuals.

A second way in which Christian individuals and communities might cease to do evil with regard to chronic or dysfunctional shame is simply to be honest about the way in which some traditional Christian practices and ideas may be implicated in the generation and propagation of shame in groups and individuals. Frequently, for example, preachers, pastors and teachers have lauded and sacralised the patriarchal family. They have seemed to suggest that nuclear family life is divinely ordained and so unquestionably good. This is to deny the possibility that families can be a locus of mass abuse, violence and danger, especially for women and children (Brock 1988; Ramsay 1991). An important part of taking responsibility for a system of beliefs and practices is to be truthful about all its implications and effects so that those who are shamed are not put in the position of having to deny their own experience or blame themselves for their situation. The denial of chronic shame and the abusive practices and experiences that often foster it is damaging to shamed groups and individuals. It should cease if Christianity is to exercise a liberative and disclosive, rather than an ideological, function. Tolstoy writes, '[T]o recognize the truth as a truth and avoid lying about it is a thing you can always do . . . you not only can but should do this, because . . . in freeing yourself from falsehood and confessing the truth . . . lies the sole welfare of your life' (Tolstoy 1936: 442). It is not only the welfare of the individual who ceases to lie that is served by fundamental honesty, even if the truth is difficult and uncomfortable.

On a more positive note, there are a number of things that can be done to promote the well-being of individuals and groups. First, it is important that Christians should have special regard to the interests of children and other groups who are vulnerable to shaming or who have been systematically shamed, stigmatised and alienated. These groups should not be exposed to beliefs and practices that are likely to damage their sense of worth or to nurture alienation. In the case of children, it is important to communicate to them a sense of their own inherent value and the significance of their own emotional experience before teaching them that they should, for example, deny themselves, be humble, or be more interested in the happiness and approval of parents and God before their own. Children should learn to listen to and accept themselves and their emotions before being introduced to the notion of a self divided by a battle between good and evil and betrayed by the physical body, particularly through sexuality. Communicating this might involve quite major revisions of liturgical texts and usage of scripture, as well as looking at the broader subject of education and nurture within the Christian community.

Too many children have been forced to walk the way of the cross and to forsake self in the valley of the shadow of religiously sanctioned abuse (Greven 1992; Poling 1991; Rubin 1994). The onus now lies on the Christian community to develop ways of building up a proper sense of selfhood in children before they are, for example, invited to meditate upon the all-encompassing, all-sufficient sacrifice of Christ. Jesus, after all, was an adult before he was required to give his own life for his friends. Notions of sacrifice and selflessness must give way to richer and more affirming views of the nascent self if unhappy, abused children are not to have their imaginations funded by 'tormenting thoughts' (Capps 1995a) which do little to help them grow into responsive and responsible adults relating fully to others in community.

A second positive thing that might be undertaken is to gain the appropriate helping skills that might allow shamed people and groups to discover their own value and their connection to others. Often, Christian pastors and others have an inadequate sense of their own personal boundaries and engage in what might be called naive, co-dependent helping (Jacoby 1994). This kind of assistance often takes the form of trying to rescue others from their misery and unhappiness. Frequently it fails; then individuals find themselves drawn into abusive relationships that may often uncannily mirror those that created a sense of shame and alienation in the first place. Rescuers find themselves turned into persecutors, or indeed into victims. Instead of helping people, they eventually affirm them in a position of shame and dependence that may be exploitative (Parkes 1990). The religious community is shot through with examples of adults and children being abused and exploited by pastors and others. Often this abuse is unwitting. Sometimes, as in the case of the 'Nine O'Clock Service' in Sheffield, it seems to be deliberate and prolonged (Howard 1996). Only if people understand the nature of personal boundaries together with the dangers of abusive, shaming relationships, and have acquired the skills that are needed to deal with these, is help likely to be real, affirming and liberating for the shamed and abused.

A third positive task might be to think of ways in which individuals and groups might be generally affirmed and integrated in liturgy and other aspects of communal and church life. This is a creative process that might take very different forms in different congregations and localities, depending on the needs of the people concerned.

Priestland asserts that the need to give love is more desperate than the need to receive it. One needs to see oneself as loving before one can regard oneself as lovable (Priestland 1986: 246). If this is the case, then one way to assist and affirm shamed individuals and groups may be to ask of them something that they can willingly give, however small, within the community. In this way, efficacy and a subjective sense of worth might be nurtured more effectively than by simply feeling sorry for people or trying to serve them.

Facilitating people and groups to become active subjects of their own lives must be part of any positive response to shame. A woman I used to know was hospitalised for a severe mental health problem for many months as the staff struggled to help her. Her recovery began, she said, when her daughter came to visit her and asked her to drive her and her own baby out into the countryside. It was this gesture of trust and dependency that awoke this woman's sense of responsibility and efficacy. All service does not consist in washing other people's feet – it may mean allowing them to do things that are really valued. The implications of this may be radical at all levels for a community that regards itself as active and 'good' while shamed groups and individuals are unhelpfully stereotyped as wholly passive victims (cf. Lamb 1996).

Lastly, it may be useful for Christian communities to counterbalance traditional teachings, images, and practices that appear to affirm dysfunctional shame and alienation with others that are more positive. This does not necessarily mean abandoning traditional ways of thinking or doing things, though this may sometimes be appropriate. (I often think that it would be very helpful, for example, if rites of penance and prayers that perpetuate a sense of non-specific badness and personal unworthiness, such as the prayer of humble access or the collect for purity in the Anglican eucharistic rite, were used much more sparingly or not at all. They distort the nature of forgiveness and acceptance as shown by Jesus in the gospels (Pohier 1985: 200ff.). Furthermore, they have amplified my own sense of defilement and terror since childhood.) Rather, I am suggesting that a greater range of images, metaphors, symbols, stories and practices might be put into circulation within Christian communities. These might allow individuals and groups to find and maintain a sense of worth and belonging. Some of them might be drawn from the Christian tradition. Others, however, could be new-minted in the interests of allowing people to find new sources of identification and affirmation.

For example, stories of contemporary abuse survivors, perhaps members of a particular congregation, might be allowed to find a place in corporate worship alongside scripture readings (Blumenthal 1993). This might allow children and others to recognise, identify and accept their own experience in the context of religion rather than feeling that they were isolated, alienated and alone. Rites might be created that affirmed the power and efficacy of human beings, their original grace and giftedness, rather than simply their unworthiness and dependence upon a critical, monarchical God. Some progress has been made in this direction by feminists who challenge the negative assumptions of traditional practices that have maintained women in a state of invisibility and implicit defilement. A lot more work needs to be done, though, before mainstream Christian denominations will feel free to experiment with worship and practice that affirms rather than questioning human worth and efficacy.

The aim of Christian practice, as I have framed it here, is to help overcome alienation and exclusion. This might help enable shamed people and groups to see themselves, others, and God, face to face. Thus they can belong properly to themselves and to others in 'ideal speech' communities of common, respectful discourse (Graham 1996). Much Christian practice has been positively antipathetic to this, from the habit of teaching people to bow their heads or kneel in the 'presence' of God in prayer or in church, to the exploitation of shame in co-dependent pastoral relationships. If people are to grow into the glorious liberty of the children of God and to take responsibility in community for themselves, their communities, and their world, changes will be needed at many levels. These will need to be specific to particular localities and groups. The desiderata I have suggested here are simply a starting point for a journey from shame and alienation into mature responsibility and proper guilt.

In addition to changing various practices, it will also be necessary to reassess the nature and content of Christian theology, symbolism and imagery.

The challenge of shame in Christian theology

Just as there is no Christian practice which can be entirely shame-free, universally liberating and non-shame-generative, there are no theological ideas or symbols that do not have the capacity to be received as shaming, or shame-reinforcing. If anything, theological symbols and images are even less governable and predictable in their effects and the understandings they generate than practices (Pattison 1996). The symbols and metaphors that comprise theology are necessarily polysemic. They can be understood and received in many different ways according to audience and context. Theological discourse has ambivalent and unpredictable effects. Some of these, as I demonstrated in the last chapter, may serve to engender and amplify dysfunctional shame. Like other kinds of Christian practice, theology has a shadow, potentially destructive, side as well as presenting light and insight. As a human construction serving particular interests, theology cannot be regarded as innocent or privileged within Christian communities. It must, therefore, be open to criticism and reformulation if this is appropriate.

Shame poses a significant challenge to theology and theologians – all those who create, perpetuate, propagate, and interpret theological symbols and ideas at any level in church or academy. The challenge is to find ways of taking appropriate responsibility for theological ideas and symbols in such a way that dysfunctional shame is not needlessly and uncritically fostered in individuals and groups. This is a huge task, the dimensions of which can only be hinted at here. I shall proceed by laying out some general considerations or desiderata that theologians might take into account in trying to construct theological images and ideas. Thereafter, I shall offer some fragmentary theological thoughts and images that have been suggestive for me in trying to come to terms with shame theologically. It will be helpful to situate the desiderata and the fragments within a clear vision of the nature and purpose of theology. It is with this that I begin.

The purpose of theology

Theology is often taken to be the abstract, theoretical academic study of ideas and traditions about the Christian God. This deprives theology of any practical force or relevance in people's lives and experience. In the present context, it will be helpful to see theology as a more engaged, evangelical activity that is, or should be, concerned with discerning and making real salvation and liberation in contemporary people's everyday lives.

Roberta Bondi, an American feminist theologian, sees theology as concerned with healing wounds and nurturing human well-being. She describes theology as 'healing work' and writes:

Theology . . . is about saving lives, and the work of theology . . . is saving work. First, it involves learning to see the ways in which false images of God, ourselves, and the world have bound us and taken away the life God intends for us. Second, it involves learning to know God as God is . . . Third, it involves imagining a future that is consistent with the God we have come to know. (Bondi 1995: 11)

Theology has a significant contribution to make in helping to free people from the shadow of religiously engendered dysfunctional shame and alienation. Part of this lies in exposing and criticising images and symbols of God that bind people and diminish their sense of life, community and responsibility. A further role is in trying to create ideas, symbols and images that provide horizons of imagination which allow people to find themselves and others more easily within an overall commitment to human flourishing (Jantzen 1998). The work of theology is never completed because people and situations change all the time. There can never, then, be a single, finished, perfect theology that invariably helps to free individuals and groups from dysfunctional shame and alienation. This is not an excuse for not starting on the work of critique and creativity that might help in the practical task of helping people to free themselves from the valley of the shadow of shame and abnegation.

Desiderata for approaching shame theologically

In trying to make Christian theological activity less alienating and more responsive, responsible and shame-sensitive, it may be helpful for theologians to have regard to the following considerations.

In the first place, it is necessary for theologians to recognise and take some responsibility for the effects that the ideas, images and symbols that they propagate may have on individuals and groups, both generally and in specific contexts (McDonald 1993). At the very least, they need to cease denying that these things may have a harmful or helpful impact upon people. However, there has been a lack of willingness to recognise what the real effects of theologies on people are.

Theologians seem to have been remarkably uninterested in the practical implications and effects of their ideas. They have not been keen empirically to study or understand them. Thus they have effectively abrogated responsibility for their own creations and activities in relation to shame, amongst other human conditions.

The point of taking responsibility for the human effects of theological ideas and symbols and of understanding what those effects might be is to modify usage if necessary. If particular symbols, images or approaches seem persistently to engender or exacerbate shame, perhaps they should be modified, limited in their use, or even completely discarded. If, on the other hand, they foster reconciliation, responsibility and worth, perhaps they should be amplified, developed or more widely circulated.

A more positive, additional role to that of modifying existing usage of symbols and ideas is the introduction of new or different processes, meta-phors, narratives and images into the theological ecology. Theology has often tended to be rather conservative and to feel bound to recycle and interpret the tradition quite narrowly. However, there is no reason in prin-ciple why it should not be more adventurous in the quest to provide usable insights and understandings that might help to overcome dysfunctional shame. At its best, theology has seen itself as part of a living process. It has risen to new challenges, frequently being willing to change emphases, governing metaphors and key interpretations. This kind of innovation and flexibility might be required to face the challenge of shame.

Even if theologians feel shy of inventing new metaphors and symbols and allowing them to supplement or supplant traditional ones, it is pos-sible that they can play an important role in ensuring that the symbolic ecology is kept in balance. This can be done by rediscovering or re-emphasising ideas and symbols that have become hidden or disregarded. Thus, for example, the tradition of original blessing and the goodness of creation and humanity could be brought into prominence to counter-balance an emphasis on sin and the Fall in Western theology in the inter-ests of reducing shame (Fox 1983; Westermann 1978).

Rebalancing the symbolic ecology can be facilitated by another theo-logical activity, that of rereading and reinterpreting traditional symbols and stories. This has been a favourite strategy for feminist and liberation theologians who have been able to find new and subversive meanings and 'dangerous memories' within the Bible and other texts (Pattison 1997a). Rereading of this kind might unearth motifs that are illuminat-ing for the purposes of understanding and dispersing dysfunctional shame and enhancing a sense of human worth.

All of the three previous approaches, creating new symbols, rebal-ancing the symbolic ecology and rereading the tradition, can contribute to creating a larger intellectual and symbolic world. Within this, it may be possible for shamed people and groups to discover meanings that cor-respond more readily and more helpfully to their experience. This broadening of theological worlds and world views creates space for people to find narratives and motifs that can appropriately mirror their experience. It provides a narrative and symbolic stock out of which people can authentically create their own stories and also be integrated into the community, discourse and grammar of faith (Lindbeck 1984; McLeod 1997). Hopefully, this may help to build up a sense of recogni-tion, worth, belonging and self-esteem.

An important part of theological responses to shame is to become more self-conscious and critical of the effects that usage of ideas and images may have in the lives of individuals and groups. Equally important is the need for theology to become more flexible, playful and experimental (Pruyser 1991; cf. Jantzen 1998). Under the aegis of the quest for unity and monolithic orthodoxy, theology in its methods and content has mirrored and served an ideology of domination and submission that has characterised patriarchal Christianity almost from its beginning (Moore 1996; Pagels 1982, 1990). Theology is now becoming a more pluralistic, permissive, porous kind of activity with more space for individuals and groups to contribute their own ideas and experiences (Pattison with Woodward 1994). This potentially allows the formulation of new, more local ways of understanding God, religion and the human condition. These may help people to liberate themselves from the shadow of shame.

Above all, theology is now in a much better position to listen seriously to specific contemporary human experiences and stories rather than feeling that those stories and experiences should be suppressed or conformed to a tradition-based master narrative (Frank 1995). Within this context, theologians have the possibility of respectfully offering 'theological fragments' from the tradition that may have considerable illuminative power (Forrester 1997: 200). With some courage and imagination, theology has the possibility of engaging with human hurt and healing in new and creative ways, enabling rather than imposing meanings, symbols and images that enlighten rather than imprison.

Theological fragments for responding to shame

I now want to offer some fragmentary images, motifs and themes that have funded my imagination (Brueggemann 1993) in thinking about beginning to respond theologically to shame. These are loose, incomplete, unsystematic and, at least in some respects, contradictory. They illustrate the difficulty of trying to reformulate or rebalance a theological system that has hitherto paid little specific critical attention to the contemporary experience of shame. They may have limited relevance and meaning for people other than myself. Nonetheless, they may provide some starting points for providing theological content for a positive response to shame. In one way or another, I have found these fragments to provide a measure of hope and solvent for chronic shame.

The fundamental goodness and value of creation and of humanity
This theological motif stands in stark contrast to the rather pessimistic, Augustinian-influenced tradition in Western theology that emphasises

the fallenness and sinfulness of humanity and creation and its need for a distinct interventionist redemptive event to put things right. A number of writers contribute to an affirmation of original worth. Westermann (1978) and Fox (1983) have highlighted the notion that in creating and continuing to create the world and humanity God blesses it and finds it good. Nakashima Brock (1988) identifies the category of original grace as a fundamental aspect of human existence. Jantzen (1998) suggests that Christian theology should be rooted in the universal symbolic imagery of natality. Blessing and grace are not then withheld and contingent events that are only available to those who self-consciously believe certain things and regard themselves as saved.

Many other theologians have pointed out that creation and redemption should not be seen as separate events. Wilson puts it best: 'Creation is universal talk about salvation. . . . Salvation is here and now talk about creation' (Wilson 1988: 162). There is a sense, then, in which God has been creating and redeeming the world and its inhabitants since the beginning of time in a single movement. Insofar as people exist and participate in life, they contribute to godly creative activity. As they join in the work of creation, they manifest aspects of the image and likeness of the creator. This kind of positive, holistic view of creation and human life is a powerful antidote to a kind of necrophilic 'worm' theology (Cumbee 1980) that dwells upon human imperfection, sin, destructiveness, death, alienation and stain. For many years, I used a versicle in worship that ran, 'I receive life from all around me: To all around me I give life' (Cotter 1987: 3). While I found it difficult to believe that the latter part of this assertion could possibly be true of me, it has acted as a powerful theological summary symbol of hope that affirms the worth of life, creation and selves – even my own self.

Salvation does not revolve around the suffering of lost individual victims
The Christian tradition of redemption and atonement has often emphasised the unique importance of the saving death and 'sacrifice' of Jesus. The efficacy released by the death of one victim creates the possibility of salvation for other individuals if they can appropriate this by faith.

The centrality of a single saving death that then makes individual salvation possible has been helpfully challenged by many feminist theologians amongst others (Carlson Brown and Bohn 1989; Grey 1989; Jantzen 1998; Brock 1988). They argue that the exaltation of victimhood can be death-promoting and life-denying. It legitimates the continual re-creation of humiliating victimhood for people, especially women, in the contemporary world: 'The glorification of anyone's suffering allows the glorification of all suffering. To argue that salvation can only come through the cross is to make God a divine sadist and a divine child abuser' (Carlson Brown and Parker 1989: 23).

In place of this kind of theology, they suggest that the significance of Jesus' death should be understood in the context of his life. This consisted in creating a living concrete community of 'saving' relationships in which people find themselves and each other. Life and resurrection in human communal relationships should therefore take precedence over the historical death of one man as a theological motif:

Resurrection means that death is overcome in those precise instances when human beings choose life, refusing the threat of death. Jesus climbed out of the grave in the Garden of Gethsemane when he refused to abandon his commitment to the truth even though his enemies threatened him with death. On Good Friday, the resurrected one was crucified. (Carlson Brown and Parker 1989: 28)

This kind of theological understanding based upon living community turns redemption into an active, ongoing, creative and reconciling human process in the contemporary world. It provides an impetus to overcoming the death-dealing alienation of shame, moving from theology based on victimhood and stain to theology based on life and creating community.

Sin understood as disobedience is not the defining differentiator between God and humanity

Much of the theological tradition has revolved around the notion that human beings are alienated from God by their individual pride and disobedience against the deity. Feminists have questioned this view. It may seem appropriate to over-assertive, detached, disconnected men who find themselves living lives of unaccountable loneliness. However, it hardly matches the situation of many women (Saiving 1979).

Nakashima Brock (1988) argues that the negative side of human existence is better characterised as brokenheartedness and sees sin as damage to persons. Brueggemann (1993: 32) sees the differentiator between God and humanity as being the latter's frailty. Theological understandings like these prompt a move away from anxiety about whether God as divine parent is pleased or angry with humanity and a move towards paying close attention to the wounds endured by specific human beings and the ruptures in human relationships. The reconnection of human beings with each other, based on understanding and overcoming of hurts, provides a basis for engaging seriously with alienated, shamed individuals and groups. The work of reconciliation and forgiveness becomes contemporary, concrete and specific and much less to do with promises of individual eternal salvation basking in the pleasure of a divine king. It is to this kind of practical this-worldly compassion that Jesus' own ministry bears witness in many ways.

God is not an oriental despot or super-father

God has been presented in the Christian tradition mainly in terms of a patriarchal ideal of kingship, patronage and tribal fatherhood (Moore 1996). Such a figure is essentially distant and authoritarian, demanding obedience and submission for his followers. He does not mind if they feel ashamed in the presence of his glory, for this is an appropriate stance in the presence of such a superior being.

Here again, feminists have been helpful in deconstructing and reconstructing images of God, broadening them so that God is a less threatening, nearer and more compassionate figure. In this connection, McFague has proposed a more organic, embodied view of God who is incarnate in the materiality of the creation (McFague 1993). This immanent, yet transcendent, God can be modelled as mother, lover and friend, rather than as father, king and judge (McFague 1987). Imagery like this helps to problematise traditional notions of God. It focusses attention on the quality of relations between entities rather than upon supposed unsurpassable differences between them. It thus helps to undergird a theology that values divine loving presence being realised in this-worldly human relations rather than fixing attention upon transcendent connections that might have no reality at all. Questioning the monarchical view of God and finding different models for this relationship is important if people are to take themselves and their human relations seriously. Again, it prompts positive engagement in expunging the alienation of shame in individuals and groups rather than attending to the metaphysics of putative ontological defilement and stain.

God's face is hidden from humanity

An important theme in traditional theology has been the importance of the presence of God as symbolised by seeing God's face (Taylor 1987). For many, perhaps most, Christians down the centuries, the presence of God has been perceived to be a joy and a delight while God's perceived absence has been accompanied by misery and despair (Pss. 22.1, 102.1, 104.29). The theological motif of the hiddenness of God's face therefore appears on first sight to be tragic, worrying, frustrating and unfortunate.

This is not necessarily the case for shamed people. For me, the sense that I was always in the critical gaze of an omnipresent God was uncomfortable and persecutory. I would have done anything to escape from the presence of this God. It is this unpleasant experience that has led me to begin to explore the possibly liberating and helpful theological motif of the absence of God.

The positive benefits of the absence of God and being able to exist outside the gaze of the Almighty have not been particularly fully explored in the mainstream theological tradition. However, there are images and instances that illustrate it. On the ceiling of the Sistine Chapel, there is a graphic picture of God's backside as he disappears into heaven having created the sun and moon. When Adam and Eve eat of the forbidden tree in the Garden of Eden, God is apparently absent. For long swathes of the Old Testament the character God does not appear to be present, leaving human beings for the most part to their own devices and only occasionally, if decisively, intervening in person (Miles 1996).

In the New Testament, too, God is not often directly present in events. Cupitt, amongst others, charts the way in which God gradually fades away as a person-like being who speaks directly to human beings without intermediaries (Cupitt 1990: 113ff.; Miles 1996). Even when characters in the Bible speak with and see God, they are not permitted to see his face lest they should die (Exod. 33.20). By an act of voluntary self-limitation, God leaves space for humans to live their lives independently of his intervening presence. In other words, it could be said that God not only guards the mystery and transcendence of God's own being, God also shows considerable sensitivity and respect for human beings and creation.

For me, this delicacy is best symbolised in what has come to be called the story of the Fall. When God returns to the Garden of Eden after humanity's primal offence and discovers the shamed Adam and Eve endeavouring to hide themselves beneath fig leaves, he does not demand that they should stand naked before him in judgment. Rather, he clothes them with coats of skins (Gen. 3.22) before casting them out of Paradise to labour and toil (Miles 1996: 36).

A possible interpretation of this event and the tradition of absence is that God respects human autonomy and even human shame. God is not just an all-seeing omnipresent 'eye in the sky'. God is also discreet, courteous, sensitive and respectful.

This motif may provide very good and liberating news for those who feel poorly enselfed, stained and alienated. A God who stands far off may provide them with the space and opportunity they need to discover who they are in relation to themselves and others. Such a God may also enable them to discover their own autonomy, efficacy and power so that they can begin to take proper responsibility for themselves and for the creation. In other words, this God allows people to grow up, to learn to trust themselves and other human beings, to make their own mistakes, to discover the limits of their powers, and to enjoy a proper sense of boundaries and possibility in relationships.

The image of the back, or absence, of God provides a powerful and necessary counterbalance to the image of the immanent, present God who takes a minute and oppressive interest in human affairs, especially personal inadequacies and wrongdoings. Far from being a cause for despair, the absence of a certain kind of God may be a cause for rejoicing amongst the shamed and victimised.

The notion of the absent God, the God who conceals his face, stands in stark contrast to many of the theological motifs hitherto discussed that have emphasised the benevolent presence of God in contemporary human relationships. This emphasises the importance of playfulness, experiment and paradox in theology that tries to relate to shame (Pruyser 1991). Theology is a discourse of human words and symbols, not direct knowledge of God in Godself. Theologians in the past have often claimed to know a good deal about the deity. However, whatever God is in Godself cannot be known to us. All we have are words and images. Often these have been used to legitimate and maintain human interests and social arrangements, frequently at the expense of the powerless and victimised. Thus, much theology has had the unwitting effect of increasing dysfunctional shame and alienation amongst those who are powerless to resist this with their own stories and images. Playing with different words and images may create space for such people to begin to talk back to the tradition, to extend the vision of God. It may help them and others to face themselves and others in community. Perhaps in this way, they might encounter a loving, respectful God face to face.

Writing of the limits of theological language and model making about the divine, McFague notes in a discussion about the face of God:

The transcendence of God frees us to model God in terms of what is of most significance to us . . . and to do so not with the fingertips but with both hands. We can do this because we know that God is not captured in nor exhausted by our models. We have given reasons for adopting one or another model . . . but correspondence with divine reality is not and cannot be one of these reasons. That is, I believe, what the transcendence of God, understood as the unavailable face of God, tells us. (McFague 1993: 193)

Theologians must model and play with images of God boldly. We must err on the margins of discourse and reality (Taylor 1987) if we are to find ways of ending the theological alienation that is the portion of those who have been marginalised in shame anyway. One of the surprising results of playing with the notion of an absent God, a God whose presence is lost, is that we may find it easier to make real the presence of God's people to themselves and each other in concrete relationship. Fragmentary, fragmented images of God might contribute more to the healing of the fragmented than the unitary God of orthodoxy. They may enable us better to move towards divinity by recognising and giving face to each other (cf. Jantzen 1998).

Jesus images the possibility of courteous, respectful, inclusive relationship that overcomes shame
There is always a danger, when discussing Jesus' life and work in a theo-logical context, of idealising the man and failing to recognise the ambivalent effects of his acts and words (Pattison 1995a). So, for example, the motif of inclusion, which was important in Jesus' ministry (Sanders 1995) and seems to denote exactly the kind of communal rec-onciliation that is needed to negate shame, may have inadvertent and divisive implications: 'The potent idea of the one and the true, the truth of unity and the unity of truth is a two-edged sword. Those who unite in truth and solidarity are divided from others who do not' (Martin 1980: 17). In many ways, the record of Jesus' life and ministry should perhaps best be regarded as a series of polysemic metaphors that are capable of multiple understandings and interpretations. Some of these interpreta-tions may be destructive for some people. Jesus' teaching and example therefore have a negative, as well as a positive, side.

It is, however, possible to highlight some aspects of what we know of Jesus' ministry in the interests of generating liberating theological motifs that may illuminate a positive response to dysfunctional shame. The aspect that I want to highlight here is, as I have already implied, that of acceptance and inclusion. Much of Jesus' ministry seems to have been concerned with creating a new community (Malina 1996; Sanders 1995) and with drawing people into this. This community has been character-ised as a Kingdom consisting of undesirables, nuisances and nobodies (Crossan 1993, 1994). The gospels are full of accounts of socially marginalised and stigmatised – that is, objectively defiled, shamed – people such as lepers and demoniacs, being healed by Jesus. They are then able to rejoin their own communities, or Jesus' community. Jesus thus appears to overcome the marginalisation of shame in general terms. This itself is a powerful positive theological motif in approaching this condition.

Jesus' integrative work is particularly prominent in the gospel of Luke where special attention is given to children, women and the poor as important groups for inclusion in the community. There are two stories in particular that I find theologically suggestive in approaching shame. In the first of these (Luke 13.10–16), a crippled woman comes to Jesus in synagogue on the Sabbath. She is bent double and unable to stand upright. She could not look into the faces of those around her and so could be metaphorically understood not to be a full member of the community. Jesus heals the woman so that she stands up straight and can see into the faces of others. She gains 'face', literally and metaphorically, and is restored to fuller citizenship and personhood in the community. The ruler of the synagogue then protests as the healing work has been done on the Sabbath. Jesus rebukes him as a hypocrite. He and his friends are then covered in confusion or more literally, 'ashamed'. That is to say that they lose face. The humble and ashamed, therefore, have been included and given their face back, whilst those who run the community have lost face and excluded themselves from Jesus' community.

The importance of this little vignette in the present context is that it provides a suggestive illustration of the reversal of shaming by integration that might be desirable within the religious community. To be a little moralistic, it might be said that a community that does not seek to give face – the recognition of respect and belonging – to the shamed is itself shamed by this. Perhaps, then, this story provides illuminating inspiration for the work of integrating shamed individuals and groups within the religious and theological communities.

The second story is that of Zacchaeus (Luke 19.1–10). Zacchaeus was a tax gatherer and thus a sinner and social outcast, and a short man who was relatively difficult to see and be seen. When Jesus visited Jericho, Zacchaeus climbed a tree to see him. However, when Jesus came to the tree in which Zacchaeus was perched, he looked upward and addressed Zacchaeus by name, calling him to come down because he needed to stay in his house. Zacchaeus hurried down and welcomed him 'joyfully'. He took Jesus to his house and then told him that he proposed to give half of his property to the poor and to pay back any he had cheated four times over. The story ends with Jesus rejoicing in Zacchaeus' salvation: 'For the Son of man is come to seek and to save that which was lost' (Luke 19:10 AV).

This story is apparently a wonderful parable of the respectful over-coming of shame and alienation. Without in any way abasing himself, Jesus looks up into Zacchaeus' face from below, thus being anything but invasive or dominating. He recognises and honours Zacchaeus' distinct subjectivity and personhood, a fact denoted by the use of the man's name. Jesus then asks for something from Zacchaeus that the latter can easily give in the form of accommodation, thus indicating that he does not despise or reject the man and affirming his efficacy and power. This recognition of personhood and inclusion in the community has the effect of making Zacchaeus want to include himself further. It is at this point, when he has been honoured and had the stain of social shame removed from him, that Zacchaeus is able to become a moral person, taking responsibility for the needs of others and respecting their rights. A lost and outcast, immoral man has been integrated into the commu-nity and moral responsibility by the conferral of respect that removes the taint of shame.

It seems to me that it is precisely the kind of shame-removing and morally empowering process figured by the story of Jesus and Zacchaeus that Christian individuals and communities need to explore and emulate today. The Lukan story may provide theological warrant, inspiration and paradigm for doing exactly that.

There are probably many other theological images and motifs, both contradictory and complementary, that might be considered and evoked in relation to constructing a positive theological response to shame. The image of Jesus and Zacchaeus, however, seems to be a particularly appo-site one with which to conclude this section, this chapter, and indeed, the substance of this book.

Conclusion

The experience of prolonged, chronic or dysfunctional shame for indi-viduals or groups is an experience of alienation and living death. In this chapter, I have tried to suggest some ways in which Christian commu-nities might change and develop to respond more sensitively and posi-tively to shame. The obstacles to this kind of response are considerable. Religious communities will need to recognise the ways in which they benefit from the exploitation of shame in the first place. They will also have to work hard to overcome dysfunctional self-idealisation. Beyond this, it will be necessary to criticise and revise the kinds of practices that persistently engender or exacerbate shame and to identify ways of acting that help to integrate people and facilitate a sense of worth. This will need to be accompanied by critical reassessment of theological approaches, symbols, images and ideas.

There is much scope here for creativity, imagination and playfulness in the cause of finding practices, stories and symbols that allow shamed groups and individuals to find themselves, each other, their community, and God. It is in such activity that contemporary Christians may help to give humanity face, bestowing valued personhood by recognising it in each other. In so doing, they may find that they are doing something that humans alone can do by giving their God a face – doing something absolutely necessary and beautiful for a God who otherwise remains invisible, isolated, unknown.

The practical and intellectual agenda outlined here is a large and imprecisely defined one. It has not been possible to pursue it very far. Nonetheless, it is to be hoped that some individuals and groups will wish to develop aspects of it in the interests of those individuals and groups whose lives are decisively shadowed by shame. The stigma and aliena-tion of shame, figured by the metaphor of stain, will not easily be removed. Inclusion, worth-giving, and acceptance will not readily be effected without considerable conscious change and effort. But did not the Son of Man come to seek and to save that which was lost? And should not his followers attempt to do likewise?

Epilogue

My main motivation for writing this book was better to understand my own experience of shame, particularly in relation to my engagement with religion. As the volume has progressed, I have occasionally illustrated it with examples drawn from my own history. It may be appropriate now to say a little about where I have been left at the end of this project.

The whole of this book has been composed under the watchful gaze of the Angel of the Judgment (see Plate 1) who appears in the Roger Van der Weyden's altarpiece for the Hospices de Beaune painted in the early fifteenth century (Gondinet-Wallstein 1990). I first saw this heavenly being in about 1990, but I felt that I recognised him and, indeed, had known him all my life. The Angel was for me a physical portrayal and externalisation of the sense of shame-producing self-surveillance that had accompanied me all my life. It was, as it were, 'his' critical gaze (or rather, my projection of that gaze) within me that epitomised my sense of shame, defilement and inadequacy. It may be that one of the innovations of the picture is precisely that it invites people to judge themselves internally rather than being judged by an external accuser (Gondinet-Wallstein 1990: 111–12).

Subsequently, I have spent many hours in Beaune staring back at my glorious persecutor. Furthermore, a miniature version of the altarpiece has been attached to the front of my word processor throughout the writing of this book as a symbol of my attempt to come to terms with shame. Whenever I look up from writing, I can, if I wish, look into the Angel's unblinking eyes, filled with a light that might have been deliberately intended to evoke divine omniscience (Gondinet-Wallstein 1990: 116). Just before I started on the main text, I tried to put my feelings of dread and discomfort about the Angel into words:

Plate 1: *The Angel of the Judgment*, part of the polyptych *The Last Judgment*, by Roger Van der Weyden, reproduced by kind permission of the Hospices Civils de Beaune © Hospices de Beaune (photograph © Paul M. R. Maeyaert).

THE ANGEL OF THE JUDGMENT AT BEAUNE

He is lovely.
Stepping out from beneath Christ's rainbow throne of judgment, this curly-
　　headed youth is the most beautiful of the sons of morning,
all decked in white, glittering cope, wings of peacock eyes.

Around him naked people are beckoned into bliss or hurled into hell.
This he knows – the balance of justice is in his own right hand.

Slowly, stately he advances, his sweet face impassive, his progress inexorable.
There is no stopping him.

To him all hearts are open.
From him no secrets are hid.
No hiding place from his gaze.
Onwards, ever onwards he comes.

He is not angry.
Nor does he condemn.
In his perfection, he does not notice the fate of humankind.
Naked souls are weighed in his balance.
They find themselves shamefully, sordidly wanting.

The angel has been walking my way for ever.
I am in his path.
I cannot flee his all-seeing eye.
No door can resist him, no screen can block the windows of the heart.
His entrance is automatic.
This lofty spirit of judgment is already within.

Will I ever see the back of him?

In personal terms, this work has been an attempt to see the back of the
Angel at Beaune, or perhaps to get to a point where I can look 'him' in
the face without flinching. The quest has been one of trying to understand and perhaps overcome a sense of dysfunctional, irrational shame
fuelled and amplified in part by religious thought and participation. I
want now to comment on the extent to which I have succeeded in this
quest.

　　In many ways, I have been surprised at the extent to which this study
has been personally transformative. I have often written, perhaps rather
glibly, of practical or pastoral theology as a transformative activity
(Pattison with Woodward 1994). However, I have been surprised by the
extent to which my views of shame, Christianity, God, and my self have
been changed (sometimes uncomfortably and inconveniently) by engaging in this work.

With regard to shame, I now see it as a much more complex and more fundamental phenomenon in human existence than I initially imagined. The stain of shame is far more deadly and far more widespread and significant as a social and individual phenomenon than I thought. I am heartened to discover that I am not alone in experiencing a profound sense of shame. There are narratives of causation and effect that help to account for shame and may open ways for solidarity and integration. However, far more academic and clinical work is needed in this area if many individuals and groups are to enjoy the fullness of human life that is figured by face-to-face acceptance and non-objectifying belonging symbolised by sharing, singing and feasting together in the Kingdom of God (Ford 1999).

In relation to Christianity, it has been very uncomfortable for me to have to acknowledge that a religion to which I have adhered all my life can itself be shame-generating and -amplifying. The Jewish scholar, David Blumenthal, said in a seminar I attended while writing this book that he felt physically sick and guilty at having to expose some of the faults, evils and inadequacies of his faith and its theology when composing *Facing the Abusing God* (1993), a work that dealt with various kinds of horrific soul- and body-destroying abuse. I think I know something of Blumenthal's real anxiety and misery from my own authorial experience. If one has placed faith and trust in an idealised system that later turns out to be not what it seems, and if one has voluntarily represented it to others as healing and beneficial, this is somewhat humiliating. It also evokes feelings of intense anxiety and loss. The loss of a vision of religion as essentially 'all good', benevolent, and ideally parental is difficult to bear. It confronts one with the need to take responsibility for oneself, one's world and, indeed, one's religious tradition. This is hard adult labour and it is appropriate – but not necessarily easy or welcome.

Much the same kind of comment might be made of my perception of God. For many years, God functioned as a kind of ideal accompanying parental presence in my life. If this perfect, all-loving and all-powerful internalised object 'God' was persecutory, hostile and critical, finding me vaguely disgusting and unsatisfactory all the time, God also made me feel wanted and important, having particular acts of obedience in mind that he wanted me to accomplish. I must acknowledge that this particular living image of God is now dead for me. The shaming, sadistic God that evoked in me a sense of profound stain has had to go along with many of the practices and assumptions that sustained his reality. This again has left a curious space and sense of loss in my life for which I still grieve. If

God is no longer so powerful, frightening and shame-inspiring, this God also seems less protective, intriguing and fascinating.

All of which represents for me a curious kind of resurrection from the death of shamed or false self that inspires fear and confusion more than happiness or joy. Perhaps I understand something of why the women who first witnessed Jesus' empty tomb were afraid rather than having any other kind of more positive response (Mark 15.8). Christianity is a reve-latory and an iconoclastic, anti-idolatrous religion with a God who has qualities of hiddenness and openness, presence and absence. I hope I can look forward, therefore, to discovering new faces or images of God that transcend my previous distortions. Alongside the image of the Angel on my word processor, at some point I wrote this quotation from Psalm 27: 'I shall see the goodness of Yahweh in the land of the living' (Ps. 27.13 JB). Not far before, in the same Psalm, the author writes, 'Of you my heart has said, "Seek his face!" Your face, Yahweh, I seek; Do not turn away from me' (Ps. 27.8 JB). Perhaps one day, like Jacob, Moses, Martin Luther (Erikson 1962) and the pure in heart of the Beatitudes (Matt. 5.8) I will see God face to face. If so, I hope to be fortified by the example of Luther who, according to Nietzsche, 'wanted to speak to God directly, speak as himself, and without embarrassment' (Erikson 1962: 97).

So to my perspective on myself. One of the implications of idealising a particular image of God as good is that this maintained me in a perma-nent state of feeling bad about myself. I failed to recognise that of God in me. In fact, I wished that 'me' did not exist and did my best for many years to eliminate what felt like a very unwanted self. I have had to come to realise that what felt like a false self that disrupted my quest for sanc-tity, obedience and holiness, is in fact not going to die. Furthermore, it is this apparently unwanted part of me, for so long covered in shame and abnegation, that embodies the spirit of life within me which must in some way be both honoured and released. If God is no longer all-good and all-powerful in the way that I used to think, I am no longer all-bad and passively helpless either. While God may seem less present to me, I feel less distant and more present to my own immediate experience. I feel less depressed; perhaps more of me is available to myself and to others.

In a strange way, I sense that I have been converted from a defensive, protective and inwardly persecutory religion founded upon fear and sado-masochistic dependence to some kind of new life that is both more mundane but more important than what I knew before. I hope it is not too pretentious to say that I find echoes of this in Martin Buber's account of his conversion from extraordinary religion to a life of everyday dialogue with humanity:

In my earlier years the 'religious' was for me the exception . . . 'Religious experience' was the experience of an otherness which did not fit into the context of life . . . The 'religious' lifted you out . . . Since then I have given up the 'religious' which is nothing but the exception, extraction, exaltation, ecstasy; or it has given me up. I possess nothing but the everyday out of which I am never taken. The mystery is no longer disclosed, it has escaped or it has made its dwelling here where everything happens as it happens. I know no fulness but each mortal hour's fulness of claim and responsibility. Though far from being equal to it, yet I know that in the claim I am claimed and may respond in responsibility, and know who speaks and demands a response. (Buber 1961: 28–30)

I can only think that this is a kind of empowerment of myself and other human beings as agents with a real sense of selfhood and responsibility that is desirable in the modern world. Perhaps human beings need appropriately to differentiate themselves from God, Jesus and the church if they are to witness to, and make real, some kind of healing and salvation that is relevant. If so, paradoxically, there may sometimes be a need for people to emancipate themselves from Christ, in the name of Christ, to do the work of Christ in the world (Pattison 1995a). To internalise Christ it may be that sometimes one has to undergo the stripping process of loss and mourning that ultimately leads to possibilities of newness of life (Harvey 1985).

It is time for me to turn my back upon the Angel and upon this long text to pass on to the next lot of claims and responsibilities that present themselves. I hope that this study may help others as well as me to claim and respond more fully and dialogically in the reality of the face-to-face community that is the human race created in, and creating, the image of God.

Bibliography

Adorno, T. W., Frenkel-Brunswick, Else, Levinson, Daniel and Nevitt, Sanford 1969, *The Authoritarian Personality*, New York, W. W. Norton.

Alves, Rubem 1986, *I Believe in the Resurrection of the Body*, Philadelphia, Fortress Press.

Alvesson, Mats and Willmott, Hugh 1996, *Making Sense of Management*, London, Sage.

Andrews, Bernice 1998a, 'Methodological and definitional issues in shame research' in Gilbert and Andrews (eds.), pp. 39–54.

Andrews, Bernice 1998b, 'Shame and childhood abuse' in Gilbert and Andrews (eds.), pp. 176–90.

Angelou, Maya 1984, *I Know Why the Caged Bird Sings*, London, Virago.

Armon-Jones, Claire 1986a, 'The thesis of constructionism' in Harré (ed.), pp. 32–56.

Armon-Jones, Claire 1986b, 'The social functions of emotion' in Harré (ed.), pp. 57–82.

Ashby, Godfrey 1988, *Sacrifice*, London, SCM Press.

Augustine, St 1972, *City of God*, Harmondsworth, Penguin Books.

Augustine, St 1991, *Confessions*, Oxford, Oxford University Press.

Aulen, Gustaf 1931, *Christus Victor*, London, SPCK.

Averill, James 1986, 'The acquisition of emotions during adulthood' in Harré (ed.), pp. 98–119.

Averill, James 1996a, 'Intellectual emotions' in Harré and Parrott (eds.), pp. 24–38.

Averill, James 1996b 'An analysis of psychophysiological symbolism and its influence on theories of emotion' in Harré and Parrott (eds.), pp. 204–28.

Bailey, James and Vander Broek, Lyle 1992, *Literary Forms in the New Testament*, London, SPCK.

Baker Miller, Jean 1986, *Toward a New Psychology of Women*, London, Penguin Books.

Ballard, Paul (ed.) 1986, *The Foundations of Pastoral Studies and Practical Theology*, Cardiff, HOLI.

Barasch, M. 1987, *Giotto and the Language of Gesture*, Cambridge, Cambridge University Press.

Barth, Karl 1961, *Church Dogmatics III.4*, Edinburgh, T & T Clark.

317

Barth, Karl 1981, *Ethics*, Edinburgh, T & T Clark.

Basile, Giuseppe 1993, *Giotto: The Arena Chapel Frescoes*, London, Thames and Hudson.

Batson, Daniel, Schoenrade, Patricia and Ventis, Larry 1993, *Religion and the Individual*, Oxford, Oxford University Press.

Bauman, Zygmunt 1993, *Postmodern Ethics*, Oxford, Blackwell.

Beck, Ulrich 1992, *Risk Society*, London, Sage.

Bendelow, Gillian and Williams, Simon 1998, *Emotions in Social Life*, London, Routledge.

Benedict, Ruth 1954, *The Chrysanthemum and the Sword*, Rutland, Charles Tuttle.

Berger, Peter, Berger, Brigitte and Kellner, Hansfried 1973, *The Homeless Mind*, Harmondsworth, Penguin Books.

Berke, Joseph 1987, 'Shame and envy' in Nathanson (ed.), pp. 318–34.

Bettelheim, Bruno 1986, *The Informed Heart*, London, Penguin Books.

Blumenthal, David 1993, *Facing the Abusing God*, Louisville, Westminster/John Knox Press.

Bly, Robert 1991, *Iron John*, Shaftesbury, Element Books.

Bolton, Gillie 1999, *The Therapeutic Potential of Creative Writing*, London, Jessica Kingsley.

Bondi, Roberta 1995, *Memories of God*, London, Darton, Longman & Todd.

Bonhoeffer, Dietrich 1964, *Ethics*, London, Fontana.

Bowden, Peta 1997, *Caring: Gender Sensitive Ethics*, London, Routledge.

Bowker, John 1987, *Licensed Insanities*, London, Darton, Longman & Todd.

Bradley, Ian 1995, *The Power of Sacrifice*, London, SPCK.

Bradshaw, John 1988, *Healing the Shame that Binds You*, Deerfield Beach FL, Health Communications Inc.

Braithwaite, John 1989, *Crime, Shame and Reintegration*, Cambridge, Cambridge University Press.

Bringle, Mary Louise 1990, *Despair: Sickness or Sin?*, Nashville, Abingdon Press.

Brock, Rita Nakashima 1988, *Journeys By Heart*, New York, Crossroad.

Broucek, Francis 1991, *Shame and the Self*, New York, Guilford Press.

Broucek, Francis 1997, 'Shame: early developmental issues' in Lansky and Morrison (eds.), pp. 41–62.

Brown, George 1996, 'Life events, loss, and depressive disorders', in Heller et al. (eds.), pp. 36–45.

Brown, Peter 1989, *The Body and Society*, London, Faber and Faber.

Browning, Don 1983, *Religious Ethics and Pastoral Care*, Philadelpia, Fortress Press.

Browning, Don 1987, *Religious Thought and the Modern Psychologies*, Philadelphia, Fortress Press.

Browning, Don 1991, *A Fundamental Practical Theology*, Minneapolis, Fortress Press.

Brueggemann, Walter 1993, *The Bible and Postmodern Imagination*, London, SCM Press.

Buber, Martin 1961, *Between Man and Man*, London, Fontana.

Burns, David 1990, *The Feeling Good Handbook*, London, Plume.

Burton, Robert 1932, *The Anatomy of Melancholy* (3 vols.), London, J. M. Dent and Sons.

Cairns, Douglas 1993, *Aidos*, Oxford, Oxford University Press.

Calhoun, Cheshire and Solomon, Robert 1984, *What is an Emotion?*, Oxford, Oxford University Press.

Campbell, Alastair 1986, *The Gospel of Anger*, London, SPCK.

Campbell, Alastair (ed.) 1987, *A Dictionary of Pastoral Care*, London, SPCK.

Caplovitz Barrett, Karen 1995, 'A functionalist approach to shame and guilt' in Price Tangney and Fischer (eds.), pp. 25–63.

Capps, Donald 1983, *Life Cycle Theory and Pastoral Care*, Philadelphia, Fortress Press.

Capps, Donald 1990a, 'Augustine's *Confessions*: The scourge of shame and the silencing of Adeodatus' in Capps and Dittes (eds.), pp. 69–92.

Capps, Donald 1990b, 'Augustine as narcissist: of grandiosity and shame' in Capps and Dittes (eds.), pp. 169–84.

Capps, Donald 1993, *The Depleted Self*, Minneapolis, Fortress Press.

Capps, Donald 1995a, *The Child's Song*, Louisville, Westminster/John Knox Press.

Capps, Donald 1995b, *Agents of Hope*, Minneapolis, Fortress Press.

Capps, Donald and Dittes, James (eds.) 1990, *The Hunger of the Heart*, West Lafayette, IN, Society for the Scientific Study of Religion.

Carlson Brown, Joanne and Bohn, Carole (eds.) 1989, *Christianity, Patriarchy, and Abuse*, Cleveland, Pilgrim Press.

Carlson Brown, Joanne and Parker, Rebecca 1989, 'For God So Loved the World?' in Carlson Brown and Bohn (eds.), pp. 1–30.

Carroll, Robert 1991, *Wolf in the Sheepfold*, London, SPCK.

Caute, David 1970, *Fanon*, Glasgow, Collins.

Chancer, Lynn 1992, *Sadomasochism in Everyday Life*, New Brunswick, Rutgers University Press.

Christ, Carol and Plaskow, Judith (eds.) 1979, *Womanspirit Rising*, San Francisco, Harper and Row.

Coate, Mary Anne 1994, *Sin, Guilt and Forgiveness*, London, SPCK.

Cole, Jonathan 1998, *About Face*, Cambridge MA, MIT Press.

Condren, Mary 1999, 'Women, shame and abjection', *Contact* 130: 10–19.

Cooter, Roger 1984, *The Cultural Meaning of Popular Science*, Cambridge, Cambridge University Press.

Corbin, Alain 1986, *The Foul and the Fragrant*, Leamington Spa, Berg.

Cotter, Jim 1987, *Prayer in the Morning*, Exeter, Jim Cotter.

Cotter, Jim 1997, *Brainsquall*, Sheffield, Cairns Publications.

Countryman, William 1989, *Dirt, Greed and Sex*, London, SCM Press.

Cox, Murray and Theilgaard, Alice 1997, *Mutative Metaphors in Psychotherapy*, London, Jessica Kingsley.

Crawford, June, Kippax, Susan, Onyx, Jenny, Gault, Una and Benton, Pam 1992, *Emotion and Gender*, London, Sage.

Crossan, John 1993, *The Historical Jesus*, Edinburgh, T & T Clark.

Crossan, John 1994, *Jesus: A Revolutionary Biography*, San Francisco, HarperCollins.

Cumbee, Dwight 1980, 'Depression as an ecclesiogenic neurosis', *Journal of Pastoral Care* 34: 254–67.

Cupitt, Don 1990, *Creation Out of Nothing*, London, SCM Press.

Danziger, Kurt 1997, *Naming the Mind*, London, Sage.

Darwin, Charles 1965, *The Expression of Emotions in Men and Animals*, Chicago, University of Chicago Press.

Davenport-Hines, Richard 1990, *Sex, Death and Punishment*, London, Collins.

Davidson, Robert 1983, *The Courage to Doubt*, London, SCM Press.

DeBlassie, Paul 1992, *Toxic Christianity*, New York, Crossroad.

Delumeau, Jean 1990, *Sin and Fear*, London, St Martin's Press.

Demos, John 1996, 'Shame and guilt in early New England' in Harré and Parrott (eds.), pp. 74–88.

Demos, Virginia (ed.) 1995, *Exploring Affect*, Cambridge, Cambridge University Press.

de Sousa, Ronald 1990, *The Rationality of Emotion*, Cambridge MA, MIT Press.

Dodds, E. R. 1951, *The Greeks and the Irrational*, Berkeley, University of California Press.

Dostoevsky, Fyodor 1958, *The Brothers Karamazov* (2 vols.), Harmondsworth, Penguin Books.

Dostoevsky, Fyodor 1994, *Demons*, London, Vintage Books.

Douglas, Mary 1969, *Purity and Danger*, London, Routledge and Kegan Paul.

Douglas, Tom 1995, *Scapegoats*, London, Routledge.

Dreyfus, Hubert and Rabinow, Paul 1982, *Michel Foucault*, Hemel Hempstead, Harvester Wheatsheaf.

Dudley, Martin and Rowell, Geoffrey 1990, *Confession and Absolution*, London, SPCK.

Ecclestone, Alan 1993, *Gather the Fragments*, Sheffield, Cairns Publications.

Eichenbaum, Luise and Orbach, Susie 1985, *Understanding Women*, London, Penguin Books.

Ekman, Paul and Davidson, Richard 1994, *The Nature of Emotion*, Oxford, Oxford University Press.

Elias, Norbert 1994, *The Civilizing Process*, Oxford, Blackwell.

Ellmann, Richard 1982, *James Joyce*, Oxford, Oxford University Press.

Ellmann, Richard 1987, *Oscar Wilde*, London, Hamish Hamilton.

Erikson, Erik 1962, *Young Man Luther*, New York, W. W. Norton.

Erikson, Erik 1965, *Childhood and Society*, Harmondsworth, Penguin Books.

Etzioni, Amitai 1995, *Spirit of Community*, London, Fontana.

Fenn, Richard 1991, *The Secularization of Sin*, Louisville, Westminster/John Knox Press.

Fenn, Richard 1995, *The Persistence of Purgatory*, Cambridge, Cambridge University Press.

Ferguson, Harvie 1995, *Melancholy and the Critique of Modernity*, London, Routledge.

Feuerbach, Ludwig 1989, *The Essence of Christianity*, Buffalo, Prometheus Books.

Fiddes, Paul 1989, *Past Event and Present Salvation*, London, Darton, Longman & Todd.

Fife, Janet 1999, 'Sexual abuse and the spirituality of the Christian survivor', *Contact* 130: 20–6.

Fineman, Stephen (ed.) 1993, *Emotion in Organizations*, London, Sage.

Fischer, Kurt and Price Tangney, June 1995, 'Self-conscious emotions and the affect revolution' in Price Tangney and Fischer (eds.), pp. 3–24.

Ford, David 1999, *Self and Salvation*, Cambridge, Cambridge University Press.

Forrester, Duncan 1997, *Christian Justice and Social Policy*, Cambridge, Cambridge University Press.

Fossum, Merle and Mason, Marilyn 1986, *Facing Shame*, New York, W. W. Norton.

Foucault, Michel 1979, *Discipline and Punish*, London, Penguin Books.

Fowler, James 1996, *Faithful Change*, Nashville, Abingdon Press.

Fox, Matthew 1983, *Original Blessing*, Santa Fe, Bear.

Frank, Arthur 1995, *The Wounded Storyteller*, Chicago, University of Chicago Press.

Freeman, Mark 1993, *Rewriting the Self*, London, Routledge.

Freud, Sigmund 1977, *Three Essays on Sexuality*, London, Penguin Books.

Freud, Sigmund 1984, *On Metapsychology*, London, Penguin Books.

Fridlund, Alan and Duchaine, Bradley 1996, '"Facial expressions of emotion" and the delusion of the hermetic self' in Harré and Parrott (eds.), pp. 259–84.

Furedi, Frank 1997, *Culture of Fear*, London, Cassell.

Gabriel, Yiannis 1993, 'Organizational nostalgia – reflections on "the golden age"' in Fineman (ed.), pp. 118–41.

Game, Ann and Metcalfe, Andrew 1996, *Passionate Sociology*, London, Sage.

Gay, Peter 1988, *Freud*, London, J. M. Dent.

Geertz, Clifford 1993, *The Interpretation of Cultures*, London, Fontana Press.

Gellner, Ernest 1985, *The Psychoanalytic Movement*, London, Granada Publishing.

Gendzier, Irene 1973, *Frantz Fanon*, London, Wildwood House.

Gergen, Kenneth 1991, *The Saturated Self*, np, Basic Books.

Gergen, Kenneth 1994, *Realities and Relationships*, Cambridge MA, Harvard University Press.

Gibson, Ian 1978, *The English Vice*, London, Duckworth.

Giddens, Anthony 1991, *Modernity and Self-Identity*, Cambridge, Polity Press.

Giddens, Anthony 1992, *The Transformation of Intimacy*, Cambridge, Polity Press.

Gilbert, Paul 1998, 'What is shame?' in Gilbert and Andrews (eds.), pp. 3–38.

Gilbert, Paul and Andrews, Bernice (eds.) 1998, *Shame*, Oxford University Press.

Gilbert, Paul and McGuire, Michael 1998, 'Shame, status and social roles' in Gilbert and Andrews (eds.), pp. 99–125.

Gilhus, Ingvild Saelid 1997, *Laughing Gods, Weeping Virgins*, London, Routledge.

Gillis, John 1988, 'From ritual to romance: toward an alternative history of love' in Stearns and Stearns (eds.), pp. 87–121.

Ginsburg, G. and Harrington, Melanie 1996, 'Bodily states and context in situated lines of action' in Harré and Parrott (eds.), pp. 229–58.

Girard, Rene 1996, *The Girard Reader*, New York, Crossroad Publishing.

Glaz, Maxine and Moessner, Jeanne Stevenson 1991, *Women in Travail and Transition*, Minneapolis, Fortress Press.

Gondinet-Wallstein, Eliane 1990, *Un Retable pour l'Au-delà*, np, Editions Mame.

Goffman, Erving 1956, 'Embarrassment and social organization', *American Journal of Sociology* 62: 264–71.

Goffman, Erving 1968a, *Asylums*, Harmondsworth, Penguin Books.

Goffman, Erving 1968b, *Stigma*, Harmondsworth, Penguin Books.

Goffman, Erving 1971a, *The Presentation of Self in Everyday Life*, Harmondsworth, Penguin Books.

Goffman, Erving 1971b, *Relations in Public*, Harmondsworth, Penguin Books.

Goldberg, Carl 1991, *Understanding Shame*, Northvale NJ, Jason Aronson.

Gordon, Howard 1996, 'Christian Identity and the Alleviation of Guilt Feelings in Depressive Illness', unpublished PhD thesis, Cranfield University, UK.

Gorringe, Tim 1996, *God's Just Vengeance*, Cambridge, Cambridge University Press.

Gosse, Edmund 1949, *Father and Son*, Harmondsworth, Penguin Books.

Gough, Tony 1990, *Don't Blame Me!*, London, Sheldon Press.

Goulder, Michael 1994, *A Tale of Two Missions*, London, SCM Press.

Graham, Elaine 1996, *Transforming Practice*, London, Mowbray.

Greene, Graham 1971, *The Heart of the Matter*, Harmondsworth, Penguin Books.

Greven, Philip 1992, *Spare the Child*, New York, Vintage Books.

Grey, Mary 1989, *Redeeming the Dream*, London, SPCK.

Gudorf, Christine 1992, *Victimization*, Philadelphia, Trinity Press International.

Guillaumont, A., Puech, H.-Ch., Quispel, G., Till, W. and Al Masih, Y. (eds.) 1976, *The Gospel According to Thomas*, Leiden, E. J. Brill.

Gunton, Colin 1988, *The Actuality of Atonement*, Edinburgh, T & T Clark.

Hans, James 1991, *The Origins of the Gods*, Albany, State University of New York Press.

Harder, David 1995, 'Shame and guilt assessment, and relationships of shame- and guilt-proneness in psychopathology' in Price Tangney and Fischer (eds.), pp. 368–92.

Hardy, Daniel and Ford, David 1984, *Jubilate*, London, Darton, Longman & Todd.

Harré, Rom (ed.) 1986a, *The Social Construction of Emotions*, Oxford, Blackwell.

Harré, Rom 1986b, 'An outline of the social constructionist viewpoint' in Harré (ed.), pp. 2–14.

Harré, Rom 1998, *The Singular Self*, London, Sage.

Harré, Rom and Finlay-Jones, Robert 1986, 'Emotion talk across times' in Harré (ed.), pp. 220–33.

Harré, Rom and Parrott, Gerrod (eds.) 1996, *The Emotions*, London, Sage.

Harvey, Peter 1985, *Death's Gift*, London, Epworth Press.

Hauerwas, Stanley 1981, *A Community of Character*, Notre Dame, University of Notre Dame Press.

Hawthorne, Nathaniel 1903, *The Scarlet Letter*, Oxford, Oxford University Press.
Heelas, Paul 1996, 'Emotion talk across cultures' in Harré and Parrot (eds.), pp. 171–99.
Heller, Agnes 1985, *The Power of Shame*, London, Routledge and Kegan Paul.
Heller, Tom, Reynolds, Jill, Gomm, Roger, Muston, Rosemary and Pattison, Stephen (eds.) 1996, *Mental Health Matters*, Basingstoke, Macmillan.
Hepworth, Mike and Turner, Bryan 1982, *Confession*, London, Routledge and Kegan Paul.
Hick, John 1966, *Evil and the God of Love*, London, Macmillan.
Hick, John (ed.) 1977, *The Myth of God Incarnate*, London, SCM Press.
Hick, John 1989, *An Interpretation of Religion*, Basingstoke, Macmillan.
Hills, Paul 1987, *The Light of Early Italian Painting*, New Haven, Yale University Press.
Hiltner, Seward 1958, *Preface to Pastoral Theology*, Nashville, Abingdon Press.
Hilton, Boyd 1988, *The Age of Atonement*, Oxford, Oxford University Press.
Hochschild, Arlie Russell 1983, *The Managed Heart*, Berkeley, University of California Press.
House of Bishops 1991, *Issues in Human Sexuality*, London, Church House Publishing.
Howard, Roland 1996, *The Rise and Fall of the Nine O'Clock Service*, London, Cassell.
Howe, Leroy 1995, *The Image of God*, Nashville, Abingdon Press.
Hughes, Gerard 1997, *God, Where Are You?*, London, Darton, Longman & Todd.
Hull, John 1985, *What Prevents Christian Adults from Learning?*, London, SCM Press.
Hunt, Geoffrey (ed.) 1995, *Whistleblowing in the Health Service*, London, Edward Arnold.
Iglesias, Immaculada 1996, 'Vergüenza ajena' in Harré and Parrott (eds.), pp. 122–31.
Jackson, Stanley 1986, *Melancholia and Depression*, New Haven, Yale University Press.
Jacobs, Michael 1988, *Towards the Fullness of Christ*, London, Darton, Longman & Todd.
Jacobs, Michael 1993, *Living Illusions*, London, SPCK.
Jacoby, Mario 1994, *Shame and the Origins of Self-Esteem*, London, Routledge.
James, William 1960, *The Varieties of Religious Experience*, London, Fontana.
James, William 1981, *The Principles of Psychology*, Cambridge MA, Harvard University Press.
James, Susan 1997, *Passion and Action*, Oxford, Oxford University Press.
Jantzen, Grace 1990, 'AIDS, shame and suffering' in Woodward (ed.), pp. 22–31.
Jantzen, Grace 1998, *Becoming Divine*, Manchester, Manchester University Press.
Johnstone, Lucy 1989, *Users and Abusers of Psychiatry*, London, Routledge.
Jones, James 1991, *Contemporary Psychoanalysis and Religion*, New Haven, Yale University Press.
Joyce, James 1956, *Dubliners*, Harmondsworth, Penguin Books.
Joyce, James 1968, *A Portrait of the Artist as a Young Man*, London, Jonathan Cape.
Kafka, Franz 1953, *The Trial*, Harmondsworth, Penguin Books.

Karp, David 1996, *Speaking of Sadness*, Oxford, Oxford University Press.

Kaufman, Gershen 1985, *Shame: The Power of Caring*, Rochester, Shenkman Books, second revised edn.

Kaufman, Gershen 1993, *The Psychology of Shame*, London, Routledge.

Kaufmann, Walter (ed.) 1976, *The Portable Nietzsche*, London, Penguin Books.

Keillor, Garrison 1985, *Lake Wobegon Days*, London, Faber and Faber.

Keltner, Dacher and Harker, Lee Ann (1998), 'The forms and functions of the nonverbal signal of shame' in Gilbert and Andrews (eds.), pp. 78–98.

Kinston, Warren 1987, 'The shame of narcissism' in Nathanson (ed.), pp. 214–45.

Kirk, Kenneth 1931, *The Vision of God*, London, Longmans, Green.

Kitayama, Shinobu, Rose Markus, Hazel and Matsumoto, Hisaya 1995, 'Culture, self, and emotion: a cultural perspective on "self-conscious" emotions', in Price Tangney and Fischer (eds.), pp. 439–64.

Kitwood, Tom 1997, *Dementia Reconsidered*, Buckingham, Open University Press.

Klassen, William 1996, *Judas: Betrayer or Friend of Jesus?*, London, SCM Press.

Klein, Josephine 1987, *Our Need for Others and its Roots in Infancy*, London, Tavistock.

Klein, Melanie 1988a, *Love, Guilt and Reparation*, London, Virago.

Klein, Melanie 1988b, *Envy and Gratitude*, London, Virago.

Koestler, Arthur 1947, *Darkness at Noon*, Harmondsworth, Penguin Books.

Kohut, Heinz 1971, *The Analysis of the Self*, Madison, International Universities Press.

Kristeva, Julia 1982, *Powers of Horror*, New York, Columbia University Press.

Kritzman, Lawrence (ed.) 1988, *Michel Foucault: Politics, Philosophy, Culture*, London, Routledge.

Kundera, Milan 1984, *The Unbearable Lightness of Being*, London, Faber and Faber.

Kuschel, Karl-Josef 1994, *Laughter*, London, SCM Press.

Laird, James and Apostoleris, Nicholas 1996, 'Emotional self-control and self perception' in Harré and Parrott (eds.), pp. 285–301.

Lamb, Sharon 1996, *The Trouble with Blame*, Cambridge MA, Harvard University Press.

Lambert, Malcolm 1998, *The Cathars*, Oxford, Blackwell.

Landman, Janet 1996, 'Social control of "negative" emotions: the case of regret' in Harré and Parrott (eds.), pp. 89–116.

Lansky, Melvin 1987, 'Shame and domestic violence' in Nathanson (ed.), pp. 335–62.

Lansky, Melvin 1997, 'Envy as process' in Lansky and Morrison (eds.), pp. 327–38.

Lansky, Melvin and Morrison, Andrew (eds.) 1997, *The Widening Scope of Shame*, Hillsdale NJ, Analytic Press.

Lasch, Christopher 1984, *The Minimal Self*, New York, W. W. Norton.

Lasch, Christopher 1991, *The Culture of Narcissism*, New York, W. W. Norton.

Lazarus, Richard and Lazarus, Bernice 1994, *Passion and Reason*, Oxford, Oxford University Press.

Lehmann, Paul 1976, *Ethics in a Christian Context*, New York, Harper and Row.

Lévi-Strauss, Claude 1972, *Structural Anthropology 1*, London, Penguin Books.

Lewis, Helen Block 1971, *Shame and Guilt in Neurosis*, New York, International Universities Press.

Lewis, Helen Block (ed.) 1987a, *The Role of Shame in Symptom Formation*, Hillsdale NJ, Lawrence Erlbaum.

Lewis, Helen Block 1987b, 'Introduction: Shame – the "sleeper" in psychopathology' in Lewis (ed.) pp. 1–28.

Lewis, Helen Block 1987c, 'The role of shame in depression over the life span' in Lewis (ed.) pp. 29–50.

Lewis, Helen Block 1987d, 'Shame and the narcissistic personality' in Nathanson (ed.), pp. 93–132.

Lewis, Michael 1992, *Shame: The Exposed Self*, New York, The Free Press.

Lewis, Michael 1998, 'Shame and stigma' in Gilbert and Andrews (eds.), pp. 126–40.

Lidmila, Alan 1997, 'Shame, knowledge and modes of enquiry in supervision' in Shipton (ed.), pp. 35–46.

Lindbeck, George 1984, *The Nature of Doctrine*, London, SPCK.

Lindholm, Charles 1990, *Charisma*, Oxford, Blackwell.

Lindsay-Hartz, Janice, de Rivera, Joseph, and Mascolo, Michael 1995, 'Differentiating guilt and shame and their effects on motivation' in Price Tangney and Fischer (eds.), pp. 274–300.

Linn, Matthew, Fabricant Linn, Sheila and Linn, Dennis 1995, *Healing Religious Addiction*, London, Darton, Longman & Todd.

Lloyd, Genevieve 1996, *Spinoza and the 'Ethics'*, London, Routledge.

Lodge, David 1981, *How Far Can You Go?*, London, Penguin Books.

Lowenfeld, Henry 1976, 'Notes on shamelessness', *Psychoanalytic Quarterly* 55: 62–72.

Ludemann, Gerd 1997, *The Unholy in Holy Scripture*, London, SCM Press.

Lukes, Steven 1973, *Individualism*, Oxford, Blackwell.

Lupton, Deborah 1998, *The Emotional Self*, London, Sage.

Lutz, Catherine 1996, 'Engendered emotion: gender, power and the rhetoric of social control in American discourse' in Harré and Perrott (eds.), pp. 151–70.

Lynch, Gordon 1999, 'Exploring the client's view', *Contact* 128: 22–8.

Lynd, Helen Merrell 1958, *On Shame and the Search for Identity*, New York, Harcourt Brace.

Macdonald, James 1998, 'Disclosing shame' in Gilbert and Andrews (eds.), pp. 141–57.

MacIntyre, Alasdair 1981, *After Virtue*, London, Duckworth.

Macmurray, John 1992, *Reason and Emotion*, Atlantic Highlands NJ, Humanities Press.

Macquarrie, John and Childress, James (eds.) 1986, *A New Dictionary of Christian Ethics*, London, SCM Press.

Mainprice, June 1974, *Marital Interaction and Some Illnesses in Children*, London, Institute of Marital Studies.

Malby, Becky and Pattison, Stephen 1999, *Living Values in the NHS*, London, The King's Fund.

Malina, Bruce 1983, *The New Testament World*, London, SCM Press.

Malina, Bruce 1996, *The Social World of Jesus and the Gospels*, London, Routledge.

Malony, H. Newton and Spilka, Bernard 1991, *Religion in Psychodynamic Perspective*, Oxford, Oxford University Press.

Margalit, Avishai 1996, *The Decent Society*, Cambridge MA, Harvard University Press.

Martin, David 1980 *The Breaking of the Image*, Oxford, Blackwell.

McCourt, Frank 1997, *Angela's Ashes*, London, Flamingo.

McDonald, J. I. H. 1993, *Biblical Interpretation and Christian Ethics*, Cambridge, Cambridge University Press.

McFadyen, Alistair 1990, *The Call to Personhood*, Cambridge, Cambridge University Press.

McFague, Sallie 1983, *Metaphorical Theology*, London, SCM Press.

McFague, Sallie 1987, *Models of God*, London, SCM Press.

McFague, Sallie 1993, *The Body of God*, London, SCM Press.

McGrath, Alister 1986, *Iustitia Dei* (2 vols.), Cambridge, Cambridge University Press.

McGrath, Alister and McGrath, Joanna 1992, *The Dilemma of Self-Esteem*, Cambridge, Crossway Books.

McGreal, Wilfrid 1994, *Guilt and Healing*, London, Geoffrey Chapman.

McKeating, Henry 1970, *Living with Guilt*, London, SCM Press.

McLeod, John 1997, *Narrative and Psychotherapy*, London, Sage.

McNeill, John 1977, *A History of the Cure of Souls*, New York, Harper and Row.

Mead, George 1934, *Mind, Self, and Society*, Chicago, University of Chicago Press.

Merton, Thomas 1972, *New Seeds of Contemplation*, London, Burns and Oates.

Mestrovic, Stjepan 1997, *Postemotional Society*, London, Sage.

Middelton-Moz, Jane 1990, *Shame and Guilt*, Deerfield Beach, Health Communications Inc.

Miles, Jack 1996, *God: A Biography*, London, Simon and Schuster.

Miles, Margaret 1988, *The Image and Practice of Holiness*, London, SCM Press.

Miles, Margaret 1992, *Desire and Delight*, New York, Crossroad.

Miller, Alice 1987a, *The Drama of Being a Child*, London, Virago.

Miller, Alice 1987b, *For Your Own Good*, London, Virago.

Miller, Alice 1991, *Banished Knowledge*, London, Virago.

Miller, Susan 1985, *The Shame Experience*, Hillsdale NJ, Analytic Press.

Miller, Susan 1989, 'Shame as an impetus to the creation of conscience', *International Journal of Psychoanalyis* 70: 231–43.

Milton, John 1969, *Poetical Works*, Oxford University Press.

Mitchell, Duncan 1970, *A New Dictionary of Sociology*, London, Routledge and Kegan Paul.

Miyake, Kazuo and Yamazaki, Kosuke 1995, 'Self-conscious emotions, child rearing, and child psychopathology in Japanese culture' in Price Tangney and Fischer (eds.), pp. 488–504.

Mollon, Phil 1993, *The Fragile Self*, London, Whurr Publishers.

Moltmann, Jürgen 1974, *The Crucified God*, London, SCM Press.

Montgomery, Jill 1989, 'Preface' in Montgomery and Greif (eds.), pp. ix–xv.

Montgomery, Jill and Greif, Ann 1989, *Masochism: The Treatment of Self-Inflicted Suffering*, Madison, International Universities Press.

Moore, Sebastian 1980, *The Fire and the Rose are One*, London, Darton, Longman & Todd.

Moore, Stephen 1996, *God's Gym*, London, Routledge.

Morley, Janet 1992, *All Desires Known*, London, SPCK.

Morris, Colin 1972, *The Discovery of the Individual*, New York, Harper and Row.

Morrison, Andrew 1983, 'Shame, ideal self, and narcissism', *Contemporary Psychoanalysis* 19: 295–318.

Morrison, Andrew 1987, 'The eye turned inward: shame and the self' in Nathanson (ed.), pp. 271–91.

Morrison, Andrew 1989, *Shame: The Underside of Narcissism*, Hillsdale NJ, Analytic Press.

Morrison, Nancy 1987, 'The role of shame in schizophrenia' in Lewis (ed.) pp. 51–88.

Moxnes, Halvor 1988, 'Honor, shame, and the outside world in Paul's letter to the Romans' in Neusner et al. (eds.), pp. 207–18.

Mruk, Chris 1999, *Self-esteem*, London, Free Association Books.

Nathanson, Donald (ed.) 1987a, *The Many Faces of Shame*, New York, Guilford Press.

Nathanson, Donald 1987b, 'A timetable for shame' in Nathanson (ed.), pp. 1–63.

Nathanson, Donald 1987c, 'Shaming systems in couples, families, and institutions' in Nathanson (ed.), pp. 246–70.

Nathanson, Donald 1992, *Shame and Pride*, New York, W. W. Norton.

Nelson, James 1992, *The Intimate Connection*, London, SPCK.

Nelson, James and Longfellow, Sandra (eds.) 1994, *Sexuality and the Sacred*, London, Mowbray.

Neusner, Jacob, Borgen, Peder, Frerichs, Ernest and Horsley, Richard (eds.) 1988, *The Social World of Formative Christianity and Judaism*, Philadelphia, Fortress Press.

Nicholls, David 1989, *Deity and Domination*, London, Routledge.

Niebuhr, H. Richard 1977, *The Purpose of the Church and its Ministry*, New York, Harper and Row.

Niebuhr, Reinhold 1964, *The Nature and Destiny of Man* (2 vols.), New York, Charles Scribner's Sons.

Nietzsche, Friedrich 1969, *Thus Spoke Zarathustra*, London, Penguin Books.

Nietzsche, Friedrich 1974, *The Gay Science*, New York, Vintage Books.

Nietzsche, Friedrich 1989, *The Genealogy of Morals and Ecce Homo*, New York, Vintage Books.

Nineham, Dennis 1977, 'Epilogue' in Hick (ed.), pp. 186–204.

Nineham, Dennis 1993, *Christianity Medieval and Modern*, London, SCM Press.

Nussbaum, Martha 1994, *The Therapy of Desire*, Princeton, Princeton University Press.

Oakley, Justin 1992, *Morality and the Emotions*, London, Routledge.

Oatley, Keith 1996, 'Emotions: communications to the self and others' in Harré and Parrot (eds.), pp. 312–16.

O'Hagan, Kieran 1993, *Emotional and Psychological Abuse of Children*, Buckingham, Open University Press.

O'Hear, Anthony 1976/7, 'Guilt and shame as moral concepts', *Proceedings of the Aristotelian Society* 77: 73–86.

Oksenberg Rorty, Amélie (ed.) 1980, *Explaining Emotions*, Berkeley, University of California Press.

Oppenheimer, Helen 1986, 'Pride' in Macquarrie and Childress (eds.), pp. 495–6.

Orbach, Susie 1994, *What's Really Going On Here?*, London, Virago.

Orwell, George 1954, *Nineteen Eighty-Four*, Harmondsworth, Penguin Books.

Osborn, Lawrence and Walker, Andrew (eds.) 1997, *Harmful Religion*, London, SPCK.

Otto, Rudolf 1950, *The Idea of the Holy*, Oxford, Oxford University Press, second edn.

Ould, Nelson 1995, 'Chronic Shame in Pastoral Theology: An American Protestant Reformed Perspective', unpublished PhD dissertation, University of Edinburgh.

Pagels, Elaine 1982, *The Gnostic Gospels*, London, Penguin Books.

Pagels, Elaine 1990, *Adam, Eve, and the Serpent*, London, Penguin Books.

Pagels, Elaine 1996, *The Origin of Satan*, London, Allen Lane.

Parker, Robert 1983, *Miasma: Pollution and Purification in Early Greek Religion*, Oxford, Oxford University Press.

Parkes, Penny 1990, *Rescuing the Inner Child*, London, Souvenir Press.

Parkinson, Brian 1995, 'Emotion' in Parkinson and Colman (eds.), pp. 1–21.

Parkinson, Brian and Colman, Andrew (eds.) 1995, *Emotion and Motivation*, London, Longman.

Parkinson, Patrick 1997, *Child Sexual Abuse and the Churches*, London, Hodder and Stoughton.

Parrott, Gerrod and Harré, Rom 1996a, 'Embarrassment and the threat to character' in Harré and Parrott (eds.), pp. 39–56.

Parrott, Gerrod and Harré, Rom 1996b, 'Overview' in Harré and Parrott (eds.), pp. 1–20.

Pattison, George 1998, *The End of Theology – and the Task of Thinking About God*, London, SCM Press.

Pattison, Stephen 1986, 'The use of the behavioural sciences in pastoral studies' in Ballard (ed.), pp. 79–85.

Pattison, Stephen 1989a, 'Review of *The Gospel of Anger* by Alastair Campbell', *Modern Theology* 5: 186–7.

Pattison, Stephen 1989b, *Alive and Kicking: Towards a Practical Theology of Illness and Healing*, London, SCM Press.

Pattison, Stephen 1990, 'To the churches with love from the Lighthouse' in Woodward (ed.), pp. 8–19.

Pattison, Stephen 1993, *A Critique of Pastoral Care*, London, SCM Press, second edn.

Pattison, Stephen 1995a, 'The shadow side of Jesus', *Studies in Christian Ethics*: 54–67

Pattison, Stephen 1995b, 'Can we speak of God in the secular academy?' in Young (ed.), pp. 35–49.

Pattison, Stephen 1996, 'Should pastoral care have aims and objectives?, *Contact* 120: 26–34.

Pattison, Stephen 1997a, *Pastoral Care and Liberation Theology*, London, SPCK.

Pattison, Stephen 1997b, *The Faith of the Managers*, London, Cassell.

Pattison, Stephen 1998, '"Suffer little children": the challenge of child abuse and neglect to theology', *Theology and Sexuality* 9: 36–58.

Pattison, Stephen in press, 'Mend the gap: Christianity and the emotions', *Contact*.

Pattison, Stephen, Dickenson, Donna, Parker, Michael and Heller, Tom 1999, 'Do case studies mislead about the nature of reality?', *Journal of Medical Ethics* 25: 42–6.

Pattison, Stephen, Malby, Becky and Manning, Steve 1999, 'I want to tell you a story', *Health Service Journal* 109(5643): 22–4.

Pattison, Stephen with Woodward, James 1994, *A Vision of Pastoral Theology*, Edinburgh, Contact Pastoral Limited.

Pattison, Stephen and Woodward, James 2000, 'An introduction to pastoral and practical theology' in Woodward and Pattison (eds.), pp. 1–19.

Patton, John 1985, *Is Human Forgiveness Possible?*, Nashville, Abingdon Press.

Patton, John 1997, 'Address to Clinical Theology Association', *Clinical Theology Association Newsletter* 69, pp. 1–5.

Perkins, Judith 1995, *The Suffering Self*, London, Routledge.

Pfister, Oscar 1948, *Christianity and Fear*, London, George Allen and Unwin.

Piers, Gerhart and Singer, Milton 1971, *Shame and Guilt*, New York, W. W. Norton.

Pines, Malcolm 1987, 'Shame: what psychoanalysis does and does not say', *Group Analysis* 20: 16–31.

Plant, Stephen 1996, *Simone Weil*, London, Fount.

Plutchik, Robert 1994, *The Psychology and Biology of Emotion*, np, HarperCollins.

Pohier, Jacques 1985, *God in Fragments*, London, SCM Press.

Poling, James 1991, *The Abuse of Power*, Nashville, Abingdon Press.

Price Tangney, June, Burggraf, Susan, and Wagner, Patricia 1995, 'Shame-proneness, guilt-proneness, and psychological symptoms' in Price Tangney and Fischer (eds.), pp. 343–67.

Price Tangney, June and Fischer, Kurt (eds.) 1995, *Self-Conscious Emotions: The Psychology of Shame, Guilt, Embarrassment, and Pride*, New York, Guilford.

Priestland, Gerald 1986, *Something Understood*, London, André Deutsch.

Pruyser, Paul 1991, 'Anxiety, guilt, and shame in the atonement' in Malony and Spilka (eds.), pp. 99–116.

Ramsay, Nancy 1991, 'Sexual abuse and shame: the travail of recovery' in Glaz and Moessner (eds.), pp. 109–25.

Rawls, John 1972, *A Theory of Justice*, Oxford, Oxford University Press.

Read, Jim and Reynolds, Jill 1996, *Speaking Our Minds*, Basingstoke, Macmillan.

Retzinger, Suzanne 1987, 'Resentment and laughter: video studies of the shame-rage spiral' in Lewis (ed.), pp. 151–82.

Retzinger, Suzanne 1991, *Violent Emotions: Shame and Rage in Marital Quarrels*, Newbury Park, Sage.

Retzinger, Suzanne 1995, 'Identifying shame and anger in discourse', *American Behavioral Scientist* 38: 1104–13.

Retzinger, Suzanne 1997, 'Shame-rage in marital quarrels', in Lansky and Morrison (eds.), pp. 297–312.

Retzinger, Suzanne 1998, 'Shame in the therapeutic relationship' in Gilbert and Andrews (eds.), pp. 206–22.

Richards, Val (ed.) 1996, *The Person Who Is Me*, London, Karnac Books.

Ricks, Christopher 1974, *Keats and Embarrassment*, Oxford, Oxford University Press.

Ricoeur, Paul 1967, *The Symbolism of Evil*, Boston, Beacon Press.

Rizzuto, Ana-Maria 1979, *The Birth of the Living God*, Chicago, University of Chicago Press.

Robinson, Simon 1998, 'Christian ethics and pastoral counselling revisited', *Modern Believing* 39(3): 30–44.

Rogers, Carl 1967, *On Becoming a Person*, London, Constable.

Rorty, Richard 1980, *Philosophy and the Mirror of Nature*, Oxford, Blackwell.

Rorty, Richard 1989, *Contingency, Irony, and Solidarity*, Cambridge, Cambridge University Press.

Rose, Nikolas 1989, *Governing the Soul*, London, Routledge.

Rowe, Dorothy 1983, *Depression*, London, Routledge.

Rubin, Julius 1994, *Religious Melancholy and Protestant Experience in America*, Oxford, Oxford University Press.

Russell, Jeffrey 1977, *The Devil*, Ithaca, Cornell University Press.

Russell, Jeffrey 1986, *Mephistopheles*, Ithaca, Cornell University Press.

Rycroft, Charles 1972, *A Critical Dictionary of Psychoanalysis*, London, Penguin Books.

Saiving, Valerie 1979, 'The human situation: a feminine view', in Christ and Plaskow (eds.), pp. 25–42.

Sanders, E. P. 1991, *Paul*, Oxford, Oxford University Press.

Sanders, E. P. 1995, *The Historical Figure of Jesus*, London, Penguin Books.

Sandler, Joseph, Person, Ethel Spector and Fonagy, Peter (eds.) 1991, *Freud's 'On Narcissism': An Introduction*, New Haven, Yale University Press.

Sanford, Linda Tschirhart and Donovan, Mary Ellen 1993, *Women and Self-Esteem*, London, Penguin Books.

Sarbin, Theodore 1986, 'Emotion and act: roles and rhetoric' in Harré (ed.), pp. 83–97.

Sartre, Jean-Paul 1958, *Being and Nothingness*, London, Methuen.

Sartre, Jean-Paul 1993, *The Emotions*, New York, Citadel Press.

Saussy, Carroll 1991, *God Images and Self Esteem*, Louisville, Westminster/John Knox Press.

Scheff, Thomas 1987, 'The shame-rage spiral: a case study of an interminable quarrel' in Lewis (ed.), pp. 109–50.

Scheff, Thomas 1990, *Microsociology*, Chicago, University of Chicago Press.

Scheff, Thomas 1995a, 'Conflict in family systems: the role of shame' in Price Tangney and Fischer (eds.), pp. 393–412.

Scheff, Thomas 1995b, 'Shame and related emotions: an overview', *American Behavioral Scientist* 38: 1053–9.

Scheff, Thomas 1997, *Emotions, the Social Bond, and Human Reality*, Cambridge, Cambridge University Press.

Scheff, Thomas and Retzinger, Suzanne 1997, 'Helen Block Lewis on shame: appreciation and critique' in Lansky and Morrison (eds.), 139–54.

Schimmel, Solomon 1997, *The Seven Deadly Sins*, Oxford, Oxford University Press.

Schleiermacher, Friedrich 1988, *Christian Caring*, Philadelphia, Fortress Press.

Schneider, Carl 1987a, *Shame, Exposure, and Privacy*, New York, W. W. Norton.

Schneider, Carl 1987b, 'A mature sense of shame' in Nathanson (ed.), pp. 194–213.

Schreiter, Robert 1985, *Constructing Local Theologies*, London, SCM Press.

Schüssler Fiorenza, Elizabeth 1995, *Jesus: Miriam's Child, Sophia's Prophet*, London, SCM Press.

Screech, M. A. 1997, *Laughter at the Foot of the Cross*, London, Allen Lane.

Seale, Clive and Pattison, Stephen (eds.) 1994, *Medical Knowledge: Doubt and Certainty*, Buckingham, Open University Press.

Selby, Peter 1991, *BeLonging*, London, SPCK.

Selby, Peter 1995, *Rescue*, London, SPCK.

Sennett, Richard 1986, *The Fall of Public Man*, London, Faber and Faber.

Sennett, Richard 1993, *Authority*, London, Faber and Faber.

Shaw, Graham 1983, *The Cost of Authority*, London, SCM Press.

Shengold, Leonard 1989, *Soul Murder*, New Haven, Yale University Press.

Sheppard, Grace 1995, *Pits and Pedestals*, London, Darton, Longman & Todd.

Shipton, Geraldine (ed.) 1997, *Supervision of Psychotherapy and Counselling*, Buckingham, Open University Press.

Shuman, Joel 1999, *The Body of Compassion*, Boulder, Westview Press.

Siegel, Allen 1996, *Heinz Kohut and the Psychology of the Self*, London, Routledge.

Smedes, Lewis 1993, *Shame and Grace*, London, SPCK.

Smith, Richard 1987, *Unemployment and Health*, Oxford, Oxford University Press.

Solomon, Robert 1992, *Ethics and Excellence*, Oxford, Oxford University Press.

Solomon, Robert 1993, *The Passions*, New York, Hackett Publishing.

Sophocles 1947, *The Theban Plays*, London, Penguin Books.

Soskice, Janet Martin 1985, *Metaphor and Religious Language*, Oxford, Clarendon Press.

Stearns, Carol and Stearns, Peter (eds.) 1988, *Emotion and Social Change*, New York, Holmes and Meier.

Stearns, Peter and Knapp, Mark 1996, 'Historical perspectives on grief' in Harré and Parrott (eds.), pp. 132–50.

Stein, Edward 1969, *Guilt: Theory and Therapy*, London, George Allen and Unwin.

Stendahl, Krister 1976, *Paul Among Jews and Gentiles*, Philadelphia, Fortress Press.

Stern, Daniel 1985, *The Interpersonal World of the Infant*, np, Basic Books.

Stevens, Richard (ed.) 1996, *Understanding the Self*, London, Sage.

Stout, Jeffrey 1988, *Ethics After Babel*, Cambridge, James Clarke.

Stowers, Stanley 1994, *A Rereading of Romans*, New Haven, Yale University Press.

Strongman, Kenneth 1987, *The Psychology of Emotion*, Chichester, John Wiley, third edn.

Strongman, Kenneth and Strongman, Luke 1996, 'Maori emotion' in Harré and Parrott (eds.) pp. 200–3.

Symington, Neville 1993, *Narcissism*, London, Karnac Books.

Symington, Neville 1994, *Emotion and Spirit*, London, Cassell.

Tambling, Jeremy 1990, *Confession*, Manchester, Manchester University Press.

Tanner, Michael 1994, *Nietzsche*, Oxford, Oxford University Press.

Tantam, Digby 1998, 'The emotional disorders of shame' in Gilbert and Andrews (eds.), pp. 161–75.

Taylor, Charles 1989, *Sources of the Self*, Cambridge, Cambridge University Press.

Taylor, Charles 1991, *The Ethics of Authenticity*, Cambridge MA, Harvard University Press.

Taylor, Gabriele 1985, *Pride, Shame, and Guilt*, Oxford, Oxford University Press.

Taylor, Mark 1987, *Erring*, Chicago, University of Chicago Press.

Theissen, Gerd and Merz, Annette 1998, *The Historical Jesus*, London, SCM Press.

Thrane, Gary 1979, 'Shame and the construction of the self', *Annals of Psychoanalysis* 7: 321–41.

Tillich, Paul 1962a, *The Shaking of the Foundations*, Harmondsworth, Penguin Books.

Tillich, Paul 1962b, *The Courage to Be*, London, Fontana.

Tillich, Paul 1978, *Systematic Theology Vol. II*, London, SCM Press.

Tillich, Paul 1984, *The Meaning of Health*, Chicago, Exploration Press.

Tolstoy, Leo 1936, *The Kingdom of God and Peace Essays*, Oxford, Oxford University Press.

Tolstoy, Leo 1995, *Anna Karenina*, Oxford, Oxford University Press.

Tomkins, Sylvan 1987, 'Shame' in Nathanson (ed.), pp. 133–61.

Tournier, Paul 1962, *Guilt and Grace*, London, Hodder and Stoughton.

Tracy, David 1987, *Plurality and Ambiguity*, London, SCM Press.

Trible, Phyllis 1984, *Texts of Terror*, Philadelphia, Fortress Press.

Turner, Frederick 1995, 'Shame, beauty, and the tragic view of history', *American Behavioral Scientist* 38: 1060–75.

van Deusen Hunsinger, Deborah 1995, *Theology and Pastoral Counseling*, Grand Rapids, Eerdmans.

Walker, Moira 1992, *Surviving Secrets*, Buckingham, Open University Press.

Walker Bynum, Caroline 1995, *The Resurrection of the Body*, New York, Columbia University Press.

Wallbott, Harald and Scherer, Klaus 1995, 'Cultural determinants in experiencing shame and guilt' in Price Tangney and Fischer (eds.), pp. 465–87.

Walton, Heather 1999, 'Passion and pain: conceiving theology out of infertility', *Contact* 130: 3–9.

Waugh, Evelyn 1962, *Brideshead Revisited*, Harmondsworth, Penguin Books.

Weber, Max 1976, *The Protestant Ethic and the Spirit of Capitalism*, London, George Allen and Unwin.

Weil, Simone 1959, *Waiting on God*, London, Fontana.

Wengst, Klaus 1988, *Humility*, London, SCM Press.

West, Angela 1995, *Deadly Innocence*, London, Cassell.

Westermann, Claus 1978, *Blessing in the Bible and the Life of the Church*, Philadelphia, Fortress Press.

Western, Drew 1984, *Self and Society*, Cambridge, Cambridge University Press.

White, Vernon 1996, *Paying Attention to People*, London, SPCK.

Whitehead, James and Whitehead, Evelyn 1994, *Shadows of the Heart*, New York, Crossroad.

Whyte, James 1987, 'Practical theology' in Campbell (ed.), pp. 212–13.

Williams, Bernard 1993, *Shame and Necessity*, Berkeley, University of California Press.

Wilson, Michael (ed.) 1983, *Explorations in Health and Salvation*, Birmingham, The University of Birmingham.

Wilson, Michael 1988, *A Coat of Many Colours*, London, Epworth Press

Wink, Walter 1992, *Engaging the Powers*, Minneapolis, Fortress Press.

Winnicott, D. W. 1974, *Playing and Reality*, Harmondsworth, Penguin Books.

Winnicott, D. W. 1990, *The Maturational Process and the Facilitating Environment*, London, Karnac Books.

Wood, Linda 1986, 'Loneliness' in Harré (ed.) pp. 184–208.

Woodward, James (ed.) 1990, *Embracing the Chaos*, London, SPCK.

Woodward, James and Pattison, Stephen (eds.) 2000, *The Blackwell Reader in Pastoral and Practical Theology*, Oxford, Blackwell.

Wren, Brian 1989, *What Language Shall I Borrow?*, London, SCM Press.

Wright, N. T. 1996, *Jesus and the Victory of God*, London, SPCK.

Wright Mills, C. 1970, *The Sociological Imagination*, Harmondsworth, Penguin Books.

Wurmser, Leon 1987, 'Shame: the veiled companion of narcissism' in Nathanson (ed.), pp. 64–92.

Wurmser, Leon 1995, *The Mask of Shame*, Northvale NJ, Jason Aronson.

Wurmser, Leon 1997a, 'Nietzsche's war against shame and resentment' in Lansky and Morrison (eds.), pp. 181–204.

Wurmser, Leon 1997b, 'The shame about existing' in Lansky and Morrison (eds.), pp. 367–82.

Young, Frances 1975, *Sacrifice and the Death of Christ*, London, SPCK.

Young, Frances (ed.) 1995, *Dare We Speak of God in Public?*, London, Cassell.

Young-Bruehl, Elisabeth 1991, *Anna Freud*, London, Papermac.

Zahn Waxler, Carolyn and Robinson, JoAnn 1995, 'Empathy and guilt: early origins of feelings of responsibility' in Price Tangney and Fischer (eds.), pp. 143–73.

Index of subjects

Index of author names

341